JOHN MUIR'S LAST JOURNEY

John Muir

JOHN MUIR'S LAST JOURNEY

South to the Amazon and East to Africa

Unpublished Journals and Selected Correspondence

Edited by Michael P. Branch

Foreword by Robert Michael Pyle

ISLAND PRESS / Shearwater Books

Washington, D.C. / Covelo, California

A Shearwater Book
Published by Island Press

Copyright © 2001 by Island Press

John Muir Papers, Holt-Atherton Special Collections,
University of the Pacific Libraries,
Copyright © 1984 Muir-Hanna Trust.

Most of the original manuscript pages contained in this book
reside in the John Muir Papers, Holt-Atherton Special Collections,
University Library, University of the Pacific, Stockton, California

Library of Congress Cataloging-in-Publication Data
John Muir's last journey : south to the Amazon and east to Africa :
unpublished journals and selected correspondence /
edited by Michael P. Branch
p. cm.
Includes bibliographical references (p.).
ISBN 1-55963-640-8 (cloth : alk. paper)
1. Muir, John, 1838-1914—Journeys—South America. 2. Muir, John,
1838-1914—Journeys—Africa. 3. Natural history—South America.
4. Natural history—Africa. I. Branch, Michael P.
QH31.M78 A3 2001
508.8'092—dc21
[B]   2001001808

British Cataloging-in-Publication Data available.

10 9 8 7 6 5 4 3 2 1

Printed on recycled, acid-free paper

Contents

List of Maps and Illustrations . . . .   *ix*

Foreword by Robert Michael Pyle . . . .   *xv*

Preface . . . .   *xix*

Introduction . . . .   *xxiii*

CHAPTER 1

Preparing for the Last Journey:

California, New York, and Boston

(26 January 1911 – 12 August 1911) *3*

CHAPTER 2

Southbound and up the Great Amazon

(12 August 1911 – 25 September 1911) *35*

CHAPTER 3

Coastal Brazil and up the Iguacu River

into the *Araucaria braziliensis* Forests

(26 September 1911 – 8 November 1911) *69*

CHAPTER 4

Southern Brazil, Uruguay, Argentina, Chile,

and into the *Araucaria imbricata* Forests of the Andes

(9 November 1911 – 10 December 1911) *102*

CHAPTER 5

At Sea, South Africa, the Zambezi River,
and to the Baobab Trees
(11 December 1911 – 6 February 1912) *127*

CHAPTER 6

East Africa, Lake Victoria, the Headwaters of the Nile,
and Homeward Bound
(7 February 1912 – 27 March 1912) *161*

CHAPTER 7

Home to America, California, and Writing:
The Fate of John Muir and His South America
and Africa Journals
(28 March 1912 – 29 December 1912) *184*

APPENDICES

Appendix A: Timeline/Locator *225*
Appendix B: Editorial Methods *239*
Appendix C: John Muir's Reading and Botanical Notes *251*
Appendix D: South America and Africa Books Owned by Muir . . .   *267*
Appendix E: Annotated List of Selected Archival Materials *269*
Appendix F: Table of Emendations *287*

Notes to Editor's Introductions *293*
Textual Notes *299*
Bibliography *313*
Acknowledgments *317*
Credits *321*
Index *323*

List of Maps and Illustrations

MAPS

The route of John Muir's last journey, August 1911–March 1912 . .   *xii*
The route of Muir's travels in South America,
     August 1911–December 1911 . . . .   *34*
The route of Muir's travels in Africa,
     December 1911–March 1912 . . . .   *128*

ILLUSTRATIONS

John Muir . . . .   *(frontispiece)*
Carleton E. Watkins photograph of Muir in San Francisco,
     circa 1875 . . . .   *xxviii*
A page from Muir's 1911 journal, showing field sketches of
     Araucaria braziliensis . . . .   *xliii*
Muir, late in his life, in the "scribble den" of his home in
     Martinez, California . . . .   *lii*
Muir beneath the palm tree at his Martinez home *15*
Muir dressed to receive an honorary degree from Yale, June 1911 . .   *25*
Muir's farewell letter, written just prior to departing for the
     Amazon *33*
Cable issued on behalf of President Taft to aid Muir abroad *45*
Muir with daughters Helen and Wanda *62*
Sketches of *Araucaria braziliensis*, including Muir's leaf calculations   *87*

Sketch of *Araucaria braziliensis,* with a cross section of the
    tree's bole *90*

Sketch of *Araucaria imbricata* forest on an Andean ridge *105*

Montagu Pass, in the Andes *109*

Journal sketches showing multiple perspectives of
    Araucaria imbricata *116*

Photograph of *Araucaria imbricata,* the monkey puzzle tree *122*

Photograph of the forest near Victoria Falls *134*

Sketch of *Adansonia digitata,* the baobab tree *148*

Photograph of Victoria Falls *150*

Sketch of a glacially carved dome near Beira, Africa *152*

Photograph of a baobab tree in an African village *156*

Photograph of an African village *162*

Sketch of the hills near Lake Victoria *168*

Photograph of baobab trees along the railroad tracks *173*

Sketch of a glacially carved valley near 'Adan *177*

Typescript journal page with Muir's editorial notes *191*

John Muir and John Burroughs, April 3, 1912 . . . .   *206*

Muir, playing with his grandchildren *218*

I've had a most glorious time on this trip, dreamed of
nearly half a century—have seen more than a
thousand miles of the noblest of Earth's streams and
gained far more telling views of the wonderful forests
than I ever hoped for.

John Muir to Katharine Hooker
From the Amazon delta at Belém (Pará), Brazil
September 19, 1911

———

Indeed it now seems that on this pair of
wild hot continents I've enjoyed the most
fruitful year of my life.

John Muir to William E. Colby
While at sea near Zanzibar, East Africa
February 4, 1912

———

I am now writing up some notes [from the journey],
but when they will be ready for publication I do not
know. . . . [I]t will be a long time before anything is
arranged in book form.

John Muir to Douglas Aimers
After returning home to Martinez, California
June 20, 1912

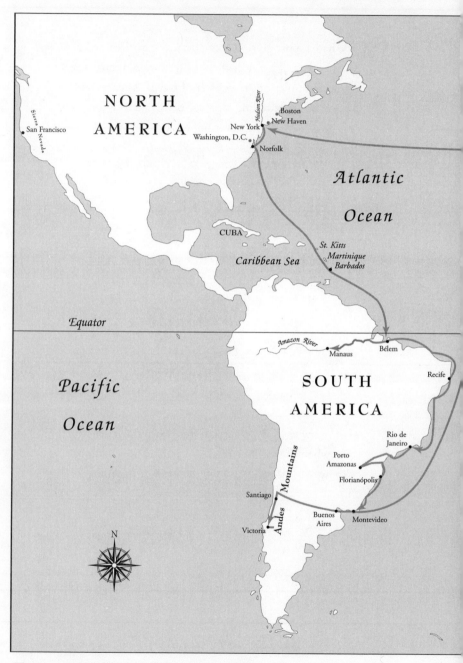

The route of John Muir's last journey, August 1911–March 1912

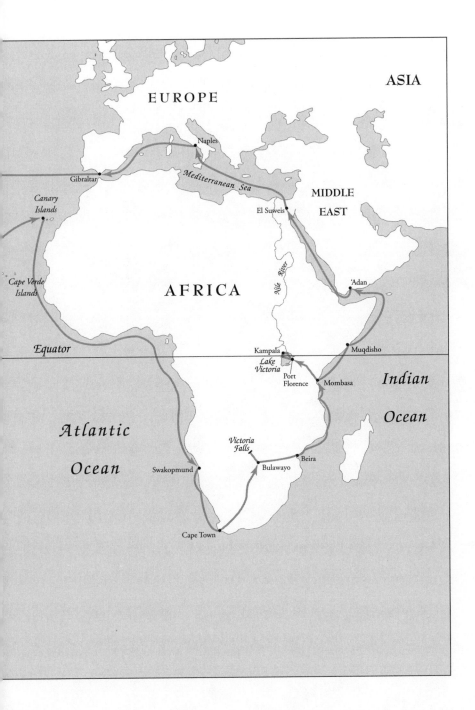

Foreword

The Journey Home

When I went off to college in the mid-1960s, my greatest desire was to be like John Muir. The Rock of western conservation was well known among the young environmentalists at the University of Washington. We recognized Muir as a true radical, at a time when many of us were playing at radicalism. Also as a genuine naturalist, which was what I most aspired to become. I probed dusty second-hand bookshops on University Way for his writings, grew my beard long out of honorific emulation, and affected a Muirish exultation in my journals. My jottings, embarrassing to read today, produced neither good writing nor good mimicry; but at least they were honest in praise of both model and topic.

A fond conceit, this, and doomed from the outset; yet in many ways, John Muir guided all I did. We had Muir's Yosemite in mind, for example, when our Conservation Education and Action Council fought for the North Cascades National Park. Focusing my revolutionary fervor on ecology as well as war, I joined Seattle Audubon Society and the local chapter of the Sierra Club, and these brought me still closer to the person of John Muir. The Audubon board meetings took place around an immense dining room table in the Capitol Hill home of Emily Haig, Grand Dame of Seattle conservationists; Sierra Club retreats also revolved around Emily, as we congregated in her country cabin on Hood Canal. When we broke for coffee and cookies at Emily's sideboard, or to gather dinner from her own oyster beds, I gazed on her eggshell face with its honeysuckle smile and conjured on this one astounding fact: Emily Haig had belonged to the

Sierra Club in San Francisco while John Muir was still president! She had known the man.

When Emily Haig shared her memories of John Muir, I shivered with a sense of reflected glory such as only a twenty-year-old idol-worshipper could manage. I recall her telling of Muir's bright eyes, his youthful stride and spring, and his indefatigable energy when brought to bear upon conservation battles. Not that he had much ready appetite for fighting or politicking. He would far rather be afield, measuring the advance or retreat of glaciers, triangulating trees, plumbing the spiritual luminosity of the Range of Light. Even then he was a celebrity for his books, but he didn't seek such exposure. For him to actually write about experience rather than live it was tantamount to torture. As a young woman in the club, Emily told me, she especially enjoyed the outings, and they were the president's favorite part too. Even so, Muir recognized the powerful force the Sierra Club might exercise in the conservation colloquy of the times. He had no idea how important it would become under a certain successor.

David Brower came north to meet with Seattle wilderness advocates soon after he had left the executive directorship of the Sierra Club and founded Friends of the Earth and the John Muir Institute. A creature of the crags as well as congressional hearing rooms, Brower had not only climbed the same peaks as Muir, but also followed his example as long-standing leader of the club. Like his predecessor, Brower had experienced a great victory and a burning loss. If beating the scheme to dam the Green River was his Yosemite, then losing the struggle for Glen Canyon—inundated beneath Lake Powell—was Brower's Hetch Hetchy. But while the loss of "the second Yosemite" would be Muir's last campaign, Brower went on to lead the successful resistance to dams in the Grand Canyon. After we met with Brower in Seattle, I imagined the historic encounter in the nearby Olympic Hotel between Muir and Gifford Pinchot—founder of the Forest Service, leader of the "greatest good for the greatest number" school of conservation, and Muir's Hetch Hetchy nemesis. Out of their fateful and bitter joust would come the major dialectic of American environmentalism. But even people who know this much have little idea of Muir's overall import.

My own sense of John Muir broadened greatly in the years that followed. Walking in the California grove of coast redwoods that bears his name (where Brower once took Rachel Carson), or flying over Alaskan glaciers that he had scaled without a single piece of modern equipment from REI, I gained a feel for the kind of world for which he fought and the terms on which he came to the land. But it took a summer as ranger–naturalist in Sequoia National Park, hiking over some of the same sugar-stone granite passes and cirques where John O'Mountains had walked, to drive home the depth of his commitment and its effect. On Morro Rock, a miniature Half Dome, I watched a white-throated swift carry a feather sky-high and drop it for another to catch, over and over, and wondered if Muir had seen the same in Yosemite. On ranger walks in Giant Forest, I paused for silence in the very glade where Muir loved to listen for what his friend John Burroughs called the "religious beatitude" of the hermit thrushes. We too heard that sweet fluting. Another walk rounded Crescent Meadow, John Muir's favorite. Rambling that emerald curl, beneath the spires of Sierra redwoods, I palped the reverence for the wild that drove John Muir to become something he might never have intended: a campaigning scientist, rather than the contemplative naturalist he might have preferred.

In doing so, Muir set the pattern for those who followed—Aldo Leopold, Rachel Carson, E. O. Wilson, and all their lot—those who have possessed both the knowledge of the natural world and the refined love for its elements that, together, turned their consciences toward selfless activism on behalf of ecological reform. For it wasn't as much his friendship with presidents, his rhapsodic language, or his reputation as the Sage of the Sierra that saved Yosemite and inspired the conservation of biodiversity ever after. It was more the fact that John Muir truly was a rigorous scientific observer and a pioneering, original student of the landscape: its geology and glacial history, its plant communities, its ecological wholeness. Muir combined a truly Thoreauvian attention to his surroundings with the robust physicality of Teddy Roosevelt and the inclusiveness of Gilbert White, the father of Natural History; and he blended them all with a literary exuberance that caught the imagination of readers and politicians alike. John Muir also had a broad worldview, concern and curiosity for the whole globe spinning in his mind. Hence, his ultimate desire to see where he had not yet been. All these elements emerge in this celebratory account of his improbable, final adventure.

Popular belief has it that Muir's last years were eclipsed by his failure to save Hetch Hetchy Valley from inundation by thirsty San Francisco: an inglorious finish to a glorious life, a final darkness at the end of the Range of Light. Yet, that wasn't all there was to it, as *John Muir's Last Journey* shows. What a surprising, thrilling discovery! A whole chapter in the man's life, almost unknown, a great gift rendered with scholarly precision and literary elegance by Michael Branch. And how like Muir, to take off for far climes, alone, at seventy-three. The great gift of this remarkable book is the wonderful knowledge that John Muir's final years were rewarded, enlivened, and brilliantly illumined—you might almost say redeemed—by one final, phenomenal Field Trip.

I never succeeded in becoming much like Muir. For one thing, lacking his litheness and comfort with gravity, I do not climb rocks. For another, no one could really be much like this Scottish-American original. But in reading his South American and African travels, so long deferred, so abundantly enjoyed, I realize anew how proper a model Muir was, and still is, for anyone who loves nature. For he did love, more than most have any idea how to do. He loved his family, friends, and all life. He loved the colors on the sea and sky, and the gift of sight he almost lost. He especially loved big round things: the clouds, the trees, the granite domes—the world itself.

A journal entry from the *Araucaria imbricata* forest of Chile says it all: "My three companions slept under tarpaulin tents, strangely fearing the blessed mountain air and dew." No one was more comfortable in the wild world than John Muir: his whole life was a journey home. We should all give thanks for the grace of going along on the last leg.

Robert Michael Pyle

Preface

In the spring of 1997 I received a thrice-forwarded electronic mail copy of a letter the Shuar people of upper Amazonia had sent to a primary school in Dunbar, Scotland, the town where John Muir was born. "No white man has reflected the spiritual essence and beauty of our natural world more profoundly than your magnificent son John Muir," wrote the representative of the Shuar. "So! It is my great pleasure to inform first the children of the spiritual home of John Muir that we hereby name him . . . Honorary Blood Brother of the Shuar-Actuar nations." Like many people, the Shuar recognized Muir's gift for perceiving the aesthetic and spiritual beauty of nature. But unlike most of us, they also knew that Muir had been to the Amazon basin and that his travels there had forged another link in the chain of environmental concern that connects people around the world—from Amazonia to Dunbar to the Sierra Nevada.

When I received that message four years ago, I had already been working for a year on Muir's remarkable but little known and previously unpublished manuscript journals and letters describing his journey to South America and Africa. The sort of textual editing and research needed to bring manuscripts to publication is painstaking work, where many hours may yield only the accurate transcription of a single line or the discovery of a single allusion. But it is also deeply rewarding. While an original manuscript is not quite a flower, it can be nearly as mysterious and lovely, with a distinctive look, feel, and even a smell that attracts some people as a species of flower attracts the hummingbird. I hope that my years of hovering above these manuscripts, so sweet even in moments of frustration, has contributed a new shade to Muir's legacy.

I live in a high desert valley on the western edge of the Great Basin, at the foot of the eastern slope of the Sierra Nevada; Muir's South America and Africa manuscripts live on the other side of the Sierra, in the special collections of the Holt-Atherton Library at the University of the Pacific in Stockton, California. Although my home and office contain cairns of reproductions of Muir manuscripts, the real treasure lies on the other side of the big hill. I have thus had the special pleasure of crossing the Sierra—whose wonders John Muir did so much to protect—on my way to Stockton to study the manuscripts housed there. But if the Sierra crest as seen from Donner Pass has offered inspiring views, views equally long and rich are to be had in the subterranean chambers of a manuscript archives. Donning white gloves to begin another day there, I always get a fresh feeling of excitement at the prospects ahead, and even the most fruitless day of archival research cannot erase the feeling of immediacy that one has when working with original literary texts just as their creator has set them down.

There is a narrative convention by which we can convey a sense of the immediacy of exciting past events by using the present tense. For example, I might write that John Muir "crawls and climbs through the tangled vines of the Amazon jungle, searching for *Victoria regia,* the giant water lily." Or, I might explain that in the archives "I find a piece of an old map, and then another, and then ten more, until the fragments resolve into a whole, revealing the map that Muir carried with him up the Amazon." This use of the present tense, which linguists sometimes refer to as the "historical present," nicely suggests the power of the artifact to collapse for a moment the time and space separating us from those who lived and died before us. Holding an original manuscript journal or letter delicately in gloved hands, I imagine I feel the movements of Muir's hand upon the page, and the past becomes present to me in ways that are difficult to understand and describe, magical to experience. There is, in such moments, what Muir's friend Ralph Waldo Emerson called an "occult sympathy" that links us imaginatively and viscerally to the past and urges us to contemplate a future when the gift of our present will be someone else's past, when the work of our day will be someone else's artifact. It has been a great privilege and challenge to work with these manuscripts, to travel with Muir to Africa and to the Amazon of the Shuar, line by line and word by word. This work cultivates, I like to think, the sort of disciplined patience and attention that Muir brought to his own botanical and geological studies. As Muir makes clear throughout the journals and letters that follow, it is good that we should recognize in this world those things that deserve to be handled with care.

A note on the structure of *John Muir's Last Journey*. I've divided the story of Muir's South America and Africa travels into seven chapters that braid Muir's journals and letters for corresponding periods between 1911 and 1912. The notes for general and chapter introductions (Notes to Editor's Introductions) are to be found near the back of the book, as are notes specific to the textual editing of Muir's archival materials (Textual Notes); explanatory notes on people, places, and allusions Muir refers to appear as footnotes to the relevant journal pages and letters. The Timeline/Locator can be used to follow Muir's daily activities and locations, while various other appendices provide additional information on related Muir materials and their editorial preparation.

M.P.B.
Reno, Nevada
April 2001

Introduction

"I am now writing up some notes, but when they will be ready for publication I do not know. . . . [I]t will be a long time before anything is arranged in book form." These words of John Muir, written in June 1912 to a friend, proved prophetic. The journals and notes to which the great naturalist and explorer was referring have languished, unpublished and virtually untouched, for nearly a century. Until now. Here edited and published for the first time, Muir's travel journals from 1911 to 1912, along with his associated correspondence, finally allow us to read in his own words the remarkable story of John Muir's last great journey.

That final journey, made by Muir just three years before his death, is the subject of this book. Leaving from Brooklyn, New York, in August 1911, Muir, at the age of seventy-three and traveling alone, embarked on an eight-month, 40,000-mile voyage to South America and Africa. He first went a thousand miles up the Amazon, then down the Atlantic coast and across the continent into the Chilean Andes before re-crossing the pampas to Buenos Aires, Argentina. From there Muir sailed east and traveled through south and central Africa and to the headwaters of the Nile before returning to New York via the Red Sea, Mediterranean Sea, and North Atlantic. Although this epic journey has received almost no attention from the many commentators on his work, Muir himself considered it among the most important of his life and the fulfillment of a dream of decades. Ever since 1867, when his first attempt to reach the Amazon had been defeated by a malarial illness, Muir nurtured the hope that he might someday study the tropical plants and trees of the world's greatest river basin.

For more than forty years Muir kept alive the dream that he might yet journey to the "two hot continents" and study their richly biodiverse flora and fauna. Despite his many literary, preservationist, and family obligations, the aging Muir at last resolved in 1911 that he must try to reach South America and Africa. So began his last great journey, the epic voyage described in the pages of this book. Muir's 1911–12 journals and correspondence allow us to travel with Muir as he explores and studies some of the most spectacular rivers, forests, mountains, and trees of the southern hemisphere. And his writings on this journey highlight a side of Muir that has been little seen or appreciated. They provide us a rare view of a Muir whose interests as a naturalist, traveler, and conservationist extended well beyond the mountains of California, and they show John Muir as an older man, a family man, a world traveler, and a naturalist with global concerns. These journals and letters thus add important dimensions to our understanding of the life and work of one of America's most accomplished and influential environmental writers, allowing us to see Muir whole.

Seeing Muir Whole

When we think of John Muir, a number of images typically come to mind. There is the Muir we associate with the glory of California's Sierra Nevada, the mountains he spent much of his life exploring and studying, and which he affectionately called the Range of Light. There is Muir the environmentalist, who helped protect Yosemite as a national park, who formed and led the Sierra Club, shaped the emergent national park idea, defined the preservationist wing of the American environmental movement, and fought to the bitter, tragic end to save the Hetch Hetchy Valley from being dammed and inundated in what became a landmark battle in American environmental history. Then there is Muir the accomplished naturalist, whose early studies in Sierra geology were the first to prove Yosemite's glacial origins, and whose later botanical studies won him the admiration of scientists worldwide. Perhaps we think of Muir the hiker, who walked 1,000 miles from Indiana to the Gulf of Mexico, or Muir the intrepid explorer, who in seven trips to Alaska—many undertaken alone or with just a few native guides—discovered dramatic features of the northern landscape: Glacier Bay, the giant glacier that now bears his name, and others. Of course Muir was also a gifted mountaineer whose many climbs, whether into a Douglas-fir crown in a windstorm, behind a Yosemite waterfall by moonlight, up the sheer face of Mt. Ritter alone, or along the dark, snowy shoulders of Mt. Shasta, have become legendary. Some may think of the young Muir who was so talented an inventor, or of the older Muir, who was the confidante of presidents and the friend of prominent journalists, artists, writers, and industrialists (such as Robert Underwood Johnson, William Keith, Ralph Waldo Emerson, and Edward H. Harriman, respectively). Finally, from these and many other remarkable experiences emerges Muir the nature writer, a man who, though he himself often described writing as an unfortunate distraction from nature and a sadly indirect way to communicate its sacredness, produced works of environmental writing that distinguish him as one of America's most eloquent and influential literary voices on behalf of the aesthetic, ecological, and spiritual value of wilderness.

Amidst these various activities and accomplishments, however, there is another Muir of whom we know far too little, and of whom scholars and admirers of Muir too rarely speak: John Muir the world traveler. Though "John O' Mountains" has been variously remembered as the wild child of the Wisconsin wilderness, the guardian angel of the blessed Sierra, and the grand old man of Alaska, his several significant journeys abroad have been largely forgotten, or in the case of his last, to South America and Africa, little known about. In order to fully understand how global were Muir's interests as a traveler, botanist, and environmentalist, it is imperative that we recognize the vital role of international travels in Muir's life and work.

In his first trip abroad, taken in 1864 at age twenty-six, Muir made a seven-month botanical excursion across the border to the wilds of Canada in order to study flowers and, perhaps in part, to avoid being drafted into service in the Civil War. Almost thirty years later, in the summer of 1893, he toured Europe, visiting Scotland, Norway, England, Switzerland, France, Italy, and Ireland, in order to meet with fellow naturalists and visit such celebrated landscapes as the glacial fjords of coastal Norway, the English Lake District, the Matterhorn, Mont Blanc, the Lakes of Killarney, and the Scottish Highlands.

A decade later, from May 1903 to May 1904, Muir toured the world, primarily in order to study trees. Traveling at first with Harvard botanist Charles S. Sargent, Muir went to London, Paris, and Berlin, then on to the Russian frontier, through the Lindula larch forest of Finland, the Caucasus Mountains near the Black Sea, and through the Volga Valley and then over the Ural Mountains onto the broad Siberian prairies. After a short visit to Manchuria, Sargent and Muir sailed down the Korean coast to Shanghai, where Muir struck out on his own. He traveled along the coast of China and on to India, where he saw the great Himalayas and the giant deodar trees near Simla. From India he sailed to Egypt, where he saw Cairo, visited the Pyramids, and steamed up the Nile to witness the picturesque scenery of its lower cataracts. From Egypt he sailed to Ceylon and on to Australia and then New Zealand, where he explored the casuarina forests of the Blue Mountains and the Mueller Glacier at the base of Mount Cook. Returning to Australia, Muir made a pilgrimage into the mountains of Queensland to study two kinds of rare coniferous trees, *Araucaria bidwillii* and *Araucaria cunninghamii,* in their native forests. After quick stops in Malaysia and the Philippines he returned to San Francisco via China, Japan, and Hawaii. Muir's world tour, made when he was already in his mid-sixties, confirmed his passion for international travel and nature study, and whetted his appetite for a voyage to South America and sub-Saharan Africa, the two major areas of the globe he had not yet seen. Though this ambitious voyage has received little attention from scholars, the fact that Muir gave a full year of his life to it suggests how important such travels are to a fully developed understanding of Muir's life and career.

Muir's final international journey—the final major journey of his life and the one he proclaimed his most rewarding—is lesser known even than the Canadian excursions and the world tour, and is the subject of *John Muir's Last Journey*.

The True Beginnings of the Last Journey

In order to understand the significance and poignancy of Muir's last journey, we must revisit his first major journey, the famed 1867 thousand-mile walk from Indianapolis, Indiana, to the Gulf of Mexico, made when he was twenty-nine years old. Having emigrated from Scotland to the Wisconsin prairies as a boy in 1849, Muir had grown up under the hard labor of the farm and the strict Calvinism of his father, but he had nevertheless developed an early love of plants, literature, and mechanical inventions. In 1860 he left the farm for Madison, where he exhibited his inventions at the state fair and subsequently enrolled as a student at the university there. Three years later he left the University of Wisconsin for what he famously called the University of the Wilderness, and went on walking and botanical tours in Iowa, Wisconsin, and lower Canada. Despite his graduation to nature study, however, Muir's poverty soon drove him to work in a sawmill and broom and rake factory near Meaford, Canada, where he remained employed until March 1866, when the factory burned down. Muir returned to the United States and was soon employed by the Indianapolis firm of Osgood, Smith, & Co. as a sawyer, machinist, and what we would now call "efficiency expert" in their carriage wheel factory.

Oddly enough, it is there, among the wheels and spokes of the industrial factory, that the story of Muir's last journey properly begins. The young Muir had begun to worry that professional and financial circumstances might compel him, he wrote, "to abandon the profession of my choice, and to take up the business of an inventor." And although he was succeeding wonderfully in his work on industrial machines and their efficient use, he was painfully aware of the imminent danger "of becoming so successful that my botanical and geographical studies might be interrupted." Then, while working late in the factory on the evening of March 6, 1867, Muir was injured in an accident that dramatically changed the course of his life. As he used the sharp end of a file to unlace the joining of a leather belt on one of the machines, the file slipped and struck his right eye, piercing it at the edge of the cornea. As Muir turned from the machine toward the window, helplessly cupping his injured eye as the aqueous humor fell into his palm and his sight began to fail, fellow sawyer Henry Riley heard him lament, "My right eye is gone, closed forever on all God's beauty."

Although Muir was able to make his way to his lodgings without help, within hours he was confined to bed, and had lost vision not only in the damaged right eye but also, through a sympathetic reaction that is typical in such injuries, the left as well. The doctor who was called concluded that Muir's right eye was irrecoverably damaged, though the left might recover. During this period of total blindness Muir mourned that "[t]he sunshine and the winds are working in all the gardens of God, but I—I am

The injury to Muir's right eye is visible in this Carleton E. Watkins photograph, taken in San Francisco, circa 1875

lost!" Indianapolis friends responded to Muir's misfortune with kind visits during which they often read to him, while friends elsewhere wrote encouraging letters. In her sanguine letter consoling him during his blindness, Muir's friend Jeanne Carr assured him that God "gave you the eye within the eye, to see in all natural objects the realized ideas of His mind. . . . He will surely place you where your work is."

Fortunately, Muir's prospects soon improved. A specialist who was called in predicted the total recovery of the left eye and, to Muir's great relief, the substantial recovery of the damaged eye as well. He began to feel better, his pain subsided, and, by slow increments, his vision returned. During the four weeks he spent convalescing in a darkened room, Muir also resolved his vocational dilemma. Despite the handsome opportunities his industrial employers offered, he began instead to plan for a life devoted to nature study. "This affliction has driven me to the sweet fields," he wrote. "God has to nearly kill us sometimes, to teach us lessons." A dream that Muir had had before the accident now became a resolve: a long botanical ramble through the American South and then on to South America. Resigning his position at the factory, he returned to Wisconsin for the summer to study flowers, complete his recovery, and take leave of his family and friends.

On September 1, 1867, John Muir, now twenty-nine years old, left Indianapolis for points south, traveling by the "wildest, leafiest, and least trodden way" he could find. "I bade adieu to mechanical inventions, determined to devote the rest of my life to the study of the inventions of God," he wrote. "I propose to go South and see something of the vegetation of the warm end of the country, and if possible to wander far enough into South America to see tropical vegetation in all its palmy glory." And so, keeping his own promise that if God should restore the gift of sight he would use it to study the beauty of the creation rather than the contrivances of man, Muir walked alone, twenty-five miles a day, throughout the autumn of 1867. After taking a train from Indianapolis to Jeffersonville, Indiana, he crossed the Ohio River to Louisville, Kentucky, and then walked a thousand miles to the Gulf of Mexico at Cedar Keys, Florida, with the intention of continuing to South America by boat. The now-famous flyleaf inscription with which young Muir began the journal of that epic walk clearly suggests his new orientation toward life: "John Muir, Earth-planet, Universe."

Although Muir's accident did not generate the idea of explorations far afield, it did inspire him to try to fulfill a childhood dream. As a boy Muir had delighted in the adventures of South American and African explorers, and had yearned someday to have such adventures himself. "Boys are fond of the books of travelers, and one day, after I had been reading Mungo Park's travels in Africa," wrote Muir in his autobiography, referring to the Scottish explorer's 1860 book *Travels in the Interior Regions of Africa*, "mother said: 'Weel, John, maybe you will travel like Park and Humboldt some day'." Muir reports that his father, always intolerant of such impractical schemes, retorted "'Oh, Anne! Dinna put sic notions in the laddie's heed'." Paternal discouragement notwithstanding, notions of international travel and exploration were in Muir's head, and even during his years on the farm, at the university, and in the factory, he had never given them up.

Even more important than Mungo Park in inspiring Muir's early dreams of international exploration was the great German explorer and scientist Alexander von Humboldt, whose work Muir read throughout his life. Humboldt gave Muir the vicarious thrill of wilderness adventure, while also modeling the kind of engaged scientific exploration that puts a premium on observation, conservation (especially forest protection), and attention to the distribution of and interconnections among species. Humboldt also served as a model of the sort of broad-minded, philosophically inclined natural scientist that Muir would himself aspire to become. And it was largely through Humboldt's account of his South American travels that Muir developed his most burning ambition: to explore and study the tropical rainforests of the great Amazon basin.

Indeed, Muir's letters from the mid-1860s demonstrate unequivocally that he developed high hopes for a voyage to South America before his 1867 industrial accident. The most telling of these letters, written to a friend on the day following his misfortune, makes clear how serious he was about the southern journey: "For weeks," he wrote, "I have daily consulted maps in locating a route through the Southern States, the West Indies, South America, and Europe—a botanical journey studied for years. And so my mind has long been in a glow with visions of the glories of a tropical flora; but, alas, I am half blind. My right eye, trained to minute analysis, is lost and I have scarce heart to open the other."

Muir's deep devotion to the planned journey is suggested by his reaction to the accident, which is to lament not blindness so much as the fact that blindness has precluded the long-dreamed-of explorations. As his vision slowly returned, Muir more fully admitted the strength of his passion for the journey. "For many a year," he commented, "I have been impelled toward the Lord's tropic gardens of the South. Many influences have tended to blunt or bury this constant longing, but it has outlived and overpowered them all."

Muir's journal of the epic walk—the first of his sixty extant journals—was posthumously published in 1916 as *A Thousand-Mile Walk to the Gulf,* and it has received a great deal of well-deserved critical attention since then. The journal covers Muir's two-month botanical ramble through the South in the wake of the Civil War. As many commentators have recognized, this first of Muir's extant journals traces both the landscapes he sees and the emotional changes that accompany his physical movement through Kentucky, Tennessee, North Carolina, Georgia, and Florida, where, in late October, his journey was stopped short by a near fatal malarial fever that left him unconscious for several days, and convalescent for several months. What has received far too little attention, however, is the fact that Muir's ultimate goal for the walk was not the Gulf of Mexico, but rather South America; even a biographer as astute as Frederick Turner leaves us with the unfortunate impression that Florida was the "destination of [Muir's] long-deferred dreams."

On the contrary, Cedar Keys was not a destination but an unplanned, illness-induced stopover on a longer trip toward the greatest of the world's river basins, as Muir's own description of his travel plan makes clear. "I

had long wished to visit the Orinoco basin and in particular the basin of
the Amazon," he wrote, describing his ambitions for a truly Humboldtian
adventure. "My plan was to get ashore anywhere on the north end of the
continent, push on southward through the wilderness around the headwaters of the Orinoco, until I reached a tributary of the Amazon, and float
down on a raft or skiff the whole length of the great river to its mouth."
Even Muir's severe illness did not daunt his ambition to reach the Amazon. As he began his long recovery during early November, he instructed
a friend to send letters to New Orleans, where he intended to go in order
to find "a boat to South America," and he asked his brother David to forward $150 to New Orleans, where he planned to pick up the travel funds
before continuing on to "the glorious mountains and flower fields of
South America," in order to see "the snow-capped Andes and the flowers
of the Equator."

When a ship arrived in Cedar Keys bound for Havana in early January,
Muir quickly decided he would add a Cuban sojourn to his plans; on that
island, Muir must have reckoned, he could recuperate more fully while
having the pleasure of studying the botany of "the fairest of West India
islands" before finding a ship bound for Venezuela or the Caribbean coast
of Colombia. However, Muir's beachcombing and botanizing along the
Cuban coast, while enjoyable, failed to restore his strength. "After passing
a month in this magnificent island, and finding that my health was not
improving, I made up my mind to push on to South America while my
stock of strength, such as it was, lasted," he wrote. Despite his resolve to
continue south, though, Muir discovered that he "could not find passage
for any South American port."

Muir later admitted the impracticality of the South America plans he
was then following: "[i]t seems strange that such a trip should ever have
entered the dreams of any person, however enthusiastic and full of youthful daring, particularly under the disadvantages of poor health, of funds
less than a hundred dollars, and of the insalubrity of the Amazon Valley."
It is quite clear, however, that at the time Muir fully intended to attempt
the adventurous plan, and that only the considerable and combined obsta-

cles of his weakened physical condition and the logistical difficulties of finding passage persuaded him otherwise. Muir finally decided, regretfully, that his ambitious journey to the Amazon could not be effected under such adverse circumstances and would have to be put on hold.

Muir's decision in that moment of postponement changed the course of his life, and radically influenced the development of American environmental concern, protection, and literature as we now know them. "I could not find a vessel of any sort bound for South America, and so made up a plan to go North, to the longed-for cold weather of New York, and thence to the forests and mountains of California," wrote Muir, who had seen a brochure boasting of the geological and botanical wonders of the Sierra Nevada. "There, I thought, I shall find health and new plants and mountains, and after a year spent in that interesting country I can carry out my Amazon plans." It proved a fateful decision, for upon his arrival in San Francisco, via the Isthmus of Panama, in late March 1868, John Muir walked into the Sierra, into Yosemite, and into history.

A Dream Long Deferred

It might be said that the John Muir we have come to know and appreciate is the figure who developed during the forty-four-year hiatus between his first and second attempts to reach the Amazon. Nearly everything we know of Muir's contributions as a writer, mountaineer, scientist, natural philosopher, and environmental advocate follows from his auspicious arrival in California. But if, after Muir's first glimpse of the Sierra, "the rest is history," then the history of Muir's life and travels as it has commonly been told remains incomplete. For during the four decades spanning Muir's better-known adventures, he continued to dream of the Amazon journey that had been thwarted in his youth, and he never relinquished hope that he might someday complete the voyage that had been so earnestly begun when he left Indianapolis in 1867.

Though Muir deeply admired the Sierra, even his much-celebrated early experiences in the mountains of California never fully eclipsed his

Amazonian ambitions. Shortly after arriving in Yosemite in the spring of 1868, Muir wrote to his brother David that he expected to resume the South America expedition in November, and to his sister Sarah he added, somewhat later and less decisively, that "a few months will call upon me to decide to what portion of God's glorious star I will next turn." Even when the "attractions of California" proved irresistibly tempting to Muir, he decided that he would only "stay another year or so" before moving on. Although Muir lingered in California, wandering the Central Valley and foothills, working various jobs, and then herding sheep into the high country during the summer of 1869, even his ecstatic "first summer in the Sierra" failed to decide the Amazon matter. In September 1869—within weeks of having descended from the experience of that famous first season in the high Sierra—he wrote to friends and relatives that he was still considering South America, and that by December or January he would probably leave California for "some other of our Father's gardens."

Yet another year passed, and in the autumn of 1870 Muir's friend Jeanne Carr wrote to tell him of a South American expedition that her son was joining and to encourage Muir to join it as well. "The Amazon and Andes have been in all my thoughts for many years, and I am sure that I shall meet them some day ere I die," he wrote back on November 4. "I thought of landing at Guayaquil and crossing the mountains to the Amazon, [then] float to Para, subsisting on berries and quinine." The fact that Muir's South American plan now called for arrival at Guayaquil, Ecuador (on the Pacific coast), rather than "anywhere on the north end of the continent" (the Caribbean coast plan of 1868) demonstrates that he had revised the plan to account for his new location on the West Coast, and therefore confirms that his intentions for the southern adventure were still very much alive. Nevertheless, it was difficult to part from "the glory of YoSemite," he explained to Carr. "I am very happy here and cannot break for the Andes just yet." Another year in California still found Muir actively considering the trip, and in the fall of 1871 he wrote to the director of the Smithsonian Institution, Clinton Merriam, offering to become a gatherer of botanical specimens in South America or elsewhere. As biographer

Stephen Holmes has recognized, but most other scholars have not, Muir "continued to write of California as merely a stopping point before his eventual continuation on to South America."

By the mid-1870s, Muir's life had begun to intertwine with the life of montane California, and his geological, glaciological, and botanical studies of the Sierra absorbed most of his attention. In the decades that followed, as he became increasingly attached to his adoptive home region, he also became an environmental scientist, advocate, and writer of international stature. By the dawn of the twentieth century, Muir knew the Sierra intimately and had described it in detailed scientific and inspiringly lyrical prose; he had made productive scientific excursions to dramatic landscapes in many other parts of the country; he had made numerous discoveries on his seven Alaskan voyages; and his 1903–04 international expedition had enabled him to study many of the most spectacular mountains, immense glaciers, and ancient forests elsewhere on "God's glorious star."

In 1908 Muir, now a national icon and a famous scientist, preservationist, and writer, turned seventy years old. His wife, Louie, had died three years earlier, and his daughters, Wanda and Helen, had begun to give him grandchildren; he had begun to excavate old dreams and memories by dictating material for his autobiography; activist work had begun to limit his opportunities to travel; and his advancing age seemed to increase the urgency of his literary affairs. In a letter of March 2, 1911, Muir described the several books he was then working on, adding that "I have also planned a book describing other Yosemites, another on mountaineering . . . one on trees, one or two on Alaska, two or three on earth sculpture, etc., two or three on travels abroad, and one on animals, etc."

Weighing his literary ambitions against the magnetic pull of wilderness travel, Muir decided, as he had so many times before, that making books would have to wait. Shortly before his seventy-third birthday, Muir responded passionately to a friend who had inquired whether he had finally given up the idea of voyaging to South America: "Have I forgotten the Amazon, Earth's greatest river? Never, never, never. It has been burning in me half a century, and will burn forever." During late winter or early spring of 1911, Muir began to plan in earnest for what he knew would be his last chance to fulfill the long-held dream of reaching the great river. Perhaps thinking of one of his favorite poetic lines—"'twill soon be dark," from Ralph Waldo Emerson's "To J. W."—Muir wrote to his friend Robert Underwood Johnson that he hoped to reach South America "before it is too late." Muir quickly squared away business at the Martinez ranch, took leave of California family and friends, and did what he could to aid the Sierra Club in its struggle to save the Hetch Hetchy Valley from damming. Having tied up what loose ends in California he could, Muir left San Francisco on April 20, 1911, bound by rail to the East.

During the three months between his arrival in New York and his August 12 departure for the equatorial rainforests of Brazil, Muir was tremendously busy. The early weeks of his visit were devoted to meetings, dinners, and talks in the nation's capital, where he lobbied President Taft, members of Congress, and other influential public figures on behalf of Hetch Hetchy. In late May he was in Boston, negotiating publication of his autobiography with Houghton Mifflin; by month's end he was back in New York, arranging with the Century Company for publication of his Yosemite manuscript, which he had not yet completed. In mid-June he spent a few days in New Haven, Connecticut, where on June 21 he received an honorary degree from Yale before returning to New York to finish the Yosemite book. Throughout July and early August Muir remained in New York, racing to complete his Yosemite manuscript, while his thoughts had already begun to head south, toward the Amazon.

In reading the many unpublished letters written to Muir in the weeks preceding his departure, it is striking how energetically Muir's friends and family attempted to dissuade him from taking the solitary voyage, even as they also seemed to realize the futility of their entreaties. "You do not know how loathe we were to let you go on this trip alone," wrote Ellie Mosgrove on April 12, "but then we who know you well forget that the world is yours and not the limited zone we call home." A few days later Henrietta Thompson wrote to her friend: "I do not quite like the idea of this trip you intend making to South America. It is so hot and there are so many snakes and big bugs and biting things generally. . . . Still, if you must follow your fate, of course you will," she writes, "and as you have said, we can trust God to take care of you wherever you go." Toward the end of June, Robert Marshall of the United States Geological Survey (USGS) wrote to Muir that "[i]f you do make that southern trip, I wish you all pleasure of course, but, if it were in my power, I would not let a man who means so much to the world, and especially to these United States, go alone." And at mid-month, unsure if Muir had yet sailed, his dear friend Katharine Hooker wrote, worried: "[A]re you melting away into a barbarous and unknown land, almost as distant in my imagination as another planet? I don't like to think of it." Even President Taft, who, like his predecessor Theodore Roosevelt, considered John Muir something of a national treasure, was concerned about Muir's welfare on the voyage. Unbeknownst to him, Taft issued a July 8 memorandum to United States diplomatic and consular officers around the world, introducing "John Muir, Esquire, a distinguished naturalist and explorer," and requesting for the traveler "such courtesies and assistance as you may be able to render consistently with your official duties."

Finally, on August 3, Helen wrote a very serious letter to her father announcing that she and her husband, Buel Funk, had discussed the matter and had agreed that Buel should accompany Muir on the long journey. "It will be a big load off my mind," writes Helen, "for I don't want to think of you away off there all alone and I will worry all the time you are gone." Knowing of Helen's frail health and her need for Buel during what was the first year of her motherhood, Muir graciously refused, explaining in a letter to Katharine Hooker that "loving darling Helen wrote anxiously begging me to take her husband with me as she couldn't bear to have me go alone. Of course I couldn't let him sacrifice his own young life for mine."

Politely dismissing the admonitions that he was too old, too ill, or too important to undertake the voyage, Muir resolved to reach the Amazon despite the objections of sympathetic friends who did not fully share his passion for wilderness. Although never resigned to the idea of his traveling alone on such an arduous and potentially dangerous journey, most who were close to Muir also realized how important the trip was to him. Typical is the August 8 letter of the recently widowed Fay Sellers, in which she worries about her friend's health and safety, but writes that "[y]ou probably know best, however, and will be happier after you have accomplished it [a voyage to the Amazon], for you have so often talked about it that you will not be contented until you have seen it."

As he contemplated the upcoming journey, Muir seems to have felt a keen sense of impending separation from loved ones, combined with a conviction that a trip so important to him as a person and as a naturalist had to be made before it was too late. To his friends and family—and particularly to Helen, his often-infirm daughter who was now the mother of an infant son named Muir—he wrote tender letters of concern offering paternal words of advice and encouragement. Muir's sense of loneliness and mortality, as well as his sense of urgency to begin the voyage, was intensified by the unfortunate loss of many of his close friends to the ravages of old age. In a poignant letter to Helen, Muir speculates on the recent deaths of three of his closest friends: "Your letter received yesterday telling our dear Sellers's death Sunday made me sad and lonely. I suppose you know that J. D. Hooker, the friend in our greatest need, was taken violently ill the day of dear Sellers's death and died Wednesday evening. And Keith too gone," he wrote, sadly. "I wonder if leaves feel lonely when they see their neighbors falling."

Given the objections voiced by his friends and family, the anguish caused by the recent deaths of several close friends, the worries about Hetch Hetchy Valley, the grueling task of completing the Yosemite manuscript, and the lonely prospect of traveling, old and alone, into the Amazon jungle, it is remarkable that Muir's journey happened at all. Despite these discouragements, Muir's resolve to visit the Amazon seems never to have wavered throughout this period. "It's kind of you to care so much about my loneliness in my travels," he wrote to a concerned friend, "but I'm always fortunate as a wanderer and fear nothing fate has in store." The subtext of Muir's comment perhaps suggests that in order to undertake the great voyage, he had first to prepare himself psychologically for every eventuality, including the unspoken possibility that he might not survive a trip to the southern continents.

Although Muir seems to have casually invited a number of friends—including, at various times, nature writer John Burroughs, USGS administrator Robert Marshall, and curator and paleontologist Henry Fairfield Osborn—to accompany him, there is no evidence that his actual plan ever included traveling companions. "Quite a number of my friends say they would like to go but they cannot. I seem to be the only one free," he notes in a July 14 letter to Marshall. And on the eve of his departure he wrote a letter to Katharine Hooker, announcing that "I start tomorrow for the great hot river I've been wanting so long to see, and alone as usual." Muir remained sanguine about his solitary travels; "oftentimes our loneliest wanderings are most fruitful of all," he commented.

On August 10, 1911, Muir finished the manuscript of his Yosemite book, and just two days later he went down to the harbor to begin what would be his last great journey. In 1868 the young John Muir had hesitantly deferred his South America journey and had instead come to New York and caught a ship to California. Now, forty-four years later, he was back, and, at long last, he was Amazon bound.

The 40,000-Mile Odyssey

Muir's epic voyage began on August 12, 1911, when he left Brooklyn and sailed south through the Atlantic and Caribbean to Belém (then Pará), Brazil, at the mouth of the Amazon. From here Muir steamed 1,000 miles up the great river, fulfilling his dream of following Humboldt's tracks into the greatest river basin on Earth. Near Manaus, at the confluence of the Amazon and Rio Negro, Muir spent an exciting week observing trees, plants, birds, and reptiles, and making a special trip into the thick jungle in search of the rare, gigantic water lily *Victoria regia*. Though the infrequency of upriver steamers prevented him from going another 1,000 miles into the interior, as he had hoped, Muir was deeply satisfied with his

Amazonian jungle experience as the completion of the trip that he had begun four decades earlier. Returning to Belém Muir then sailed to Rio de Janeiro, where he admired the glacially sculpted landscape and the view from the surrounding mountains before continuing south along the Brazilian coast.

From Santos Muir began his quest to find a rare tree of the *Araucaria* genus, *Araucaria braziliensis*, which he knew to be native to southern Brazil. First described by Jussieu in 1789, the *Araucaria* is a genus of South American and Australasian evergreen, and is a striking tree with regularly whorled branches, long boles, and a flattened crown. Some species of the genus grow up to 90 meters tall while others are thought to exceed 1,000 years in age. One of Muir's primary goals in visiting South America was to investigate several rare species of this unusual tree. First he sought *Araucaria braziliensis* (also known to scientists as *Araucaria angustifolia*, and known by common names including pinheiro, candelabra tree, and Parana pine), a tree native to subtropical forests at elevations of 500 to 1,800 meters. Muir was fascinated by this tree, the seeds of which (when not planted by birds such as the blue gralha) provide food for a diversity of animals including humans, monkeys, preás, agoutis, ouriços, serelepes, tirivas, and maitacas. Now far off the routes taken by the few tourists who visited this region during the early twentieth century, Muir traveled by rail inland from Santos and then by small steamer up the Iguacu River into the heart of the Brazilian wilderness, where he at last found vast forests of *Araucaria braziliensis*. He remained in the forest for more than a week, spending nearly every hour of daylight, regardless of the weather, making precise observations of the unusual tree in its native habitat.

Having studied *Araucaria braziliensis* Muir returned to the coast and sailed south to Montevideo and then Buenos Aires. From coastal Argentina he began the second of the great tree quests of his voyage, traveling west across the South American continent to Chile, where he hoped to find the even more rare cousin of *Araucaria braziliensis, Araucaria imbricata*, the so-called monkey puzzle tree. We now know that *Araucaria imbricata* (also known to scientists as *Araucaria araucana*), which is currently protected as an endangered species, grows in southern Chile and southwestern Argentina at elevations of 950 to 1,050 meters. Muir, however, had no certain information about where the tree might be found, and instead simply followed his botanist's instincts five hundred miles south, from Santiago to Victoria, where he intended to begin his search for the tree. After an arduous mountain journey through rough terrain and up to snowline, Muir at last discovered the forest he had crossed the continent to see. He spent an ecstatic day studying and sketching the monkey puzzle tree before sleeping out beneath its branches in the Andean night. Delighted with his observations of the monkey puzzle forest, Muir was soon off again, returning to Santiago and then back across the pampas to Buenos Aires. From Buenos Aires he returned to Montevideo seeking a ship bound for South Africa.

The second major phase of Muir's journey began in early December, when he sailed for South Africa, via the Canary Islands—then a grueling thirty-five-day ocean voyage that clearly suggests Muir's deep desire to study the flora and landscape of the African continent. After spending Christmas and New Year's at sea, Muir at last arrived in Cape Town in mid-January 1912.

From coastal South Africa Muir began yet another great tree pilgrimage—this time to *Adansonia digitata,* the African baobab—traveling inland by rail to search for the tree near the famed Victoria Falls of the Zambezi River. Named for French botanist Michel Adanson, the baobab is a genus of large, evergreen or nearly deciduous trees, classified in the family Bombacaceae, that are native to Africa and Australia. *Adansonia digitata* (called monkey bread tree, dead rat tree, and upside-down tree, as well as the African baobab) is among the largest of the world's great trees. Though it reaches a maximum height of only seventy-five feet, its swollen, bottle-shaped trunk grows to sixty feet in diameter—a girth second only to Muir's beloved Sequoia. The baobab provides important habitat for various animals on the otherwise barren savanna, and the unusual character of its wood allows large specimens to contain up to 30,000 gallons of water. This giant tree has unusual, pendulous, waxy, white flowers that bloom at night and are pollinated by nocturnal animals including lemurs and fruit bats, and its large, gourd-like "monkey bread" fruit (which is actually too hard to be cracked by monkeys) is eaten by baboons. Among the oldest living things on earth, the baobab is believed to live up to 2,000 years. Little wonder that Muir was so determined to find this remarkable tree, or that he so delighted in studying the baobab when at last he found it growing near Victoria Falls. Indeed, after observing and sketching the baobab Muir declared the experience one of the most rewarding of his life.

Traveling to the southwestern coast of Africa, Muir sailed north to Mombasa, in present-day Kenya, where he began the next leg of his journey. In early February he went inland by rail across the wildlife-rich Athi plains to Nairobi, and then on to the shores of Lake Victoria. Taking a small boat across the great lake, Muir studied central African flora on his way to Ripon Falls, where he felt privileged to see the waters of the Nile beginning their 3,000-mile course to the sea. Muir then returned to coastal Africa, where he spent a few days studying trees as he prepared for the long homestretch of his journey.

In late February Muir sailed north: through the Indian Ocean and Red Sea, then through the Suez Canal and across the Mediterranean Sea to Naples, where he visited sites including Pompeii and Mount Vesuvius. On March 15 Muir began the final leg of his travels, first plying the sea along the mountainous coast of Spain, then sailing through the Straits of Gibraltar into the North Atlantic. After weathering unusually severe storms at sea, John Muir arrived safely back in New York on March 27, only a few weeks shy of his seventy-fourth birthday. He had traveled 40,000 miles since leaving America the previous summer, and had not been ill a single day.

"The Most Fruitful Year of My Life"

During his eight-month, 40,000-mile journey to South America and Africa, Muir recorded his observations in three pocket-sized travel journals, with a fourth small journal book devoted to notes gleaned from his reading of books and pamphlets about the botany, zoology, and geology of the "two hot continents." Like his earliest extant journal, which records the thousand-mile walk to the Gulf, this last of Muir's sixty extant journals was carried with him through forest and field, and includes both precise scientific observations and general philosophical ruminations. In addition to written descriptions of flora, fauna, and landscapes both wild and domestic, the journals are also replete with field drawings of the

A page from Muir's 1911 journal, showing field sketches of Araucaria braziliensis

mountains, sunsets, and, especially, the rare trees Muir felt so privileged to witness during his journey; here, in delicate pencil sketches that are sometimes as small as a thumbnail and rarely larger than a playing card, Muir has left minute renderings of towering peaks, sweeping savannas, and gigantic ancient trees. That his techniques of observation and engagement with nature were visual as well as textual is suggested by the number of sketches included—more than 160—and by their organic relationship to the text: the journal pages typically combine written and pictorial representations in referential association.

These journals allow us to travel with Muir as he journeys up the great Amazon, into the jungles of Southern Brazil, to snowline in the Andes, through South and Central Africa to the headwaters of the Nile, and across six oceans and seas in order to reach the rare forests he had so long wished to study. In their words and images, Muir's journals provide us a rare opportunity not only to see *what* Muir sees, but also to see *how* he sees—to glimpse not only the wild and domestic landscapes of the southern continents, but also to see how the fully mature John Muir observed, considered, and represented the beauty of the equatorial and subequatorial regions to which he made his final pilgrimage. We see the private John Muir, a man who remained by sensibility and inclination an observer, recorder, and student of nature even as he was called upon to serve a public role as the reluctant hero of the American movement for wilderness preservation.

Despite their tremendous value and importance, Muir's 1911–12 travel journals have received very little attention from scholars, many of whom have remained unaware of the journals' existence; until now this material has been unpublished and therefore practically unavailable to most students and admirers of Muir's work. Even the voyage recounted in the pages of these journals has rarely received attention, despite the fact that Muir himself described the 1911–12 journey as the most rewarding of his life. A perusal of sixteen biographical and critical studies on Muir published between 1924 and 2000 shows that Muir's last journey has received a *total* of fewer than a dozen pages—and that out of the more than 4,000 pages of analysis collectively contained in these studies. In her seminal 1938 book, *John of the Mountains: The Unpublished Journals of John Muir,* Linnie Marsh Wolfe included nothing from Muir's international travel and field journals, and subsequent Muir editors have followed suit, thereby solidifying a monolithic and distorted view of Muir simply as the patron saint of the Sierra. It is striking, too, how often Muir's travel plans, travels, and travel journals have been discussed inaccurately by those scholars who have discussed them at all. And while there is limited value in enumerating these various errors, distortions, and omissions, they are important as indicators of how little earnest attention has been paid to Muir's international travels and to what those travels suggest about his concerns as a naturalist, writer, environmentalist, and person.

Why have we ignored Muir's international travels, and how do the journals from his South America and Africa voyage help us to achieve a more complete and more nuanced view of Muir's life and character? One important reason we have largely ignored Muir's travels may be that, as Hall and Mark suggest, Muir scholarship is often "Americo-centric and [therefore] fails to recognize the broader significance of much of Muir's work" outside the landscapes of North America. As with Henry Thoreau, the saunterer who asserted at the start of *Walden* that he had "travelled a good deal in Concord," we like to think of Muir as an angelic vagabond whose wanderings encompass our home ground and help to imaginatively chart our American wilderness. We involuntarily think of Muir not as a spokesman for the beauty of "God's glorious star," but rather as an advocate for the part of the planet we like to call our own.

While this identification with Muir as an *American* nature writer, explorer, and preservationist is understandable, Muir's international travels and nature studies remind us that his allegiance was not to Wisconsin, California, or America, but to Earth. As he put it in an entry in his botanical and reading journal from the voyage (in which he paraphrased Hall Caine, whose book *My Story* he was then reading), "[c]at-like devotion to home, believing one's own country the best, is an amiable fallacy." Even before the South America and Africa journey Muir's literary ambitions encompassed his international travels, and he affirmed in a letter of March 1911 that among the books he earnestly planned to write were "two or three on travels abroad." As the inscription to the first extant travel journal of "the wanderer"—as Muir often called himself—so powerfully reminds us, his address was not Yosemite Valley, California, but "John Muir, Earth-planet, Universe." Regardless of how we choose to see him, Muir saw himself as a citizen of Earth first, with other sentiments of membership and affiliation subordinate to that primary self-identification.

The journals of Muir's last journey clearly show that his appreciation for natural beauty and his desire to study plants in their native habitats transcended national borders. So, too, his environmental concern, as when he laments that the Andean forests "are being rapidly destroyed" by comparing the effects of irresponsible timber practices in Chile to those he has seen in other parts of the world. "Lumbermen rent to buy large tracts; cut the most valuable . . . then ruthlessly burn all that's left; nine-tenths or so," Muir explains, sadly. "Dry limbs and brush are piled around every tree and the burning goes on until nothing but black monuments are left of all the flowery leafy woods. . . . Only on a small scale can even New Zealand show equal tree desolation." And so, too, his work as a natural scientist, for Muir so loved rocks and ice and trees that he would seek them in any wilderness, including the "noble palmy ice land" of the subequatorial jungle. The various and precise tree studies contained in these journals demonstrate that Muir was an accomplished botanist whose impressive expertise and passion led to successful botanical studies far beyond the Range of Light. For example, Muir's desire to study rare species of *Araucaria* and his uncanny ability to find them in remote wildernesses distinguished him even from professional South American botanists, who knew very little about the growth of the unusual trees in their native forests. It should take nothing away from our sense of Muir's genuine love of the Sierra to expand our awareness, as Muir himself did, to include the beauty, study, and protection of the natural wonders of other lands.

It is also likely that those interested in Muir have hesitated to examine the 1911–12 materials because they are the record of an old man's experiences. Societal preference for youth and vigor has perhaps predisposed us to freeze Muir in visions of a young man who scaled cliffs and rode avalanches. Although Muir was almost thirty when he first saw Yosemite, in his mid-fifties when he founded the Sierra Club and published his first book, and even older during several of his voyages to Alaska, we persist in imagining him primarily as the indefatigable mountaineer, crucified on the face of Mt. Ritter, meditating in freezing sublimity on Mt. Shasta, or clinging, "with muscles firm braced, like a bobolink on a reed," in a storm-tossed Sierra treetop. When we do tell the story of the older Muir, our narrative is too often limited to the Hetch Hetchy battle, and to a narrow account of that battle which martyrs Muir to the cause of wilderness preservation by directly attributing his death to the loss of the treasured valley.

Perhaps it is to Muir's credit that he has achieved a form of eternal youth in our collective imagination. Like Thoreau, Muir appeals to the idealized part of each us that would be strong, wild, independent, holy, and free of the corruption—if not also the responsibility—of civilized life. Of course it helped that Muir maintained a sprightliness and enthusiasm until close to the end of his life, and that he was unusually active and vigorous even as a septuagenarian. It is also the case that our preference for the image of a youthful Muir is conditioned by Muir's own oeuvre, since the books he published during his lifetime—including, notably, his autobiography—are based primarily upon experiences and journals of the young Muir. Nevertheless, picturing Muir only on summits and in treetops endorses a cult of youth that deprives us of a full understanding of his accomplishments as a person, writer, and naturalist.

Even if we prefer not to think of it, Muir did travel in trains, steamships, and automobiles, and he did grow old and feel the weakening in his body, and he did suffer from the loss of his wife and the death of many of his closest friends. And, as any of us would, Muir worried about his physical demise and meditated on his mortality. But one of the lessons of Muir's 1911–12 journals and correspondence is that he also bore up under the weight of these losses and troubles with remarkable strength of body and character. That the seventy-three-year-old Muir chose to undertake this ambitious voyage to South America and Africa alone—and that he did so with such vigor, passion, pleasure, and success—suggests a courage and independence every bit as impressive as the youthful strength we are more accustomed to associating him with. The South America and Africa journals help us to see Muir as a different kind of hero, one whose endurance and intellectual curiosity carried him into far fields of adventure even as he aged.

Corollary to our hesitancy in thinking of Muir as an old man is our hesitancy in thinking of him as a social man—a person whose connections with and dependencies upon family and friends were deep and earnest. The popular narrative of Muir's life is shaped by the conventions of a romantic wilderness aesthetic that typically figures him as a solitary hero who exchanged his human connections for an apotheosis in the high Sierra. For many, the name John Muir conjures visions of a man who preferred to be alone, who loathed to leave the woods for the defilement of civilization, and who, with a blanket and a little bread and tea, could exist apart from and above the emotional connections that bind humanity together. We prefer Muir of the Sierra wilderness to Muir of the Martinez orchards, Muir of intrepid solitude to Muir the collaborator and colleague, Muir of the wild to Muir of the domestic world that includes family and friends.

One of the contributions of Muir's South America and Africa journals—and, especially, his correspondence—from the voyage is that they remind us of what a loving man Muir was, how genuinely he missed his family and worried about their well-being, how deeply attached he was to his daughters and his grandchildren, how generous he was with the many people for whom he cared. Muir did travel alone on his last voyage, but he also met and befriended many fellow travelers whose company and hospitality he enjoyed. He did value solitary nature study, but he also frequently admitted that he felt lonely and far from home. Muir's late journals and correspondence re-humanize Muir by reminding us that he was a brother, husband, father, grandfather, friend, neighbor, orchardist, and businessman, as well as a scientist, adventurer, and writer—not just an iconic representative of American wilderness but a fully developed human being with genuine affections, ambitions, and fears.

These South America and Africa journals also make a valuable contribution to our understanding of Muir's literary style and aesthetic sensibility, and they introduce a provocatively wide range of literary subjects. Although—and in part *because*—the 1911–12 journals were never finally crafted for publication, they demonstrate the spontaneous energy and insight of Muir's field observations. Written from train cars and steamer decks, houses and hotels, parks and botanical gardens, and the deep jungles, forests, and swamps that Muir described as places "according to my heart," these daily observations and sketches show us Muir in the field rather than at his desk—in the moment rather than in the mode of literary retrospection that so often characterizes his often heavily revised published work. In introducing this first publication of Muir's last journal, I would echo the sentiment expressed by William F. Badè in introducing the initial publication of Muir's first journal, that of the thousand-mile walk to the Gulf: "If the record, as it stands, lacks finish and adornment, it also possesses the immediacy and the freshness of first impressions." Indeed, readers today sometimes find the literary "finish and adornment" of Muir's published work too Victorian in its stylistic excesses, and even Muir was aware of his penchant for sentimental hyperbole, once describing the process of revising his own "adjectivorous" prose as a painful but necessary exercise in "slaughtering gloriouses."

In place of the wrought (and occasionally overwrought) prose of his finished literary work, these more sparse and more meditative field journals show us Muir in conversation with himself rather than in performance for an audience, and therefore offer unique insight into his perceptions and representations of landscapes—including domestic and agricultural landscapes—before the self-conscious rhetorical mediation that characterizes his published books. The Haiku-like compression and intensity of some of Muir's brief journal notes often suggest an aesthetic and literary sensibility that differs provocatively from that of the effusive wilderness psalmist of the early Sierra journals. It is also interesting to contrast the austere reportage and precise scientific observations of Muir's journal entries with the more emotional account of his travel experiences that emerges from the letters he wrote while wandering abroad.

The 1911–12 journals also expand Muir's literary subject, for they provide us an unusual opportunity to examine his impressions of tropical rather than temperate flora, equatorial rather than northern glacial geology, and human culture rather than strictly natural history. He delights in the fecundity and impenetrable verdure of the Amazonian rainforests, despite the fact that his contemporaries associated the region primarily with malaria, savages, and man-eating reptiles. He remarks on the kindness of the South American people and is constantly appreciative of the generosity of the traveling companions he meets along his way. As a glaciologist and geologist he expresses his joy at finding "so clear and noble a manifestation of ice-work at sea level so near the Equator," where he is thrilled to discover "glacier domes feathered with palms instead of hemlocks and spruces and pines." In Africa he hunts not for big game, as did his friend Theodore Roosevelt, but for the bigger game of the rare, immense baobab tree, noting appreciatively after having at last found a representative of the species that he had enjoyed "one of the greatest of the great tree days of my lucky life."

The various ocean voyages that were part of Muir's last journey also give us an opportunity to read Muir's descriptions of seascapes rather than landscapes, the latter of which comprise the vast majority of his nature writing. His descriptions of dolphins, whales, seals, seabirds, flying fish, and ocean waves, light, and storms provide interesting insights into his nautical travel experiences and the aesthetic sensibility through which he understood and represented those experiences.

When he set out for the Amazon in the summer of 1911, Muir commented to friends that "[t]he world's big, and I want to have a good look at it before it gets dark." Before his travels were even halfway through he wrote home to report that "I've had a most glorious time on this trip, dreamed of nearly half a century—have seen more than a thousand miles of the noblest of Earth's streams and gained far more telling views of the wonderful forests than I ever hoped for." And near the end of his journey, he unequivocally affirmed that "I've had the most fruitful time of my life on this pair of hot continents." As for the landscapes, plants, and animals he felt so privileged to have seen on his journey, he wrote happily that "the new beauty stored up is far beyond telling." When John Muir arrived back in New York in late March 1912, he was a just a few weeks shy of his seventy-fourth birthday. He had been away for seven and a half months, during which time he had traveled 40,000 miles, sailed for 109 days, crossed the equator six times, and studied the rivers, jungles, forests, plains, mountains, and rare trees of the southern continents he had longed to see.

"We all travel the milky way together, trees and men," Muir once wrote, after riding out a Sierra windstorm in the wildly pitching crown of a towering Douglas-fir. "Trees are travelers, in the ordinary sense," he philosophized. "They make many journeys, not extensive ones, it is true; but our own little journeys, away and back again, are only little more than tree-wavings—many of them not so much." Muir, a man who traveled to trees and who felt trees travel, thought of his own wanderings as a motion as natural and exhilarating as the tossing of a spruce crown in the wind. As Muir told a reporter for the *Buenos Aires Herald,* who interviewed him as he passed through the city in early November 1911 on his way to the Andes, he was not yet ready to give up his "present occupation." "And what may that be?" asked the reporter. "Tramp," replied Muir, adding that, even at his advanced age, he was "still good at it." And he *was* good at it, for Muir's own tree-wavings took him through the wilds of South America and Africa and brought him home safely to California on his seventy-fourth birthday. Less than three years after returning from his last journey, John Muir's long, productive life came to an end; and when he died, peacefully, on Christmas Eve, 1914, some of his voluminous unpublished manuscripts lay within his reach.

When Muir left Indianapolis in September 1867 with his sight restored and his vision of life clarified, he was bound for the Amazon. When he arrived there in September 1911 after the forty-four-year detour that became most of his adult life, he at last fulfilled a very dear and nearly life-long dream. And if the first of his extant journals had begun with the orienting declaration "John Muir, Earth-planet, Universe," his final journal, here published for the first time, affirms that the pledge Muir once made in blindness was faithfully kept, and that he remained, until the end, a student, lover, and citizen of Earth.

Muir, late in his life, in the "scribble den" of his home in Martinez, California

JOHN MUIR'S LAST JOURNEY

CHAPTER I

Preparing for the Last Journey: California, New York, and Boston

26 January 1911–12 August 1911

THE YEARS LEADING up to his final journey were remarkably active ones in John Muir's life as a traveler, naturalist, activist, family man, and writer. As the twentieth century dawned, Muir was a vigorous man of sixty-one, engaged in studies of geology, glaciology, botany, and palaeontology around the American West and—between May 1903 and May 1904—tree studies around the world. Just before that travel abroad he camped with President Theodore Roosevelt in Yosemite and just after his return he worked hard to win the seventeen-year battle to have responsibility for the protection of Yosemite Valley shifted from the state of California to the federal government. In Muir's private life during this period, the frequent illness of his teenage daughter Helen was a pri-

mary concern, but not the only one. In late June 1905 his wife, Louie, suddenly became ill with what turned out to be a lung tumor, and she died in
early August of that year. Now alone, Muir wandered between the old
family ranch in Martinez and various natural history studies in the field
and at Stanford University and the University of California, Berkeley.

Though punctuated by periods of loneliness, the years following Louie's
death were rich and active ones for Muir, filled with happy family occasions and numerous travels with friends. In the summer of 1906 his eldest
daughter, Wanda, married Thomas Rae Hanna and moved into the adobe
house immediately behind Muir's own house on the Martinez ranch. The
following summer Muir made extensive trips to the Hetch Hetchy Valley
with the Sierra Club and with his friend the artist William Keith. In the
summer of 1908 Muir dictated his autobiography at the Pelican Bay, Ore-
gon, lodge of his friend, the powerful railroad magnate and financier
Edward H. Harriman.

In 1909 Muir, now in his seventies, continued his remarkably active
schedule of travels and explorations, making a six-week trip to the South-
west and visiting the Grand Canyon with fellow literary naturalist John
Burroughs. Later that year he traveled to the lower Colorado River with
Harriman, to Yosemite with Burroughs, to Hetch Hetchy with the Sierra
Club, and to Daggett, California, where Helen was now living in hopes
the desert air would improve her health. In October he toured Yosemite
with President Taft, and Hetch Hetchy with Secretary of the Interior
Richard Ballinger. Muir's family life also had its blessings. Although
Helen was ill with typhoid during the spring of 1909, she recovered well
and was married to Buel A. Funk in October of that year. By 1909 Wanda
had already given Muir his second grandchild.

These were also remarkably productive years for Muir as a writer. *Stickeen,* his famous dog story, was published in 1909, and in 1910 he completed the manuscript of *My First Summer in the Sierra* and began work on
several other book projects. Although 1910 was a year busy with travels in
California and the Southwest, Muir returned four times to Los Angeles to
lodge and write at the home of his wealthy friend John D. Hooker, the

amateur astronomer and retired ironmaster. Muir's friendship with the Hooker family was vitally important to him during these years. Much of his best writing from this period was accomplished not in the "scribble den" of the old Martinez ranch house, but in the garret of the Hooker's home on West Adams Street in Los Angeles, and many of his most expressive letters from the South America and Africa journey were written to J. D. Hooker's wife, Katharine, who was widowed several months before Muir sailed for the southern continents.

Muir's earnest preparations for a trip to South America began in early 1911. He was then seventy-two years old and the grandfather of three: Wanda's sons, Strentzel and John Hanna, and Helen's infant son, Muir Funk. Nevertheless, he had decided to go east to begin his long sea voyage to the Amazon. He also hoped to use the East Coast portion of the trip to lobby representatives in Washington (and prominent men everywhere he could) on the need to preserve the endangered Hetch Hetchy Valley, and to arrange for publication of the several books he was then working on. After doing what he could on both counts, Muir reckoned, he would be free to take an Atlantic steamer south to the Amazon and beyond in order to study the great trees of the only major parts of the world he had not yet visited.

By January 1911 the outline of Muir's plan was shaped, though the details of the trip east and journey south were as yet uncertain. Muir's friend and Yosemite ally Robert Underwood Johnson, an editor at *Century Magazine*, was already soliciting from him any essays that might come out of the planned Amazonian travels. "Don't forget that we want your impressions of South America," reminded Johnson in a January 18 letter to Muir, to which Muir responded, in the January 26 letter included in this chapter, "[m]y impressions of South America, that you mention may be a long way off yet, but I hope to make that journey before it is too late."

Muir's correspondence from early 1911 is also replete with concerns about Hetch Hetchy Valley, the fate of which had already been a matter of contention for more than a decade. Requiring additional water sources to satisfy a booming population, the city of San Francisco had attempted to

gain rights to the Valley since 1901 but had been energetically opposed by
Muir and his Sierra Club allies, who argued that the location of Hetch
Hetchy within Yosemite National Park (established in 1891) made it invi-
olable by urban commercial interests. The stakes in the Hetch Hetchy
fight were high: if the city won and the Valley was dammed, it would assert
the anthropocentric standard of the greatest good for the greatest number
of people; if the Sierra Club won and the Valley was saved, it would assert
the preservationist standard that national parks were sacred ground that
should be protected in perpetuity.

In 1911 Muir was cautiously optimistic about efforts to preserve Hetch
Hetchy from industrial incursion. In a January 27 letter to the family of
Herbert Gleason, the photographer whose work illustrates the first edition of *My First Summer in the Sierra,* he wrote that "[a]ll continues to go
well as far as I know with the Sierra Club in its work, especially with reference to the preservation of Hetch-Hetchy." By February 15, however,
Muir informed his friend the palaeontologist and natural history curator
Henry Fairfield Osborn that "the Hetch-Hetchy question" remained unsettled, and he correctly guessed that a great deal of "hard fighting" was
still ahead for the preservationists. Six weeks later Muir was palpably disgusted with renewed efforts to destroy Hetch Hetchy, and on March 31 he
sent letters of protest to a number of high-ranking federal officials, including President Taft himself, to whom he wrote, with characteristic candor,
that "the San Francisco thieves and robbers are still at work, bent on
destroying some of the grandest of God's handiwork in the Yosemite
National Park." However, letters would not be enough, and Muir was
already preparing to go east to lobby on behalf of "Hetch Hetchy immortal business" before sailing for South America.

In mid-February Muir returned from Los Angeles to Martinez to han-
dle business at the ranch, though he was back in L.A. briefly on March 21
to attend a dinner honoring his friend Theodore Roosevelt, whom he had
guided through the Yosemite wilderness in 1903. Attending the dinner
were "a party of about a dozen gentlemen," which included host Arthur
Fleming, Roosevelt, and John Burroughs. Muir was also invited to Roo-

sevelt's lecture later that evening, "A Zoological Trip through Africa"—a topic of considerable interest to Muir, who seems already to have been considering whether to extend the planned South America journey so far as Africa.

Returning to Martinez after what he called "a very brilliant and in every way Rooseveltian affair," Muir took up his South America travel plans with new resolve. In his correspondence from this period there is a sense of urgency that confirms his commitment to reach the Amazon—a desire for South American travel mixed with a fear that if he did not go at once he might miss his opportunity to go at all. During late March and early April Muir settled matters at the ranch, arranged his manuscripts a bit, and wrote some final letters urging loved ones to take special care in his absence. On the evening of April 20 he left San Francisco, bound for New York on a private railcar provided courtesy of the family of his friend E. H. Harriman, whom he eulogized in a booklet entitled *Edward Henry Harriman,* and with whose family he often corresponded.

Although we have no details of Muir's trip to New York, it is certain that after his arrival he wasted little time in getting to Washington, D.C., and lobbying on behalf of Hetch Hetchy. As early as May 8, Muir was already able to inform William Colby of the "good luck" that had allowed him to preach the preservation of the Valley in meetings with President Taft, Secretary of the Interior Walter Fisher, Speaker of the House Champ Clark, Congressman Joseph Cannon, and "lots of senators and representatives." In a letter included in this chapter Muir wrote to Katharine Hooker that "[e]ver since my arrival on this crowded side of the continent I've been in a dizzy whirl of National Park work, book publishing arrangements, South American plans, visits, receptions, dinners, etc." "In particular," he noted, perhaps in explanation for delays in his planned departure for the Amazon, "I feel bound to do all in my power for the Hetch Hetchy Valley ere I vanish in the wilderness of the other America."

In addition to ambitious lobbying work to preserve the endangered valley, Muir was also busy arranging for publication of the several books he then had in progress. His first book, *The Mountains of California,* had been published by the Century Company in 1894, but Houghton Mifflin had published *Stickeen* in 1909 and had *My First Summer in the Sierra*, which would come out in June 1911, already in press. Nevertheless, Muir had decided to return to the Century Company for the publication of "a Yosemite book"—which he sometimes referred to by the tentative title "Yosemite Valley and Other Yosemites"—that he was even then rushing to finish before leaving for South America. On May 13 Muir traveled from New York City to Rochester on the Harrimans' private railcar, and within a few days had continued on to Boston to discuss with Houghton Mifflin possible terms of publication for his autobiography. Although Century was also interested in the autobiography, Muir ultimately decided—after some negotiations regarding advance serial publication—to contract with Houghton Mifflin, which eventually brought out *The Story of My Boyhood and Youth* in March 1913.

In addition to visiting New York, Washington, and Boston, Muir also spent a few days in New Haven, where, on June 21, he received an honorary degree from Yale University. Although Harvard had likewise honored him in 1896 and the University of Wisconsin had done so in 1897, Muir seemed to enjoy the Yale ceremony particularly, and he composed a number of charming, comically self-deprecating, mock-heroic missives, such as the June 27 letter to Charlotte Kellogg that is reproduced in this chapter.

Though Muir often referred to himself as "the wanderer," his desire to wander to South America was being delayed by a number of obligations, the most urgent of which was the need to finish the manuscript of the Yosemite book before "vanish[ing] in the wilderness of the other America." His letters throughout June and July routinely refer to the Yosemite book and his need to complete it as soon as possible. In a July 14 letter to John Burroughs, Muir explained that he had intended to work on the book in the offices of the Century Company in New York City but that the extraordinary heat of the summer of 1911 had driven him to the Hudson highlands, where he had decided to work in the cooler, more comfortable surroundings at Castle Rock, his friend Henry Fairfield Osborn's summer house at Garrison on the Hudson, near West Point. Muir was working almost constantly during July, and he now routinely declined social and professional invitations in order to remain at Castle Rock and finish his Yosemite book in time to sail for the Amazon by mid-August.

Amidst this physical separation from his family and friends, and laboring beneath the burden of the summer heat and worries about the fate of the treasured Hetch Hetchy Valley, Muir was working at a frenetic and exhausting pace. Though he often cautioned his daughters against overwork, Muir was himself a stubborn and often indefatigable worker, as his efforts during July and early August clearly show. His letters to his family before the journey, several of which are included here, tend to emphasize his physical preparedness for the journey. On the very day of his departure he reassures Helen: "Don't fret about me, for I've been so well fed, etc., that in spite of hard work I'm perfectly well." Other letters, such as his August 2 missive to Katharine Hooker, however, reveal the work regimen under which Muir had placed himself during the months prior to sailing: "Have been at work every morning for weeks and weeks at 5:00 to about 8:00 p.m. Fell asleep day before yesterday pen in hand though can't sleep much in bed."

Having worked approximately 100 hours per week for almost two months straight, Muir completed the manuscript of the Yosemite book on the evening of August 10, leaving him less than two days before he sailed for the Amazon. The final words of that book, published the following April under the title *The Yosemite*, are among his most famous: "These temple destroyers, devotees of a ravaging commercialism, seem to have a perfect contempt for Nature, and, instead of lifting their eyes to the God of the mountains, lift them to the Almighty Dollar. Dam Hetch Hetchy! As well dam for water-tanks the people's cathedrals and churches, for no holier temple has ever been consecrated by the heart of man." Having ended the book with those powerful lines, Muir deposited his manuscript with the Century Company, packed his bags, wrote a few quick letters, and, by the morning of August 12, 1911, was ready to sail out of Brooklyn Harbor, bound for the great Amazon at last.

Correspondence

Los Angeles, California
January 26, 1911
Robert Underwood Johnson[1]

Dear Mr. Johnson,

I am glad you are going to give me a memorandum of your relationship to Yosemite Park and other parks. Do not make it too short, as I want everybody to know that in particular you invented Yosemite Park.

On receipt of your letter of Jan. 5th I wrote immediately to your son-in-law, Mr. Holden, at the Fairmont Hotel, San Francisco, giving him my address and saying I hoped to meet him here, but I have not yet heard from him.

I shall be glad to see Mr. Scott here.[2]

My impressions of South America, that you mention, may be a long way off yet, but I hope to make that journey before it is too late.

---

[1] Robert Underwood Johnson (1853–1937), editor, writer, diplomat, and civic activist, was a friend and collaborator of JM's. Johnson, who met JM in 1889, was for forty years an editor at *Century Magazine* in New York City. He published many of JM's essays and articles on environmental preservation there, and lobbied for protection of Yosemite and other important American wilderness regions. It was Johnson who first suggested the idea of a Yosemite National Park, and the "memorandum" here mentioned is a reference to JM's request that Johnson provide him a reminiscence of his role in creating Yosemite Park so that JM might accurately represent the facts in his book *The Yosemite* (Century Company, 1912), which he was then writing. Johnson remained an influential defender of Yosemite for a quarter century, and he was largely responsible for persuading President Cleveland's administration to form the influential Forest Commission of the National Academy of Scientists (often termed the Sargent Commission), which resulted in the protection of 21 million acres of America's forests. Johnson was also a poet of some distinction, an early member of the American Academy of Arts and Letters, and, later, Ambassador to Italy. Because of his encouragement of JM's writing about South America and Africa—and his role in the Hetch Hetchy controversy—Johnson is particularly important to the story told in *John Muir's Last Journey*. In "John Muir As I Knew Him," a reminiscence Johnson presented at a meeting of the American Academy of Arts and Letters on January 16, 1916 (a little over a year after JM's death), he declared that "the world will look back to the time we live in and remember the voice of one crying in the wilderness and bless the name of John Muir."

[2] "Mr. Scott" was a senior editor at *Century Magazine*, whom Johnson had told JM would soon be visiting San Francisco.

I am trying dictation and in the story of my life I find I can do something in the way of composition, though of course it has to be recast often.[3]

Glad you had such a splendid time at the Academy and wish I could have been with you.[4]

Don't work too hard, now that you are Editor, since blessed Gilder left you.[5]

Hoping to see you ere long, I am,

Ever faithfully yours,

John Muir

———

Los Angeles, California
February 11, 1911
Charlotte Kellogg[6]

Dear Mrs. Kellogg,

I'll take our first train which if on time leaves here at 6:45 and arrives San Francisco about 8:30 so I may catch your 9:00.

I want to go to the *Araucaria imbricata* forests[7] and across Brazil and to

[3] The project that was eventually published as *The Story of My Boyhood and Youth* (Houghton Mifflin, 1913).

[4] The American Academy of Arts and Letters (which Johnson helped establish in 1904), the activities of which Johnson often reported to JM.

[5] Richard Watson Gilder (1844–1909), American poet and senior editor of *Century Magazine,* was upon his death succeeded by Johnson.

[6] Charlotte Hoffmann Kellogg (1864–1946) was the wife of Vernon L. Kellogg (1867–1937), a zoologist and professor of entomology at Stanford University. Charlotte Kellogg was the author of a number of books, including *Women of Belgium* (1917), *Jadwiga, Queen of Poland* (1936), *Pacific Light* (poems, 1939), and *Paderewski* (1956), and she worked in war-relief efforts during World War I, including service in occupied Belgium during 1916. It should be noted that Charlotte and Vernon Kellogg were not related to Dr. Albert Kellogg (1813–1887), the California botanist who wrote *Forest Trees of California* (1882) and with whom JM explored the Sierra in the fall of 1873.

[7] In this letter JM introduces the genus of rare tree that would occupy so much of his time and imagination during the 1911–12 journey and which receives so many references throughout this book. There are at least nineteen species of *Araucaria.* Most species are tropical (many are endemic to New Caledonia and Malaysia), and many are threatened with extinction. The genus is said to have been named for the province of Arauco in southern Chile. Muir had long read about *Araucaria* and had, during his 1903–04 world tour, taken pains to study two Australian species, *Araucaria bidwillii* and *Araucaria cunninghamii*, in the mountains of Queensland.

South Africa and to Stanford Kellogg.[8] The last seems most difficult of the three. Should I live through them all then "it's home and it's home and it's home I would be,"[9] if ever I'm to have a fixed home this side of the great river.

Ever yours,
John Muir

Los Angeles, California
February 15, 1911
Henry Fairfield Osborn

Dear Mr. Osborne,[10]

No end of obstacles jumped up in my way last fall when I was planning to be with you and the Harrimans,[11] for glorious visits and some most interesting Hetch Hetchy work.

As subsequent letters and journal entries make clear, JM spent considerable time seeking, and then studying, documenting, and sketching, *Araucaria braziliensis* in the forests of southern Brazil. Because of its value as lumber, only a small fraction of the pre-settlement forests of *Araucaria braziliensis* has survived, and much of what remains is very near where JM saw it, in what is now Brazil's Iguaçu National Park. The other species of *Araucaria* JM sought in South America was the one mentioned in this letter, *Araucaria imbricata* (now known to scientists as *Araucaria araucana* and bearing the memorable common name monkey puzzle tree). More rare than its Brazilian cousin, *Araucaria imbricata*, which is now protected as an endangered species, grows in southern Chile and southwestern Argentina at elevations of 950 to 1,050 meters. JM discovered a forest of *Araucaria imbricata* growing at the Andean snowline near Victoria, Chile. Forests of this unusual tree have been preserved within Argentina's Lanin National Park. Given JM's tremendous influence on the national park movement—a movement that began in the United States but has since spread around the world—it is fitting that both species of *Araucaria* that JM traveled to South America to study are now preserved in national parks there.

[8] Probably a reference to Vernon Kellogg, to the Kellogg family generally, or to the Kellogg's home near Stanford University.

[9] JM's allusion is to the poem "Loyalty," by Scottish poet, anthologist, biographer, and novelist Allan Cunningham (1784–1842), which begins with the following lines: "Hame, hame, hame! Oh hame I fain wad be, / O hame, hame, hame, to my ain countrie!"

[10] JM occasionally misspelled Osborn's name, as he does here, by incorrectly adding the letter "e" to the name. JM's friend Henry Fairfield Osborn (1857–1935) was chief curator of the American Museum of Natural History and was the first curator of the Museum's Department of Vertebrate Paleontology, which opened in 1891. Osborn was also a professor at Princeton (1881–90) and Columbia (1890–1909).

[11] The family of Edward H. Harriman (1848–1909), the railroad magnate and financier whose Harriman expedition to Alaska JM had joined in 1899. At the request of Harriman's wife, made after her husband's death in 1909, JM wrote the small book *Edward Henry Harriman* as a tribute (New York: Doubleday, Page, & Co., 1911). JM remained friends with the Harriman family until his death.

I have been shut up in a garret this winter, writing on three different books, one of which, a little journal, is now in the press, a volume of auto-biography, and a book on Yosemite Valley and other Yosemites. The greater part of the time I have been half sick with the "grip" as usual,[12] but I hope to be with you in the spring.

By the enclosed "Resolution" you will see that the Hetch Hetchy question is still far from being settled,[13] and I look forward to a good deal of hard fighting about next May,[14] for the proponents of that damming scheme are still hard at work with plenty of money, leaving no stone un-turned that they think may give them a chance to complete this grand national robbery. I trust, however, that President Taft and Secretary Ballinger will stand fast and that the right will triumph.

With warmest regards to Mrs. Osborne and all the family, I am,

Faithfully yours,

John Muir

———

Martinez, California
March 2, 1911
Betty Averell [15]

My dear Betty Averell,

Your letter came perilously near charming me across the continent leav-

---

[12] The "grip" (often spelled "grippe") is now known as the "flu."

[13] The resolution JM mentions has not survived with the letter; since several important documents regarding the Hetch Hetchy controversy were being produced at about this time, it is not possible to know with certainty which resolution is referred to here. For a description of documents that might correlate to JM's reference, see Jones (ch. 5).

[14] JM probably expected this fighting in May because President William Howard Taft's Secretary of the Interior Richard Ballinger had granted the city of San Francisco until June 1, 1911 (a deadline later extended several times by Ballinger's successor, Walter Fisher), to present its case for damming Hetch Hetchy.

[15] "Betty" is Elizabeth Averell, daughter of Mr. and Mrs. William H. Averell, of Rochester, New York. W. H. Averell was the brother of Mary Williamson Averell, who was the wife of Edward Henry Harriman. Elizabeth Averell (then a teenager) had been among the passengers on the *George W. Elder* when it sailed—with JM, John Burroughs, and many other famous naturalists aboard—to Alaska on the famous Harriman expedition of 1899. During that expedition JM used the affectionate term the "Big Four" to refer to Dorothea Draper, Betty Averell, and Betty's cousins Mary and Cornelia Harriman.

ing all cares to gang tapsalterrie,[16] as Burns sings. Yes, I learned that Will was going East 2 or 3 weeks ago when at Los Angeles I called to see him and get tidings of you.

I'm glad to hear of the tribute to the memory of Mr. Harriman. None I know deserves more. The whole country is his monument.

You mention your aunthood and mother's grandmotherhood, while I have been grandfathered thrice. My daughter Wanda has a pair of boys 2 and 4 years of age, and the other day darling Helen got a boy.[17] This quarter dozen of youngsters and the almanac offer startling proofs of age. Yet, strange to say, I am almost wholly unconscious of the fast flying years, and if possible feel younger than I did while writing my first Sierra journal in the summer of 1869, thirty years before I first saw you. This, in part, is the reward of those who climb mountains and keep their noses outdoors.

You ask what I'm doing. I'm correcting the book proofs of my *First Sierra Summer,* to be published in April, putting finishing touches on a Yosemite book and a first volume of a sort of Autobiography begun at the Harriman Pelican Lodge. It begins with my school days in Scotland, tells of going to America, life on a farm in the Wisconsin Woods, and ends at the close of my four years course at the Wisconsin University. To complete the Autobiography will probably require 8 or 12 years. I have also planned a book describing other Yosemites, another on mountaineering, illustrated by some of my own wandering, scrambling excursions, one on trees, one or two on Alaska, two or three on earth sculpture, etc., two or three on

[16] JM's allusion is to Robert Burns's 1784 song "Green Grow the Rashes, O," the fourth stanza of which (that is, the third stanza following the opening chorus) reads: "But gie me a cannie hour at e'en, / My arms about my dearie, O, / An' war'ly cares an' war'ly men / May a' gae tapsalteerie, O!" (Most scholars also attribute to Burns the bawdy version of this song which is included in *The Merry Muses of Caledonia.*) The spirit of Burns's line is repeated in a slightly different form in his 1785 poem "To a Mouse," which includes the famous lines "The best-laid schemes o' mice an' men / Gang aft a-gley."
[17] JM and his wife, Louisa Wanda ("Louie") Strentzel Muir (1847–1905), had two children. Their first child, Annie Wanda (1881–1942), married Thomas Hanna in 1906 and had six children: Strentzel (1907–1973), John (b. 1909), Richard (1912–1992), Robert (1914–1958), Jean (1919–1976), and Ross (b. 1922). Their second child, Helen Lillian (1886–1964), married Buel A. Funk in 1909 and had four children: Muir (1911–1970), Stanley (1912–1962), John (1914–1973), and Walter (b. 1916). Thus, in March 1911 Wanda's "pair of boys" would have been Strentzel and John, and Helen's new baby would have been Muir Funk, who was born on February 2, 1911.

Muir beneath the palm tree at his Martinez home

travels abroad, and one on animals, etc. The trouble is that when impor-
tuned long ago to write, write, I said I couldn't spare the time until too old
to climb mountains. The mountains are still calling, though somehow I've
been persuaded to make a beginning on the endless weary word-work.

But it grows late and this letter is growing unconscionably long and
book manuscript-like. Give my love to your mother, brother, and sister,
and to Mrs. Harriman and the Osborns.

Affectionately yours,

    J.M.

P.S. Have I forgotten the Amazon, Earth's greatest river? Never, never,
never. It has been burning in me half a century, and will burn forever. For

you must know, dear Betty, that even water and rocks, everything God possesses, burns like the stars in His love.

I've been up to the eyes in plodding word-work all winter in Hooker's garret,[18] whence I often ran last summer to see you. Long ere this I had hoped to be with you, the Harrimans and Osborns and all those blessed tribes who with unfailing sympathy have been so much to me. But struggle as I may to let my heart have its way, Fate has held me fast here doubled up at a desk making it appear that the greater our freedom the more firmly are we guided and bound.

Los Angeles, California
March 31, 1911
William E. Colby[19]

Dear Mr. Colby,

It must make every honest man grunt to have this eternal Hetch-Hetchy question bob up as if not a word had been written or spoken on the subject before. I have written to Taft, Kent, and the new Secretary, as you suggested.[20] All we can do, as far as I see, is to watch and be ready for every action that the unweariable thieves and robbers invent.

---

[18] After his wife's death in 1905, JM often did his writing at the homes of various close friends. During much of 1910 JM had been writing at the home of John D. Hooker on West Adams Street in Los Angeles.

[19] William Edward Colby (1875–1964) was a San Francisco attorney and environmental activist who served as the secretary of the Sierra Club from 1900 to 1946 and was the recipient of the Club's first John Muir Award, given in 1961.

[20] "Taft" is twenty-seventh US President William Howard Taft (1857–1930). "Kent" is Progressive Republican Congressman William Kent of California (1864–1928), who served in Congress from 1911 to 1917. Kent was sympathetic to environmental causes, and he eventually presented the redwood grove now called Muir Woods, which was then his family's private property, to the United States. The "new Secretary" is Secretary of the Interior Walter Lowrie Fisher (1862–1935), who took office in 1911. JM's letters to these public officials were written on March 31, the same day as the letter to Colby.

Send me a word every day or two telling Keith's condition,[21] and when you see him always assure him of my love.

I expect to be in San Francisco about the middle of April.

Faithfully yours,

John Muir

———

Los Angeles, California
March 31, 1911
Helen Muir Funk [22]

Darling Helen,

I was so glad to get your postal and letter telegram, and your letters of March 28th and 29th, all of them assuring me that you were well and growing stronger in the blessed desert air.

One thing I want to warn you about, and that is against the baby taking cold. You know that he has been breathing air of a regular temperature ever since he was born, until you suddenly took him up to an elevation of 2,000 feet[23] and into a house, which, unless you exert extreme care, you cannot keep anywhere near an even temperature, making it all the more necessary that you guard against having him too thinly covered, and against drafts. Your house, with its thin walls, is easily heated by the sun, and chilled by the wind at night. You cannot therefore be too careful. And again, remember what I told you about boiling all the water that you drink. If these things are watched and attended to with eternal vigilance I have not the slightest doubt but what you will all thrive.

As for myself, I am all right, but already feeling lonesome in not having you where I could walk to you in your room at the hospital, and also feel-

[21] A statement of concern for his friend, the artist William Keith (1838–1911), who was then very ill. JM was great friends with Keith, a fellow Scot, whom he had met in Yosemite in 1872 and with whom he had often traveled. The death of the artist later that year grieved JM greatly.

[22] JM's youngest daughter, Helen Lillian Muir (1886–1964), who had married Buel A. Funk (1889–1934) in 1909.

[23] JM's daughter Helen, her husband, Buel Funk, and their new baby, Muir Funk (1911–1970) had moved from Hollywood to Daggett, California, on the edge of the Mojave Desert, where it was hoped that the drier climate would improve Helen's health.

ing that in a week or two I must be on my way east. You know I never like to travel, and somehow I feel less and less inclined to leave home than ever. Still, I must do the best I can. I will have an easy trip to New York anyhow. Do not know when I will get back.

I gave Mrs. Jones your message. Also Mrs. Thompson; and soon I will see Mrs. Sellers.[24] All who know you send love.

Don't forget to write. I will send you word when I leave here, so you may direct your letters to the old home.

Ever your devoted father,

John Muir

P.S. Hope Tom will come round by and by.[25]

––––––

San Francisco, California
April 20, 1911
Vernon L. Kellogg

Dear Kelloggs three,[26]

I am starting out on a long journey. I leave for New York in a private car this evening.[27] Have gotten all arrangements made and will visit Boston, and Washington, and perhaps South America, before I return. I regret very much that book writing has prevented me from being able to visit you before leaving.

Very affectionately yours,

John Muir

P.S. Will write. Address c/o R. U. Johnson, Century Magazine, Union Square, New York

––––––

[24] Alice S. Jones, wife of Mr. Fred Jones and niece of John D. Hooker, who lived in the Hooker home where JM was then staying and to whom JM playfully referred as "Alice-hark-the-lark." Henrietta Thompson, who served JM as typist and literary secretary during his lengthy stays in Los Angeles. Fay Sellers, wife of JM's Pasadena friend Col. A. H. Sellers, whom he met in Yellowstone in August 1885.
[25] Presumably Thomas R. Hanna (1881–1947), who had married JM's eldest daughter, Annie Wanda Muir (1881–1942) in 1906.
[26] The "Kelloggs three" are Vernon L. Kellogg, his wife Charlotte Hoffmann Kellogg, and their daughter Charlotte Jean Kellogg (elsewhere referred to by JM as "Jean").
[27] The Edward H. Harriman family's private railroad car, *Arden*, which the family had made available for JM's journey east.

Washington, D.C.
May 8, 1911
William E. Colby

Dear Mr. Colby,

I came here last Thursday on Hetch Hetchy immortal business with R. U. Johnson, and so far have had what looks like good luck. Had a long hearty telling talk with the President, three with Sec. Fisher. Lunched with speaker Champ Clark and his wife and daughter and of course got in Hetch Hetchy and Yosemite Park and parks in general, ably seconded by Johnson. Smoked and talked over the whole Hetch Hetchy history with immortal Joe Cannon[28] in his private room in the capitol. Saw lots of senators and representatives and made an hour and a half speech on Hetch Hetchy and parks at a grand dinner of the influential Boone & Crockett Club,[29] standing beside the chairman and Secretary Fisher. This being the fourth time that I have met Sec. Fisher he must now know our side of the question fairly well.

I never imagined I could stand so much dining and late hours. What with getting my Yosemite book finished and the other placed for publication I may not get off on my S. American trip until near the end of next

[28] "Sec. Fisher" is Walter Lowrie Fisher (1862–1935), a Republican urban reformer who was particularly influential in Chicago. Through his work with the Conservation League of America and the National Conservation Association Fisher became a friend of Gifford Pinchot, President Theodore Roosevelt's Chief Forester, and James R. Garfield, Roosevelt's Secretary of the Interior. In 1911 President Taft appointed Fisher Secretary of the Interior, a post held until 1913, when he returned to law practice and conservation work in Chicago. "Champ Clark" is James Beauchamp Clark, Kentuckian, agrarian Democrat, orator, and legislator, who served as Speaker of the House of Representatives from 1911 to 1919. The "immortal Joe Cannon" is Joseph Gurney Cannon (1836–1926), Republican Congressman from Illinois, who served a total of forty-six years in Congress, nearly continuously from 1872 until his retirement 1923; known for his iron-fisted rule as Speaker of the House, "Uncle Joe" Cannon was so exploitative of his political power that his methods gave rise to the term *Cannonism.*
[29] Founded in 1887 by Theodore Roosevelt, the Boone & Crockett Club is a sportsman's organization that focuses on hunting, outdoor ethics, and the promotion of wildlife research and associated conservation efforts.

month. My address will be as at present until at least the middle of June, c/o R. U. Johnson, The Century Co., Union Square, New York.

Send me a few copies of the Hetch Hetchy pamphlet.[30]

Ever Faithfully Yours,

John Muir

P.S. Have dedicated "My First Summer" to the Sierra Club.

————

Rochester, New York
May 14, 1911
Helen Muir Funk

Darling Helen,

I'm so glad to be able to share in your gladness through your letters, and never am weary in thanking heaven for your health, and little boy's health, and Buel's. Long may you all live and love whether in desert or town.

I came here last evening from New York with Mrs. Harriman and Carol in the Private Car *Arden*. Am here only for a day or two at the Averell's on the way to Boston to see about the publication of the Autobiography, etc. After Boston I return to N.Y., there to remain until about the end of June when I go to New Haven for a day or two at Yale.[31] Then I hope to get off to S. America. In the meantime I'll try to finish my Yosemite book in Mrs. Harriman's garret.

I had a great time in Washington, as I think I wrote you. Hereafter I'll be comparatively quiet and may get some work done other than Yosemite and Hetch Hetchy. My address will be No. 1, East sixty ninth St., New York, N.Y. c/o Mrs. E. H. Harriman or to the Century Co. as before— until I sail.

Heaven bless you darling and all who love you.

Your devoted Father,

John Muir

————

[30] For more information on the various "Hetch Hetchy pamphlet[s]" distributed by the Sierra Club, see Jones (ch. 4).
[31] JM had been invited to New Haven to receive an honorary degree from Yale; he did visit New Haven for several days, and received an honorary Litt.D. degree on June 21, 1911.

My dear Mrs. Hooker,[32]

Your note of May 17th just received on my return from Boston, and I'm so glad to get your San Francisco address to which letters may now fly straight from heart to heart.

The above will be my address until the first week of July though any letters sent in Johnson's care will reach me here. I am stopping with the Harrimans, a grand place and the perfect home in which now that the greater part of the Hetch Hetchy Washington work is done I hope to finish the Yosemite book. Ever since my arrival on this crowded side of the continent I've been in a dizzy whirl of National Park work, book publishing arrangements, South American plans, visits, receptions, dinners, etc. In particular I feel bound to do all in my power for the Hetch Hetchy Valley ere I vanish in the wilderness of the other America.

The interest taken in my simple work seems wonderful, and wonderful too it seems that I have been able to endure weeks of late hours and extravagant lionizing with no apparent injury. After a dinner the American Alpine Club is arranging for me,[33] and the cap and gown affair,[34] I may get some real work done. I long to hear from you. How bravely are you endur-

---

[32] JM wrote many letters—usually addressed to "my dear friend"—to Katharine Putnam Hooker, wife of JM's dear friend, the retired ironmaster, inventor, amateur astronomer, and philanthropist John Daggett Hooker (1838–1911). Katharine Hooker was the author of three books of Italian travel, *Wayfarers in Italy* (1902), *Byways in Southern Tuscany* (1918), and *Through the Heel of Italy* (1927). J. D. Hooker, a descendant of Reverend Thomas Hooker of Massachusetts, was a member of the California Academy of Sciences and is perhaps best known for having financed the famous Hooker telescope at the Mt. Wilson observatory—the most powerful astronomical instrument of its day. The Hookers had been great friends to JM, and JM corresponded regularly with the family, especially in the years following J. D. Hooker's death in 1911.

[33] The American Alpine Club, founded in 1902, is an organization of mountain climbers devoted to exploration and scientific study of high mountain and polar regions, dissemination of knowledge regarding mountains and mountaineering, and conservation and preservation of mountain regions and climbing areas. The dinner the Club arranged in JM's honor was held at New York's Hotel Manhattan on June 17, 1911; the talk Muir gave at the event was later published in the *Sierra Club Bulletin* (vol. 12 [January 1924]: 43–46).

[34] The ceremony at which JM received an honorary Litt.D. degree from Yale.

ing your heavy load.[35] The letter you inquire about with various enclosures was duly received, and you may rest assured that communication is now perfectly reliable.

You say you seem to have lost me altogether. You should know that while I live such loss is impossible. All Hookers are in my heart to stay, you and Marian[36] the deepest of all.

It's kind of you to care so much about my loneliness in my travels, but I'm always fortunate as a wanderer and fear nothing fate has in store. Have no plans as yet but will probably go straight to Para and up the great river as a beginning. Anyhow and anywhere, I'm faithfully, affectionately,

Your friend,

John Muir

———

New York City
May 30, 1911
Helen Muir Funk

Darling Helen,

Your letter received yesterday telling our dear Sellers's death Sunday made me sad and lonely.[37] I suppose you know that J. D. Hooker, the friend in our greatest need, was taken violently ill the day of dear Sellers's death and died Wednesday evening. And Keith too gone. I wonder if leaves feel lonely when they see their neighbors falling.

Mrs. Harriman is exceedingly kind. I'm trying to finish the book on Yosemite before I set out for the other America. I got a copy of "My First Summer" from the publishers two or three days ago. It looks well. In a week or so it will be in the stores.

---

[35] JM here refers to the illness of Katharine's husband, John D. Hooker. Although the timing, location, and tone of the letter make clear that JM could not have known of it, John D. Hooker died on May 24, 1911—the very day that JM wrote this letter.

[36] Dr. Marian Osgood Hooker, born in 1875, was the Hookers' daughter and a physician and scientist who published a number of books on technical and scientific subjects.

[37] During this period JM learned of the deaths not only of Col. A. H. Sellers, John D. Hooker, and William Keith, but also of Henry Hooker, Jeanne Carr, his sister Margaret, Edward H. Harriman, Catharine Merrill, and Francis Fisher Browne.

I'm so glad your little boy is thriving and is so dear a child. I haven't heard from Wanda since I left California. Give my kindest regards to Buel and his mother and that little girl.

　　Devotedly your Father,
　　　　John Muir

———

New York City
June 13, 1911
Hooker family

My dear, dear friends Hookers,

　　I'm so glad your brother is with you, and hope ere this you have all gone to the healing soothing mountains. Surely the melancholy business affairs can be left to lawyers by this time.[38] Anyhow don't let your hearts be troubled. All that's worth while you have in abundance with God's peace and love.

　　Every day I feel anxious to be with you in case I might be able to help in some way. Write a word or two often. I may not start on the Amazon trip for nearly a month trying to complete the Yosemite book.

　　Remember me to Alice and Fred.[39]

　　Ever faithfully affectionately yours,
　　　　John Muir

P.S. I sent a letter to your San Francisco address.

———

New York
June 27, 1911
Charlotte Kellogg

My dear, dear Mrs. Kellogg,

　　In re-re-reading your charming letter of May 25th[40] telling in such sprightly witty triumphant style your happy mothery housekeeping I

[38] That is, affairs having to do with the settlement of the estate of John D. Hooker.
[39] Alice and Fred Jones, Mrs. Hooker's niece and her husband, who lived in the Hooker home.
[40] The letter here referred to may be found in the MP (I/A/20/11340).

always feel that you are working too hard. I know that mother-love radium can work miracles just as Nature-love radium of the Scotch kind lifts mountainous bodies with only crumbs of bread to the highest summits as if they were light as thistledown. But somehow I always feel that those I love most should have good rest and good substantial meaty nourishment and avoid exhausting work.

No doubt you have found enough but too much work and care with too little rest. Pray be kind and pitiful to yourself but watch Jean's gums and lance them if necessary.

I've been this side of the continent two months—have done lots of National Park work at Washington and book work here and in Boston, wildly interrupted by endless dinners, lionizing, etc. Am now trying to hide in Prof. Osborn's log writing den in a hickory grove to finish a Yosemite book before leaving for S. America. Perhaps I told you that Yale wished to give me a degree, and as it was in great part for saving God's parks I ventured to accept hoping their action might help to make public opinion for Yosemites.[41] I went to New Haven on the morning of June 20th and was received and entertained with wonderful cordiality and taken to the ball game in the afternoon.

Though at first a little nervous on account of the approaching degree ceremonies I quickly caught the glow of the Yale enthusiasm. Never before have I seen or heard anything just like it. The many alumni classes assembled from all the country were clad in wildly colored uniforms, and the way they capered and danced, sang and yelled, wheeled and doubled quadrupled and octopled their flying ranks is utterly indescribable. Autumn leaves in whirlwinds are staid and decorous in comparison. Surely nothing in the golden coronation glory over the sea could surpass it in uncontrollable fraternal alma mater gladness and loyalty.

The next memorable morning we donned our academic robes and marched to the great hall where the degrees were conferred. I had perhaps the best seat on the platform, and when my name was called I arose with

[41] In other words, JM accepts the degree because he hopes his appearance at Yale might help to galvanize public support for national parks generally.

a grand air befitting the occasion, shook my academic plumes into finest fluting folds and stepped forward in awful majesty and stood rigid, serene and solemn as an ancient sequoia while the orator poured praise on the honored wanderer's head. And I think I had better leave the wanderer in this heroic attitude. With love to you friends three I am,

Ever faithfully, affectionately,

John Muir

Muir dressed to receive an honorary degree from Yale, June 1911

Garrisons on the Hudson, New York
July 14, 1911
John Burroughs

Dear John Burroughs,

When I was on the train passing your place I threw you a hearty salute across the river but I don't suppose that you heard or felt it.[42] I would have been with you long ago if I had not been loaded down with odds and ends of duties, book making, book selling at Boston, Yosemite and Park affairs at Washington, and making arrangements for getting off to South America, etc., etc. I have never worked harder in my life, although I have not very much to show for it. I have got a volume of my autobiography finished. Houghton Mifflin is to bring it out. They want to bring it out immediately but I would like to have at least part of it run through some suitable magazine, and thus gain ten or twenty times more readers than would be likely to see it in a book.

I have been working for the last month or more on the Yosemite Book, trying to finish it before leaving for the Amazon, but I am not suffering in a monstrous city. I am on the top of as green a hill as I have seen in all the state, with hermit thrushes, woodchucks and warm hearts, something like those about yourself.

I am at a place that I suppose you know well, Professor Osborn's summer residence at Garrisons, opposite West Point. After Mrs. Harriman left for Arden[43] I went down to the Century Editorial Rooms where I was offered every facility for writing in Gilder's room, and tried to secure a boarding place near Union Square, but the first day was so hot that it made

---

[42] As he rode the rails south from Boston back to New York to prepare to leave on his journey, JM would have passed fairly near the home of his friend, fellow nature writer John Burroughs (1837–1921); Burroughs's home and his famous writing cabin, Slabsides, is on the Hudson River near West Park, New York. Henry Fairfield Osborn's summer home, Castle Rock, at Garrison on the Hudson, where JM was then writing, was not far from Slabsides, but JM's hectic schedule in finishing the Yosemite book and preparing for the South America voyage prevented him from visiting Burroughs on this trip.

[43] Arden (also "Arden House") was the Harriman family estate, located in the Ramapo Highlands, ten miles west of the Hudson River and forty-five miles north of Jersey City. When Edward H. Harriman purchased the tract from James Parrott in the summer of 1885, it comprised 8,000 acres. Later expanded by additional land purchases, Arden eventually came to occupy an area of thirty square miles, making it one of the largest estates in the East. The Harrimans moved to Arden in the fall of 1886.

my head swim and I hastily made preparations for this comfortable home up on the hill here, where I will remain until perhaps the 15th of August when I expect to sail.

Nothing would be more delightful than to go from one beautiful place to another and from one friend to another but it is utterly impossible to visit a hundredth part of the friends who are begging me to go and see them and at the same time get any work done. I am now shut up in a magnificent room pegging away at the book, and work as hard as ever I did in my life. I do not know what has got into me, making so many books all at once. It is not natural.

I had a note from Mrs. Ashley the other day acknowledging the receipt of my "First Summer in the Sierra" and with it a very warm invitation to visit her at Middletown. I should think that she would get more out of the book than out of myself. I ordered a book sent to Miss Barrus[44] at the same time so probably she has received hers also, but I think it was sent to her address in New York at her brother-in-law's. They will of course forward it. As you know I dislike traveling but my studies drag me and I cannot help it, so I have to go on and on, heaven knows where.

With all good wishes for your big and happy family, I am ever,

Faithfully your friend,

John Muir

Garrisons on the Hudson, New York
July 14, 1911
Robert Marshall[45]

My dear Mr. Marshall,

Many thanks for your promptly sending me the maps and for your kind wishes for my Amazon trip. You must be suffering with the heat down

[44] Mrs. Ashley was a friend of Dr. Clara Barrus, Burroughs's physician, friend, and literary executor; JM had met both women in February 1909 when they accompanied Burroughs and JM on a study of petrified trees in the North Forest, Arizona.

[45] This is not the Bob Marshall (1901–1939) who co-founded the Wilderness Society but rather Robert B. Marshall, a Sierra Club activist and friend of JM's who was with the United States Geological Survey. The maps mentioned in the first line of the letter were sent by Marshall to help JM with his work on the Yosemite book he was then writing.

there. We have been very hot also but I am comfortably located in Prof. Osborn's place about a thousand feet above the sea, overlooking the Hudson and surrounded with a close growth of trees. I have been hard at work and am still working on the Yosemite Book but many interruptions causes very slow progress. Still I hope to get the thing off my hands before I go South. I expect to sail direct for the Amazon August 15th and wish you could go with me. Quite a number of my friends say they would like to go but they cannot. I seem to be the only one free, but heaven knows, I am tied up pretty hard now about the printing of books. I hope you will get out to your mountain work, hope indeed that you have already gone and escaped the dreadful heat of the last week or so. It is now cooler here. Give my love to Mrs. Marshall and the blessed children when next you write to them, and with all good wishes, I am as ever,

Faithfully your very friend,

John Muir

———

Garrisons on the Hudson, New York
August 2, 1911
Houghton Mifflin Co., Boston

Dear Sirs,

In reply to your last letter of recent date, I leave for South America on the 15th of this month, and it seems unlikely that I shall be able to make satisfactory arrangement for the serial publication of my *Boyhood and Youth* at present.[46] You stated that you could probably arrange for publication with McClure or some others. In any case I have made up my mind to delay publication until time has been given for its serial publication. I have spent about a week on it and have, I think, greatly improved it; one

[46] As he explained in a number of letters, JM was determined to have his autobiography appear serially before it was published in book form in order to expand his audience. Despite Houghton Mifflin's hurry to bring the book out, JM prevailed, and parts of the autobiography appeared in four issues of the *Atlantic Monthly* during 1912 and 1913 (vol. 110, nos. 5 and 6; vol. 111, nos. 1 and 2; also see Kimes, items 311–14) before Houghton Mifflin brought the book out in March 1913.

advantage of delay. I have been so very busy completing the Yosemite Book that the Century Company is to bring out that I have had very little time for anything else. I appreciate what you say as to the uncertainty of life, but this uncertainty unfortunately applies to publishers also and probably, all things considered, it will be better to postpone the publication of my little Boyhood Book until I return from my South American trip.

Faithfully yours,
John Muir

————

New York
August 2, 1911
Katharine Hooker

My dear everlasting friend,

I'm so glad to see by your letters that you are finding your way, aiming straight ahead in newness of life. God's best good luck to you my word of farewell. I leave Philadelphia on the fifteenth of this month for the Amazon direct,[47] all alone as usual. I'm well but very tired finishing Yosemite book. Have been at work every morning for weeks and weeks at 5:00 to about 8:00 p.m. Fell asleep day before yesterday pen in hand though can't sleep much in bed. Hope to rest on way to the great hot river.

You have time to write me a line of goodby to above address.

Heaven's peace be yours dear Katharine, so devoutly prays,

Your very friend,
John Muir

————

[47] As we know, JM ultimately left for the Amazon on August 12, 1911, and from Brooklyn rather than Philadelphia.

Garrisons on the Hudson, New York
August 10, 1911
Helen Muir Funk

My brave darling Helen,

It is awfully good of you to offer to give up Buel[48] but it would never do to leave you and the baby. I would only fret all the more. It was too late anyhow as it turns out for my ship, the *Dennis* of the Booth Line,[49] sails Saturday morning instead of Wednesday morning. I will be all right anyhow. It is now half past six in the evening and I have just finished the Yosemite book and start for Brooklyn tomorrow morning to get aboard so as not to be left in the morning. I am all right only tired. Have been up at about half past four for the last three or four weeks and at work about five. I will rest on the way down to the Amazon. Send me a letter to Para, Brazil, South America, and I will probably get it sometime. I will give you other addresses as soon as I know them.

Give my love to Wanda and the little boys and ask Tom to send to Para the letter or two that he said he could furnish as introductions to his friends.

Now darling take care of yourself and do not fret about me as I am all right. Goodby, ever,

Your devoted father,

John Muir

———

[48] Helen had written her father on August 3 (I/A/20/11459) to encourage him to take her husband, Buel Funk, along on the voyage. Helen explained to her father that her concern for his health and safety would be allayed if he would allow Funk to travel with him.

[49] Here "Booth Line" refers to the Booth Steamship Company (formally named Alfred Booth and Company), founded by Alfred and Charles Booth, who launched the first ship of their line in 1866. During this period the Booth Line did considerable business to and from northern Brazil, so it is not surprising that the *Dennis,* bound for the Amazon, would have been a Booth ship.

Garrisons on the Hudson, New York
August 10, 1911
Katharine Hooker

My dear friend Katharine H.,

I hope that ere this reaches you, you and Marian will be in the pines with your brother, breathing their strength and peace and pure fountain love. I know by your last letter that you need the mountains. So I pray you, anywhere in the Sierra sugar pine woods, or a little higher in the balsam firs. Oh dear! how glad I'd be to go with you. Skimming across the continent would seem only a mere street ride. But I start tomorrow morning for the great hot river I've been waiting so long to see, and alone as usual though plucky loving darling Helen wrote anxiously begging me to take her husband with me as she couldn't bear to have me go alone. Of course I couldn't let him sacrifice his own young life for mine. Got Yosemite book done this eve. Though for a month I've been at work by 5:00 a.m. Goodby. Remember me to all who love you.

Affectionately yours,
John Muir

———

New York
August 12, 1911
Loulu Perry Osborn [50]

Dear friend Mrs. Osborn,

Your kindness is endless. Many waters cannot quench it [51]—not even Avalanche Lakes or Amazons. [52]

I'm so glad you are all enjoying your mountain trip. The day your letter

---

[50] "Loulu" Osborn is Lucretia Thatcher Perry Osborn (1858–1930), the wife of JM's friend Henry Fairfield Osborn. JM's note implies his gratitude for the Osborns' hospitality, for it was at Castle Rock, their cool, quiet summer home in the Hudson highlands, that he was able to finish his Yosemite manuscript before departing on his voyage to South America and Africa.

[51] JM's biblical allusion is to Song of Songs 8:17, with its lovely celebration of the power of love: "Many waters cannot quench love; / rivers cannot wash it away."

[52] The places that JM and the Osborns would be traveling that summer, respectively: the Osborn family to Avalanche Lake in Glacier National Park in Montana, and JM to the "great river" in Brazil.

from 8,500 above arrived news from Cook made me hurry.[53] The *Dennis* sails this morning, the 12th instead of 15th. Nevertheless the book is triumphantly done and in the publisher's hands, while I'm in Virginia's,[54] who in genuine Osborn style is making all kind arrangements imaginable to launch me straight for my way. So that in an hour or two I'll be fairly off.

But as to Taft and Hetch Hetchy I could do nothing for want of time before leaving. Later however I may manage it. Possibly through the Sierra Club.

My address will be Para, Brazil, c/o Booth Steamship Co.

Goodby, love to you all,

John Muir

———

New York
August 12, 1911
Helen Muir Funk

Darling,

In an hour or two I'll be sailing straight to the Amazon. Mr. Osborn's servants here and the Professor's man are all at my service and I'll be taken to the ship from here in an auto. I'll write often. Don't fret about me, for I've been so well fed, etc., that in spite of hard work I'm perfectly well. Love to all. Write to David. I'm so hurried. Dear dear child, Goodby.

My address will be Para Brazil, care of The Booth Steamship Company.

Ever your loving,

Father

———

[53] Thomas Cook & Son, the international travel company begun by Thomas Cook in 1845 and established under the name Thomas Cook & Son in 1871, when Thomas's son John Mason Cook joined his father as a business partner. Cook & Sons was the major international travel agency throughout the first quarter of the twentieth century, and continues in business today. Here JM has to hurry because he is informed by Cook & Sons that his steamer, bound for Brazil, will leave three days earlier than expected; the steamer *Dennis* did indeed leave Brooklyn at 11:00 a.m. on August 12, 1911.

[54] The Osborn's daughter, Virginia Sturgis Osborn (b. circa 1880), who apparently saw JM off in New York.

New York
August 12, 1911
David Gilrye Muir [55]

Dear brother David,

  In an hour or two I'll be off for the Amazon.

  Goodby and love to all,

    John Muir

———

*Muir's farewell letter, written to his brother David just prior to departing
for the Amazon*

[55] Named for JM's maternal grandfather, this David Gilrye Muir (1840–1916) was JM's
younger brother, and the fourth of the seven Muir children.

The route of Muir's travels in South America, August 1911–December 1911

CHAPTER 2

Southbound and up the Great Amazon

12 August 1911–25 September 1911

NEARLY FORTY-FOUR YEARS after his first, ill-fated attempt to reach the Amazon, John Muir began his journey to the "great hot river." When the steamer *Dennis* sailed from Brooklyn Harbor that August morning in 1911, Muir was already seventy-three years old, traveling by himself, and uncertain of exactly where his voyage would take him. Indeed, isolated comments in his correspondence hint that he wondered whether he would return at all. It was a voyage he was committed to making nevertheless, and one he embraced with great enthusiasm.

After taking on coal at Norfolk, Virginia, the *Dennis* steamed south through the subtropical Atlantic and the Caribbean, stopping briefly at Barbados on August 22. Muir's journal entries during this first leg of the southbound journey are sparse, suggesting that perhaps—as he had so often promised in his letters to concerned family and friends—he was using the sea voyage as an opportunity to recover from the strenuous pace he had kept in the months prior to leaving New York. After a week at sea, however, Muir began to describe the scenes and weather in more detail. On August 25, for example, the wet weather of the equatorial Atlantic prompted him to speculate that "[r]ain seems wasted on the sea, but of course it must require irrigation for various purposes, to keep the globe in wholesome useful order, and in beauty." Some of Muir's observations are richly detailed, while others are characterized by a haiku-like compression and intensity, such as his August 26 note, "[s]ilvery flying fish glittering among the blue waves."

On August 27 Muir crossed the equator for the first time on his voyage. The following morning, as his ship steamed toward the Amazon delta, he was greeted by an augury of land in the form of a butterfly. Approaching the port town of Belém ("Para"), Brazil, Muir noted the density and beauty of the forest, in which he saw "[m]any magnificent dome-headed giant trees looming in most imposing grandeur above the crowded multitude of palms." The next day he disembarked and went into Belém, where his considerable fame, advanced age, and engaging personality combined to make him welcome among prominent citizens including bankers, surgeons, engineers, steamer line agents, and American diplomatic officers.

In Belém Muir also initiated his natural history studies. His method of botanical study throughout the trip was first to prepare himself by reading extensively on the flora that most interested him, then to examine those species growing in botanical gardens and city parks, and, finally, to locate and study the desired trees and plants within the richer context of their native habitat. Given this methodical approach, it is not surprising that the morning of August 30, his first full day in port, found Muir in the Belém Botanical Gardens studying Amazonian plants, and that by afternoon he was observing trees in the city park. The highlight of Muir's visit to the Botanical Gardens was his opportunity to study *Victoria regia,* a white-flowering giant water lily he hoped to find and observe in its native habitat along the Amazon itself.

September 1 marked Muir's first views of the Amazon he had so long wished to see. On that morning, he was awake and on deck by 4:00 a.m., that he might "see as much as possible of the river scenery." As the ship passed through the Narrows on its way into the river's main channel, Muir reveled in the "magnificent exuberance of tropical vegetation," noting that he could nearly touch the trees as the steamer swept by them on its way upstream. Throughout the Amazon voyage Muir recorded his observations of the trees and plants he studied from the deck of the steamer, and commented on weather, water color, geological formations, and the many "butterflies, moths, dragonflies [that] are enlivening the air." Muir's journals from the Amazon leg of his journey are, nevertheless, more the work of a traveler than a scientist. Perhaps because, as a naturalist, Muir found himself a stranger in a strange land, his descriptions of the Amazonian rainforest are often impressionistic—concerned more with appreciating the beauty of the place than enumerating the myriad species inhabiting it. And Muir's journalistic eye was trained not just on nature. He also noted the artifacts of human culture—both native and colonial—that he observed along the river: the homes, crops, ranches, and villages of Portuguese settlers, and the huts, canoes, plantings, and hunting and fishing activities of the native peoples.

After five days on the great river, during which he made a number of friends among his fellow passengers but stopped only once, at the village of Itacoatiara, Muir arrived at the town of Manaus, near the mouth of the Rio Negro. His meditations on scenes and scenery at Manaus, then a booming port, focus upon the dominant industries of rubber tapping and trading, and reflect on the debilitating and often fatal malarial fevers in the area—comments that remind us of the very real risks that Muir, already a septuagenarian, was willing to run in order to visit the Amazon basin.

The Amazonia into which Muir traveled in 1911 was a place of terrific and often abhorrent contradictions. On the one hand it was, as Muir recognized, the greatest wilderness on earth: a 3,900-mile-long river with more than 1,000 tributaries draining a watershed the size of the United States, and the basin of which contains the largest, wildest, and most biodiverse forest on the planet. On the other hand, this immense wilderness also had a four-hundred-year history of colonial incursion—an incursion led by Spain but followed by Portugal, France, Prussia, Germany, and England. On the one hand, the Amazon contained in unimaginable richness the solitude, beauty, and freedom that Muir so deeply valued. On the other, the watery heart of the basin was being invaded by a soaring rubber economy whose presence resulted in environmental destruction and in the displacement and enslavement of the native peoples upon whom the industry's profits depended. The Manaus Muir visited was no longer a modest Portuguese fort town; it had, almost overnight, become a decadent boomtown of 100,000 inhabitants. In the thirty years previous to Muir's arrival, the income in the town had risen nearly thirtyfold, creating a city that, although still isolated from the centers of the civilized world, could afford to import extravagances from every corner of the globe. As a naturalist, Muir was indeed entering what was (and, despite catastrophic deforestation, still is) the largest and least-inhabited forest wilderness on the globe; as a tourist, however, he was following active arteries of trade to the capital of a vast empire of rubber tapping and trading.

Muir made a number of friends in Manaus, where he received warm hospitality from several wealthy, prominent citizens. On September 10, Muir took an ambitious day trip in search of the remarkable *Victoria regia* in its native habitat. Accompanied by a party of his new friends, he first took a steam tug across the Rio Negro and entered a reedy bay. Next the men boarded skiffs and traveled up a shallow, vine-draped, and tree-strewn channel into the heart of the watery jungle. The thickness of the forest required that they frequently pull the skiffs through a tangle of vines and branches. When the wall of rainforest vegetation became impenetrable, the men were forced to turn back before reaching the lagoon where the rare lily was said to grow. Though disappointed by his failure to reach the wild *Victoria regia*, Muir nevertheless described the day as a "wonderful experience" that introduced him to "the great size and beauty of the trees, birds, butterflies" of Amazonia.

Despite the many generous traveling companions he met along his way, Muir's comments and letters suggest that he was sometimes lonely during his voyage. A moving example of his need to maintain emotional contact with his faraway family and friends—a kind of contact through fond memory that he often referred to as "heart-sight"—occurred on September 11, when Muir happened to notice, on the shelf of a home where he was then lodging, a tattered copy of *Wayfarers in Italy,* the book his dear friend Katharine Hooker had published in 1902. "It seemed," wrote Muir, "that my friend was actually present in the flesh."

Muir had traveled 1,000 miles up the Amazon and had already purchased a ticket to sail another 1,200 miles to Iquitos, Peru. However, long delays associated with finding a boat on which to continue his trip so far upriver persuaded Muir to return to coastal Brazil and pursue his studies southward. On September 12 he reboarded the *Dennis* and left his Manaus friends, sailing through a wild thunderstorm before enjoying clear weather and fine forest views on the two days following. Muir arrived at Belém on September 15 and the next morning went to the Botanical Gardens for the third time, where he measured the growth that had occurred in the *Victoria regia* specimen during his two-week trip upriver. He spent the week following his return to Belém dining with friends, taking walks, studying trees in the Botanical Gardens and city parks. He also used this time to study the geography and history of South America, to review his Amazon journal notes, to read letters forwarded to Belém from New York, and to write a number of letters to family and friends.

Muir's extant letters from this period display unalloyed enthusiasm for the diversity and sublimity of Amazonian scenery. Late-August letters to his daughter Wanda and friends the Osborns reassure them of his good health and suggest his deep feelings of connection with them, despite the intervening distance. To Loulu Perry Osborn he writes that "[t]he more I see of our goodly Godly star the more plainly comes to sight and mind the truth that it is all one like a face, every feature radiating beauty on the others." Upon returning to Belém in mid-September Muir wrote a series of letters extolling the remarkable beauty of the Amazon River wilderness he felt so privileged to have witnessed. He put it best in a letter to Katharine

Hooker: "I've had a most glorious time on this trip, dreamed of nearly half a century—have seen more than a thousand miles of the noblest of Earth's streams and gained far more telling views of the wonderful forests than I ever hoped for."

Journal

1911

Aug. 12

Left Brooklyn, N.Y., 11:00 a.m. Stopped several hours opposite the Statue of Liberty. Thence sailed for Norfolk, Va., for coal.[1]

Aug. 13

Arrived 4:00 p.m. in charge of pilot in broad shallow muddy Chesapeake Bay. Went alongside grand steel coal bunkers—very high. The coal was shot down into the ship's bunkers at the rate of about 1,000 tons per hour, but it required the labor of twenty Negroes for over twenty-four hours to trim it.[2]

Aug. 15

Sailed for Barbadoes 11:00 p.m. Shores of bay low. Several forts. Traces of Civil War. Large number of vessels from far countries.

Aug. 16

Out of sight of land since 3:00 p.m. yesterday. Last evening the sky was overcast, heavy, leaden, with gloomy, straw-colored clouds wonderfully

---

[1] In their chronology of JM's South America and Africa voyage, Hall and Mark indicate that JM spent August 13–15, 1911, in Baltimore. I find no evidence supporting this claim, as it seems certain that JM was in Norfolk, Virginia, during these several days.
[2] That is, to adjust the ballast and cargo so as to make the ship as stable and as fast as possible.

enlivened with lightning along the eastern horizon. Very little thunder heard. The sea is heaving in long, low swells intermingled with beautifully sculptured hollows of innumerable wavelets, each one of which had its own little hollow and ridge some of them breaking in purple and violet foam. One wonderful jet black cloud mass overhead, the sky back of it light blue, white and yellow smoothly brushed, or rippled with mackerel clouds. Most of day muddy dingy clouds, cumuli, like those of tropics.

Aug. 17

Almost same next morning, 17th, and evening. Glorious tree-like clouds along the horizon.

Aug. 18

Nearly same this morning, only whiter and more luminous. Rows of pillared masses and dense black clouds with white cumuli above them.

Aug. 19

Almost cloudless. Sea without a single speck of foam. Wonderful circle of dark blue water. Sky pale around horizon.

Aug. 20

Sea ornamented with whitecaps, mostly wide apart. Ship pitching eighteen or twenty feet. Dull yellow sunset. Sooty clouds, mostly small.

Aug. 21

Christopher Island close at hand on the left (E.). The ridges of a mountain volcano fringed with palms and its skirts dappled with pale yellow-green sugar fields. A long row of volcanic islands stretching southward. The highest about 6,000 feet. Fine to see land after a week of round blue water days. Lovely blue levels, varying in tone. Very few birds, flocks of glittering flying fish, and glorious clouds. Expect to be at Barbadoes to-morrow p.m. This evening at 5:00 p.m. a grand cloud, white above, dark beneath, and rain torrents like hair streaming from it into the sea in our wake. A calm, serene, glowing crimson sunset back of a rocky mountain, jagged range of sooty black fired on the edges. Great experience to rest on the "watery bosom" of the sea, as Lamb says.[3] Passed Martinique about midnight.

Aug. 22

Magnificent clouds to the northward, pure silvery white, with very deep caves, caverns, and canyons full of shade. A glorious sight. Most northward. Arrived at Barbadoes at 3:30 p.m. Left 6:30 p.m. Barbadoes English colony. Beautiful island. Not mountainous. Land rising in ter-races—fertile. Sugar cane principal crop. Palms, mango trees, and alligator pears, etc. About one hundred steerage passengers came aboard for Para, and five cabin.[4] Had to be rowed a mile or more to ship at anchor. A lively scene getting aboard. Mostly Negroes. Made still livelier by little, sinewy, lithe, brown and black boys diving for nickels. One dived from upper deck of steamer. Another dived from his little skiff, passed under the keel and bobbed up on the other side. The weather showery so did not go ashore, though most of our fifty passengers on way to work on railroad around Madeira Falls did.

Aug. 23

Dark, showery most all day. "Regular Amazon weather," said the waiter at our table.

Aug. 24

Beautiful sunrise barred with bright clouds. Magnificent cumuli with white fluffy edges resting on level dark-slate or sooty-colored masses.

---

[3] JM's allusion is to "Ellistoniana," by English essayist Charles Lamb (1775–1834), in which Lamb wrote: "It was as if by one peremptory sentence he had decreed the annihilation of all the savoury esculents, which the pleasant and nutritious-food-giving Ocean pours forth upon poor humans from her watery bosom." "Ellistoniana," a remembrance of the recently deceased Robert William Elliston (1774–1831), was first published in the *Englishman's Magazine* in August 1831.

[4] That is, five cabin passengers. Steerage passengers, whose fare was considerably lower than that of the more comfortably situated cabin passengers, usually traveled on the underdeck, near the rudder, or just forward of the main cabin.

Cumuli of every shape, many like leaning, wind-bent trees, others erect, with horizontal filmy high clouds back of them, mostly whitish. At 4:00 p.m., rain back of the vessel's course S.E. and N.W. Another shower ahead. Very black, now. Lat. 10 deg. N. Quite warm, of course, but not oppressively so. Small showers have been falling from detached clouds all around the horizon since noon or before.

Slight rain at sundown and later.

Aug. 25

Fine, calm, clear. Glorious white, fluffy, woolly cumuli, much divided up to 1:00 p.m. Smaller and dull, rainy in distance ahead and on either hand. Sea rippled and dimpled with small waves; few curl-topped, spangling, throbbing. Toward evening, heavy rain lasting about ten minutes stilled the small wavelets on the sides of the larger waves, which were mostly unbroken swells that made the ship pitch to height of about twenty feet, while the pattering of the rather large raindrops whitened all the sea and made it look oily. There was no lightning, though the temperature was high. Lat. about 6 deg. N.

Cleared partially at sunset. Rain seems wasted on the sea, but of course it must require irrigation for various purposes, to keep the globe in wholesome useful order, and in beauty.

Aug. 26

Fine, clear morning. The clearest sky since leaving New York. Only faint whitish pencilings on northern horizon. Sea dark blue, far from black. Silvery flying fish glittering among the blue waves. No whitecaps, though moderate swell from S.E. Our course S. nearly.

At 9:00 a.m., a broad swath of spangles on the swelling weltering waves to the eastward. Close in beds and clusters in foreground with sharp slender needles like those of crystals, quivering, dancing, up-flashing like those made by the plash of hail or heavy raindrops. In the distance the wide-apart spangles are in mirror-like masses—only quick big flashes visible while those in foreground fairly quiver and sparkle in close clusters, adorning every wave like beds of bright rejoicing flowers rising from the watery soil, maturing in rich crops of light, ever dying, ever renewed in endless harvests only a fraction of a second apart—seen or unseen covering all the broad seas.

Aug. 27

Cloudy. Sky and water dim all day. Many flocks of flying fish? At noon we were less than two hundred miles from the mouth of the Amazon. Waters slightly greenish from particles of the river mud, some of them brought down from the Andes thousands of miles distant.

Crossed equator a few minutes past 6:00 p.m. Much fun at meeting held in the cabin to pass judgment on unfortunates who had been found guilty of crossing the line for the first time.[5]

We arrived opposite the light ship about 9:00 p.m. Took pilot and proceeded an hour or so and came to anchor. On account of dangerous shifting currents of the river delta, the charts are unreliable, says Captain Tocque.

Aug. 28

Started at daybreak. Land in sight on our left. Low, flat and densely tree-clad; a few fishing boats in sight, schooners, etc. One large freight steamer. Water yellow. Sky dimly cloudy. Expect to reach Para this afternoon at 2:00 p.m.

At 10:00 a.m. a butterfly came aboard. Land distant about four miles. Warm, but less oppressive than New York weather a month ago.

Sixty or seventy miles on left coast as we approached Para of glorious forest, very dense. Many magnificent dome-headed giant trees looming in

---

[5] It has long been traditional to recognize the crossing of the equator with various forms of ritualistic celebration, usually accompanied by hazing of those who are crossing "the line" for the first time. Although the ritual has taken numerous forms, a general sense of it may be derived from a comment Mark Twain made in his 1897 book *Following the Equator: A Journey Around the World* (New York: Harper & Brothers): "In old times a sailor, dressed as Neptune, used to come in over the bows, with his suite, and lather up and shave everybody who was crossing the equator for the first time, and then cleanse these unfortunates by swinging them from the yardarm and ducking them three times in the sea."

most imposing grandeur above the crowded multitudes of palms. A few openings on ascending ground, twenty or thirty miles from Para, with pale yellowish beach and many buildings. Breezy places of resort for pleasure and rest from the hot city. Cumulus clouds ranged above the forest. Some of the domed trees solid, half-hemispheres of verdure. Others with openings through their vast crowns. Some with clear tall shafts, and a wide half-circle of dense foliage, like umbrellas, one hundred and fifty feet wide, for sunshades or rain. Lots of palms in recesses along shore, and in coves of the lower woods.

Arrived at Para about 4:00 p.m. Very warm evening.

Aug. 29

Dead air alongside of dock. The Chief Engineer attached electric fan to current and the steward enclosed my bed in mosquito netting. The little eight-inch fan I had brought from New York kept the air stirring all night so that I slept comfortably notwithstanding the heat.

P... W. H. Taft

July 8, 1911.

To the

    Diplomatic and Consular Officers

       of the United States.

Gentlemen:

    By direction of the President I take pleasure in introducing to you John Muir, Esquire, a distinguished naturalist and explorer, who is about to proceed abroad.

    I commend Mr. Muir to your attentive consideration and cordially beseek for him such courtesies and assistance as you may be able to render, consistently with your official duties.

    I am, Gentlemen,

       Your obedient servant,

CB/Da.

Cable issued on behalf of President Taft, requesting US Consular officers to aid Muir abroad

Called on our American Consul, who kindly offered his services in every possible way. Was introduced by Mr. Sanford, a graduate of Yale University.[6]

Aug. 30

Visited with Mr. Sanford the banker, Mr. Ross, and other friends of his. In the afternoon rode to the end of the car line to a City Park full of magnificent trees growing naturally, the ground simply cleared of underbrush and made accessible by smooth roads and trails. This is one of the most interesting city parks I ever saw. Along the walks at intervals were seats where views of the finest trees were to be seen. All the walks were bordered with ferns and lycodopium. Dined with Mr. Ross and Mr. Southgate, the agent for the Booth line of steamers. Returned aboard the *Dennis* about 9:00 p.m.

Went to the Consul with letters in the morning with Dr. Housepian, the ship's surgeon,[7] and got money changed. Also in the forenoon, before going out to the Park, had an interesting time in the Botanical Gardens. Got names of wonderful ferns and palms, ceibas, etc. *Pandanus veichii.* Stems prickly. Leaves eight feet long and four inches wide, serrated. *Hevea brasiliensis, Ceiba pentandara* Euphorbiaceae *Parkia Pendula,* an umbrella-like leguminous tree. *Ochroma lagopus,* one of the malva family, called cotton tree. Another *Hura crepitans,* one of the Apocciniaceae, *Guadua superba,* magnificent bamboo. *Cycas circinatis,* some of the fronds eighteen inches wide, ten feet long. About three hundred divisions a quarter of an inch in width in the leaf. Palm-like stem one foot in diameter, eight feet

---

[6] According to Yale alumni records, the "Mr. Sanford" who JM so often mentions is Frederic Henry Sanford (1867–1927). After receiving his B.A. from Yale in 1889, Sanford worked for the War Department, studied law, and was admitted to the bar in 1894, though he never practiced. In that year he moved to Brazil to become a rubber exporter, a trade he engaged from Belém (1894–99) and, later, upriver at Manaus (1899–1903). He was US Consular Agent at Manaus from 1901 to 1903, and after a stint in the Bolivian rubber trade returned there in 1906, where he served as the head of the rubber exporting house of Adelbert H. Alden until 1913. After a year in Switzerland he returned to the United States and became a partner in the import-export firm of H. A. Astlett & Co. until his retirement in 1927.

[7] Probably Dr. Moses M. Housepian, a Syrian-born physician and ship's medical officer who died in New York in 1952.

long, terminated by a magnificent yellow bud. The whole plant palm-like. About sixty fronds. In a large tank a *Victoria regia*[8] with leaves about four feet in diameter and with raised edges four inches high, bright green above, brown and prickly beneath. Old leaves were somewhat eaten off and frayed on the edges. The young leaves very beautiful. One flower is just opening. When fully opened it will probably be about six inches in diameter. Pure white. Some of the leaves of this magnificent lily are said to be seven or eight feet in diameter, with flowers ten or twelve inches in diameter, when growing naturally in lakes on the margin of the Amazon.

Very heavy thunderstorm from 5:00 to 6:00 in the afternoon. A huge black cloud covering all the sky. Storm began when the cloud covered only one half the sky. Big plashing raindrops falling in torrents.

Aug. 31

In the forenoon went to the gardens again. Admired the *Theobroma* tree, with its red flowers about one half inch in diameter growing in clusters of hundreds, like huge warts on the branchless leafless trunk. These flowers are sessile and grow on the smooth bark down to the very ground. In the Zoological Gardens I was greatly amused at one of the monkeys holding out his hands through the bars and begging for something to eat. I handed him a peppermint lozenge, something that so excited his curiosity that he probably had never before seen anything of the sort. He first smelled it, then held it back and critically examined it, touched the end of

---

[8] This is JM's first mention of the *Victoria regia* (later renamed *Victoria amazonica*), a giant water lily native to the Amazon region. This beautiful nymphaeaceous plant, first described in 1836, has leaves up to eight feet across, and fragrant, white-pink flowers with fifty or more petals up to eighteen inches wide. JM very much wanted to see this plant, and he considered it one of the goals of his Amazon journey to do so. As we'll see, on September 10, while upriver on the Amazon, he went to great lengths to try to find the lily growing wild in vine-tangled lagoons near Manaus; and on September 16, the day following his return to Belém, he once again visited the Botanical Gardens to investigate changes in the *Victoria* specimen growing there. Though JM was unable to locate the great lily in the Amazonian wilds, he considered his pursuit of the plant one of the high points of his Brazilian excursion. Henry Thoreau, whom JM deeply admired, also knew of *Victoria regia* and used it to symbolize his own quests as a naturalist; in his August 1862 essay memorializing Thoreau shortly after his death, JM's friend Ralph Waldo Emerson praised Thoreau's acuity as a naturalist by relating that Thoreau "told me that he expected to find yet the *Victoria regia* in Concord" ("Thoreau," *Atlantic Monthly*, vol. 10, no. 58, pg. 244).

his tongue with it very cautiously as though afraid it might be poisonous, rubbed it between his hands, then picked up a small stick and gave it a good rubbing with the stick, then tasted it again. Evidently he had never tasted anything like it before. Another thunder shower. After dark all the sky was at short intervals illumined with sheet lightning.

Expect to start for Manoas at 4:00 p.m.

Sept. 1

Rose early, about 4:00 a.m., to see as much as possible of the river scenery. About 7:00 a.m. we anchored in the "Narrows," a narrow channel lined with palms, so narrow in some places that we could almost reach the outleaning trees as we swept past them. Wonderfully beautiful. Nowhere else had I ever seen such magnificent exuberance of tropical vegetation. On the immediate margin of the river the palms greatly outnumbered all other trees.

Sept. 2

For miles, over one half of the trees in sight are covered with red flowers in upright panicles. Noticed a few trees that had been killed by fire on a bluff near an old settlement in which the walls of a fort are still visible.[9] This abandoned settlement is on the north side of the river. A round tree-covered hill was visible above the level forest about two miles back from the river bank and about two miles below the fort on the left bank of the river. Large number of trees of moderate size about seventy-five feet high, with slender trunks, gray in color, had masses of white flowers. Others, about the same size and form, had rose red flowers. Possibly these may be colored leaves. Nearer views show both red flowers and green leaves almost

---

[9] Several waves of missionary effort and colonial enterprise in the Amazon basin depended upon the strategic placement of garrisons and forts along the river. Following failed efforts by the Dutch and English, the Portuguese eventually established a network of jungle forts—a network that represented a form of Portuguese colonial control that was ratified by the Treaty of Madrid in 1750. Though Portuguese in control, many of these fortresses were actually built by Italians on models of eighteenth-century European fort design that had been heavily influenced by the French. See Murillo Marx's "Brazilian Architecture in the XVIII and Early XIX Centuries," in Damián Bayón and Murillo Marx's *History of South American Colonial Art and Architecture* (New York: Rizzoli, 1989).

hidden beneath the dense masses of flowers. All shades of red, dull and bright rose. One species of tree made complete circles set at right angles to line of sight, densely leafy on the outside, but showing the sky through the center. A row of flat-topped bluffs or hills made an interesting show on the left bank about 8:00 this evening.

All day the red-flowered trees formed the most striking and characteristic feature of the forest. The palms, so characteristic of the woods for two hundred miles above Para, are almost wanting today. Palm thatched houses of the Indians occur at intervals of a mile or two on both banks. A canoe of course, for travel and fishing. Some of these Indian settlers had cleared a little space in the dense growth for a few banana trees.[10] Lots of naked children come running down to the water's edge to see the ship go by. A little rubber is collected at these lonely settlements for trade at stations of the Portuguese that occur at wide intervals, for calico, tobacco, coffee, coal oil, etc. These Indians are said to keep their lamps lighted all night for superstitious reasons.

Meadow-like openings are becoming common. Passed sandstone bluffs with high ground back of them on the south side of the river. The strata horizontal. Very warm. Wind abaft, making almost dead air.[11] At sunset a flock of the celebrated Brazil mosquitoes came aboard, and invaded the dining room, where we were seated at the tables, causing lively slapping and clapping, in defending ourselves from their stings. The clapping was so continuous that a stranger might fancy that a speaker was being cheered. The dead mosquitoes were piled on the tablecloth at the side of each plate and each seemed to be as anxious to make good use of the sport that he seemed to enjoy it, each claiming a greater number of the game than their neighbors. At night slept well under my net fanned by my little electric wind mill, that I had brought from New York. Many of the passengers were kept awake nearly all night.

---

[10] Although the diversity of indigenous cultures in the Amazon basin makes identification of these "Indian settlers" difficult, most likely they are of the Arua (Aruan) or Waiãpi peoples. As JM steamed upriver, it is likely he would also have come into contact with the Mura and Manao (Manoa) peoples.

[11] That is, the wind was blowing toward the ship from the stern at about the same velocity as the ship was moving, thus making it feel as if the air was still.

Sept. 3

Mosquitoes this morning have vanished from the deck, swept off by a fine breeze from the sea. A few are still in the rooms below deck. A good many butterflies, moths, dragonflies, etc., are enlivening the air. Many extensive bright yellow-green meadows, with the lakes in the center of them, occur in lagoons cut off from the river, at time of high water. Several houses are visible on the higher portions of the margins of these lagoon meadows, belonging to Portuguese peddlers. Some of these houses seem quite large and substantial with red-tiled roofs, the tiles said to have been brought all the way from Lisbon. Some of these settlers keep large droves of cattle, and on the highest portion of the banks there are groves of the *Theobroma* and banana. We passed Santarem about 10:00 last evening, and Obidos this morning, old Portuguese villages situated on sandstone bluffs. The red-flowered tree is here less abundant. Some of them are very large and like most other trees grow round-headed in age. The slender, delicate little palm, abundant lower down the river, are now left far behind. Some of this species have only from three to six fronds and stems only about an inch or an inch and a half in diameter. Many white wasp nests are hanging on the branches of the trees like fruit. A few of the nests are very large, black in color, or grayish.

Magnificent cumulus clouds adorned the sky last evening. There was but little rain or thunder. A very large tree, with smooth light gray trunk, with broad buttresses near the ground, was seen to fine advantage on the edge of openings. Probably Ceibas.

Sept. 4

Reached Itacoatiara[12] about 10:00 a.m. this morning. It is situated near the mouth of the Madeira River. Most of our passengers left us here, after undergoing much examination of baggage. They went aboard the steamer Montenegro to go to the head of navigation of the river at Porto Velho to

[12] The village of Itacoatiara, originally established in 1759 as a missionary settlement of Abacaxis Indians from the Madeira River, became important in the early twentieth century as an outpost convenient to the Madeira-Mamoré railway.

work on the railroad,[13] which now, I am informed, will soon be completed; around two hundred and fifty miles of rapids to a long stretch of navigable water which extends to Bolivia. Two hundred miles is now finished, leaving only fifty, on which the greater part of the roadbed has been completed. Mr. Burns is going on to Manoas in charge of wireless telegraphs which are now in working order, but it seems that the Brazilian Government will not allow the line to be worked until the law has been complied with. All that is required, it seems, is the purchasable goodwill of certain officials. The franchise for the wireless is also opposed by the cable company, which has its line from Para to Manaos along the bed of the river.[14] The cable is oftentimes broken by sunken trees carried along the bottom of the river in the time of high water.

[13] The railroad to which JM refers here and in subsequent passages is the infamous Madeira-Mamoré railway, dubbed the "Devil's Railroad" because during its construction at least 10,000 people died (perhaps many more—estimates of the project's death toll vary widely)—most of malarial fevers, though some of starvation, Indian attacks, dysentery, pneumonia, or violent brawls. The five-year construction of 227 miles of track through Earth's densest jungle was an internationally celebrated engineering accomplishment, though the human cost of the project was memorialized in the Brazilian truism that each of the railroad's ties rested upon a human skull. JM's observation that the workers bound for the railroad project "were far from merry" indicates that the men were well aware of the dangers that awaited them in what some called *o inferno verde*—the "green hell." As JM notes, the Madeira-Mamoré was built in order to circumvent a series of impassable falls on the Madeira River, thus effectively connecting the landlocked, rubber-rich jungle of Bolivia with the Atlantic Ocean via a 2,000-kilometer water route down the Madeira and Amazon Rivers. The railroad was thus designed to open a lucrative trade route by which rubber— then the region's most valuable export commodity—could be removed from the otherwise inaccessible reaches of the Bolivian jungles. After several false starts on the project, the Madeira-Mamoré was begun in earnest in 1907, when the government of Bolivia hired the American construction company May, Jekyll & Randolph. It is a tragic irony that the railroad, built at such an exorbitant human cost, was completed in 1912—the very year South American rubber prices peaked and then began to plummet as competition from plantation-grown rubber in other parts of the world destabilized the Amazonian rubber economy. Too expensive to maintain, the railway received little use and was consequently nationalized by Brazil in 1931 and ultimately decommissioned in 1972.
[14] Submerged telegraph cable such as that connecting Belém to Manaus was developed in the 1840s and 1850s, and the first submarine transatlantic cable was laid in 1858. "Wireless" technology (later called "radio") was developed in the early years of the twentieth century, and by 1909 most passenger ships were equipped with the new communications technology. By the second decade of the century, wireless had begun to compete with conventional telegraph technology, as JM's note suggests. JM often appropriated the vocabulary of radio-telegraphy, as in his January 31, 1912, letter to his friends the Osborns, which he closes by sending them "wireless, tireless love messages."

The Captain, Mr. Burns, and myself had a merry goodbye from the passengers who left us. As they pulled away to the steamer that was to take them up to the Madeira they hurrahed in fine style and sang: "He's a Jolly Good Fellow." But many of those poor fellows were far from merry, and were perhaps singing to keep their own courage up, for malarial fevers are extremely fatal along the railroad line in the heart of the tremendous wilderness. Itacoatiara is a small village three or four miles from the mouth of the Madeira. There are four or five steamers lying here. The greater part of the difficulty in making this railroad, as I have said, is in clearing the roadbed, and only about fifty miles more of track are required to be laid. The larger stumps were blown up with dynamite, but both roots and branches of most of the trees are so full of sap that they would not burn. They had to be cut up into small pieces. A good many granite hills had to be blasted through, which furnished material for filling in the swamps. In all this long line of rapids the vertical descent is only about three hundred and fifty feet. The navigable part of the river above the rapids flows through a rich country for agriculture. Sometimes during the building of this railroad over ten percent of the workmen were in the hospital, and enormous quantities of quinine have been required. The malarial fever here is of so deadly a kind that some deaths followed after only three days of sickness.

Mr. Stone, an American, has a large cattle ranch near Itisotiara. I saw hundreds of cattle feeding on open grassy ground, on which grew tall-but-tressed Ceibas. Mr. Stone also raises large quantities of cacao. He came here after the Civil War, with other disgusted Southerners, Brazil being then a slave state. He with others has made a fortune here although slavery for many years has been abolished. The land here is on a low plateau of red sandstone, the edge of which touches the river and forms bluffs about seventy-five feet high for many miles. For a hundred miles or so below this town there are many Portuguese settlers, with patches and strips of cacao and bananas. Some of the cacao plantations are only made up of low bushes six or eight feet high. The Indian settlements are only solitary huts, with a few banana trees and palms, but it was pleasant to see bright flowers in pots in front of these little huts. And of course all have canoes, tied to a bush. Some of them nicely painted. Many of them were seen in their canoes with very long bows and arrows standing erect in the prow, fine muscular manly figures watching to get a shot at fishes or turtles disturbed by our steamer when running close to the bank to escape the strong current. There is about one of these native huts per mile on both banks. Few of those homes had less than four or five children.

Sept. 5

Arrived at Manaos about 9:00 a.m. A showy town claiming a population of about 100,000 inhabitants. Many remarkably fine buildings, appearing strange in the midst of the greatest forest wilderness in the world. The town is situated near the mouth of the Rio Negro on the left bank about nine miles above the confluence with the main river. The river here is so broad it looks more like a large lake than a river. Water in the harbor is about thirty-five fathoms in depth. The docks therefore are floating on iron pontoons. In the rainy season the rise of the river is about forty feet. It is now falling. Has fallen about twelve feet below high water mark. It begins to rise in April and to fall in August. The confluence with the Amazon is strikingly marked by a line of drifting leaves, and huge sods of water plants, and uprooted trees that look like islands, but most strikingly by the contrast in color of the two streams. The Negro water is very dark, almost pure black, but in bucketfuls it appears to be coffee-colored, while that of the Amazon is tawny-colored with mud particles from the Andes and to some extent from crumbling bluffs along its lower course, both in the mass and in small quantities. Dark chocolate or coffee-colored Negro water is like that of many streams and lakes of the heathy Scotch highlands; a decoction of peat bogs and swamp. Many of the Florida streams and of the low coastlines in the Southern States are of this same Rio Negro color. Strange to say, the mighty flood of the Rio Negro suddenly disappears beneath the great yellow Amazon flood. The steamship in crossing this abrupt line churns up some of the dark water in detached masses which float for a few minutes on the surface of the yellow water with a very striking effect.

Sept. 6

This morning the air was pleasantly cool and clear, and at midday there was an Indian-summerish haze around the horizon, making distant objects indistinct though there was not a single cloud in the sky. The cargo of our steamer is being discharged by a crew of Indian stevedores, strong able fellows naked to the waist. Their bright chestnut colored skin shining like ripe fruit. They receive the high wages of two dollars and a half per day with board and are hired to serve the Company permanently. They are extremely strong and able and work with a will. The business of all this Amazon region is founded on rubber. Into this rubbery wilderness thousands of men, young and old, rush for fortunes, half crazy, half merry, daring fevers, debilitating heat, and dangers of every sort, etc. Most of the rubber is collected by Indians who tap the trees over a great extent of territory and bring in their rubber in their canoes. My friend, Mr. Sanford, has been living on the Amazon at Para and Manoas for some ten years. He hopes to leave the country with a satisfactory fortune within the next two or three years from now. He has had yellow fever and many attacks of malarial fever, and he now considers himself almost immune from further attacks. The climate, however, is in general so depressing that he, with nearly all the other merchants, go to the North every year or two for a new stock of health and recreation. Manaos is never free from yellow fever, but it is not regarded as so deadly as some of the forms of malarial fever. With due precautions as to health and careful protection from the many species of poisonous mosquitoes, temperance in eating, drinking, etc., one may get rich and escape to a livable climate long before life's sundown. Yellow fever, once very prevalent in Para has within the last year been almost wholly banished by methods similar to those employed in Havana and New Orleans[15] with such marked success. Steps are being taken to banish fevers from Manoas also. The temperature is not usually very oppressive except in midday hours. Below the Rio Negro the average width of the

---

[15] Methods for the eradication of mosquito-borne diseases then consisted primarily of the use of dikes and levees to drain the wetlands that were once adjacent to the cities JM mentions.

river is about three or four miles. Masses of raggedy slow-growing cumuli arise early in the morning sometimes lasting all day, thickening toward evening with more or less lightning. No rain during the last few days. Large flocks of white egrets, ducks, parrots, etc., are seen almost all the way up from Para. Buzzards are never absent. The Manoas Theater, the Catholic Cathedral, and Customs House are magnificent buildings. About fifty steamers are in sight from the deck of the *Dennis* near the dock, lying at anchor here. Many of them comparatively small, to run up branches of the river for the collection of rubber, carrying oil, flour, and canned goods for trade.

Fine noon breeze coming off the river. Handsome cumuli around the horizon, their heads leaning upstream, with the prevailing wind. Dim, white, filmy horizontal belts of clouds back of them. Sky above, fine blue.

Sept. 7

Mr. Sanford called for me at 7:00 this morning. Went ashore with him and rode to the suburb called "The Flores," seven or eight miles by trolley, and thence enjoyed a long walk by a narrow path in the natural forest. Returned to town about half past ten. After resting and cooling, Mr. Sanford guided me to Col. May's residence[16] to breakfast at noon. A grand meal. Champagne and other fine wines, liquors, etc. The Colonel is an exceedingly active and enterprising Kentuckian. He is the builder of the Madeira River railroad. After breakfast Col. May took me to ride about town in his auto. Then called for Mr. Sanford and returned to May's to dinner. Mr. Sanford invited me to sleep at his cool, airy house. Met other able gentlemen, one of whom, Mr. Suabie, invited me to go up the river in his launch into a lagoon to see *Victoria regia* next Sunday, the 10th. Dinner at Robardias', Agent for the Booth Company.

It is perfectly wonderful to me how kind people are to this stranger.

---

[16] "Col. May" is presumably the "May" of the American construction company of May, Jekyll & Randolph, which in 1907 was hired by the Bolivian government to build the Madeira-Mamoré railway.

Sept. 8

Breakfast at Mr. Sanford's. Remained in the house until noon, when Mr. Sanford took me to Mr. Robardia's to lunch and also to dinner.

Sept. 9

After lunch went with Mr. Sanford and Mr. Robardia to see a sawmill, the electric machinery for supplying the city, the foundry, etc. Mr. Scott, a sturdy Scotchman from Montrose, was the engineer.

Mr. May called for me at 5:00 p.m. and drove me around town, then to his home to dine and stay all night and go to see *Victoria regia* next day.

Sept. 10

Went to the river landing, met the two brothers Suabi, got on board their steam tug, a fine swift boat, proceeded to their fine residence in a cove near town, and took on baskets and boxes of food and drink, and steamed out into the broad Rio Negro. Crossed diagonally to the mouth of a bay, about five miles below the town, and proceeded to its head through tall reedy grass which had creeping root-stalks which gradually accumulate sediment. Then the company, Mr. Sanford, Col. May, his chief engineer, a fine fellow, the two Suabis, and tug employees got into two skiffs and pushed up a wonderful Igarape[17] over-arched with tall leafy flowing trees. The water of the river has been falling rapidly during the last few days and of course the channel through the woods was correspondingly low. We had to duck beneath innumerable ropy lianes and tree branches, dodge the fallen trees, creep beneath them, or pull the skiffs over the tops of them.

At length, after miles of this strange Igarape work, we were stopped by an extensive jam of fallen trees and compelled to turn back after trying to go afoot through the vine-tangled woods and to the open lagoon, where the wonderful *Victoria regia* was growing. The ground was so muddy and the vines so dense that the company declared it was going to be impossi-

---

[17] "Igarape," a word first published by Amazonian explorer Alfred Russell Wallace in 1853, refers to a tributary or channel—what we might call a "creek"—that is just wide enough for travel by canoe.

ble to get to the lagoon, although it was only a few miles distant, and return to the tug before dark. So, sad to say, this grand trip, so full of promise, was in the main a failure. The Suabi Brothers had visited the lagoon the month before without difficulty when the water was five or six feet higher. Nevertheless, it was a wonderful experience for me. The great size and beauty of the trees, birds, butterflies, etc., the luxuriance of the vines and underbrush, etc.

After returning to the tug we ran out to a submerged island, tied up to the limb of a tree and ate our luncheon. Thence to the Suabi residence, beautifully located. Lots of dogs, birds, monkeys, etc., running free about the house, or secured in large cages. Many good books too. Thence back to the Sanford home in automobile. A memorable day.

As an incident of the trip, we caught a chameleon,[18] swimming a mile or so from land. It seemed quite tame and was easily captured. A beautiful creature about five feet long, the large scales arranged in striking order. Claws very sharp. The length of tail three and a half feet. Lives in trees. Was perhaps searching for a sand bank to deposit its eggs; so the sailors said. This handsome reptile was said to be good to eat.

The great river was ruffled here and there with a slight breeze, reflecting the blue sky like fairyland.

Sept. 11

At Mr. Sanford's fine residence all day. Reading. Looking over Mr. Sanford's little library, scanning the titles. I noticed one dingy, much-used book, partly hidden by the frame of the case. Opened the glass door, and joyfully read the name "Katharine Hooker—*Wayfarers in Italy.*" It seemed as if my friend was actually present in the flesh. What wonderful luck I had in this vast wilderness of strange floods and forests. Went out by a long, round-about trolley way through the woods to Mr. Gordon's. A Scotchman. Dined with him. He is at the head of a Rubber Company. Very fine dinner.

---

[18] JM's description of the "chameleon" suggests that his party had captured a common green iguana *(Iguana iguana)*, a tropical, omnivorous, largely aquatic, oviparous lizard that attains lengths of six feet and is a common food source in Central and South America.

Sept. 12

At 7:00 a.m. Mr. Sanford took me out to the *Dennis* for my return to Para, to sail at 10:00 a.m. He then returned to the city and with Mr. May, Dose, McFarland, and Robardia, and with other most kind friends came out on the Company's tug with hearty good wishes to see me off. Mr. Sanford especially has been a very brother in every way. Col. May gave me a pressing invitation to go as a guest with him up the Madeira and over the railroad. This I was eager to accept as I would see so much of the forest in near views, but when I inquired when he would start he informed me that it would be in about a month, and that it would be perhaps another month before I could return to Manoas. This I judged was too long a time to spend in one place when I had so great a journey before me in other parts of the continent. The same difficulty in regard to time prevented me from going, as I intended, to Iquitos, twelve hundred miles further up the river, to which point, indeed, I had already purchased a ticket, but the steamship on this line belonged to another company and I was informed that perhaps it would be a month or so before one of these steamers on the upper river would start from Manoas for Iquitos. That the trip would be very long, requiring from ten to twenty days; that perhaps still another month would be required to return to Manaos. So that in either of those two trips I would have to remain on the upper river for at least two and perhaps three months. Concluding that I could put in the time to better advantage I reluctantly set out on the return journey to Para.

Fine sail down the black Negro and tawny Amazon. I watched with increasing interest the meeting of those two great streams, the black and the yellow. Endless variety of treetops. Great smooth dense gray-green domes amid others dark green, with loose, fairy, feathery umbrellas, upheld and outspread by a network of small branches and branchlets, which were invisible at a little distance. Other treetops were perfectly flat tables of verdure, or evenly divided and outspreading, over-curling like feathery antennae.

In the afternoon a wild rain and windstorm. The air was darkened with flying scud torn from the river wave-tops. Looked like a blur of driving desert sand. Only once before have I seen anything like it in the tremendous speed of the wind. That was on the Columbia River. Heavy thunder lasted about fifteen minutes. It seemed as if the steamer must be blown out of the river. Beautiful sunset. In one place before the storm I saw many brush fires.

Sept. 13

This morning we are passing many beautiful bays in the forest walls around which there are a considerable number of farms and cattle ranches, where the ground lies twenty or thirty feet above the river floods.

Passed Obidos at 11:00 a.m. Red-topped trees very abundant.

In the afternoon, raggedy cumuli leaning upstream, on the sea wind. Extensive meadows, a characteristic feature of the river scenery hereabouts.

Sept. 14

Warm. Light wind. Wonderful domed trees. Many of them orchid-laden. A good many *Hevias* in sight. Mostly rather small, which have been spared, and thus brought to light in the little clearings.

At noon palms very abundant and form the greater part of the forest in the Narrows, which we entered about 8:00 a.m. Palms more and more abundant.

The innumerable islands, great and small, in the broad delta of the river, are mostly covered by these noble palms, almost to the exclusion of other trees. Forty or fifty miles below the Narrows the species that form the bulk of the palm woods are very tall and massive. Magnificent specimen of the great dome-headed *Ceiba* noticed today forms almost a semi-circle of perhaps one hundred and fifty or two hundred feet in diameter, rising into the open sky above the palms and other trees. Foliage pale. The branches radiating in regular order from the center, like the spokes of a huge wheel. One of the domed forms had the outer dense rim of leaves upheld by radiating limbs like the spokes of a wheel but covered with leaves with but few branchlets visible. A fine specimen of this kind was seen about eighty miles above Para. Wonderful sunset. A smooth globe of beautiful fire.

Sept. 15

Arrived at Para about 6:00 a.m. Left ship about 8:00 a.m. with Mr. Aimers, a good Scot from Galashiels. Went to banker's. Drew thirty pounds sterling. Got invitation to stop at their house until steamer sails south. Very pleasant here in roomy house. Fine garden.

Sept. 16

Cool. 66 deg. After tea went to Botanical Garden.

Macrobium acaciafolum. Fine large pinnate leaves. Leguminous.
theobroma speciosum spreng. Cacao. 6 inches diameter.
Theobroma bi-color H.B.K. Cacao of Peru.
Large cordate leaves.
Cassia, large tree—fine leaves.
castilloa uleia—large tree.

The *Victoria* flower failed to bud. The young leaf doubled in diameter. Now three feet. A young one has appeared, about eight inches diameter— heart-shaped—in rolled margin covered with red bristles, something like broad moccason.

Malisia paraensis, Herb. Leaves 12 inches long, 7 wide. Handsome tree.
Chrysophillum excelsumrsorva of Peru. Fine large tree. Glossy leathery obcor-
    date leaves.
Bombax. Large tree, long petioled, 7-parted leaves, round-headed.

Sept. 17

Got letter last evening from Katharine and Marian Hooker, Mrs. Sell-ers, Mrs. Thompson, Mr. Chamberlain and telegram from the Kelloggs. All forwarded from Castle Rock by Osborns. Held for postage at Para. Spent the day in the quietest way, reading, etc.

Sept. 18

Received another lot of letters forwarded by Osborns. Answering let-ters most of day. Find the Duff home comfortable in every way.

Sept. 19

Writing letters and looking over notes.

Sept. 20

Reading. Studying maps. Planning trips. Wishing I was on my way South, yet so much at home here.

Sept. 21

Studying world geography.

Sept. 22

Took walk alone and got lost. Found way home by taking new bearings from the Botanical Gardens. Had good time studying *Ceiba pentandra* trees, a magnificent row of them planted along one side of a public square. Very large. Six to eight feet diameter above the wide-straddling buttresses. Wide-spreading large branches, now nearly leafless, but dotted and tufted with cottony fruit, called cotton tree sometimes, as well as the Okroma. Leaves narrow. Three or four inches long. Some just opening. Trees very fruitful, five or ten thousand pods on single tree, with seeds. Down now flying. Some pods green. Belongs to the *Apoccinia*—dogbane. About sixty years old.

   Zutahy—ecica—leguminous. Round-headed tree. Dense summit.

Sept. 23

At home all day reading *Harnsworth History of South America*,[19] etc., etc. Making lists of books for the many friends I've found here and at Manoas, etc., etc.

Sept. 24

Fine ride in auto with Mr. Aimers for three hours. Along streets lined with palms. Very striking. Walk in fine shady park and Botanical Gardens.

---

[19] JM's reference is to one of the several editions of *Harmsworth History of the World: The Life-Story of the Earth and of All Nations, Told in Eight Grand Divisions* (London: Carmelite House, 1907). Volume 8, which covers the Americas, includes substantial discussion of the Maya, Nahua, Toltec, and Aztec peoples, as well as Mexican and Spanish colonialism in South America.

Sept. 25

Sao Paulo arrived last evening. Leaves tomorrow morning at 8:00, for Rio. Go downtown with Mr. Aimers, get ticket, 291 milreis. Wrote letters. Returned to Duff home for luncheon, packed, and bade a most grateful goodbye to Mr. Duff and Mr. Cole who have been incredibly kind to me. Never left a friend's home with greater obligation and regret.

Went on board at half past five with Mr. Aimers, who looked after everything.

Muir with daughters Helen and Wanda (and unidentified man), to whom he wrote many of his letters while traveling abroad

Correspondence

Para, Brazil
August 29, 1911
Wanda Muir Hanna

Dear Wanda,[20]

I got here yesterday afternoon. Had a fine smooth sail all the way and feel better than when I started.

Will go on up the river on the 31st. May be on the great river about a month.[21] I'll write again ere going south. Weather here less oppressive than in New York—feel quite well. Take precious care of the big happy boys.[22] Tell them I'll be back to see them and tell stories next spring. Hope Tom's crops[23] and plans are prospering.

Please hold my mail until I get home. Remember me to the neighbors. Love to all.

Your devoted father,

John Muir

---

[20] JM's eldest daughter, Annie Wanda Muir (1881–1942), who married Thomas R. Hanna (1881–1947) in 1906. As the letters in this book might suggest, the correspondence between JM and his youngest daughter, Helen, was more frequent and perhaps more tender than his correspondence with Wanda, particularly during this period. There are several possible reasons for this. First, Helen was infirm almost from birth, and seemed to require a special parental care and attention that JM often tried to provide through letters. Also, during this period Helen lived in Hollywood and then in Daggett, California, a physical separation that made frequent correspondence necessary in order to sustain a strong relationship, whereas Wanda and her family lived on Muir's property, in the adobe house out behind his own. Many letters between JM and Wanda are collected in *Dear Papa: Letters between John Muir and His Daughter Wanda,* edited by Jean Hanna Clark (Wanda's daughter and JM's granddaughter) and Shirley Sargent (Fresno, Calif.: Panorama West Books, 1985), though it is telling that *Dear Papa* contains no letters written after 1906, even though JM lived until late 1914.

[21] As it turned out, JM spent only a fortnight on the Amazon; although he was holding a ticket all the way to Iquitos, Peru, he did not go further upriver than Manaus, Brazil, because of the difficulty of finding timely passage. In particular, JM was anxious to begin searching for *Araucaria braziliensis* and *A. imbricata* in southern Brazil and in Chile, respectively.

[22] Wanda and Thomas Hanna's first two children, sons Strentzel and John.

[23] Thomas Hanna's fruit orchards on the Strentzel ranch in Martinez.

Para, Brazil
August 29, 1911
Loulu Perry Osborn

Dear Mrs. Osborn,

Here at last is The River and thanks to your and Mrs. Harriman's loving care[24] I'm well and strong for all South American work in sight that looks like mine.

Arrived here last eve after a pleasant voyage—a long charming slide all the way to the equator between beautiful water and beautiful sky.

Approaching Para had a glorious view of fifty miles or so of forest on the right bank of the river. This alone is noble compensation for my long desired and waited for Amazon journey even should I see no more.

And it's delightful to contemplate your cool restful mountain trip which is really a part of this equator trip. The more I see of our goodly Godly star the more plainly comes to sight and mind the truth that it is all one like a face, every feature radiating beauty on the others.

I expect to start up the river to Manoas in a day or two on the *Dennis*. Will write again on my return before going south and will hope to get a letter from you and Mr. Osborn, who must be enjoying his well earned rest. How often I've wished him with me. I often think of you and Josephine[25] among the Avalanche Lake[26] clintonias and linnaeas. And that lovely boy[27] at Castle Rock. Virginia played benevolent mother delightfully[28] and sent me off rejoicing.

My love to each and all; ever, dear friend and friends,

Faithfully, gratefully,

John Muir

---

[24] JM is here thanking his friends for their hospitality during the months in New York preceding his voyage.
[25] Probably Lucretia ("Loulu") Perry Osborn's sister Josephine Adams Perry, who was married to Junus Spencer Morgan.
[26] Avalanche Lake was the site of the Osborns' summer trip to Glacier National Park in Montana.
[27] Probably one of the Osborns' two young sons.
[28] The Osborns' daughter, Virginia Sturgis Osborn (b. circa 1880), apparently helped see JM off from New York.

Para, Brazil
September 18, 1911
Helen Muir Funk

Darling Helen,

I fondly hope you and Buel and the precious son are well, safely through the summer in the pine woods of the mountains.

I'm well and have enjoyed a glorious trip of more than a thousand miles up the great river enriched with the spoils of the greatest of all the world's forests. Had far more telling views of the trees than I ever hoped for. The river is everywhere immensely wide, yet for hundreds of miles the steamer ran so close to banks I could almost touch the outreaching branches. I was a week at Manoas on the Rio Negro, wandered in the wonderful woods, got acquainted with the best citizens and had a good telling time every way. They even gave me a champagne dinner and many others hardly less notable, trying to lionize me almost like my own country friends though at first I felt dreadfully lonesome. Couldn't speak a word of Portuguese.

Here too I'm faring wonderfully well in the house of a Scotch banker.[29]

I got back to Para on the 15th and am waiting for a steamer to Rio. May have to wait a week, learning what I can of the adjacent country in the meantime. From Rio I plan to go to Buenos Aires. Thence up some of the rivers and across the Andes to Valparaiso, etc.

Be very careful of your health darling. I'll be home in the spring. God bless you.

Ever your devoted father,

John Muir

––––––

[29] The banker is presumably the previously mentioned "Mr. Duff," who, on an uncataloged scrap discovered in the MP, is further identified as "A. Duff."

Para, Brazil [30]

September 19, 1911

William Colby

Dear Mr. Colby,

I hope you all had a good time this summer, the usual Sierra Club luck. When I left New York August 12th the Hetch Hetchy looked comparatively safe as far as I could see.[31] But the wicked, whether down or up, are never to be trusted, so we must keep on watching praying fighting overcoming evil with good, as we are able.

I've had a glorious time up the Amazon. In about a week from above date I hope to be on my way to Rio de Janeiro. Thence I intend going to Buenos Aires, sail up the Uruguay and La Plata, cross the Andes to Valpariso, and southward along the Araucarian forests, etc., then perhaps to South Africa to see its wonderful flora, etc. May be home in the spring.

My kindest regards to Mrs. Colby and the great pair of boys[32] and to the Parsons,[33] and all the club you see.

Faithfully yours,

John Muir

------

[30] An excerpt from this letter was published in the *Sierra Club Bulletin* 8.3 (Jan. 1912): 214. It is also listed in the Kimes bibliography, item 306.

[31] JM's optimism about the fate of the Hetch Hetchy came in part from a change in Secretaries of the Interior that was then taking place, as Richard Ballinger, who had alienated conservationists, resigned and was replaced by President Taft's appointee, Walter Fisher.

[32] The Colby's two sons, Henry Vrooman and Gilbert Winslow.

[33] Edward Taylor Parsons (1861–1914) and Marion Randall Parsons (1880–1953) of San Francisco, close friends of JM's who were Sierra Club activists and comrades in the Hetch Hetchy battle. Edward Parsons, who worked for the Sherman-Williams Paint Company, was a mountaineer and outdoorsman who served as Club Director from 1904 to 1914, and was succeeded in that role by his wife, Marion, who served from 1914 to 1938. Edward Parsons was also an avid photographer, and part of his legacy to American environmental history is his important collection of more than 2,000 photographs, taken in the Sierra between 1901 and 1913. Marion Parsons, who was also a distinguished mountaineer, helped JM, during the final year of his life, to organize and edit his Alaska manuscripts—posthumously published as *Travels in Alaska* (Houghton Mifflin, 1915); indeed, it was the work of Marion Parsons in completing the organization of the manuscript after JM's death that allowed for its publication as a book. Marion Parsons also published various articles and one book, *Daughter of the Dawn* (1923). The Parsons' work was honored by naming a 12,120-foot mountain in Yosemite's Cathedral Range Parsons Peak—a mountain first ascended by Marion Parsons in the late 1920s or early 1930s.

Para, Brazil
September 19, 1911
Katharine Hooker

Ill in bed—dear dear friend no wonder to those who know the cruel burdens Fate has heaped on head and heart these long weary years.[34]

Yet the news seems almost incredible for your bodily strength always appeared to be beyond change or disease like crystals or sunshine. Of course you need absolute rest. Lie down among the pines for a while then get to plain pure white love-work with Marian, to help humanity and other mortals and the Lord—heal the sick, cheer the sorrowful, break the jaws of the wicked,[35] etc. But this Amazon delta sermon is growing too long. How glad I am that Marian was not with me, on account of Yellow fever and the most rapidly deadly of the malarial kinds so prevalent up the river.

Nevertheless I've had a most glorious time on this trip, dreamed of nearly half a century—have seen more than a thousand miles of the noblest of Earth's streams and gained far more telling views of the wonderful forests than I ever hoped for. The Amazon as you know is immensely broad, but for hundreds of miles the steamer ran so close to the bossy leafy banks I could almost touch the outreaching branches—fancy how I stared and sketched.

I was a week at Manaos on the Rio Negro tributary—wandered in the wonderful woods, got acquainted with the best of the citizens through Mr. Sanford a graduate of Yale—was dined and guided and guarded and befriended in the most wonderful way, and had a grand telling time in general. I have no end of fine things for you in the way of new beauty. The only fevers I have had so far are burning enthusiasms but there's no space for them in letters.

Here however is something that I must tell right now. Away up in that wild Manaos region, in the very heart of the vast Amazon basin I found a

[34] The foremost "cruel burden" to which JM refers was the recent death of Katharine Hooker's husband, John D. Hooker.
[35] An allusion to Job 29:17, which refers to Job's work for justice: "And I broke the jaws of the wicked, and plucked the spoil out of his teeth."

little case of books in a lonely house. Glancing over the titles none attracted me except a soiled volume at the end of one of the shelves, the blurred title of which I was unable to read, so I opened the glass door, opened the book, and out of it like magic jumped Katharine and Marian Hooker, apparently in the very flesh. The book needless to say was *Wayfarers in Italy*.[36] This joy-shock I must not try to tell in detail for medical Marian[37] might call the whole story an equatorial fever dream.

Dear, dear friend again goodby. Rest in God's peace.

Affectionately,

John Muir

––––––

[36] In this letter JM's loneliness is mitigated by his chance discovery of a copy of his friend Katharine Hooker's Italian travel book, *Wayfarers in Italy* (San Francisco: D. P. Elder and Morgan Shepard, 1902). A copy of the book, inscribed to JM from Katharine Hooker in June 1907, is in the MP at UOP.

[37] The Hookers' daughter, the physician and scientist Dr. Marian Osgood Hooker.

CHAPTER 3

Coastal Brazil and up the Iguacu River into the Araucaria braziliensis Forests

26 September 1911–8 November 1911

W ITH A GREAT SENSE of appreciation for the Amazon basin and the friends he had made on his trip upriver, Muir left Belém on the morning of September 26, southbound for Rio de Janeiro on the steamer *Sao Paulo*. The passage to Rio took ten days, with brief calls at Fortaleza, Recife, and Salvador, and Muir seems to have enjoyed both the ocean and port aspects of the trip. Most of his journal entries for this period describe the brilliant sunsets and cloud formations, the physical geography near port towns the ship stopped at, and wildlife sightings on the open ocean. Most striking, on September 30 he recorded seeing a "[m]agnificent wing-shaped pair of foam-masses made by the diving of whales." "Fifteen or twenty feet of their tails were visible, black, gleaming, as they plunged," he wrote. "Two, swimming within a few rods of each other, rose and spouted and plunged together for fifteen or twenty minutes. Never before saw such lofty foam splashes made by animals, pure white in the sunlight."

Arriving in Rio de Janeiro on the morning of October 7, Muir spent four days in the city, walking the streets, traveling by cog railway to the top of nearby Corcovado Mountain, and—as he did in every town that afforded the opportunity—visiting the Botanical Gardens. As a geologist, he was captivated by the beauty of Rio's glacial scenery, which, though so near the equator, reminded him of the ice-carved mountains of Alaska, Yosemite, and the Swiss Alps; as a proponent of Thoreauvian austerity and idealism, however, the frenetic commercialism of the town led him to lament that strenuous efforts to amass "so-called wealth" amounted to little more than an "energetic fuss for bread and semi-pleasurable amusements, and dress-duds, etc., out of all reasonable proportion to the real pleasures of life."

On October 10 Muir left Rio on a different steamer, the *Voltaire*, southbound for Santos. All the way south from Belém Muir had his heart set on reaching the Uruguay River, where he hoped to find one of those rare South American trees that he had specifically hoped to study, the *Araucaria braziliensis*. But on his trip from Belém to Rio Muir had met a Mr. Harell, who was on his way to work at a lumber camp on the Iguacu River, deep in the forests of the Brazilian state of Paraná. After exchanging various descriptions with Harell, Muir concluded that the "Brazilian pine" that grew in the interior Paraná wilderness was actually the long-sought *Araucaria braziliensis*. Aboard the *Voltaire* Harell introduced Muir to Mr. Bouchet, Superintendent of the Paraná Lumber Company, who invited Muir to accompany the company sawmill party to Paraná's lumber mill and surrounding forests.

Muir arrived in Santos Harbor on October 11, and the following day went by rail with the sawmill party over the steep coast range to São Paulo. Outside São Paulo Muir delighted in his first glimpse of a few isolated specimens of *Araucaria braziliensis*. The next day he continued by rail to Porto Amazonas, on the Iguacu River, where he lodged at the home of a Portuguese farmer. Muir's quest for the *Araucaria braziliensis* began in earnest on the 15th, when he boarded the little river steamer *Iguassu* for his trip into the heart of the Paraná wilderness. After sailing down the Iguacu all night and up one of its tributaries the following morning, Muir arrived at the mill, in the midst of what indeed proved to be a nearly unbroken forest of *Araucaria braziliensis*.

Unlike Muir's thwarted Amazonian quest for the *Victoria regia*, his search for the *Araucaria braziliensis* was an unequivocal success. He seems to have spent nearly all the daylight hours of the next week in the forest that he fondly described as "a place according to my heart." His journals for this week are replete with detailed observations and careful sketches, reminding us that Muir's field journals were never exclusively diaries; they were also repositories of important natural history observations. The fastidiousness of his field observations of the *Araucaria braziliensis* is best evidenced by the journal entry and accompanying drawings for October 23, which document Muir's "analysis of the leafy tufts forming the ends of the branches" and careful counting of specimen branches, branchlets, and leaves, which led to his calculation that the number of leaves in the crown of a single tree is "about 3,491,152." Like his visit to the Amazon, Muir's week with the *Araucaria braziliensis* fulfilled a long-held dream. "Most interesting forest I have seen in my whole life," he exclaimed on October 24. "Formal, yet variable, and always impressive with auld-lang-syne Sequoia-like physiognomy."

Muir finally left the Paraná lumber camp on October 24, sailing up the small Rio Negro tributary of the Iguacu River to the village of Rio Negro, from which he boarded a train the next day for Curitiba. When Muir's train broke down he used the unexpected delay to study trees and add botanical notes to his journal. After an uncomfortable night on the train—during which he nevertheless enjoyed observing *Araucaria braziliensis* by starlight—and a few hours sleep after his 2:30 a.m. arrival in Curitiba,

Muir wandered the town parks and forests. On the evening of October 26, Muir tells us, he "[b]ade goodbye to all my *Araucaria* friends," as though speaking of the trees as well as of the men who guided him to the forest, "and felt very lonely."

The next morning Muir traveled by rail through spectacular "wild glacial scenery" to the small coastal town of Paranaguá, where he arrived by late morning. He experienced an early example of Hollywood exportation when he was taken by a friendly German to see "a moving picture show, which illustrated a California stage robber scene." After botanizing around the gardens of Paranaguá the following morning, Muir boarded the steamer *Sirio,* southbound for Montevideo, Uruguay, a voyage frequently punctuated by Muir's appreciative and vivid observations of the glacial geology of the southern Brazilian coast. During his two-day stay in Montevideo, Muir visited with the American Consul, Frederic W. Goding (a cousin of Muir's California friends Alfred and Fay Sellers), and studied trees in the Montevideo Botanical Gardens.

Soon back at sea, Muir sailed to Buenos Aires, Argentina, during the night of November 6. He spent a quick two days in Buenos Aires, during which he gave an interview to the *Buenos Aires Herald,* visited with mountaineer Annie Peck, dined with the American Consul and other prominent citizens, received forwarded letters, drew additional travel funds from a local bank, made plans for the next leg of his journey, and, of course, studied plants and trees in the Buenos Aires Botanical Gardens. Surprised and pleased by his warm reception and the interest of the local newspaper in his visit, Muir commented in his journal that "my fame has traveled thus far, though I am not acquainted with a single person in the whole of this great city."

The warm reception Muir received throughout his travels is attributable to a number of factors. By 1911 the name John Muir was internationally known among geologists, botanists, and conservationists: Muir had proven the glacial origins of Yosemite and had discovered glaciers and bays in remote Alaska; he had done pioneering tree studies in the Sierra

Nevada; he had helped win protection of Yosemite as a national park, and in 1911 he still served as the founding president of the Sierra Club. However, at least some of Muir's international "fame" was the product of the July 8, 1911, memorandum sent by President Taft to all US diplomatic and consular officers around the world, introducing the distinguished naturalist and requesting for him special assistance during his travels (though Muir appears to have been unaware of the memorandum until sometime in November 1911). In addition to his fame, Muir's advanced age and engaging personality were factors in the warm reception he received: some of the friends he made along his way meant simply to help an old man who was far from home; others found that Muir's wit, learning, and sense of adventure made him a companionable fellow traveler.

Only four of Muir's letters from this Belém to Buenos Aires leg of his journey are extant, and all are written to his daughter Helen. Though brief and often hurried, these letters confirm that Muir was enjoying his voyage in good health, that he was delighted with the success of his journey into the *Araucaria braziliensis* forests, and that he was deeply fascinated by the sub-equatorial glacial geology of coastal Brazil. And even while pursuing his own ambitious errand so far from home, Muir remembered his family, asking Helen to send money from his account to his Dunbar cousin Margaret Lunam, as he did each Christmas: "Tell her in the letter ½ is for herself, the other ½ for the poor," he instructed. In his last letter from this period, written to Helen on the eve of his departure from Buenos Aires, he informs her of his mission on the next leg of his journey: to cross the Argentinean pampas and ascend the Andes in search of the extremely rare monkey puzzle tree, *Araucaria imbricata*.

Journal

Sept. 26

Left Para at 8:30. Mr. Aimers came down to see me off. Vast send-off to a Senator. Brass band playing, the crowd hurrahing. A lot of girls in white, with huge hats and hobble skirts, etc. All the French notions plus Portuguese. Colored like flamingoes. Politics more intensely displayed than in US which is saying very wildest stuff imaginable.

Color of Amazon water distinct all day. Dull black cloudy evening. Bright stars at night, except around horizon. Slept pretty well.

Sept. 27

Fine clear morning. White fluffy-edged cumuli, dull pale haze around horizon. Lovely blue above. The sea white-capped sparsely. Colored slightly with the finest of the Amazon mud particles. Ship pitching. One pure white bird skimming through the even curly-topped swells. Fine ship, built in Scotland. Cadaverous very un-Scotch-flavored food. Dish of yellow, slimy, ointment-like stuff, perhaps intended for custard instead of porridge, at 6:00 a.m. with coffee and cakes. Breakfast at 10:00. Lunch at 1:30. Dinner at 5:00. Supper at 8:00. All these meals made up of stuff deadly undesirable.

Sept. 28

Lovely breezy exhilarating morning. Few dim clouds low around the horizon. Water beautiful pale blue. Fine sky all day. Few clouds. Stiff breezes. A headland in sight at 1:00 p.m. Sunset huge ball, easily stared at without hurt to eyes. Magnificent wing-like clouds on either side of the setting sun. Red glowing patch on dull leaden black. The sun as it touched the horizon was bright orange above dull orange below.

Sept. 29

Anchored last evening about 11:00. Within two or three miles of Ceara.[1] Moved in at 6:00 this morning, within less than a mile of the town and discharged large lots of freight; flour, clocks, a piano, a cotton gin, etc., etc., and took in large lots of baled cotton, said to be of fine quality. The so-called harbor is only a wide exposed bay. All freight is lightered.[2]

The town is built on yellow sand dunes. Population about 60,000. All the coast is lined with sand dunes for at least twenty-five miles east and west of the town, the dunes rising into hills one hundred feet or so high, darkened here and there with low shrubs and trees. Back of the coast the land rises in a plateau with mountains three or four thousand feet high at a distance of thirty-five or forty miles. The city has a few fine buildings. Most of them, however, are low. One story. Red in color. Many in the suburbs nearly buried in drifting sand. Large number of palms on each side of town. Probably coconuts.

We left this port at 2:30 p.m. Charming breezy day. Few wispy clouds drifting up the coast. Sunset as usual, the sun a red smooth globe. Very large disc clearly defined until within a degree or so of the horizon, when it is quenched in a leaden haze, and black clouds.

Sept. 30

Fine breezy day. Almost cloudless at sunrise, and two or three hours after. Then fleecy wisps and bundles. Sunrise pink and purple and yellow. Sea whitened with wave-tops. Magnificent wing-shaped pair of foam-masses made by the diving of whales. Fifteen or twenty feet of their tails were visible, black, gleaming, as they plunged. Two, swimming within a few rods of each other, rose and spouted and plunged together for fifteen or twenty minutes. Never before saw such lofty foam splashes made by animals, pure white in the sunlight. Porpoises also were in numerous

---

[1] Now called Fortaleza, this port on the coast of the Brazilian state of Ceara is about 700 miles southeast of Belém.

[2] That is, transferred from the ship to a "lighter"—a flat-bottomed barge used to transport cargo between the hold and the wharves.

droves.[3] A considerable number of fishermen on the foamy sea on rafts with sails, six or eight miles from the shore, now appearing on the tops of waves, now vanishing between them. A boat also braving the rough sea.

Land in sight all day. The shore low and tawny with sand dunes. Sunglow a red ball within three or four diameters of the horizon, changing as it sank low in a dense cloud bar.

Oct. 1

Arrived at Pernambuco before daylight. Entered harbor a little after 6:00 a.m. Delightful breezy day. A long sea wall, built on a reef composed of broken coral and sand a mile or more long, which encloses a narrow harbor of equal length. Waves breaking outside. Very picturesque. A broad belt of beautiful green water, contrasting with the deep blue beyond it, caused, no doubt, by coral particles worn from the reef. It reminds me of the Great Barrier Reef of North Australia, inside of which I passed on my voyage from Sydney to Port Darwin.[4] A large number of steamers here from far and near. The best from Germany and England. The city fronting on the finely curved bay is picturesque. Very old. Not very clean. Red-tiled buildings. Some imposing in size and architecture. Fine residences in background. Population said to be about 200,000.

Our ship, *Sao Paulo,* discharging flour and petroleum all day.

Oct. 2

Wondrous bright clear morning. Scarce a cloud in all the sky. Light sea breeze. Lovely weather. So hot in the city streets. Finished unloading and took on heavy cargo of sugar and cotton. Finished about 10:00 p.m. and sailed for Bahia.

---

[3] Here, as elsewhere in the journal, JM is probably not seeing a species of porpoise but rather a species of dolphin—in this case probably the common dolphin *(Delphinus delphis)* or perhaps the bottle-nosed dolphin *(Tursiops truncatus).* At one point in the journal JM uses the term *dolphin* for what is obviously the same animal, thus suggesting that, like many today, JM may have used the two terms interchangeably.
[4] The passage JM describes took place from March 30 to April 11, 1904, during his 1903–04 world tour.

Oct. 3

Cool, cloudy morning. Grand cumuli mountains in long ranges with dark lead-colored horizontal belts or blurred with showers into nimbus masses. Lovely pale blue patches showing between the lofty cumuli, all gradually darkening. Cool rain without thunder from noon until 3:00 p.m. A general evenly-distributed dark gloomy storm. At 4:00 p.m. clearing. Land in sight at 11:00 a.m. Sea dark pure blue. Clouds like rocks, trees, flowers, birds, reptiles, beasts, etc. Inky sooty black on pale yellow sky, burning on the edges. The rocks often with window openings of innumerable forms, most striking near the sunset.

Oct. 4

Arrived Bahia Todos Santos 6:00 a.m. Showery until 8:30 a.m. Wide and beautiful bay. City on bluff in a crescent five miles long. About a half circle. Business part of the town at the foot of the bluff. Very imposing. Palms and other trees mixed with the houses, especially at the curving extremities and on bluffs. The ground hilly back of the bluffs; not visible from the ship.

At night the town lavishly lighted with large electric plant in rows along the waterfront and in clusters on the bluff so close together that the rays interlock, with striking effect. A beautiful city, by night or by day. The harbor is narrow but a mile or two in length, formed by a sea wall built on a coral reef. Water outside the wall shallow on which the waves break before reaching the wall. Water green with disintegrated particles.

Oct. 5

Cumulous clouds in the morning. Almost perfectly clear after 10:00 a.m. until after sundown. This is the first evening without the ordinary sooty multiform clouds since leaving Norfolk. Sunset delicately beautiful with pale yellow arching films. Water all day violet blue.

Oct. 6

Cloudless until near sunset. Then foggy. Solid black near the horizon. Sun when within twenty minutes of setting passed an opening in the solid dark cloud. The opening veiled with gauzy films through which the sun shone bright red. Fairly painting a clearly defined road over the waves of bright scarlet from the ship to the horizon.

Three albatrosses followed the ship in the forenoon. The air nearly chilly in the morning. Memorable day.

Oct. 7

Arrived at Rio about 7:30 a.m. Approached the harbor entrance about 6:00 a.m. Wonderful view of glacier-sculptured rocks draped in rain and mist like those in Alaska. Yosemite domes, glacial monuments common. All the scenery, every feature of it, as glacial as Alaska, or that of Yosemite, or of Switzerland. Rainy all day. Went to Hotel Avanido with Mr. Mendel. Had luggage wheeled up from the sea wall. Had to come a mile or more in boat through the waves, as in most South American ports. Had long walks about the city. Called on the American Consul, Mr. Lay.[5] Could learn but little about steamers for Santos.

Oct. 8

Rainy in the forenoon. Walked down to the landing at the sea wall to seek news of Mr. Harell, who was detained on board by rain. Sky cleared about 1:30 p.m. Went up the Corcovado Mountain by trolley and cog railroad. Extremely interesting trip, in wide, all-around views of glacial landscapes. Only the palms on these rocks seem strange. The celebrated Sugar Loaf, perhaps about two thousand feet in height, as seen from the top of the cog railroad, is most wonderfully formed. It is indeed a very striking rock from any direction. The base is like the Yosemite dome in color, concentric structure and form; a truly wonderful counterpart of Yosemite dome.

After descending the Corcovado I sauntered along the Praia Flamingo.

[5] Julius Gareché Lay (1872–1939), American diplomat, entered the consular service in 1889, and was appointed as Consul for Rio de Janeiro in 1910. JM may have been especially interested in talking to the Consul because Lay had, a few years earlier, served as the Consul in Cape Town, South Africa—a place toward which JM would shortly be headed.

Many Sunday family groups were enjoying themselves in the beautiful gardens, while many others were speeding past in automobiles on the fine road around the Bay, enjoying the cool evening. Boys and young men playing ball. Children nicely dressed running gracefully about the gardens and statuary and the monuments. Magnificent scenery, from here as well as from the mountain top, from which nearly all the Bay is outspread in sight. It is very extensive and full of islands like the harbor of Sitka.[6]

Oct. 9

Heavy rain, with cold wind and lightning last evening at 10:00. Rained pretty steadily after 8:30 this morning until noon. Fair but cloudy in the afternoon. Went to Botanical Gardens with Mr. Harell and party.

The views of the mountains along the magnificent avenues of royal palms are peculiarly striking. Never before saw (Yosemite and Alaska) glacial domes and cliffs amid palms and tropical plants in general. As a Botanical Garden this one ranks far from high. Many plants unnamed, while those that are have the letters of many of the names weathered off. But as a City pleasure park it is very fine. The bamboo avenues here are the finest I have ever seen, although in Ceylon many of the bamboos are taller. The Garden is situated at the foot of the Corcovada Mountains toward the southern extremity of the fine Praia.

In the forenoon bought a ticket to Santos on the steamer *Voltaire*, 10,000 ton ship. Very tired, with long walks and waits.

Oct. 10

Sailed for Santos at 5:00 this afternoon. Went aboard with Mr. Mendes at 8:30 in the morning. Found Mr. Harell, who introduced me to Mr. Bouchet, Superintendent of the Parana Lumber Company, owning nearly a million acres of *Araucaria* forest, which I hope to see. I am cordially invited to travel with Mr. Bouchet's party. This will save me a long trip up

---

[6] On Baranof Island, in the Alexander Archipelago of southeastern Alaska. Muir had been in this part of Alaska on several of his northern excursions.

the Uruguay River. The only definite information that I have of the *Araucaria braziliensis,*[7] which I was determined to find, was from Prof. Branner,[8] who showed me two photographs taken somewhere on the upper Uruguay River, in which a few groups of these trees were seen in the general forest of the region. But on my way from Para to Rio I made the acquaintance of Mr. Harell, who, with a party of eight or ten, was on his way to work on a large mill that was about completed in the State of Parana, situated about three or four hundred miles to the west of Curytiba. I inquired what kind of timber they were going to cut and they said it was called Brazilian pine, but that he had never seen any of those trees. He told me, however, that from a description he got from one of the mill men who had been in that work there, they were trees perhaps one hundred feet high without limbs; that the limbs were all in a bunch at the top. I had little doubt from this description that they were the trees I was in search of, and said I would be very glad to go to the mill in their company if they would allow me, and he said he had no doubt that I would be welcome there.

All the four days I have spent in the wonderful Rio bay and city and surrounding mountains have been purely Alaskan in weather and general scenery of glaciated rocks, clouds, winds, rains, drizzly changeful blinks of sunshine, rounded wave-fringed islands, misty ragged clouds, dark gloomy lowering.

Entering the wonderfully picturesque harbor with its mist-capped dome fringed with wave foam, I seemed to be entering an Alaskan fjord, and in leaving the bay this evening the same dark rainy blowy cold weather

---

[7] For a description of the *Araucaria* genus generally and the *braziliensis* species specifically, see the footnote for JM's February 11, 1911, letter to Charlotte Kellogg.

[8] After studying at Maryville College and at Cornell, gifted and prolific geologist John Casper Branner (1850–1922) made his first geological expedition to Brazil in 1874. Fifteen years later he and Alexander Agassiz organized the famous 1889 Branner-Agassiz expedition to Brazil. Branner returned to Brazil again more than twenty years later, when he worked for the Brazilian government, to study the geology and biology of the Amazon delta region. Branner also served as Professor of Geology at University of Indiana (1885–87), State Geologist of Arkansas (1887–92), president of the Geological Society of America (1904), and second president of Stanford University (1913–17).

reminding me of many a dismal night in Southeastern Alaska, when I was trying to find a sheltered landing back of an island. While in sunny afternoons the great domes of solid granite, with concentric structure and dark streaks marking the courses of rain streams in shallow slow-flowing films reminded me of Yosemite domes that are as yet scarcely influenced by post-glacial weathering. In particular, there is a rock toward the south end of the Bay, perhaps 2,500 feet high, that is an almost exact counterpart of the notable Fairview Dome of the Tuolumne Meadows. That this noble bay is an unchanged piece of Nature's glacial handiwork I have no doubt.[9] The granite of this region, out of which the harbor has been eroded, is extremely hard and coarse-grained. I am greatly surprised to find so clear and noble a manifestation of ice-work at sea level so near the Equator; to find glacier domes feathered with palms instead of hemlocks and spruces and pines. Little did I dream that in "rolling down to Rio," as Kipling says,[10] I was rolling down into a noble palmy ice land. A single day, a single hour here, is well worth a hard lonely care-laden journey around the world.

As for the city, it is grand, as busy, commercial places go. Many fine churches, cathedrals, business structures, where multitudes of money changers are trying hard to gain so-called wealth, merely making a living, doing bread chores, etc. Many steamships and sailing vessels dot the bay and line miles of wharves, making an admirably energetic fuss for bread and semi-pleasurable amusements, and dress-duds, etc., out of all reasonable proportion to the real pleasures of life.

---

[9] According to Jürgen Ehlers, author of *Quaternary and Glacial Geology* (New York: John Wiley, 1996), studies have shown, "by dating of volcanic deposits that there had also been early glaciation in South America. Patagonia was repeatedly glaciated between 3.0 and 1.8 million years ago. The glaciation of the Southern Andes reached its largest extent about 1.0 million years ago" (451).

[10] JM here alludes to "I've Never Sailed the Amazon," the poem appended by English Nobel laureate Rudyard Kipling (1865–1936) to his 1900 short story "The Beginning of the Armadilloes." The second stanza of the poem reads as follows: "Yes, weekly from Southampton, / Great steamers, white and gold, / Go rolling down to Rio / (Roll down— roll down to Rio!) / And I'd like to roll to Rio / Some day before I'm old!" The sentiment expressed in the final lines of this stanza would have resonated with JM, who, at age seventy-three, was fulfilling his lifelong dream of visiting South America. That he found such clear signs of glacial geology in the region was an unlooked-for pleasure to him.

Oct. 11

Arrived Santos about 4:00 p.m. At the dock about 5:00. Very cold all day. 69 deg. at noon, and cloudy with sprinkles of rain. Fine glacial scenery all along the coast between Rio and Santos, as far as I saw it. That is, from 6:00 a.m. to 5:00 p.m., about one hundred and twenty-five miles. Many outlying islands, some mere rock, very ornamental, fringed or wholly covered with never-failing foam. The showiest of all the white water lilies.

Santos Harbor is located a few miles up the river, in the midst of magnificent mountain scenery. The stevedores loading coffee along a mile or two of steamer lined wharves make a lively scene. The bags of coffee are carried on the porters' backs, and they form long lines like ants, running, working by the piece. Here nearly all of the celebrated Brazil coffee is shipped to all parts of the world.

Went to Pensoa / Saxonia[11] with the sawmill party. Very fortunate to find guides so kind. Hotel queer, but comfortable.

Oct. 12

Rainy and misty on the mountains. Alaska weather and scenery continued as far as I have seen. Interesting railway ride to Sao Paulo. The road is well built by an English company. Extremely costly. Many steel bridges and tunnels solidly arched, and the cuts on the mountainside solidly reinforced with well-cemented masonry wherever there is the slightest danger of a landslide. Wide cement gutters for drainage of mountain slopes. The road crosses the coast range at a height of about 2,600 feet. Part of grade is so steep that the train is hauled up by steel cable. The mountains densely tree-clad. Trees mostly small. Beyond the mountains there is a plateau, diversified with hills and groves and meadows. A good cattle region. Many villages. Was delighted to discover specimens of *Araucaria braziliensis* on the plateau fifteen or twenty miles from Sao Paulo, growing among other trees and bushes.

Left Santos at 10:15 a.m. Arrived at Sao Paulo 12:50. Went to hotel close to railroad station. Stayed until 4:00 p.m. of the next day, October 13th.

[11] "Pensoa / Saxonia" may be the name of the modest hotel at which JM stayed this night in Santos.

Oct. 13

Rainy all day. Took walks in wide, double avenue, shaded with trees. Seats beneath them. Left Sao Paulo at 4:20 p.m. in sleeper. Saw a few *Araucaria*s before dark.

Oct. 14

Drizzly morning. *Araucaria*s in hundreds and thousands. Wondrous sight. Seems to bear fire better than other trees, yet it has evidently been driven to rocky hilltops. At 11:00 a.m. still winding among hills of general prairie tableland. Fine grassy cattle country. *Araucaria*s on the hills very telling, along white cloud horizon. The old trees flat-topped, the young arrowhead shaped. Some in hollows, all ages and shapes. Some double-headed. Flat or up-curved or dome-shaped. All the branches naked. Small branchlets fall off. Those of young trees all aspire.

Some of the trees have the lower limbs curled up over those above them, with three tufts longer in the center, like birds in a saucer-shaped nest. No end of forms. All of them picturesque when old. The lower branches drop off when dead, though they remain for years after the leaves fall. Saw a few that had been fire killed. The bare branches of those that had only dropped their leaves make strikingly picturesque heads. Soon all drop off, leaving only desolate blackened pillars. Each branch of the living old tree forms at the end a dome of foliage like the domes of whole trees. Very few of the limbs divide; saw only one all day.

Passed through extensive forest today about noon. Later the country was one wide prairie with *Araucaria*s only here and there along the streams and crowning hilltops in detached groves. Wonderful effect made by the crowns of umbrella tops rising above each other. Fair and sunny in the afternoon, with magnificent white cumuli here and there, on which the *Araucaria*s were most strikingly relieved. Saw a few tree ferns along the streams and meadows, the tallest about ten feet high; three or four inches in diameter. Crown of fronds two or three feet wide. A good many *Araucaria*s are now in flower.

Arrived at Port Amazons on the Iguassu River. Mr. Smith met us at the railroad junction with a special train to take us to the river landing. Was warmly welcomed by Mr. Smith, who is Superintendent of the mill, a Californian who knows many of my old friends.

Oct. 15

Stayed last evening at Port Amazons at the home of a Portuguese farmer, who has a thrifty orange grove and vegetable and flower garden, and a fine *Araucaria* grove of ten or fifteen acres back of the house. The tallest of the trees are about one hundred and twenty feet high, and between two and three feet in diameter. There is no lack of hopeful quick-growing seedlings and saplings for the renewal of the forest after those trees are removed. Bark of the stumps grows an inch or two after the tree has been felled, making a shallow pan of the top of the stump that may contain several quarts of rain water.

Oct. 16

Left Port Amazons last evening at 2:30 on the little river steamer *Iguassu*. Sailed downstream on the river of the same name until 8:00 this morning. Then up a tributary, less than an hour's sail, to the mill.

Oct. 17

Out all day in the woods. Nearly all the trees are *Araucaria*s, forming almost pure forests. They are now in flower. Male flowers from three to seven inches long, one inch in diameter. Female flowers about two inches in diameter. One specimen tree that I carefully measured was about two and a half feet in diameter four feet above the ground, one hundred and twenty-five feet high, and the crown was about fifty-five feet in diameter. The first limb was at a height of about eighty feet. Some of the knots of the limbs that had fallen off toward the head of the clear part of the trunk were not yet overgrown by the wood rings. A good many tree ferns are growing in the moister parts of the woods, from one to one and a half feet in diameter of trunk, and fifteen to twenty feet high. Fronds five feet long, one and a half to two feet wide. Several other species of ferns were growing on their trunks. There are also a good many palms in the woods, with trunks eighteen inches in diameter and sixty feet high. The bark of *Araucarias* usually about half an inch thick, and towards the top peels off in thin sheets, something like birch bark. But it is always much thicker towards the base of the tree and forms a good defense from grass fires. On some of the older trees the bark is two or three inches in thickness nearly to the top.

I found a tree that had been blown down by the wind which, at a height of forty feet from the ground, was divided into three nearly equal shafts, which ascended nearly parallel to each other only a few feet apart. The two outer divisions again divided, and all together united in a head one hundred and thirty feet high.

I found fine clumps of a species of cane, thirty feet high. Very slender, growing on stream banks. This cane, though common, covering nearly all the ground on thousands of acres, only along the streams are any living ones to be found; said to die naturally at the age of seven years. Lumbermen complain of the trouble the dense growth gives them.

Oct. 18

Warm. Most of the sky cloudy, but no rain fell.

Oct. 19

Warm. Fine cumuli in the afternoon, when the temperature fell to about 65 deg. Have been in the woods all day, a place according to my heart.

Oct. 20

Cloudy. Cleared about 11:00 a.m. Delightful day. Out in the woods four miles from the mill. Found a tree a hundred and fifty-seven feet high, four feet four inches in diameter; bark five inches thick.

Oct. 21

North of the mill there are many fine palms and tree ferns. Found a felled *Araucaria* with abundance of young cones and flowers on both upper and lower branches. The *Araucaria* is monoecious.[12]

Oct. 22

Out on logging road. Fine views of flat-topped woods on the ridges. Many small bogs and meadows.

Oct. 23

Out beyond end of logging road four or five miles from mill, in magnificent primeval *Araucaria* woods. Some of the hill slopes of considerable extent have been swept by fire, killing every tree, leaving only blackened charred monuments. The ground now taken by a dense growth of bushes.

Measured a dead prostrate tree three feet three inches in diameter at four feet above the ground and two feet in diameter one hundred feet above the ground, and one foot six inches in diameter one hundred and eight feet above. All decaying tree trunks are inhabited by a species of black ants about half an inch long. A tree felled a few days ago had limbs finely curved thirty and one half feet long. Five inches in diameter at the base. The tufts of terminal leafy branchlets are about two feet in diameter; the same in length. In general form they are like the crown of the tree that they belong to, the many small crowns making one large one. One branch that I minutely examined was five inches and a half in diameter at the base. The crown of the tree it belonged to had sixty-one branches four and a half to six and a half inches in diameter at the base. Diameter of the trunk two feet above the ground was three feet. Ninety-six feet above the ground the diameter was twenty-two inches. Bark on the stump two and one-half inches.

In analysis of the leafy tufts forming the ends of the branches I counted thirty-eight branchlets. Second and third branchlets two hundred and

[12] Hermaphroditic; having pistillate and staminate flowers on the same individual tree.

ninety-two. Leaves in the branch crown 57,232. Number of leaves in the whole crown about 3,491,152. Each leaf about an inch and a half long, an inch wide at base, flat tapering to a sharp prickly point. White violets are very abundant in shady parts of the woods. Measured a tree one hundred and thirty-five feet high, three feet in diameter. Another, one of the tallest that I found, was one hundred and fifty-seven feet high, four feet three inches in diameter, bark four to five inches thick.

*Araucaria*s rock in the wind and move the branches up and down and horizontally. Of other species of trees scattered through the *Araucaria* woods, one has very small yellowish leaves and round heads with graceful

Journal sketches of Araucaria braziliensis, *including Muir's calculations of the number of leaves in the tree's crown*

slender branchlets. Another larger species has wide glossy leaves which sparkle in the sun, making a dazzle of sun-glow when shaken by the wind. On the sides of wet meadows grows a chocolate-colored fern, like an *Espidium*, the fronds about four feet and six inches high, simply pinnate. Very handsome. The ribs of the fronds green.

The black ants mentioned above cut off great quantities of the *Araucaria* leaves, marching in double columns, each ant with a large leaf over its head, going to their nests in the ground or in old rotten logs. One column going to nests, the other to the tree they are at work on. The leaves are neatly snipped off, as if cut with a pair of scissors. Of what use the ants make of the great piles of leaves thus carefully gathered from a height of from one hundred to one hundred and twenty or thirty feet above the ground I was not able to make out. They simply seem to be designed only for protection to their nests, the leaves being very prickly, sharp-pointed.

A composite plant, with three angles, shrubby stem, and white flowers without rays, makes dense growth around the margins of meadows, five or six feet high. Back of these, where the ground is dryer, the common pteris[13] forms luxuriant growth three or four feet in height.

An *Araucaria* only thirteen inches in diameter at the ground was eighty-seven feet long, and twelve inches in diameter at fifty feet above the ground.

Oct. 24

Cloudy. Magnificent cumuli about noon. Mill running. Leave this hospitable camp about 6:00 this evening. Most interesting forest I have seen in my whole life. Formal, yet variable, and always impressive with auld-lang-syne Sequoia-like physiognomy. Tree ferns and palms make large part of primeval forest. More tree ferns than palms or trees of other species and yield most of the forest shade. Crowns of *Araucaria* trees cast little shade. Many species of herbaceous ferns both on the ground and the tree

[13] The genus *Pteris* is a common fern of the Pterideæ family.

trunks. Fine mint and large lily-like plants in flower, purple. Many mosses. Saw a squirrel, very like the Douglas, darker, redder, perhaps smaller. Must be well fed.

Oct. 25

We arrived at the village or town of Rio Negro about 6:30 this morning. Twelve hours sail up the river of same name. Fine stream; picturesque brushy banks. *Araucaria* trees common, on low flooded ground as well as on hills. Magnificent views of *Araucaria* crowned hills and slopes from high streets. Have been trying to sketch some of them. Here we take train for Curytiba at 1:20 p.m. Expect to arrive about 8:00.

Gliding up the Rio Negro, banks draped here and there with living canes, beautiful green tufts alternate along the stem at joints five or six inches apart. Stems very slender, green, elastic while alive, but become brittle when dry and soon fall and decay on the ground. This species is said to fruit and die in fifteen years from the seed.

At 3:00 p.m. we are still at Rio Negro, the railroad engine having broken down. Have been sauntering along the river bank studying the trees. The *Araucaria* is very thrifty, growing on the rich bottom land; the branches covered with ferns and orchids. Other trees are still more lavishly adorned. The large red-flowered *Amaryllis* is in great abundance. A composite shrub six or eight feet high covered by very smooth bark on the main stems, three inches in diameter. It covers densely large areas, subject to fires. No ray flowers. A young *Araucaria* about fifty feet high has a head nearly globular, about thirty-five feet in diameter. In young vigorous trees, say seventy-five years old, seventy or eighty feet high, each tuft at the end of the main limb makes a distinct head readily seen at a distance of half a mile or so. The young leaves are paler green than the old. Only the tips of tuft combined with the crown, however, show distinctly yellow. The general color is dark green. Here at Rio Negro the young trees growing on the river bottom are the finest I have so far seen. A row of *Araucaria* crowning the top of a ridge about three miles distant make a striking effect.

6:00 p.m. and no sign of train. Fine rosy, purple evening. Train came at last. We left Rio Negro at 7:30 and arrived at Curytiba at 2:30 on the morning of the 26th. Spent miserable night on the hard shabby cars.

Oct. 26

Went to a hotel and had three or four hours sleep. The *Araucaria* distributed as far as I could make out in the starlight most of the way.

Walked about town after a late breakfast. Noticed fine *Cryptomeria*s in gardens and also in dry, dusty parks. *Cupressus* also, and *Thuja,* with *Eucalyptus.* Streets roughly paved.

Araucaria braziliensis *with a cross section of the tree's bole*

Paid my respects to Mrs. Smith, charming lady born in the redwood region of California, at Eureka. Bade goodbye to all my *Araucaria* friends, Bouchet, Smith, Perry, Goodyear, and felt very lonely.

Oct. 27

Started at 6:30 a.m. for Paranaguay. Glorious ride through Yosemite scenery. Mr. Mitchell kindly took me to the train this morning, procured my ticket, and saw me off.

Araucaria scattered along the road from the outskirts of Curytiba over all the plateaus, though most of the larger trees have been cut for lumber. Passed a small sawmill where the trees were most abundant.

Many small farms showed patches of *Araucaria* on stony hills. Few of these saved trees are over a hundred feet high. *Araucaria* is a very straight erect tree. Shows no trace of wind on its crowns. Few winds are strong enough to rock them, much less to bend the trunk, or uproot them. They keep their heads level even when the trunk is leaning. A few are to be seen at the foot of the mountain on an alluvial bottom, around the harbor.

Sketched a fine broad-headed tree about sixty feet wide and high, in the middle of one of the streets in Paranaguay. It is fig-like, thick branchlets. Young leaves red and purple opening in circular flower-like rosettes on the end of the upturned branchlets.

The scenery is wonderfully fine at the head of the glacial canyon down which the railroad winds.

A noble rock, 1,500 or 2,000 feet high, looming through the fog and misty rain. A fine broad waterfall beside it. And a cascade on the main stream a few hundred yards farther up the tremendous gorge. Couldn't see the bottom of it and the other features were shifting, but saw enough to assure me that this wild glacial scenery must be ranked with that of California and the Alps and Alaska.

Arrived at Paranaguay at 10:30 a.m. Had no difficulty in finding the Johnsker Hotel, to which I was directed by a kind German in Curytiba. Two small boys carried my satchels, balancing them daintily on their heads, trotting along jauntily as if they were empty and were enjoying them as ornaments, showing forth the dignity of money-earning labor. Here I have to wait for the steamer *Sirio*, no word of which has yet arrived. Through a letter to the hotel keeper by the aforementioned German at Curytiba I was made acquainted with a young German who speaks English. Thinking that I must be putting in my time in a rather gloomy way, he took me this evening to a moving picture show, which illustrated a California stage robber scene.[14]

Oct. 28

Around Paranagua in gardens and in a small park there are many species of palms. One in particular, the traveler's tree, shaped like one immense fan. Another, with beautiful triangular leaflets on its broad frond-like leaves, and magnificent drooping swaying tassels of male and female flowers or fruit. Fruit about five eighths of an inch in diameter. Trees about sixty feet high. The largest about two feet in diameter of trunk. Leaves twelve feet long and two feet broad. A few of these are on the waterfront growing with Royal palms, the latter much taller.

Waiting for the *Sirio*. Purchased a ticket to Montevideo for 155 Milreis. Steamer was advertised to sail at 3:00 p.m. today, but did not sail until after midnight. Long waiting in the dark at wharf and out in the Bay on the tender. Not allowed to get aboard until after 9:00. Good little ship. Got a berth in a cabin with a handsome young officer of the Brazilian Navy who speaks English.

Oct. 29

Charming weather. Sun rising over the sea in purple haze. Grand sight. Mountains along the coast about 2,000 or 3,000 or 4,000 feet high, like those of Alaska in form and sculpture, with palms instead of conifers. Houses with small clearings here and there all along the coast. Arrived

---

[14] The prevalence during the first decade of the twentieth century of short western films that include conventional scenes such as the stage robbery make it extremely difficult to identify this film. However, the "moving picture" JM saw would likely have been one of the many films patterned after Edison studios' influential 1903 movie, *The Great Train Robbery*.

about 11:00 a.m. at San Francisco, about half way up a beautiful bay. Mountain scenery magnificent. Purely glacial. In an hour or two left San Francisco for the port of Ityhaya. Arrived about 5:00 p.m. This is a still grander bay than the one we have left. Had to wait for a pilot before crossing the broad wave-beaten bar. While still several miles out we noticed a sharply defined line between the ocean and the greenish-yellow river water, poured into the bay at its head.

We lay here all night.

Oct. 30

Started for Florionopolis at 4:00 a.m. It is situated on a narrow strait between the mainland and Santa Catarina Island. Beautiful, like the island passes of the Alexander Archipelago.[15] Town not large. Noticed several brush fires, burning on the high surrounding mountains, sending up great pillars of smoke. Arrived here at 11:00 a.m. Departed for Rio Grande de Sul at 5:00 p.m. Wonderful clouds at sunset. Black, craggy, edged with gold. Orange, etc.

Oct. 31

Calm. Almost cloudless. Pale thin mists most of the forenoon. Sea wondrous smooth. No land in sight after 5:00 p.m. Clouds to the westward toward noon. Sea shimmering, spangling. Temperature pleasantly cool, about 70 deg. in the shade. Toward sunset noticed massive, lead-colored cloud toward the land, spreading rapidly, causing sudden darkness and fall in temperature, followed by grand lightning and thunder and roaring wind and rain. A truly magnificent storm, buffeting our little ship and making her reel and shudder. Lasted in wild extravagant torrents with lightning illumination of the solid blackness at half minute intervals for half an hour or so. Then died down to a steady continuous rainstorm.

[15] In southeastern Alaska.

Nov. 1

Foggy up to 11:00 a.m. Anchored an hour or so. Then crept slowly ahead. Fog again settled down. Turned back on our course, heaving the lead.[16] Anchored again, fearing grounding on the Rio Grande de Sul bar. 11:30 a.m. again groping our way to the entrance of the lagoon to reach the town of Rio Grande. We must cross the bar within an hour or so or lie outside until tomorrow, so it is reported, says the Captain. Sky cleared about noon and the low, sandy coast came in sight. A tug came out to guide us through the pass over the bar. Arrived at the town a little before 1:00 p.m., and anchored a few hundred yards from the long sea-wall among a large number of ships loading and discharging. Very heavy rain and thunderstorm about 3:00 p.m. A grand black windy affair. Most of the first-class passengers went ashore to see the town. Quite imposing, but the noble glacial mountain scenery of all the ports S. of Rio Janeiro wholly wanting. Only level delta sands from the mountain streams at head of the lagoon, a continuation of the Rio Grande de Sul from its mouth near Port Allagre one hundred and fifty miles from the bar. This Patos lagoon runs parallel to the ocean coast through the midst of a vast sand delta deposited toward close of the glacial period by many streams descending from a mountainous range extending parallel to it. The larger streams enter at the head of it.

Nov. 2

Cool and cloudy. Temp. 60 deg. Discharging cargo. Mr. Hector J. Tilley left the *Sirio* here. Will miss his companionship.

Calm, clear, lovely day just closing. Not a hill, however small, or hint of any mountain, though many rise in a continuous chain parallel to the vast low sand plain divided by the long lagoon of Patos, telling of many a roaring water stream from quick-melting glaciers. The *Sirio* cargo for this town has been discharged, and that for Pelotas and for Port Alegre has been transferred to another of the Government steamers. A good many of

---

[16] That is, taking soundings to ensure sufficient depth for navigation.

the passengers have also left us for Alegre, and a few new ones have come aboard from Rio Grande for Montevideo. We expect to sail tomorrow at 4:00 a.m.

Nov. 3

Left Rio Grande this morning about 6:00. Sky cloudless, save few wisps and curls low down along western horizon, unchanged up to 1:00 p.m. Lagoon water muddy. Forms distinct line with open sea several miles out. A remarkably broad and bright belt of flashing, sparkling spangles in the wake of the sun, at their best in size and number about two and a half hours after sunrise. We expect to reach Montevideo tomorrow evening. Brazil is said to form a vast plateau 1,000 to 3,250 feet above the sea level, worn into low wide valleys and grooves by glacial and stream action. Grassy meadows and prairie-like plains are outspread between groves and forests on hills and ridges, excepting the mountain ranges and the heart of the immense basin of the Amazon where all the surface is forested or covered with bushes and separate groves. The highest mountains are said to be on the coast range toward the sea, and in the center forming two long chains, separated by the basins of the San Francisco and Paraguay Rivers. The Eastern Sierra follows the coast from Cape St. Roque, and ends in the Rio Grande del Sul. This chain is divided in two, the Sierra de Mar and Sierra de Mantiquiara. Their culminating points are Orgaos, 7,232 feet high to the north of Rio de Janeiro, and Itatiaya, about 9,150 feet, in the Sierra de Mantiquiara, and this last is the highest point in all Brazil. The Serra do Espiuhaco follows the east side of the basin of the San Francisco. Its culminating points are Itacolomy, 5,694 feet; Caraca, 6,356 feet; Piedade, 5,794 feet; and Itambe 5,924 feet. The Serra Central is formed by the group of mountains of Goyaz and of Minas Geraes to the west of the San Francisco River, and is united to the Serra Oriental by a ramification in Minas Geraes and is called Serra Bertentes. This chain is composed of two grand branches, Serra Canastera, 4,166 feet, and Serra Mattodacorda, of which the culminating points are the Montes Pyreneus, 7,774 feet. The grand plateau of Parana extends over a great part of the state of the Rio

Grande del Sul, of Santa Catarina, of Parana, of Sao Paulo, of Mines Geraes, of Goyaz and the highland of Mattogroso. Its greatest altitude is
about 3,350 feet. The immense plain of the Amazon comprehends a great
part of Mattogroso and of Goyaz, and the states of Para and of the Amazons and of Maranhao. The plateau of San Francisco lies to the west of the
river of that name. In the western region of the State of Minas Garaes and
Bahia. Its greatest altitude is 6,200 feet. Between the sea and the mountains there is a low and narrow strip of land.

The hydrographic system of Brazil is largely developed. We cite above
all the Amazon, the King of Rivers, with a course of 5,400 kilometers, of
which 3,800 is in Brazil, and its affluence of large rivers. On the left Bank
the Aca, the Jupura, the Rio Negro, all more than 1,000 kilometers. The
Jary, the Jananda, the Araguay. On the right bank the Javary, the Jutahy,
the Jurua, the Teffe, the Coarym, the Purus, the Madeira, the Tapajoz, the
Hingu, the Cotantins. Several of these have courses of 1,500 to 3,000 kilometers. Among the other rivers we notice the Gurupy, the Puryassu, the
Pindare, the Mearim, the Itapicura, the Paranahyba, the Jaguariba, the
Mossoro, the Assu, the Parahyba del Norte, the Capiberive, the Ipojuca,
the Formoso, the Mandahu, the Sao Francisco. This last has a length of
3,000 kilometers and crosses the states of Minas Gereaes, Bahia, Pernambuco and Algoas. Also the Vassa-Barris, the Itapicuru do sul, the Pearaguassu, the Contas, the Jaquitimhonha, the Mucury, the Doce, the Parahyba do Sul, the Iguapo, the Tiffucas, the Tubarao, the Ararangua, the
Mempituba, and the little river Chuy that forms the extreme original
frontier. Of other rivers that have their sources in these Brazilian territories and fall into the La Plata, these are the Uruguay, which takes its source
in the State of Santa Catarina; the Parana, which comes from Minas
Gereaes, with its numerous affluents, of which one, the Iguassu, comes
from the State of Parana; and the Paraguay, which has its source in Parythain. At the extreme north is the Oypock which separates Brazil from
French Guinea.

In the afternoon about 4:00 a black thunderstorm came suddenly from
the west. Magnificent clouds with strange fringes hung threateningly over

the sea. Soon took all the sky. Caused a sudden fall of temperature from high wind. After sunset lightning made a glorious show in the darkness, the whole heavens ablaze, and ever and anon zigzag streaks seemed to be discharging into the sea. At 9:00 p.m. still dark and rainy but wind abating and the lightning stopped.

Nov. 4

Clear, and cool enough for an overcoat. Passed two lighthouses about 6:00 in the morning. Expect to reach Montevideo about noon. At 11:00 a.m. the sky began to grow dark, threatening rain. Anchored a mile or two out from the pier, as usual. Landed in drizzling rain in small boat, with eight others, men, women and children. Short delay in customs house, and thence up to the grand Hotel Barcelona. I gladly following for the sake of one of the party, Mr. Graite, a German from Cleveland, Ohio, who speaks English. Fairly comfortable.

Nov. 5

Found my way to the American Consulate to see the Consul, Mr. F. Goding, who is a cousin of Mrs. Sellers and was very kind.[17] All day in his pleasant rooms. Went to luncheon and dinner with him. Returned to hotel about 11:00 p.m., having spent the afternoon with him in the Botanical Garden. Saw many fine trees, especially *Erythrina christagalli*, a most interesting tree, which at first glance I took for a weeping willow, and which is so-called here, although belonging to the Liguminosae.

Nov. 6

With Mr. Goding all day. Procured a ticket to Buenos Aires. Mr. Goding placed me aboard the steamer at 10:00 p.m. and introduced me to Mr. Bright, a fellow passenger, who is to take care of me, thus making all easy.

[17] Frederic Webster Goding (1858–1933), diplomat, physician, entomologist, and inventor, was a cousin of Muir's good friends Alfred and Fay Sellers. Goding was American Consul at Montevideo from 1908 to 1913, and was in charge of the American legation in Montevideo for a short time during 1911.

Nov. 7

Arrived Buenos Aires at 7:00 a.m. Steered by Mr. Bright through the Customs House and to the Royal Hotel. Received letters at the American Consulate which had been forwarded from Para by Mr. Aimers. One from Helen, one from Houghton Mifflin with Acct. Sales and check. Cordially received at the Consulate, by Mr. Bartelman, Consul.[18] The Vice-Consul General, Mr. Hazeltine, took me to the Zoological Gardens in the afternoon. Received cards from several other officials. Interviewed by Mr. Huxton for one of the newspapers. Had long talk with Miss Annie Peck, the mountaineer,[19] who called in the evening and showed many Andean photographs. Mr. Huxton wishes to call tomorrow with a photographer to get a picture to accompany his newspaper article.[20]

Cold, gloomy rainy day.

Nov. 8

Drew forty pounds at London & Plate River Bank. In the afternoon went to the Consulate, the Legation, and Agricultural Department with Mr. Hazeltine. Mr. Huxton called at my hotel after dinner, with a photographer, and obtained the pictures he desired for the *Herald* newspaper; so my fame has traveled thus far, though I am not acquainted with a single person in the whole of this great city.

---

[18] Despite JM's incorrect spelling, the Consul referred to is American career diplomat Richard Milne Bartleman, born in 1863, who served as Consul General at Buenos Aires from 1909 to 1914.

[19] American Annie Smith Peck (1850–1935) was a classicist who became a prominent explorer, mountain climber, and lecturer. Peck achieved major climbs in Europe, Mexico, and South America, and she explored the high-elevation wilderness near the source of the Amazon. The high point of her mountaineering career came in 1908 when, after several previous attempts, she achieved the first ascent on Peru's Mount Huascarán—a peak that, at nearly 22,000 feet, is considerably higher than Denali. In recognition of her achievements, the Lima Geographical Society named the north peak of Huascarán's twin mountain "Cumbre Ana Peck" in her honor. Peck also published several books, and JM's personal library contained a copy of her book *A Search for the Apex of America* (New York: Dodd, Mead, 1911). The Andean photographs JM mentions are certainly the nine postcards with photographs of Andean villages and mountains that are now included with the uncataloged memorabilia in the MP at UOP.

[20] This article was printed in the *Buenos Aires Herald* on November 15, 1911 (see Appendix E).

Correspondence

Para, Brazil
September 26, 1911
Helen Muir Funk

Darling Helen,

The hardest part of my big trip is done. I go aboard the steamer *Sao Paulo* today for Rio de Janeiro and am quite well with loving hopes you and your little family are also well. Have made lots of friends and have fared astonishingly well every way.

Give this news to Charlotte and Wanda. Am in great haste. Address your next letter to Buenos Aires, Argentine Republic, S. America, c/o American Consul. With all devoted love wishes,

Your wandering father,
John Muir

———

Rio de Janeiro, Brazil
October 10, 1911
Helen Muir Funk

Darling Helen,

I've been here 3 days and leave today for Santos. Thence I go inland 4 or 5 hundred miles to look for *Araucaria braziliensis* in the state of Parana. Rio harbor is a glacial fjord. A glorious place. I'll return to Rio from the woods thence go to Buenos Aires. Thence to Valparaiso, etc.

I'm feeling quite well and of course fondly hope you and family are.

I wish you would tell Buel to send $100 to Mrs. Margaret H. Lunam, Westfield, Dunbar, Haddingtonshire, Scotland.[21] By postal order of course

---

[21] Each year as the holiday season approached, JM sent a charitable gift to Maggie Lunham, his cousin in Scotland, typically instructing her, as he does here, to donate half of the gift to the poor of JM's native Dunbar. That JM remembered to do this even while traveling in South America suggests the concern he maintained for his family, even while pursuing adventures of his own.

and tell her in the letter ½ is for herself the other ½ for the poor. Buel will charge to my account of course.

   With all love darling,
      John Muir

———

Para, Brazil
October 28, 1911
Helen Muir Funk

Darling Helen,

   Hope you're all well. Am just leaving Paranagua for Montevideo on steamer *Sirio*. Have had glorious time in forests of *Araucaria braziliensis*, in state of Parana, and am quite well.

   Love to all,
      J. M.

———

Buenos Aires, Argentina
November 8, 1911
Helen Muir Funk

Darling Helen,

   I arrived here yesterday and received your long letter from Martinez telling the health and general well-being of your little family and of Wanda's.

   Your letter with others was forwarded from Para. My next address will be Cape Town, South Africa, c/o American Consul.

   Tomorrow morning I take train for Chile for a view of the Andes and *Araucaria* woods. Then return here and find a way to far off South Africa, thence home.

   Of my Amazon trip I have already written you. Had glorious times among the rocks and waters of Rio de Janeiro Bay (as glacial as those of Alaska) and in the Parana *Araucaria braziliensis* woods and the fjords between Santos and Rio Grande de Sul.

Everybody kind, find lots of friends and am not unknown to fame even this far from home.

God bless you darling. Love to Wanda and all others old and young, friends as well as relatives.

Ever your devoted father,

John Muir

———

Southern Brazil, Uruguay, Argentina, Chile, and into *the* Araucaria imbricata *Forests of the Andes*

9 November 1911–10 December 1911

BY EARLY NOVEMBER Muir was planning his final month in South America. He was deeply satisfied with his Amazonian travels, and with his successful excursion to the *Araucaria brazil-iensis* forests of southern Brazil. Now he was excited about seeing the breadth of the continent on his way to the Andean highlands of western South America. Muir's journal for this leg of the journey is less fragmentary and more narrative than previously—rich with the descriptive fruits of close observation, and emotionally engaged in a way that makes clear how rewarding he found these travels. His familiar literary voice emerges in his condemnation of the destructive forestry practices he witnessed, and his characteristic love of adventure animates his letters describing his own South American experiences.

Muir's trip from Buenos Aires, Argentina, to Santiago, Chile, was the beginning of another quest to find a rare South American tree he had long wished to study—*Araucaria imbricata*. The monkey puzzle tree, so named because, as Muir explained, "its prickly needles render ascent impossible to the monkey," was even more rare than its Brazilian cousin, *Araucaria braziliensis*. Nevertheless hoping he would somehow find the little-known monkey puzzle forests, Muir set out by rail on the morning of November 9, westbound for Chile in search of clues.

Crossing the continent through the picturesque Argentinean pampas, Muir noted both the openness and the agricultural richness of the land. More striking to his geologist's eye was the treeless, glaciated eastern escarpment of the Andes, which he ascended the following day. After spending the night in the western foothills of the range, Muir continued by rail to Santiago. With assistance from US Minister Plenipotentiary Mr. Fletcher—who, under directions from President Taft, took great pains to make him feel at home—Muir went to the Santiago Botanical Gardens, where he consulted with the Director about *Araucaria imbricata*. Muir learned what he could, and was shown a photograph of his arboreal quarry, but was disappointed that even the Director had never seen the rare monkey puzzle tree in its native forests, nor could shed much light on where they might be found.

After a day of rest, during which he lodged with Mr. Fletcher and enjoyed wonderful views of the snow-capped Andes from his bedroom, Muir returned to the Botanical Gardens. Combining what he already knew and what he was able to learn about the tree—including specific details regarding the soil conditions, elevation, and temperature range in which it grew—Muir determined to seek the monkey puzzle tree to the south, where he thought it might grow near snowline on the western slope of the Andes. He boarded a train that same day, and he spent all night riding the rails another 500 miles south, to Victoria.

Muir's hosts in Victoria were the Smiths, local loggers and ranchers to whom he was recommended by a teacher he had met in Santiago. Following a two-day delay caused by stormy weather, on November 18 he proceeded by horse and buggy across raging streams, up bad roads, and into the high mountains. Although most of the region remained thickly forested, Muir deplored the wanton destruction of trees he witnessed in several places. Here Muir's journal demonstrates that its author is not only a traveler and botanist, but also a preservationist with global concerns. The larger trees, he lamented, "have simply been burned and killed so that they stand melancholy, black monuments, some of them nearly a hundred feet high." In late evening, Muir finally arrived safely at the Smiths' mountain ranch, the base camp from which his trek to the monkey puzzle forests would begin.

The next day Muir wandered in the surrounding forests, studying trees and sketching "eight great white volcanic cones, ranged along the axis of the mountains." Though he marveled at the richness of the Andean forests, he continued to lament the catastrophic deforestation he observed. "Dry limbs and brush are piled around every tree and the burning goes on until nothing but black monuments are left of all the flowery leafy woods," he wrote, sadly. "Only on a small scale can even New Zealand show equal tree desolation."

On the foggy morning of November 20, Muir, on horseback and accompanied by a small party, pushed higher into the mountains. Near snowline, he finally spotted the trees he had come so far to see growing along a ridge high above a glacier meadow. Although the slope was so steep that one of the horses fell and rolled in attempting to climb it, the septuagenarian Muir dismounted and scrambled to the top of the 1,000-foot-high ridge so he could walk among the trees. "A glorious and novel sight, beyond all I had hoped for," he writes, "[y]et I had so long dreamed of it, it seemed familiar." He slept that night beside a stream, under the sky, and beneath the canopy of the rare trees. Muir studied and sketched the monkey puzzle trees all the following day before descending to the Smiths' mountain ranch in the evening. The next day he returned to Victoria, and from there to Santiago, and then back across the continent to the Atlantic coast.

Muir arrived in Buenos Aires the night of November 27 and was invited to dine and lodge with many prominent citizens of the city. Muir's interests, however, were not at dinner parties but across the sea in South Africa, where he feared that the plants and trees he longed to see there might wither with the changing season before he could arrive to study them. Although Muir had long considered a voyage to South Africa, remarkably he had no firm plans for such a trip when he left for the Amazon in August, and it is unclear precisely when he determined upon sailing from South America to South Africa.

Forest of Araucaria imbricata *on an Andean ridge*

But determined he was, and he began seeking passage to Africa on his first full day in Buenos Aires. Indeed, when he had difficulty lining up a steamer from Buenos Aires, Muir declined a number of invitations to various prestigious social gatherings planned in his honor, and instead sailed to Montevideo on November 30 in search of a ship bound for South Africa, which he eventually found. While in Montevideo Muir once again received hospitality from Frederic Goding and others, and on the evening of December 7 he favored the YMCA with a "short talk" which, in keeping with his notorious loquacity, "lasted two hours." Although no written record of Muir's talk survives, P. A. Conard, Secretary of the Montevideo YMCA, later wrote to thank Muir, noting that "to hear from the heart of so notable a scientist as yourself an expression of a vital and stalwart faith, coupled with a humble reverence, is a wonderful lift to the convictions and faith of us all."

On December 9 Muir bade his friends goodbye and went aboard the *Kurakina* as the ship coaled up in a drizzling rain. When he awoke around daybreak the next day, his ship was already fairly out to sea and he was bound for the other of the two "hot continents" he had so long wanted to see.

Muir's extant correspondence from this period is particularly rich, and suggests how fondly he remembered his family and friends and how rewarding he found his adventures in Uruguay, Argentina, and Chile. Although Muir had now been away from his California home for more than seven months—and had been traveling abroad for four months—he writes enthusiastically of all he had seen in South America, even as he makes plans to extend his journey with a visit to Africa. In a November 29 letter to his friend Henry Fairfield Osborn he asks if Osborn might not join him in South Africa, yet also recognizes that he "must not complain, for oftentimes our loneliest wanderings are most fruitful of all." To daughter Wanda, Muir writes words of concern for her health, while also assuring her that "[a]ll sought for I've found, and far more."

But it is Muir's December 6 letter to Katharine Hooker—one of the many moving letters he wrote to her during his journey—that best captures his excitement at the success of his South American travels. After praising the beauty of the glacial landscapes around Rio de Janeiro, Muir described his trip to *Araucaria braziliensis* in Brazil: "Just think of my joy in these noble aboriginal forests—the face of every tree marked with the inherited experiences of millions of years." In closing this letter, written shortly before he sailed for Africa, Muir commented, "It's perfectly marvelous how kind hundreds of people have been to this wanderer, and the new beauty stored up is far beyond telling."

Journal

Nov. 9

Start for Santiago at 8:20 a.m. Reach Rufino, nearly a fourth of the distance, at 4:30 p.m. The whole plain an almost dead fertile level soil all the way. Millions of cattle, sheep and horses. Never before saw so many in so short a ride, or anything like it. Only slight undulations, five or ten feet high, are visible. One vast, rich, green, grass sod, slightly interrupted with corn and wheat fields, and alfalfa fields, and comparatively rare small orchards. Houses wide apart. Barbed wire fences. Many small shallow lace-like pools. Haying going on now. A hundred miles or so and farther from Buenos Aires. A good many patches of thistles and mustard, especially near the city, and a hundred miles west of it. The road is very muddy, but much drier soil and of course better roads from four to five in the afternoon. With such a vast bed of fertile soil no wonder Buenos Aires is large and wealthy. Fine day. Few clouds, mostly fluffy white masses with cumulus buds here and there. Never before saw so great and uniformly level a piece of green. Large blocks of alfalfa, patches of *Eucalyptus* a feature of the landscape until near dark.

Nov. 10

Foothills in sight at 6:00 a.m. Ground sandy and rough with *Artemisia, Atroplex,* etc. Exact counterpart of Arizona plateau and desert foothills. Settlers industriously cutting the brush, cording the small stems and roots for firewood; leveling the ground, and irrigating for all sorts of crops; planting miles of Lombardy poplars for windbreaks. Extensive vineyards here. The vines look well. They are planted close, about three by one or two foot, like those of Switzerland on glacial gravel.

Changed cars at Mendoza at the foot of the Andes. Left there about 9:00 a.m., two hours late. Charming plants on the foothills. Rough stony immense beds of glacial gravel, covered with shrubs, with bright yellow flowers, covering large areas, adjacent to the main foothills. Many of the plants have purple flowers and red, but best of all are the pure white flowers of a low round-headed upright species of cactus. The flowers look like those of *Nymphia odorata* but larger. Another smaller species also has white flowers. In little more than an hour after leaving Mendoza we suddenly entered the foothills of the great Range; mountains in size, following a small river, muddy like a mining stream. A section of the river bank at the mouth of a canyon showed very rough beds at the base, containing large boulders and sand and light gravel on the upper half. Pretty regularly stratified. Magnificent mountains, lofty, but mostly rapidly disintegrating metamorphic slate. Snowy peaks, with but little snow, and very few small glaciers in last stage of decadence. Not a single tree was seen all the way up to the summit and down the other side into the town of Los Andes. A small, thorny, stubborn shrub with papilionaceous flowers and slender terete compound leaves,[1] common in the canyon bottoms, and in some cases ascending up the slopes where the material is not too shifting to allow it to strike root. In the Pass there are a great many filled-up lake basins, a striking characteristic on both flanks of the Range. Saw only one

---

[1] Flowers of the family Leguminosae and compound leaves that are approximately cylindrical or slightly tapering in shape.

Montagu Pass, in the Andes

glacier lake near the summit and only a very few scraps of meadow on east side. The glacier lake is on the west side near the summit. Toward the lower end of the Pass on the west side there is a magnificent lake basin, well watered and very fertile. Especially fertile is the one in which Los Andes and several other villages lie amid green pastures, farms, vineyards, orchards, through which we pass on our way to Valpairaiso and Santiago.

Nov. 11

Stopped last night at Los Andes. Started for Santiago about 6:00 a.m. Arrived at 10:30 a.m. having changed cars at Las Viegas. The way mostly rocky and hilly or mountainous. Little water. Most of the stream channels dry. On the hills, however, there are a few small trees and shrubs, and the tall cactus, *Cereus chilensis,* rather slender, which forms the most striking and telling feature of the rather scrawny vegetation, giving no hint of the beauty and fertility of the basin valley in which the great city of Santiago and its neighboring villages lie. From the railway station I took a cab to the Hotel Oddo, engaged a room, had luncheon, and drove to the American Legation. On the strength of my credentials from President Taft I was cordially received by Mr. Fletcher, Minister Plenipotentiary from the US,[2] who, to my surprise, invited me to take a room in his house, directed his auto driver, who speaks English, to get my baggage from the hotel and take me to the Botanical Gardens to search for information concerning *Araucaria imbricata.* The Director of the Gardens took pains to give me a general description of its distribution so far as known. He also presented me with a fine photograph of old trees, which he said must have come from somewhere near Conception, but he had never seen any of the trees of this species growing naturally, and of course could give me no definite information as to how to reach them. He said that he had heard that the timber was very hard and was seldom made use of. Therefore many had escaped the axe. He promised me letters of introduction to friends in the town of Conception.

Nov. 12

Enjoyed this charming home and entertainment. The Legation is a magnificent house situated on the Avenida, famous for its length and beauty. The house is full of good books. Mr. Fletcher is not only a very accomplished gentleman, but kind. Told me the house and everything in it was mine and to stay as long as I could. Never shall I forget the views of

---

[2] Remarkably successful American diplomat Henry Prather Fletcher (1873–1959) was a practicing attorney who, on the outbreak of the Spanish American War, enlisted as a private in Theodore Roosevelt's Rough Riders and went to fight in Cuba. In 1902 he began a long career as a diplomat, and by 1921 he was charged with the entire reorganization of the US Foreign Service and its personnel. Fletcher had been appointed US Minister to Chile in late 1909, and he became the first US Ambassador to Chile when the US legation there was raised to embassy rank in 1914. For his service in South America, Fletcher was decorated by the governments of Chile, Peru, and Ecuador.

the snowy Andes from the balcony of my bedroom window. Glorious group of lofty mountains, snow-laden and ice-laden. The principal peaks are the Altar, Poloma, and Polomba.[3]

Nov. 13

Went again to the Botanical Gardens in search of more definite *Araucaria* information. In the afternoon went to Mr. Rice's school, which is under the auspices of the M. E. Church.[4] Mr. Rice, who has traveled much down the coast, informed me that a Mr. Smith, a lumberman, owning several sawmills, and well acquainted with the forests to the southward, was the most likely man to direct me to the woods that I was in search of, and kindly telegraphed Mr. Smith to meet me at the train, at Victoria. Engaged a berth for me on the train which leaves Santiago in the evening at 5:30.

Nov. 14

Left Santiago in Pullman car at 5:40 p.m. for Victoria, about five hundred miles to the Southward, hoping from that point to reach the *Araucaria* forest said to extend along the Andes near the snow line. Until after dark the road lay through a fine level fertile valley, abounding in all sorts of orchards, vineyards, and grain fields.

Nov. 15

Heavy rain during the night. Still cloudy this morning and drizzly. Am now in fine valley with hills and mountains visible in every direction.

---

[3] The most prominent of those peaks is the altar-shaped Cerro Altar, a massif within the Parque Nacional Sangay, on the Chimborazo/Morona-Santiago provincial border in central Ecuador. The highest of Altar's two volcanic peaks is 17,300 feet.

[4] Probably the Methodist Episcopal Church, established in America in 1784. Motivated by a shortage of ordained preachers in America, John Wesley ordained Thomas Coke as Superintendent of "the brethren in America," and the "brethren" formally became the Methodist Episcopal Church at a meeting in 1784–85. Like most other Christian denominations, the Methodist Episcopal Church was active in missionary efforts in the southern hemisphere.

About 8:00 a.m. I am passing through rolling green hills. Extensive wheat fields and pastures. A beautiful region. Hundreds of miles of Lombardy poplars. Sand dunes in broad belts here and there. Arrived about 9:00 a.m. at Victoria and was welcomed by the Smiths mentioned above, as if one of the family.

Nov. 16

Thursday. Clearing. The ground beginning to dry, but the roads back into the country are reported to be impassable.

Nov. 17

Fine weather. Breezy, and the ground drying rapidly. Hope to be able to start for the mountains tomorrow.

Nov. 18

Sky almost cloudless. At noon the mountains, a noble row of snowy peaks and domes, were in full view along the Eastern horizon. Most of them solid, immaculate white down to the foothills. A broad level plain in front, lightly or heavily timbered, furrowed with small stream-courses, and strewn with moraine material. Detached hills and mountains to the westward of the town of Victoria are uniformly tree-clad except where cleared for wheat fields. These coast mountains are perhaps upward of 1,000 feet in height and finely-sculptured. The soil on the plain or plateau is apparently deep and somewhat sandy. A great part of it sown to wheat, which looks well and is now about a foot high. The town of Victoria covers a large area. The streets wide, which, excepting the business part near the Plaza, are in a wretched condition, unpaved and cut into ruts and ridges, with mud-beds and dust-beds alternating with the weather. Crops are said to suffer frequently from drought. The storm of the 14th and 15th, which has rendered the roads all but impassable, was said to be exceptional. Glad to get off at last mountainward, though have greatly enjoyed this hospitable home. Start in buggy at 3:30 p.m. Light buggy, drawn by two horses and driven by one of Mr. Smith's sons. Extremely bad road.

Much of it is corduroyed with crooked logs. Bridges also over many streams are in very bad condition. So much so that the middle of the road is shunned and the travel passes on either side, fording the streams now often belly deep to the horses, and bordered with mud about as deep. Several places we nearly lost both horses and buggy. Heavy timber on either hand as far as the eye could reach. Very few fields have been cleared. Only the smaller trees have been uprooted; the larger ones have simply been burned and killed so that they stand melancholy, black monuments, some of them nearly a hundred feet high, forming the most untidy and ragged fields imaginable. A species of lily of a striking red color common along the fences. Arrived at 6:30 at the Smith ranch, some fifteen miles from Victoria, and was welcomed by another of Mr. Smith's many friends.

Nov. 19

I wandered through broad wheat fields a mile or two from the ranch house and obtained magnificent views of eight great white volcanic cones,[5] ranged along the axis of the mountains. Spent the day sketching them. Sketched all in outline. Tree-like Madrona, 3.9 inches. Smooth thin bark, reddish outside. Pale where flakes have been recently shed off. One of the Myrtaceae? Probably myrtus. Small leaves. Tree prostrate; one hundred forty feet long, four feet diameter. Unknown species; probably beech—the most important genus of the forest trees hereabouts. Six species in Chile; five of them large; one called Roblo makes the best lumber. *Podocarpus chilense,* one of the most notable, and Laurelin. Both large and very handsome trees. So is *Persia lingue* of the shrubs. *Berberis, Pernettia, Cytharoxylon, Homatia, Azarole, Embothrium.* By far the most showy and influential is the last, with its crimson flowers in telling masses, adorning every open space, especially grassy meadows. This fine bush stands erect about from five to ten feet high. There is also a flowery parasite, very showy, which lavishly adorns the boles of the trees. Upon the whole I

[5] JM is probably observing one of two high ranges of volcanic peaks in the western Andes near Victoria: that leading toward Volcan Copahué (9,800 ft.) to the north, or, more likely, that leading toward Volcan Llaima (10,040 ft.) to the south.

think I never passed through a finer forest of round-headed hardwood trees. The average height can hardly be less than 100 feet; many of them are far taller, 125 to 140 feet. But they are being rapidly destroyed. The ground they are growing on is comparatively level, rising gradually to about 6,000 feet above the sea. Soil fairly fertile. Lumbermen rent to buy large tracts; cut the most valuable, Robley, etc., then ruthlessly burn all that's left; nine-tenths or so. Dry limbs and brush are piled around every tree and the burning goes on until nothing but black monuments are left of all the flowery leafy woods. Then wheat is sown around the stumps and rubbish and scratched and reaped with sickles. The raggedest Canadian backwoods fields are smooth and soothing in comparison. Only on a small scale can even New Zealand show equal tree desolation.

Nov. 20

Foggy morning. At 6:00 a.m. packing for the lofty ridges where grows *Araucaria imbricata*. Last evening rode over to John Hunter's, who has a sawmill. Kindly gave up work to guide us to the forests I've so long wished to see. Hard but glorious day. Camped before sunset. Rode through magnificent forest of round-headed trees, some of them evergreens. Where soil is well watered the average height of the principal trees must exceed a hundred feet. Some nearly one hundred and fifty feet high. Our party consists of Mr. Smith, Mr. Williams, Mr. Hunter, myself, two Chilean packers, all well-mounted, well-clad and provisioned.[6] After crossing many hilly ridges and streams, ferny and mossy and spacious meadows,

---

[6] In *Happenings: A Series of Sketches of the Great California Out-of-Doors* (Porterville, Calif.: W. P. Bartlett, 1927), W. P. Bartlett mentions that JM, whom he met in 1912, "gave me a brief resume of his adventures in two continents, in search of the genus Araucaria. Particularly, he spoke of his trip to the Province of Araucaria, in Patagonia, after he had failed to get directions at the Botanical Gardens at Santiago, Chile. The Patagonian Indians guided him to great forests of *Araucaria Imbricata*, the 'Monkey Puzzle Tree,' 'growing,' he said, 'much finer than in any plantings we have been able to make.' There they stand, in great forests, in their primitive majesty. The Indians treated him with great kindness." Although JM's enthusiasm for the wild *Araucaria imbricata* forest rings true, the rest of Bartlett's recollection is questionable. Although JM mentions being accompanied by "two Chilean packers," he makes no mention in any letter or journal of traveling with "Indians," let alone being guided by them to the elusive monkey puzzle forests.

came in full sight of a ridge 1,000 feet high bordering the south side of a glacier meadow, the top of which was fringed with the long-sought-for *Araucaria*. Long scramble up the steep grassy slope and brush. One horse fell and rolled. Traced the ridge a mile or two, admiring; then descended long cane-covered S. slope to the bottom of another glacier meadow valley by the side of a brawling bouldery stream and encamped beneath an *Araucaria* grove. *Araucaria* in scattered groups or singly all way down and up S. slope and fringing the horizon all around. A glorious and novel sight, beyond all I had hoped for. Yet I had so long dreamed of it, it seemed familiar. My three companions slept under tarpaulin tents, strangely fearing the blessed mountain air and dew.

The bark of the trees varies very much in thickness and pattern. On some it is smooth; on others deeply cut into squares or rhombs like alligator skins, from half an inch to nearly two inches in diameter.

Nov. 21

I traced the South ridge above our camp, sketching and photographing six views of the ancient forest.[7] Obtained a male and female flower and cones and started on the return trip to the Smith ranch, by a way several miles to the southward of the way we came up, thus obtaining new views of the magnificent round-headed forest trees extending over the whole plateau as far as the eye could reach, and interrupted only by small grassy prairies and meadows. I think it is without exception the tallest forest of round-headed trees that I have ever seen, averaging mile after mile over a hundred feet in height. Many beautiful trees and shrubs were in flower, especially around the meadow and prairie openings. One shrub in particular, usually eight to ten feet in height, was covered with brilliant scarlet flowers, making a magnificent border to the forest. Many of the trees, too, had their trunks and larger branches adorned with ferns of many species and beautiful parasites and epiphytes.

---

[7] JM's journal is replete with striking sketches of the *Araucaria imbricata*, but his photographs of the trees appear not to have survived.

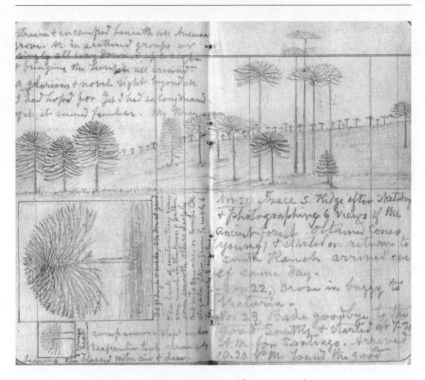

Journal sketches showing multiple perspectives of Araucaria imbricata

Arrived at the Smith ranch in the evening of the same day as left the *Araucaria* woods. We noticed in several places a lone *Araucaria* growing in the beech and laurel groves, especially on the edges of the groves, six or eight miles from the lower edge of the main *Araucaria* belt.

Nov. 22

Returned in buggy to Victoria.

Nov. 23

Bade goodbye to the good Smiths and started at 7:20 a.m. for Santiago. Arrived at 10:20 p.m., thus obtaining views of the region passed during the night on the way to Victoria. At the station, although so late in the evening, I found Mr. Fletcher's automobile awaiting me, and in a few minutes I was in his palatial home, glorying in my triumphant success in seeing the grand forest of Southern Chile.

Nov. 24

Went to the Botanical Gardens, and in the evening addressed Dr. Rice's scholars.

Nov. 25

Started in the afternoon for Los Andes. Arrived 10:30 p.m. and stayed overnight at the large hotel.

Nov. 26

Started at 6:20 a.m. across the Andes. Wonderful ride through tunnels and around innumerable mountainsides. Our short train hauled by two locomotives specially fitted for the steepest grades and shortest curves. One of the locomotives was attached to the rear of the train. Arrived at Mendoza at the foot of the range about 10:30 p.m. Changed cars and continued journey to Buenos Aires.

Nov. 27

Arrived at Buenos Aires at 7:20 p.m. Drove to Royal Hotel.

Nov. 28

Went to the American Consulate. Received a few letters which had been forwarded from Para. Went to the Legation. Met Mr. Bliss, the American Minister,[8] with whom I had quite a conversation, concerning this wonderful city, and wonderful republic. Got lost on my way back to

---

[8] American diplomat and philanthropist Robert Woods Bliss (1875–1962) graduated from Harvard and began his career in the diplomatic service in 1900. From 1909 to 1912 he was Secretary of the American Legation in Buenos Aires. He later served in many other posts around the world, and was called out of retirement to serve as a consultant to the Department of State during World War II.

the Hotel. After wandering three or four or five miles, and making scores of inquiries, was at last successful in reaching my hotel quarters.

Had many visitors and invitations to dinner, etc., but was unable to find any information concerning a suitable steamer for South Africa. Drew thirty pounds on my credit letter.

Nov. 29

Received invitations to the St. Andrews dinner and Thanksgiving Reception at the US Legation tomorrow evening and afternoon, but had to decline both, as well as an invitation of Mrs. Bliss to luncheon, on account of eagerness to find steamer to Capetown before the vegetation withered.

Nov. 30

Packing up. Taking leave of many friends, and starting for Montevideo. Got off at 10:00 p.m. Was guided and put aboard the steamer for Montevideo by Mr. Shubert, Secretary to Mr. Bartelman, Consul-General. A fine fellow.

Dec. 1

Arrived at 7:00 a.m. and drove to Consulate. Thence to the Hotel Pyramedes.

Dec. 2 to Dec. 5

Hunting ship to Capetown. On December 5th bought ticket to Teneriffe on the *Kurakina,* which is advertised to sail on the 8th.

Dec. 6

Mr. P. A. Conard, Secretary of the Y.M.C.A. of Montevideo, has been inviting me most deftly and wooingly to address the Association before I sail. He was ably seconded by Dr. Goding, and since he has been so kind and has served me in so many ways, I had to consent to give a short, informal talk, on the evening of the 7th. Weather very warm.

Dec. 7

Weather becoming still warmer. Lightning and rain in the evening. The short talk that I had promised lasted two hours. All seemed to enjoy it. Was introduced in a very flattering way by our American Minister, Mr. Nicolay Grewstad,[9] who, by the way, gave me a fine dinner on the 5th. At the close of the lecture nearly all the audience came forward to thank me and be introduced after the Minister, in English, and the President of the Association, in Spanish, had thanked me for my most novel, poetical and altogether wonderful speech. Never was this wanderer more heartily cheered.

Dec. 8

No word of the *Kurakina*. Heavy storm of wind and rain with lightning. Two ships wrecked near the harbor this evening.

Dec. 9

Our ship arrived. Harbor still rough. Got aboard at 5:00 p.m. Had to go out on tug three miles or so. Accompanied to the pier by Dr. Goding and Mr. Bright in a carriage. The Dr., who is American-Consul here, has been wondrous kind. Made me his guest since I arrived from Buenos Aires and looked after me in every way. Ship still coaling up to 11:00 p.m. Drizzling rain all day.

Dec. 10

Awoke about 5:00 a.m. Surprised to find that we were fairly off on our long voyage. Montevideo out of sight. So smoothly were we sailing through the muddy estuary water, that I was not aware that we had left port. Dull, foggy, most all day, with blinks of sunlight and showers, and thus ends my long, memorable, successful South American trip, and begins

---

[9] The Minister referred to is Norwegian-born journalist and diplomat Nicolay Andreas Grevstad (1851–1940), who was appointed Envoy Extraordinary and Minister Plenipotentiary to Paraguay and Uruguay by President Taft in 1911.

my voyage to Africa. Nothing surprises me more, in looking back upon my long journeys through South America, than the kindness that I have met almost everywhere, and from all kinds of people. The Brazilians seem naturally to be kind and polite, and all the Consuls and Ministers to whom I applied for information at once made me feel at home and offered their services in everything connected with my interests. I was much struck in crossing the Andes on my way to Chile by an old German lady beside whom I sat in the dining car at dinner. She could not speak a word of English, but she watched my plate, passed everything that she thought I would like, and when we came to the dessert of fine peaches she carefully pared and sliced them for me in that Trans-Andean dining car, pitying me, I suppose, because I could speak no German. Her husband, however, who sat opposite to me, told me at the beginning of dinner to tell him what I wanted and he would order it in Spanish. Of the extraordinary kindness of everybody I met in Brazil I have already spoken.

Correspondence

Santiago, Chile
November 14, 1911
Wanda Muir Hanna

Dear Wanda,

Just a word to let you know that I fondly hope you are all well.

So far I've been wonderfully successful in my studies, etc. Am just starting south in search of *Araucaria* woods and expect to return in a week or two to Buenos Aires and sail thence for South Africa.

Ever devotedly yours,

John Muir

P.S. Don't let the boys forget me. Remember me to the Reids, Swetts[10] and all who care to hear from me.

————

Buenos Aires, Argentina
November 29, 1911
Helen Muir Funk

Darling Helen,

I was so glad to get your cheery newsy letter of the 26th of October on my arrival from Chile after a long hard, hard but most successful hunt for *Araucaria imbricata*.

Both Buel and the baby will doubtless be somebody some day. As for yourself you have always been a wonderful shining somebody since your first appearance on this planet.

I crossed the Andes from here three or four weeks ago to Santiago. Thence went south 4 or 5 hundred miles to Victoria, thence up the mountains to the snow and found a glorious wild *Araucaria* forest feathering the ridges and filling the glacier valleys and camped among them. Guess how happy I was and how I stared at and admired these ancient trees I've so long dreamed of and what long stories I'll have to tell you. It's perfectly wonderful how kind everybody has been to me, and how lucky I've been. All I came to seek I've found and far, far more, while though often tired and bewildered in towns where strange languages were spoken some friendly soul always came to my help as if sent express from heaven and in a few days or hours I would find myself at home or even famous.

My S. American work is all done. My health is better than it was when

[10] The Reids were the family of JM's sister Margaret (1834–1910), who had married John Reid in 1860, and who had died the previous summer; the Reids had moved to Martinez in 1891 to help manage the Strentzel-Muir properties. The Swetts were the family of JM's friend John Swett, the California educator, whom JM had met in the mid-1870s, and with whose family he lived on several occasions during the 1870s. In the early 1880s Swett bought Hillgirt, the ranch adjacent to JM's, and thus became not only JM's fast friend but also his Martinez neighbor. In May 1913, several months before Swett's death, both John Swett and JM received honorary degrees from the University of California, Berkeley.

Araucaria imbricata,
the monkey puzzle tree

this grand trip was commenced, and now I'm only waiting here for a ship to float me to South Africa, and when I've had a look at the peculiar flora and fauna there and the rocks I mean to turn homeward. I'm glad you are keeping all my friends informed of my wanderings. Give them my love. Wanda I hope is well ere this. I fear she works too hard, and frets. No letter from her has yet reached me. I got your long good letter from Martinez and sent reply to Martinez in Tom's care.

I can give no address now, so I'll not expect to hear from you again until I reach New York.

God be with you darling, so ever prays,

Your devoted Father,

John Muir

Buenos Aires, Argentina
November 29, 1911
Henry F. Osborn[11]

My dear Professor Osborn,

Your letter dated September 25th makes me very happy, it's so full of hearty good news and good work all so inspiring—all the family well, tingling with Rocky Mountain radium and God's best love. No wonder you are rejoicing in the fine cretaceous work ahead of you. I should have greatly enjoyed being with you on the Red Deer River trip. And would that the confounded Titanothere had been out of the way leaving you free for South America and South Africa. But we must not complain, for oftentimes our loneliest wanderings are most fruitful of all.

I've had a glorious time in this fine wild America. All I came to seek I've found and far, far more. Two days ago I returned from a trip across the Andes in search of *Araucaria imbricata*—found magnificent forest of it 4 or 5 hundred miles S. of Santiago near the timber line. I'll tell the story when I get back. Now I'm waiting for a ship to S. Africa. How glad I'll be to see you all again. Love to each and all once more goodby. I'll write from the Cape.

Ever faithfully yours,
John Muir

———

[11] Osborn's letter of September 25, 1911, (I/A/20/11501) told of the family's recent trip to Avalanche Lake, in Glacier National Park, Montana, which accounts for the "Rocky Mountain radium" to which JM alludes. Osborn also reported taking a small boat 250 miles down the Red Deer River in southwestern Alberta, Canada; as a vertebrate palaeontologist, Osborn observed promising formations where he expected to find upper cretaceous fossils on subsequent expeditions, hence JM's reference to "fine cretaceous work ahead." The "confounded Titanothere" is a reference to Osborn's rather monumental work on titanotheres—that is, fossils of mammals of the family Brontotheriidae. Osborn later published parts of his titanothere research in 1913, 1916, 1923, and 1925, but his major work in the field, published in 1929, was *The Titanotheres of Ancient Wyoming, Dakota, and Nebraska* (Washington, D.C.: USGS). According to Osborn's letter, it was urgent work on the titanothere research that prevented him from joining JM on the journey to South America.

Buenos Aires, Argentina
November 30, 1911
Wanda Muir Hanna

Dear Wanda,

I've not heard from you direct since leaving New York on this long trip south. Helen however has kept me in touch with you all. I've just returned from a long trip across the Andes in Chile and received a lot of letters that had been forwarded from Para, Brazil, one of which from Helen more than a month old brought the distressing news that you had been seriously ill but reassuring me that you were better and would soon be well. I fondly hope that this has proved true. For several years you have worked too hard. You must be careful else you may bring on life long trouble. Do I pray take warning.

I've been very successful in my S. American wanderings. All sought for I've found, and far more, as I'll explain when I get home. I'm now waiting for a steamer for South Africa. Tell the Postmaster to hold my mail until further instructions. Don't let the fine boys forget me. Remember me to all the Valley friends.[12] Good Luck and best wishes to Tom.

Ever your devoted father,
John Muir

————

Montevideo, Uruguay
December 6, 1911
Katharine Hooker

My dear friend,

Your letter of Oct. 4 from San Francisco was forwarded from Para to Buenos Aires and received there at the American Consulate. Your and Marian's letter dated Aug. 7th was received at Para, not having been quite in time to reach me before I sailed, but forwarded by Mrs. Osborn. I can't think how I could have failed to acknowledge them. I have them and oth-

[12] That is, the Reids, Swetts, and other of JM's Martinez neighbors in the Alhambra Valley.

ers with me and they have been read times numberless when I was feeling lonely on my strange wanderings in all sorts of places.

But I'm now done with this glorious continent at least for the present, as far as hard journeys along rivers, across mountains and tablelands, and through strange forests are concerned. I've seen all I sought for and far, far, far more. From Para I sailed to Rio de Janeiro and at the first eager gaze into its wonderful harbor saw that it was a glacier bay as unchanged by weathering as any in Alaska—every rock in it and about it a glacial monument though within 23° of the equator and feathered with palms instead of spruces, while every mountain and bay all the way down the coast to the Rio Grande de Sul corroborates the strange icy story. From Rio I sailed to Santos and thence struck inland and wandered most joyfully a thousand miles or so, mostly in the state of Parana through millions of acres of the ancient tree I was so anxious to find, *Araucaria braziliensis.* Just think of the glow of my joy in these noble aboriginal forests—the face of every tree marked with the inherited experiences of millions of years. From Paranagua I sailed for Buenos Aires. Crossed the Andes to Santiago Chile, thence south four or five hundred miles. Then straight to the snowline and found a glorious forest of *Araucaria imbricata,* the strangest of the strange genus.

The day after tomorrow, Dec. 8th, I intend to sail for Teneriffe on my way to South Africa. Then home some way or other, but I can give no address until I reach New York. I'm so glad your health is restored, and now that you are free to obey your heart and have your brother's help and Marian's cosmic energy your good doing can have no end.

I'm glad you are not going to sell the Los Angeles garret and garden.[13] Why, I hardly know. Perhaps because I'm weary and lonesome with the long hot journey ahead and I feel as if I was again bidding you all goodby. I think you may send me a word or two to Cape Town, c/o the American

---

[13] JM here refers to the Hooker family house on West Adams Street, the home where JM spent so much time and did so much writing, especially during 1910. Katharine Hooker had considered selling the home after her husband John D. Hooker's death in May 1911.

Consul. It would not be lost, for it would follow me. It's perfectly marvelous how kind hundreds of people have been to this wanderer, and the new beauty stored up is far beyond telling. Give my love to Marian, Maude and Ellie, and all who love you.

I wish you would write a line now and then to darling Helen. She has a little bungalow of her own now at 233 Formosa Avenue, Hollywood Cal.

It's growing late and I've miserable packing to do. Goodnight. And once more, dear, dear friend,

Goodby,

John Muir

———

CHAPTER 5

At Sea, South Africa, the Zambezi River, and to the Baobab Trees

11 December 1911–6 February 1912

I N A REMINISCENCE of John Muir published in the *Sierra Club Bulletin* in 1916, Muir's close friend Henry Fairfield Osborn commented that, before leaving New York in the summer of 1911, Muir "had little intention of going on to Africa. It was impulse that led him from the east coast of South America to take a long northward journey in order to catch a steamer for the Cape of Good Hope." As Muir sailed away from Montevideo before dawn on December 10, he was beginning not only another major phase of his last journey, but one perhaps even more arduous than the South American phase had been. Although Muir's decision to sail to Africa was less impulsive than Osborn implies, the urgency of Muir's desire to visit the other "hot continent" is clearly suggested by his

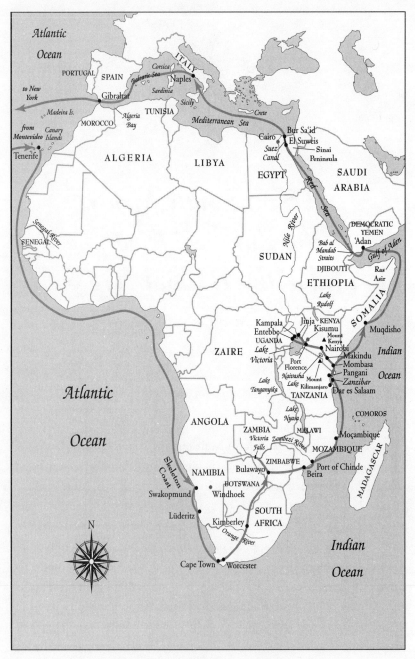

The route of Muir's travels in Africa, December 1911–March 1912

willingness to engage passage to Cape Town via the long, northern route to the Canary Islands—a passage which, though presumably the only option immediately available, required him to undertake a month-long, 10,000-mile sea voyage in order to reach a port that was but 4,000 miles due east from Montevideo. Muir's ambitions for the Africa journey were various: to tour one of the only parts of the world he had not yet visited, to observe native African flora, to see the wildlife of the central African plains, and to reach the headwaters of the Nile. His primary goal, however, was to find and study another of the world's great trees, *Adansonia digitata*, the African baobab.

Of course, the first leg of Muir's African journey does not concern Africa at all but rather the long sea voyage necessary to reach Cape Town via Tenerife. It would take Muir seventeen days sailing northward to reach the Canary Islands, and another seventeen days sailing southward to reach the Cape of Good Hope. The journal suggests that during his first week at sea Muir was resting up from his South American adventures, enjoying the spaciousness of the open ocean, and delighting in describing the sea life he observed. On December 12, for example, he wrote that "[t]he small wrinkle-like wavelets and scallops which fret the surface of the large swelling waves are throwing off sunlight in myriads of sparkles and flashes delightfully enlivening" and later he described two species of albatross that followed the ship, "flying with scarce a wingbeat, in graceful loops, thirty or forty miles an hour."

On December 19, Muir crossed the equator for the second time on his voyage. As the days wore on, he also seems to have become more contemplative. He often noted the incantational sounds of the water, wind, or the "low beating of the engines," and seems to have taken renewed interest in the night sky. "Stars and nebulae as bright and impressively seen as when viewed from mountain tops," he notes. And if Muir saw the sky from what seemed a mountaintop, he also saw what seemed mountaintops in the sky. Muir's passion for tree study comes through even in his projection of arboreal forms onto the ambiguous shapes of the clouds, which he variously describes as "trees," "tall, tree-like pillars," "pines and spruces," "groves of conifers," "feathery branches," "palms," and "rows of trees bordering a river."

Despite Muir's contemplative delight in the infinitude of sky and sea, he grew restless and irritable as the long sea voyage progressed. On December 18 he remarked that his fellow passengers were "sorely put to wits end to pass yesterday without cards in observance of the Sabbath." "Not a glint of science visible," he concludes. The diction of several subsequent entries suggests Muir's fatigue with the "sooty," "dull," "formless" environment which he called "[t]he region of rain and doldrums." "Sky all day like that of yesterday," he remarked on Christmas Eve, "[s]ame as usual, set in dull, black, shapeless horizon fog-bank."

After more than a fortnight at sea, on the day after Christmas Muir at last saw the nearly 13,000-foot Canary Island peak Pico de Teidè come into view. That afternoon he was in port in Tenerife and delighted to walk on land again, remarking that he soon "felt at home on this wild, rugged zigzag sculptured volcanic island." The following day, however, Muir booked passage on the *Windhuk* of the Dutch East Africa steamship line, and by night he was once again at sea, this time southbound for Cape Town. As the new year of 1912 began, Muir was still at sea, far from home and now going even further afield. On January 3, Muir crossed the equator for the third time on his voyage.

Early January was uneventful, and Muir's terse journal entries suggest that he was once again settling into the enforced inactivity of the sea voyage. On January 10 the *Windhuk* sailed down the Skeleton Coast and stopped briefly at "Squakum" (probably Swakopmund, Namibia) to unload passengers headed to the diamond mines at Windhoek, Namibia. Only three days later Muir was delighted to sight Table Mountain looming above Cape Town.

Within hours of disembarking Muir was at the city's Botanical Gardens studying South African trees. Over the next several days he wrote letters, enjoyed the beauty and fragrance of blooming flowers, and walked the city streets and gardens observing native plants and trees. By the 16th Muir had resumed his intercontinental search for rare trees, traveling by

rail toward Victoria Falls in search of *Adansonia digitata,* the African baobab tree.

As he journeyed from the coast, Muir admired both the cultivated and
the wild South African landscapes, which often reminded him of Southern California and Arizona. Farther inland he began to see various South
African fauna, and he stopped briefly at the diamond mining town of Kimberley before continuing north through the desert, then green hills, and
finally the plateau that is shared by present-day northern South Africa,
eastern Botswana, and southern Zimbabwe. After stopping in Bulawayo,
Muir arrived at the celebrated Victoria Falls of the Zambezi River, on the
border of present-day Zimbabwe and Zambia, near their common border
with present-day Botswana and Namibia.

In Victoria Falls Muir was fortunate to find a young African boy who
knew of the baobab and guided Muir to a grove within a few miles of the
falls. Here Muir studied and sketched the immense specimens of the
"long-dreamed-of *Adansonia digitata,*" and his lengthy journal entry for
this day includes precise descriptions of the baobab's massive trunk and
branches, its slender, green fruit and smooth, delicate leaves, and its
extraordinary bark. In his journal Muir describes his meeting with the
baobab as "one of the greatest of the great tree days of my lucky life." After
this experience of "wild baobab and Zambesi joy," Muir's general plan was
to return to the coast and work his way north to what is now Kenya, and
then inland once again to explore the Victoria Lake region and the headwaters of the Nile. For two days he was eastbound by rail to Beira,
Mozambique, on the Indian Ocean. He reveled in the glacial landscapes
through which he passed, equating the surrounding landforms to those of
his beloved Tuolumne meadows, and noting that he "[n]ever before saw so
great an assemblage of glacial rocks, noble in size and form."

After spending several days in Beira, Muir there rejoined the *Windhuk*
which, on January 28, headed north through a torrential "roaring gale" up
the southeastern coast of the continent. Over the next nine days the
Windhuk made calls at a number of east African ports; at last, on the afternoon of February 5, Muir arrived at his next destination, the coastal city of

Mombasa. Although he had only a single day to rest and plan his inland journey, Muir spent the day as only a passionate botanist would. His journal entry for February 6 reads, in its entirety: "Been out in the hot sunshine measuring and sketching baobabs. Some five of them were fifteen feet in diameter or over."

Muir's Africa journals are remarkable for their detailed, appreciative record of the geology, flora, and fauna of what had, until just a few decades before Muir's trip, been a "dark" continent in the sense that its interior deserts, mountains, and jungles remained little traveled and poorly understood by European explorers. Little wonder that Muir admired Scottish missionary David Livingstone, who became the first white to cross tropical Africa only in 1855, or that he would be thrilled by his visit to the headwaters of the Nile, which had been discovered even later in the nineteenth century.

But if Muir's Africa journals are remarkable for what they include, they are perhaps equally remarkable for what they omit. In particular, Muir visited Africa during the tumultuous period when European nations were actively competing for control of the African continent, and when native Africans were, with varying degrees of success, attempting to cast off the yoke of repressive colonial regimes. Although the Arab influence on east Africa had been strong since the seventh and eighth centuries, extensive colonial occupation of the continent began with the Portuguese during the sixteenth century and quickly spread to include the Dutch, English, French, Danes, and Swedes, who dominated large portions of Africa and who extracted vast natural resources while also supporting an extensive slave trade by which millions of Africans were exported to the Americas and to Arab countries before the slave trade ground toward a halt in the 1870s—just decades before Muir's visit.

Beginning in the late 1870s the continent was subject to a wave of imperial partition that resulted in its near-total colonization by competing European powers that now included the Germans, Belgians, and Italians. The famous Berlin Conference of 1884–85 effectively divided what remained of Africa among several European nations. Native Africans often resisted these colonizing schemes—even as various European colonizers also clashed over territorial control—and many of the fiercest battles for control of Africa were being fought at about the time Muir visited the continent. For example, as Muir sailed down the southwestern coast of Africa in early January, he mentions that some passengers leave his ship to go to the German settlement of Windhoek; he does not mention that only a few years earlier the infamous German General von Trotha, working from Windhoek, had committed what many consider the first genocide of the twentieth century when he nearly exterminated the Herero and Nama peoples who resisted the cruelties of German imperialism in southwest Africa. Later that month, as Muir traveled by train through southeastern Africa, he made extensive notes regarding the beauty of the region's landscape; he does not mention the Boer War, which, less than a decade earlier, had raged through that region, costing at least 20,000 lives on the British side alone. In February and March Muir sailed along the northeast and northern coast of Africa, frequently noting his anxiousness to return home; he does not mention that just months before his passage the Italians had invaded Libya in a conquest effort that, as it turned out, would last another twenty years.

Given Muir's pacifist demeanor and his strong reaction of moral repugnance to the early events of World War I—which he called "monstrous" and "horrible"—it is difficult to understand the omission of African colonial conflicts from his journal. This may be due to his preference for the natural over the cultural landscape; indeed, political and even cultural commentary is nearly absent in most of Muir's travel journals. Muir may also have seen his journey as an escape from the grinding political conflicts surrounding the Hetch Hetchy controversy. In any event, Muir's journals from Africa make clear that the history of most concern to him was natural history.

Muir's correspondence from Africa is particularly interesting because it simultaneously looks backward and forward, taking stock of the pleasures of the journey as it unfolds while also clearly looking forward to a loving homecoming with the friends and family whom he had kept in "heart-

Forest near Victoria Falls

sight" during his voyage. As early as the day after his arrival in Cape Town, Muir wrote to daughter Helen that "after a look at this continent the whole trip will be done. Then I hope that for me never, never more shall I seek another foreign shore." However, this was written after a grueling month at sea; when he wrote Helen again a fortnight later, after seeing the baobab trees, his tone was rather different: "I've had the grandest time imaginable. 'Kings may be blest but I'm glorious'."

To his friends the Osborns he voiced deep appreciation for the providential success of his journey. In an expression that appears in variants throughout the correspondence from this period, Muir writes that "[i]t seems that I've had the most fruitful time of my life on this pair of hot continents." A similar letter to Katharine Hooker, written from Zanzibar Harbor on February 2, begins with a "langsyney" expression of affection, but moves quickly to a celebration of "the wonderful places I've been wandering in, all of them full of immortal good things." "Fain I would write about it," he notes, "but it's utterly unletterable." As he prepared to journey to Lake Victoria and the headwaters of the Nile, Muir was already counting his blessings—both the blessing of his journey and the blessing of the loved ones toward whom he would soon travel on what he called the "longstretch homestretch" of his journey.

Journal

Dec. *11*

Foggy most of the day. Water still showing trace of the mud of the Great La Plata. Ship heaving over wide swells. Stars bright and crowded.

Dec. *12*

Fine, calm, clear morning. Few fluffy white clouds around horizon. Not a whitecap in sight, though wide waves keep our ship solemnly pitching. The small wrinkle-like wavelets and scallops which fret the surface of the large swelling waves are throwing off sunlight in myriads of sparkles and flashes delightfully enlivening. A few albatrosses, two species, are following the ship. Long, narrow-winged birds. The larger, mostly white. The others, slate-colored. Flying with scarce a wingbeat, in graceful loops, thirty or forty miles an hour. Ship heaving solemnly across the waves at a speed of eleven knots. The different kinds of birds that follow the ship seldom alight on the water, and increase in numbers toward land. Fine yellow sunset.

Dec. *13*

Dull sky. Dark, rainy-looking clouds overhead. Pale misty around horizon. At 8:00 a.m., brightening gaps of blue overhead. White fluffy-edged cumuli with dark bars around the horizon. Not a whitecap in sight. Not a wing visible in the sky or fin in the ocean, as far as I can see, at 8:30 a.m. At noon, growing cloudier. Only a few blinks of sunshine. No birds about the ship, though the land is not far off. Heavy swells vanishing. Yellow sunset. Glorious view into the depths of the heavens, between 9:00 and 10:00 p.m.

Dec. 14

Rather dark, grayish morning. Wind moderate. Nearly ahead. Warm. Clouds watery-looking. Horizontal bars and wisps in front of ragged-edged cumuli. No birds, though opposite Rio de Janeiro. Ship steady. Scarce a whitecap. Slight shower at evening. Passed four or five steamers southbound.

Dec. 15

Fine morning. Cooler. Wind moderate from the north. Clouds, dull strips and bars and ragged blotches, purple and yellow, look as if put on with a brush. No birds. Few whitecaps. No sounds much above a whisper, from small waves brushing the ship's side, and the wind above, and the low beating of the engines; not heard unless listened for.

Dec. 16

Sea this morning indigo. Large flock of flying fish, glittering silvery in the sunlight. No birds. Clouds filling half the sky or more. A few massive cumuli, with dark storm-belt sending down rain fringes here and there; light northeast breeze. Few small whitecap spots far apart. Last evening conversing with a young man in the second-class I found that he knows the writing of Darwin, Huxley, Tyndall and Heckel.[1] None that I have met among the first-class passengers seem to have any definite notions on any branch of science. One old gentleman from North Argentina, a sugar planter, etc., with extensive farms eight hundred miles from Buenos Aires,

---

[1] British biologist Charles Darwin (1809–1882), British biologist Thomas Henry Huxley (1825–1895), British physicist John Tyndall (1820–1893), and German biologist Ernst von Haeckel (1834–1919), all of whom were supporters of evolutionary theory.

speaking of Old England, said that its worn-out fields were so old that Adam and Eve might have been born there more or less. Clouds toward sunset assumed the grand and striking forms so characteristic of tropical sunsets. Dense, dark, ash-gray masses, picturesquely sculptured like old castles, turreted, etc., burning in tones of red, dull orange, bright red or glowing, some sending up towers like trees, or streaming with fluffy ring-lets and banners, variously tinted, no two alike in form or color. Between the large masses there are groups of tall, tree-like pillars, not unlike pines or spruces, of the same sooty black as the great crags, looking like groves of conifers of different species. Others broad-headed, with wide-spread feathery branches and sprays like palms. Yellow horizontal sheath and bars back of them, with jets of fiery red on the edges. Some serrated, the teeth glowing red and gold. This is the first of the tropic sunsets I have seen since leaving Rio. Sky from 9:00 to 10:00 in the evening wondrous clear. Stars and nebulae as bright and impressively seen as when viewed from mountain tops.

Dec. 17

Sunday. Breezy. Lots of massy whitecaps enlivening the indigo waves. Few clouds, hazy and indefinite in form. No inhabitants, sea or sky, visible. Church of England services conducted by the Captain in the dining room, in impressive manner. Collection taken up for Seamen's Fund.[2] Dull evening. Sooty western clouds, mostly in form of long rows of trees bordering a river. No gleam of sun fire back of them. All the sky clear at 10:00 p.m.

Dec. 18

Fine morning. Light N.E. breeze as usual. Very few whitecaps. A few flying fish flashing silvery here and there. No birds though only about a

---

[2] A 1798 provision required the master of every vessel arriving into the United States from a foreign port to pay a duty—equal to twenty cents per month for each seaman employed by that vessel—to a discretionary fund that was then used to benefit sick or disabled American seamen. It would seem that the collection JM describes was voluntary, and was probably an act of charity associated with Christmas, then only a week away.

hundred miles from shore. Sooty cumuli now bright white in morning sunshine. No sound of wind save low whispering. Ship gliding smoothly like a star. Engine heartbeats barely audible. Our dozen cabin passengers sorely put to wits end to pass yesterday without cards in observance of the Sabbath. Not a glint of science visible. Dull sky at 6:00 p.m. Sooty clouds ill-defined, the top of only one of them all glowing almost white.

Dec. 19

Dull leaden sky. Cottony wisps drifting front of hazy, all-embracing half-translucent cloud films. Glints of sunshine at intervals. Sea wondrous calm. Ship gliding silently. The sea hereabouts is said to be nearly 15,000 feet deep.[3] No birds. One ship in sight. The region of rain and doldrums. Expect to cross the line about midnight. Showers falling around the horizon. Half an hour before sunset the sun looked like a copper ball.

Dec. 20

Calm unbreezy, though a heavy, weltering swell keeps the ship slowly solemnly heaving. Cloudy, but with many openings for the sun to sow broad swaths of spangles and sparkles. About 8:00 a.m. I saw a dolphin pursuing a flock of flying fish over a wide area. They made heavy plashes as they leaped out of the water. These plashes looked like whitecaps. The fish fly considerably faster than the ship is sailing, 11½ knots. Some flocks fly all one way, along the ship's course, or in the opposite direction, occasionally scattering upward as if blasted, radiating from a center. Magnificent sunset. The forms of Chinese dragons seemed to have been gathered from these tropical sunset clouds.

Dec. 21

Thin translucent gray haze. Light N.E. breeze with heaving swells. Broad swath of spangles beneath the sun after 10:00 a.m. to 4:00 or 5:00 in the afternoon. A few whitecaps at wide intervals. No birds or fishes. Sun

---

[3] Given JM's general route and the proximity of the equator ("the line"), this notably deep part of the Atlantic is probably the Pernambuco Abyssal Plain, off the eastern tip of South America but just south of the northwestern sweep of the Mid-Atlantic Ridge.

a copper-colored globe sharply defined for an hour or so until within a half hour of the horizon, when it vanished in a formless mass of black clouds. The stars as usual came out in glorious brightness by 9:00 or 10:00 p.m.

Dec. 22

At 6:30 a.m., sea wondrous calm. Heaving swells without a single foam-bell. Suddenly a breeze made them all break forth in full, white bloom for a few minutes, all the sea like one vast bed of starry lilies, to last perhaps for ten or fifteen minutes, crop succeeding crop in endless order. Not a cloud visible except indistinct bars along the horizon to the eastward. Dolphins getting breakfast from 7:00 to 8:00 a.m. Flying fish making short flight against the wind at a speed of ten or twelve knots. Afternoon breezy. Cooler. Sudden change in temperature. Very grateful. Night darkness now comes on shortly after 6:00 p.m. Sunset as usual in formless cloud banks. Fine, breezy, starry evening.

Dec. 23

Clear, cool morning. Temperature on deck 73 deg. Wondrous reviving. Sea in a brisk welter, whitened with breaking wavelets. Not a cloud, and but little haze, even on the horizon. A wide swath of dazzling brightness beneath the sun. A few flying fish. Some of them making vigorous flights of fifty to a hundred yards against the wind at a speed of ten or twelve miles an hour. Others glinting, flashing from wave-top to wave-top. Brighter than usual all day. Dazzling before noon, beneath the sun, but dim around the horizon toward evening. Clear overhead with most beautiful lace pattern of cirrus, delicate beyond description, pure white on azure, with bits of mackerel form here and there. The sun yellow and dull red half an hour before night, lost in dark shapeless cloud mass fifteen or twenty minutes before setting. Wind continues steadily from N.E.

Dec. 24

Bright, breezy cloudless; wind increasing in speed, raising a fine crop of whitecaps. Flocks of flying fish but not a bird of any sort. Sky all day like that of yesterday. Same as usual, set in dull, black, shapeless horizon fog-bank. Most of the passengers putting forth efforts to invent methods to get rid of the dull Sabbath hours, sadly missing their usual games of shuffle-board, card-gambling, quoit pitching.[4] Toward midnight a group of the ship-hands sang Christmas Carols around the cabin with fine effect.

Dec. 25

Dawn rosy, the color quickly fading after sunrise. Sea with but few foam-flecks; dull; lead-colored. Wind as usual from the N.E. Wonderful steadiness. Sun setting in fine colors, crimson and every tone of red, yellow and blue in bars and feathery masses, level or sloping. The only brilliant sunset sky since leaving Montevideo.

Dec. 26

Cool, calm morning. The celebrated Peak of Teneriffe in sight. Expect to arrive about 3:00 p.m. Arrived at 4:00. Got ashore at 5:00 in steam launch, through fine, tumbling, dancing waves; guided to Camachos Hotel; soon felt at home on this wild, rugged zigzag sculptured volcanic island, with its famous peak, 12,700 feet high, springing abruptly out of the sea.

Dec. 27

Fine cool climate here. Enjoyed sound sleep last night. Engaged passage to Capetown on Dutch East Africa steamship *Windhuk.* At 5:30 p.m. awaiting her arrival, but she did not appear until about 7:30 p.m. Got aboard about 7:45. Was given a fine cabin on the promenade deck with door and window open to the sky. No difficulty getting aboard from the launch.

---

[4] A rough equivalent of the game of horseshoes, quoits was a game in which a quoit—a flattened ring of iron or circle of rope (the latter more likely aboard a ship)—was tossed at a pin in an attempt to ring the pin or to come as close to it as possible.

Dec. 28

Calm weather. Scarce a cloud. Not a white top in sight. The little 5,000-ton ship steady as if at anchor in harbor. Pleasant change from *Kurakina*, in food, service, bedding, etc.

Dec. 29

Cloudy and wondrous calm. A few gulls. Not a wave in bloom.

Dec. 30

Still cloudy and calm. Slight heaving swells. Passed two large steamers of the Castle Line, bound for England. Faster than ours by two or three knots an hour. At 5:30 p.m. Cape Verde is nearly abeam. Low brown shores; lofty white fringe of up-lashing waves on shore. Lighthouse on peak. We are now nearly opposite the mouth of the Senagel River in Africa. Large herds of porpoises plunging around the ship.

Dec. 31

Dull leaden sky. Feels like rain. Wind from the S.W. making whitecaps here and there. Few gulls and porpoises. Toward noon sky half clear overhead. White wispy cirrus, dark bloody nimbus around horizon. No rain reached us. Warmer. N.E. wind light. Grand New Year Dance kept up hours beyond midnight.

1912

Jan. 1

Sky seemingly cloudless, save a few cottony tufts on thin mellow haze. No birds or fishes, as we are now far from land. At 3:00 p.m. almost clear overhead. Brilliant swath of spangles. A few clouds taking definite form as if getting ready for sunset. Black, sooty sundown as usual. Yellowish glow for half an hour before the disc sank beneath the sea line.

Jan. 2

Cloudy. Warm rain falling here and there, near the horizon. Still wondrous calm. Warmer of course now that we are within three and a half degrees of the equator. Bright towards noon, from sunbeams pouring through between well-formed cumuli. Sun a coppery globe an hour or so before vanishing in sooty horizon clouds.

Jan. 3

Heavy massive clouds, dark with white, fluffy edges, dazzling, glowing, under the sun about 8:00 a.m. Rain from 8:30 to 9:00 a.m. Wild show in honor of Neptune, while crossing the line. Irreverent baptisms by sham priest, etc.[5] Dancing to music by the band.

Jan. 4

Cloudy and dull. Wind making whitecaps. Sun making glorious breadth of silver light and lily spangles on waves far and near, darkening toward sunset as usual. Sun with ray-less light, wading like the moon through drifting clouds.

Jan. 5

Dull, sooty clouds, with white edges, covering most of the sky until toward noon. Light showers. Gloomy afternoon. No waves in bloom.

Jan. 6

Heavy swells. Ship heaving. Sea glassy smooth. Big glistening waves, delicately dotted and dimpled with raindrops. Strangely streaked surface of sea in general. Beautiful cloud-glow between bars of solid black.

Jan. 7

Sea heaving our ship, considerably the highest waves of the trip. Wonderful burst of sun-fire from between bars of cloud of solid dark half an hour before sundown.

[5] See chapter 2, footnote 5.

Jan. 8

Cold enough for overcoats. Fine N.W. wind. Ship pitching. Cloudy nearly all day. Sun as usual lost in sooty clouds half hour before sunset. Wonderful fiery glow behind cloud bars a few degrees above horizon. No clear sunset for a month.

Jan. 9

Foggy and drizzly most all day, and strange to say, cold. Sea lighter blue, from land particles. Expect to arrive at Squakum, a German settlement, early tomorrow, where most of our first-class passengers leave us, to go back into the interior about three hundred miles to diamond and gold mines at a village called Windhuk. A farewell dinner was given them this evening. The dining room was elaborately decorated. A few goodbye speeches full of hearty good wishes were made, and replied to by one of the passengers, after which the room was darkened and a band of grotesquely disguised waiters, stewards, etc., marched in and made the round of the tables. The nose of each illuminated by an electric bulb.

Jan. 10

Arrived about 4:30 a.m. and dropped anchor a mile or more from shore. The sunrise clouds like lace curtains. The sky greenish back of them. Of fine tones. The shore low and sandy tawny. Not a tree in sight, but fine exulting fringe of breakers and hills a thousand or two thousand feet high in the distance. The city is a shapeless drizzle of buildings, desolate looking. The altitude of Windhuk, the terminus of a railroad from this port, is said to be about 5,000 feet. We have taken on board about a dozen first and second class passengers for Capetown, and a large number, 100 or more, third class; a curious assortment of Negroes chiefly. We left Squakum about noon.

Jan. 11

Arrived at Rudiret Bay about 8:00 a.m. The harbor is quite extensive and picturesque. The rocks very resisting but extremely barren. Not a tree in sight. Charmingly sculptured like those of Alaska bays. Grand mountains about a hundred miles inland. Took on a considerable number of passengers and left for Capetown about noon. Another ship of the same line, the one Roosevelt sailed to Mombasa on from Naples,[6] left on her home trip from this port an hour earlier. Saw a merry group of seals at play here near the mouth of the bay.

Jan. 12

High head wind. Magnificent waves. The whole sea like wild, solemn, onrushing river. Waves about fifty to seventy-five feet apart, the breaking waves fading to a beautiful green. Wild stormy day.

Jan. 13

Calm again. The famous Table Mountain in sight this morning, which, with picturesque ranges to right and left of it, form a truly magnificent background for the Cape city. Arrived about noon. Got ashore about 2:00 p.m. and drove to the Mt. Nelson Hotel, situated at the base of the lofty Table Mountain. After luncheon, strolled through crooked streets to the Botanical Garden. Hope to start inland toward Victoria Falls of the Zambesi about the 15th or 16th.

Jan. 14

Spent the day writing letters. Fine, breezy, bracing, sunny weather. Charming plants in bloom in the Hotel gardens. Along some of the streets the shade trees are fine, thrifty oaks, the English oak, *Quercus pedunculata*. Acorns singly or in twos or threes or fours, dangling like cherries by slender stem. They are now ripe. There are also many fine specimens of *Eucalyptus ficifolia* now in flower, making masses of showy crimson. The European sycamore and the *Grevellia* from Australia thrive here also. So also do the people. Most all young cheeks that I have met on the streets are in full, rosy bloom. No town that I have ever seen has so wonderful a background.

---

[6] JM here alludes to Roosevelt's famous African safari of 1909. The ship to which JM refers would have been the Dutch East Africa steamer the *Admiral,* by which Roosevelt and his party arrived in port in Mombasa on April 21, 1909.

Jan. 15

Bright, breezy. Purchased ticket to Naples via Victoria Falls, Beira, Mombasa, the Victoria Nyanza, Aden, Red Sea, and the Mediterranean.

Jan. 16

Fine weather. Left for Victoria Falls about 12:30 p.m. Fine ride along sand flat at base of mountains, gradually rising. At 5:15 at Worsuster. Beautiful town, in long beautiful, level, boulder-strewn glacier valley, in some places several miles wide, perhaps a hundred miles long or more. Finely sculptured mountain range on both sides. Water rather scarce, small streams. Like valleys in S. California. Small vineyards here and there. Grapes ripe. Grain harvested.

At the head of this long mountain-walled valley, our heavy train of a dozen coaches, drawn and pushed by two powerful engines, climbed on wonderful grades (7 or 8%) and curves out upon a vast plateau like those of Arizona in flora bounded by level-topped buttes and peaks. Saw small black monkey walking slowly and indignantly away from the passing train near the head of the pass. Not a cloud in the sky until near sundown when beautiful crimson horizontal plumes decorated the lower sky all around. A most glorious day in every way. The stars shone bright as we sped on over the apparently boundless plain.

Jan. 17

Glorious sunrise. Cloudless. All day on great plateau. Soil red and tawny. Ant nest, dome-shaped, narrow, eighteen inches high. Saw man on horseback driving a flock of ostriches. A remarkable sight to me. Crossed only one river by a fine steel bridge. The Orange River, I suppose. Arrived at Kimberly about 7:20 p.m. Marvelous city, of enormous gray dumps of material hoisted from the diamond beds. Left Kimberly and the diamond pits at 8:30 p.m. Dry desert, seemingly endless.

Jan. 18

Wonderful change. All the broad plain or plateau green and even flowery here and there, and dotted with bushes and small trees. Mimosa, etc. Some of them in flower. Gradually increasing in size and number until they darkened the landscape in the distance like forests. Only a few rounding hills or low mountains visible in the vast expanse. At 10:00 a.m. ran suddenly into a region of rounded glaciated hills of metamorphic slate out of which we emerged in about an hour to a wide plain, green and flowery with dark forested mountains in the distance. Ground near the track densely covered with bushes, mostly with yellow-green foliage. Here the first trees were found, twenty to thirty feet high, eighteen inches in diameter, with lavish undergrowth of bushes. This plain, with its low forest, extends with great regularity for one hundred and fifty miles or more. The train had been running through it at twenty miles speed over six and a half hours, and now, at sundown, there is no sign of reaching the limit of this strange forest and plain, a smooth sandstone plain, apparently boundless. Only a small group of peaks to the westward, seen about 6:00 p.m. A red sandstone in rounded moutonnée masses and ridgy pavements show here and there through the almost continuous tufted sod of grasses like Buffalo grass.

Jan. 19

Cloudy and cool. Magnificent sunrise. Huge compound wing-shaped masses of clouds, changing to deep velvety maroon and magenta. A truly glorious spectacle. The same nearly level plateau. Green, lightly forested, stretching on and on with no boundary in sight save the sky. No mountains visible. A sea of verdure. Arrived Bulwayo about 7:00 a.m. Scrawny breakfast at station. Walked through the town. Forest becoming more varied. Tall palms common, and the low, pale green dwarf species. The ground hillocky.

Jan. 20

Arrive at Victoria Falls station at 7:00 a.m. and have enjoyed a wonderful day, wonderful in many ways; one of the greatest of the great tree days of my lucky life. Inquiring at the hotel if there were any baobabs in the neighborhood,[7] the manager said that he had never heard of a baobab. I explained that it was a large tree, one of the largest of the great trees of the world, and that I had heard that some of them grew at no great distance from here.

After many anxious inquiries I found a bright Negro boy guide who led me direct to the long-dreamed-of African *Adansonia digitata.* I found a large number at a distance of only about a mile or a mile and a half from the head of the Falls, and not over half a mile back from the bank of the river. I discovered specimens showing their different forms, varying from twelve to twenty-four feet in diameter. Most of them about seventy-five to ninety feet high and very wide-spreading, the main branches large, often four to six feet in diameter, gradually dividing into comparatively slender branchlets; many of them drooping, and well-clad with rather pale-green five to seven or even nine-fingered leaves. I found a few of the fruits that had fallen on the ground and also some of the wilted flowers. The flowers are white, circular, and about six inches in diameter. This grand tree was first discovered by Michael Adanson[8] of the West Coast near Sierra Leone. It also extends considerably to the north at the head of the Senegal River. I afterwards found it in great abundance at Mozam-

[7] Although it was primarily his desire to find and study the giant African baobab *(Adansonia digitata)* that brought JM to the Victoria Falls area to begin with, this is his first mention of the famous tree in his journal. So squat is the baobab, and so root-like its branches, that it has sometimes been called the "upside-down tree," and African legend has it that when God was creating Africa he became angry that the baobab would not grow where he wished it to, and so in frustration tore up the tree and thrust it back into the ground, crown first. Large baobabs are thought to contain up to 30,000 gallons of water, and in times of drought, elephants eat all parts of the tree they can reach in order to maintain hydration; indeed, feeding elephants often undermine the foundations of the tree, causing it to fall, and in some cases falling upon the animal itself, thus leaving both tree and pachyderm dead.
[8] French botanist Michel Adanson (1727–1806) studied in France before living in Senegal from 1748 to 1953, and publishing a natural history of Senegal in 1757. He was one of the leading taxonomists of his age, and his 1763 book *Familles Naturelles des Plants* proposed a classification system that, though eventually superseded by the Linnean system, was among the most influential botanical taxonomic systems of the eighteenth century.

Journal sketch of Adansonia digitata, *the baobab tree*

bique, Zanzibar, Desersalaan, Panga, and Mombasa on the East Coast. A red-flowered species *A. madagascariensis* is found on the island of that name. A third species has been found in Australia, *A. gregorii.* It is often called monkey-bread tree. Also cream of tartar tree, from the pleasantly acid juice of the fruit furnishing a refreshing drink. This wonderful tree belongs to the malvaceae.[9] The timber is so soft and spongy that it has no

[9] That is, the Malvaceae family. In the current system of taxonomic nomenclature, *A. digitata* is part of the Bombacaceae family.

merchantable use, though I was informed that large rain-water tanks were sometimes dug in the broad body of the living tree. It grows scattered here and there among other trees in the general forest, and is easily recognized by its remarkably smooth skin-like bark, and its massive trunk and branches. Altogether I measured and sketched about a dozen specimens. The fruit is green, about six inches long and three in diameter, hanging straight down, and very conspicuous. The leaves are thin, delicate, and smooth. About three to four or five inches long and wide. The bark is gray in color, wonderfully smooth, shining, wrinkled here and there, and slightly corrugated horizontally, but with no furrow like the bark of most other trees. It looks like leather, or the skin of the hippopotamus. On my return trip I noticed a good many in the woods from the car window seventy miles or more to the southward of the falls. On the return trip to Bulwayo I enjoyed the company of Captain Murray, who has charge of the mounted police through a large part of Rhodesia north and south from the Victoria Falls. He kindly promised to send me photographs of the most telling of the Rhodesian trees. Took me to his headquarters at Bulwayo and arranged for my journey to Beira.

Jan. 21

Arrived Bulwayo at 7:00 this morning, having left the Falls at 12:20 p.m. yesterday. Enjoyed view of part of the forest that I had passed through at night on my way North. The baobab is the most interesting feature of the forest for seventy miles south of Victoria Falls. Went to Grand Hotel, Bulwayo. The town is spread over a large level area. The buildings sparsely sprinkled. Will take long to form continuous streets. At hotel all day, resting after wild baobab and Zambesi joy. Strange tree. In bark like skin of elephant. Corrugated and wrinkled like skin of hippopotamus. Very smooth and glossy. Gray, whitish some places. Beautiful five to seven-parted leaves. Huge limbs but well clothed with leaves. So striking in size and form it is easily recognized at a distance of several miles.

Victoria Falls, on the Zambezi River

The Falls too are grand and novel, and are already drawing large numbers of tourists from all parts of the world. Smoke-like spray is ever ascending, watering the woods in the neighborhood with constant drizzling showers. Large area near the Falls called the "Rainy Woods."

Among the other notable trees of the baobab forest is the Mopani, a fine, large leguminous tree with hard, valuable wood. The Maruba, another large tree, the fruit of which is edible. *Erythima tomentosa*, something like the baobab at a distance, also leguminous. Kigelia has fruit shaped like sausage two feet in length. This large tree is also seen at Victoria Falls. Common in equatorial Africa. It has a sturdy trunk with rough furrowed bark like an oak. Purple tulip-like blossoms. Also three species of palms.

Jan. 22

Drew twenty pounds on credit letter and left Bulwayo at 2:00 p.m. for Beira. Grand simple-featured landscape. Wide valleys with sparse forests, picturesquely interrupted by small prairies. The trees not large. Mostly kept down by grass fires. Glorious cloud range of peaks and battlemented mountains over the Shangane Hills, crisp and pure in white domes and pale blue. The most beautiful ever beheld, like vast glaciers. Rain and lightning at night. Many hills or kopjes.[10] They look glacial in trend and form in general. Most of them granite. Weathered on summits into boulders which disintegrate, forming ruinous piles, but with many over-flowed pavements. Distance not great from Bulwayo to the Rhodes 10,000 acre National Park,[11] where these granite hills and domes assume their wildest form. The whole country hereabouts has evidently been glaciated. At one of the stations passed this afternoon there is a circular hut with walls of corrugated sheet iron and roof thatched with reeds like those of the natives, with a signboard at the door, inscribed as follows: "Post Office. Telegraph Office. Postal Order Office. Savings Bank."

Jan. 23

Fine cool morning. The wide plateau carved into more and more interesting forms of valleys, undulating plains, prairies, and crumbling kopjes. A tree with slender branches manages to keep its flat head level or nearly so. Probably a species of Mimosa. At noon we are passing through a picturesque region of long smooth ridges and domes and craggy hills, with luxuriant and grassy flowery vegetation. In the afternoon until dark at 7:40

---

[10] Dating from the mid-nineteenth century, the word *kopje*, a variant of *koppie*, simply means "a small hill."

[11] Formerly Rhodes-Matopos National Park, now Matobo National Park, this large park and wildlife preserve is in southwestern Zimbabwe, thirty miles south of Bulawayo, in the Matopos Hills. Within the park, at Malindidzimu Hill (also called "World's View"), is the burial place of Cecil J. Rhodes (1853–1902), the British philanthropist who established the famous Rhodes Scholarship. Rhodes became wealthy and powerful as a result of diamond mining in South Africa, and at one time he held colonization rights over the entire region of Africa subsequently known as Rhodesia.

Muir's sketch of this glacially carved rock near Beira, Africa, bears a striking resemblance to Yosemite's Half Dome

we were running between two granite mountain ranges of massive glacial sculpture; domes, long ridges of smoothly-rounded unflawed forms, a hundred miles or more of granite illustrating every kind of glacial sculpture, many specimens of which are as striking as those of the Tuolumne meadows. Never before saw so great an assemblage of glacial rocks, noble in size and form. Nearly all of them massively domed, or broadly ridged and naked. Many pavements along track. Beautiful flowery vegetation, here and there. The very daintiest of little palms with only a single leaf from a big root-stalk. This, if possible, is a more gloriously fruitful day than the immortal baobab and Zambesi Falls 20th.

Jan. 24

Arrived at Beira this morning at 9:40. Low, swampy, sandy delta ground. The street cars here are run by a span of Negroes instead of a span of mules. Met the Postmaster General, Mr. Ayere, and Mr. Stokes, who was a friend of Sir J. D. Hooker, the great botanist.[12] Mr. Stokes told me that when he was a little boy Sir Joseph frequently trotted him on his knee.

Stopped at Savoy Hotel. Beautiful trees in front of it. Mostly Royal Ponciana, now in flower. Legumes two feet long when mature. Nearly all the shade trees in Beira are *Cassurina*s from Australia. A very dull town. Hot, dim, cloudy, muggy, all day. Rank, lush grass on the low flats, extending from the base of the mountains to the sea. Palms and other trees abundant along the banks of a small stream. Some extensive corn fields called meales, groves and half meadows and forest, not unlike those of New England. The average height of the mountains between Salisbury and the Beira lowlands nearly 5,000 feet. That is, the stations along the railroad track.

Jan. 25

The *Windhuk* arrived this evening.

Jan. 26

Went aboard this afternoon by motor boat. Secured a fine, airy cabin on the promenade deck near my old quarters and now feel at home.

Jan. 27

Still discharging cargo. Mostly coke from Europe. Taking on sugar and copper ore. Weather very sultry.

---

[12] Not to be confused with JM's Los Angeles friend John D. Hooker, Joseph Dalton Hooker (1817–1911), traveler, naturalist, and Director of the Royal Botanic Gardens at Kew, was a fellow Scot and one of the world's leading botanists. He served as president of the Royal Society (1873–78), and was so accomplished a scholar of plants that in 1907, on the bicentenary of Linnaeus's birth, the Swedish Academy of Sciences awarded him a specially struck Linnean Medal declaring him "the most illustrious living exponent of botanical science." JM took a botanical trip with Hooker in California in the summer of 1877, during which the men discovered the Twinflower *(Linnaea borealis)*, the first of its kind discovered in California. Hooker's memory would have been quite present to JM in January 1912, since the great botanist had just died the month previous.

Jan. 28

Completed cargo about 1:00 p.m. Too late to get out over the harbor bar. Anchored a few miles from town until 10:00 p.m., time of high tide. Then sailed for Chinde on the delta of the Zambesi. This day has been oppressively hot and steamy. Sultry towards evening. All the sky ablaze with sheet lightning, and streaked at short intervals with thundering zigzag lightning, accompanied with torrents of rain and a roaring gale that raised high waves and whitened all the sea with spray.

Jan. 29

Arrived off the Port of Chinde at the mouth of the Zambesi about 10:00 a.m. Large tender came out over the bar, bringing many passengers, mostly colored, and also discharging many, a hundred or more, of the same mixed races. The sea was very rough and all the passengers had to be hoisted in a closed circular wicker cage holding about a dozen. Weather continues sultry. Heavens all afire with chain lightning. Saw a magnificent arc of vivid chain lightning, spanning the sky from horizon to horizon. The curve of the arc almost perfect from East to West. Never before have I seen a horizontal flash of this sort.

Jan. 30

Cooler. Sky clearing. All congratulate on reviving change. Expect to reach next port of call, Mozambique, this afternoon. Arrived at 6:30 p.m. Discharging and taking on cargo by yelling at willing savages until after midnight. Very sultry with lavish lightning. Departed for Zanzibar about 1:30 a.m.

Jan. 31

North wind. Cloudy hot afternoon. Land in sight most of the day.

Feb. 1

Hot. North wind. Sky half clear. Clouds shapeless, melting into a sort of meteorological mud. Color of sea beautiful blue.

Feb. 2

Arrived at Zanzibar at 6:00 a.m. Fine day though hot. Clouds beginning to take regular tropical form. The sun this evening set clear, like a glowing copper-colored ball. The first visible sunset in the last two weeks. Zanzibar a beautiful town picturesquely situated in glorious woods and gardens. But with a woeful, slave-ful history.[13] Taking on cargo all day. Sailed for dar es Salaan.

Feb. 3

Arrived at dar es Salaan early this morning. Joyfully discovered several fine baobabs on the harbor bluff among palms and mangoes. Went ashore. Saw eight of these fine trees. Largest about twenty feet in diameter. Later discovered eight or ten more at a distance of three or four miles, the setting sun shimmering on their big trunks, bringing them into relief between their broad-domed heads. The harbor wonderfully picturesque. A lovely place.

Feb. 4

Cloudy morning. Steamy. Returning to Zanzibar for the mail. Discovered two or three baobabs on the low delta coast bluffs. Detached islets. Some quite small, with overhanging shores, like ships, all densely leafy. After stay of two hours, sailed for Panga and arrived in the afternoon. A small town in a lovely picturesque bay. Distant mountains in sight over low sandy shores. Many great baobabs along the bluffs, mingled with mangoes, etc. Houses beneath some of them, and gardens. A few in the town. Shipped large quantities of cotton. Loading all night.

Feb. 5

Sailed for Mombasa at 8:00 a.m. Expect to arrive about 2:00 p.m. Fine breezy morning, but the weather equatorish. Arrived at half past two. Went to Grand Hotel, airy, but dusty, distant about three miles from the port. The road very beautiful. Passing through an almost pure forest of

[13] Zanzibar was the primary coastal trading post for the Arab-run African slave trade, which continued until the late nineteenth century.

Baobab tree in an African village

baobabs. Town on a coral plateau. No soil. Hundreds of grizzly, stunted but huge-trunked trees. Few of the branches are in leaf on account of drought, but they all hold on to life. A few on good soil at dar es Salaan were abundantly leafy and well developed in every way.

Feb. 6

   Been out in the hot sunshine measuring and sketching baobabs. Some five of them were fifteen feet in diameter or over.

Correspondence

Cape Town, South Africa
January 14, 1912
Helen Muir Funk

Darling Helen,

I fondly hope you are well, and the boy and father. I almost feel as if on the home stretch now that I've reached this outlandish place, for after a look at this continent the whole trip will be done. Then I hope that for me never, never more shall I seek another foreign shore.[14]

My plan now looks comparatively simple. A trip from here of 2,000 or 3,000 miles past the Victoria Falls of the Zambesi and return to the Cape. Thence up the East Coast to Mombasa and perhaps a visit to Lake Nyanza, back to Mombasa and thence home by Aden, Naples or Genoa, and New York. Three months ought to be enough for the whole longstretch homestretch. Tell all my friends who may inquire that my next address will be New York, c/o The Century Company, Union Square. And be sure Darling to have a long letter awaiting me there telling all the home and family news. I expect to start for the Zambesi region in a day or two. Goodby Darling, I'll write again soon. Remember me to all my friends that are near you in your new home. Send me Charlotte's address. Perhaps she has gone to London with her husband. I suppose you often see Mrs. Sellers, Mrs. Thompson, Mrs. Jones, and others of the Hooker clan.

Ever devotedly your father,

John Muir

---

[14] The journey JM was then on indeed proved to be his final foreign travel.

Near Mozembeque and Madagascar, Indian Ocean
January 31, 1912
Helen Muir Funk

Darling Helen,

I hope you are all well. I've had the grandest time imaginable. "Kings may be blest but I'm glorious," etc.[15] Left Capetown Jan. 16th arrived Victoria Falls on the 20th. Wandered about in the woods that fringe them dripping with spray and through the Baobab woods. Thence to Beira on the East coast 150 miles or so from the mouth of the Zambesi. Glorious glacial sculptured mountains, hundreds of miles of granite domes, ridges, peaks like those about Yosemite and Tuolumne. A vast unletterable lot of them. At Beira caught the good *Windhuk* that I left at Capetown and am now on my way to Mombasa where I'll again leave her for a three week trip to Lake Victoria, returning in time to catch the steamer *General* of the same line due at Mombasa on the 27th of Feb. Then home I go via Suez, Naples, and New York. Arriving California about April or May. You see then Darling that after a look at the lake region all the rest of the trip will be only easy homegoing hoping all the way to find you well. Wanda's health is a source of anxiety, hope as I may. Love to all who love you. This letter will go direct to Europe by this ship.

Affectionately your father,
John Muir

———

Near Zanzibar, East Africa
January 31, 1912
Mr. and Mrs. Henry Fairfield Osborn

Dear Friends,

What a lot of wild water has been roaring between us since those blessed Castle Rock days. But roll and roar as it might you have never been out of heart sight.

---

[15] JM's allusion is to his beloved Robert Burns (1759–96), the sixth stanza of whose classic poem "Tam o' Shanter," written in 1790, reads as follows: "Care, mad to see a man sae happy, / E'en drown'd himself amang the nappy! / As bees flee hame wi' lades o' treasure, / The minutes wing'd their way wi' pleasure: / Kings may be blest, but Tam was glorious, / O'er a' the ills o' life victorious."

How often I've wished you with me on the best of my wanderings so full of good things guided by wonderful luck, or shall I reverently thankfully say Providence. Anyhow it seems that I've had the most fruitful time of my life on this pair of hot continents. But I must not try to write my gains, for they are utterly unletterable both in size and kind. I'll tell what I can when I see you, probably in three months or less. From Cape Town I went north to the Zambese Baobab forests and Victoria Falls and thence down through a glacial wonderland to Beira, where I caught this steamer and am on my way to Mombasa and the Nyanza lake region. From Mombasa I intend starting homeward via Suez and Naples and New York fondly hoping to find you well. In the meantime I'm sending lots of wireless tireless love messages to each and every Osborn, for I am,

Ever faithfully yours,

John Muir

Zanzibar Harbor, East Africa
February 2, 1912
Katharine Hooker

Dear Friend,

Los Angeles days begin to look langsyney[16] and the sea and continent spaces between us awfully wide. Nevertheless you have always been in sight—heart sight—and oftentimes I've thought of you and Marian in the midst of infinite work wishing you were able to enjoy some of the more accessible of the wonderful places I've been wandering in, all of them full of immortal good things. My luck throughout all the trip has been wonderful, clearing ways through everything, guiding apparently as stars are guided. Anyhow it seems that on this pair of hot wild continents I've had the most fruitful time of my life. Fain I would write about it, but it's utterly unletterable.

---

[16] JM's neologism "langsyney" invokes the nostalgic sentiment of Robert Burns and the ballad "Auld Lang Syne," the title of which means, roughly, "the good old times." Here JM intends to say that he feels far from home, and that he misses the time spent with the Hooker clan at their West Adams Street home in L.A.

I'm now on my way from Beira to Mombasa, after a grand trip to the Baobab forests of the Zambesi and Victoria Falls, and the magnificent glacial rock scenery of southern Rhodesia.

From Mombasa I intend to make a short trip into the Victoria lake region, then home via Suez, Naples, and New York.

This note goes direct to Europe on the *Windhuk,* so you will have time to write me at New York c/o The Century Company, Union Square. I'll be reading book proof there probably for several weeks.

With love to all who love you I'm,

Ever faithfully your friend,

    John Muir

————

Near Zanzibar, East Africa
February 4, 1912
William Colby

My dear Colby,

I've had a great time in South America and South Africa. Indeed it now seems that on this pair of wild hot continents I've enjoyed the most fruitful year of my life. Some happy California day I'll try to tell you about it. I'm now on my way from Beira to Mombasa after a grand trip to the Zambesi Baobab forests, Victoria Falls, and the magnificent *glacial* rock scenery of southern Rhodesia.

From Mombasa I intend to make a short trip into the Victoria lake region then home via Suez, Naples, and New York hoping to find you and all the Sierra Club and its friends and affairs hale and happy and prosperous.

Ever faithfully yours,

    John Muir

————

CHAPTER 6

East Africa, Lake Victoria, the Headwaters of the Nile, and Homeward Bound

7 February 1912–27 March 1912

B Y FEBRUARY 1912 Muir had already begun to turn his mind homeward, though he still would have a number of gratifying experiences and adventures ahead of him in what is now Kenya and Uganda. Although the greatest of his tree studies were finished, he continued to describe, sketch, and photograph the baobabs he found and continued to observe local flora and fauna wherever he went. The last leg of his last journey, the "longstretch homestretch," would take Muir across Lake Victoria, to the headwaters of the great Nile, across the wildlife-rich Athi plains, then through the Indian Ocean, the Mediterranean Sea, and the North Atlantic Ocean before reaching American shores.

Muir left the port city of Mombasa on February 7, bound inland by rail for Nairobi. After a rough train ride made somewhat palatable by companionable fellow travelers, he arrived in Nairobi the following day, having seen "hundreds or thousands of hartbeests and other antelopes" as well as "wild ostriches" on the Athi plains southeast of the city. After resting for a day he continued inland by rail through the scenic mountains of what is now the Kenyan Highlands to Port Florence, south of Kisumu on the shore of the eastern arm of Victoria, Earth's second largest lake.

From there, Muir boarded the small steamer *Clement Hill*, which headed across the great lake toward Entebbe, Uganda. Arriving in Entebbe the next morning, Muir seems to have begun measuring trees within moments of disembarking. Later he visited the Uganda Protectorate and the Botanical Gardens, where he studied plants, met with the head gardener, and was given specimens of native African flora.

View of an African village

The following day Muir was transported seven miles inland to Kampala in a jinrikisha pulled by three African men who sang as they followed the road through banana orchards and wild papyrus swamps. Of all the lines the Africans presumably sang, two in particular seemed addressed directly to the homesick naturalist: "The white man . . . is looking at the birds in the trees" and "The white man's far from his cold, cold home." Muir lodged that night in Kampala and traveled the next day, February 14, to Jinja, where he visited nearby Ripon Falls, the outlet of Lake Victoria and, more importantly, the headwaters of the Nile River. Muir was entranced by the beauty of the falls and commented on the crocodiles he saw sunning themselves on the bank, "while fishes in large numbers are constantly springing in wide curves in their attempts to ascend the cascade to enter the lake."

Thirteen hours aboard the little steamer brought Muir back across the lake to Port Florence, where he studied nearby trees before boarding a train for the return trip to Mombasa. The train ran through terraced bluffs, then steep mountains, glacial cirques, and "gorgeous and fluting ravines in close succession," and the following day took him through the Naivasha Lake region, then past Nairobi and out onto the Athi plains below the Yatta Plateau. Rain had obscured the long views on Muir's journey west to Lake Victoria, but clear weather on his return trip allowed him to see not only vast herds of wildlife near the tracks, but also features of the distant landscape, including the immense Mt. Kilimanjaro and Mt. Kenya.

Muir spent five days in Mombasa before beginning his long sea voyage homeward. Despite the great heat, he used those days precisely as we might expect, by taking every opportunity to study trees—African palms, the luxuriant vegetation of mangoes, and the "so-called almond trees," among others. Most important to Muir during these sweltering African days, however, was his final opportunity to observe the baobab tree, which he studied, sketched, and photographed on February 20 and 21. The next day Muir packed for his journey home, and by the evening of the 23d he was aboard the Dutch East Africa line steamer *General,* northbound through the Indian Ocean.

As Muir's ship sailed through rough weather, north along the coast of present-day Somalia to "Wubuschi" (probably Muqdisho, Somalia), he crossed the equator for the sixth time on his voyage. Although many of his fellow passengers became seasick during this stormy passage, Muir seems to have fared perfectly well. The steamer next took him to Ras Asir—old Cape Guardafui on the eastern tip of present-day Somalia—where he enjoyed picturesque views of the wave-beaten cape, with dramatic table-lands and high mountains behind. On February 28 the *General* rounded Ras Asir and sailed west into the Gulf of Aden.

The next day Muir, in port at 'Adan in present-day Democratic Yemen, admired the "[w]onderfully sculptured sharp-pointed crenelated peaks" along the coast before sailing again, through the Bab el Mandeb strait and into the Red Sea. On March 1 Muir noted an interesting series of islands he calls "the Twelve Apostles" (perhaps Jazâ'ir az Z'ubayr) and admired a beautiful red-yellow alga through which the ship passed: "[f]ine hair-like tresses of delicate filament, turned up from a considerable depth."

For the next two days Muir could not see land, though he had the coast of present-day Ethiopia, Sudan, and Egypt on the port beam and present-day Saudi Arabia on the starboard. As the weather turned colder, Muir at last sighted land on March 3, as his ship approached Râs Muhammad, the cape at the southern tip of the Sinai Peninsula. That night the *General* sailed into the Gulf of Suez, where the next day Muir enjoyed views of the "lofty hills" along the Egyptian coast before docking at El Suweis.

From this port fifteen of Muir's fellow passengers disembarked and took a train to El Gîza, less than one hundred miles inland, to see the great pyramids before rejoining the *General* the following day at Bur Sa'id, on the Nile River delta where the Gulf of Suez enters the Mediterranean Sea. Considering the hard traveling—by boat, train, skiff, horse, buggy, and on foot—Muir was willing to endure in order to visit particular species of trees, it is interesting that he chose not to join the travelers who, by taking a short train ride, had the opportunity to witness one of civilization's most celebrated creations. Although Muir had seen the pyramids in 1903, dur-ing his world tour, the emphases of his journal suggest that he would have ranked the monkey puzzle and baobab trees well above the pyramids in his own list of the world's wonders.

Beginning with his passage through the Suez Canal and into the Mediterranean on March 5, Muir's journal entries become increasingly cursory—despite his visiting some spectacular sites in Italy. His correspondence during this last leg of his journey is apparently also scant: only three Muir letters from this period are extant, and these are brief notes to apprise family and friends of the timing of his scheduled arrival in New York. Though Muir now had "homegoing" on his mind and he may have been fatigued from his long travels, there is a more likely explanation for the paucity of his letters and brevity of his journal entries during the final weeks of his voyage. In all his correspondence regarding the voyage, never did Muir describe in any detail the nearly two weeks he spent in Italy and the Mediterranean, nor did he seem to consider the activities of those weeks particularly important. Muir was devoted to the idea of visiting the two "hot continents" and, having done so, seemed to see the Mediterranean leg of his journey, and even northern Africa, as little more than the way home. The brevity of these early March entries suggests that Muir never intended to include serious treatment of the Mediterranean in the book of South American and African travels that he hoped—in vain, as it turned out—to publish during his lifetime.

Muir left Naples on March 15, this time aboard the Hamburg-American line steamship *Kaiserin Augusta Victoria*. The ship sailed across the Tyrrhenian Sea and through the Strait of Bonifacio between Sardinia and Corsica and then close along the glacially carved mountains of coastal Spain, stopping for a half day at Gibraltar. Unfortunately, the ten-day North Atlantic crossing that followed was through weather so fierce that, according to Muir, the captain of his ship declared the passage the worst he had experienced in forty trips. Muir's final journal entry reads simply: "Arrive at New York, after my very long voyage, one hundred and nine days sailing, having crossed the equator six times."

John Muir was nearing his seventy-fourth birthday when he sailed into New York on March 27th, successfully completing an epic voyage halfway around the world that had begun almost eight months earlier. He had traveled 40,000 miles and had crossed the equator six times. He had visited the Amazon and Rio Negro and studied the plants and trees of the Amazonian rainforest. He had found *Araucaria braziliensis* growing along the Iguacu River in the wilderness of southern Brazil. He had crossed the South American continent and ascended the Andes to discover rare forests of *Araucaria imbricata,* the monkey puzzle tree. He had sailed 10,000 miles to reach South Africa, and studied and sketched the immense *Adansonia digitata,* the African baobab tree. He had seen the Athi plains and the great Lake Victoria, and had stood at the headwaters of the Nile. And now, by way of the halcyon Mediterranean and the stormy North Atlantic, he was back in America. It was time to ride the rails back to California, Martinez, and the writing life. John Muir's South American and African dreams, held fondly ever since his failed attempt to reach the Amazon in 1867–68, had at last been fulfilled. "On this pair of wild hot continents," he affirmed in a letter written from the deck of his ship as it sailed past Zanzibar, "I've enjoyed the most fruitful year of my life."

Journal

Feb. 7

Start at noon for Antebbe, Uganda. Heavy rain in the morning. Baobabs common along the railroad for twenty or thirty miles, but smaller as the coast is left, though the soil is good. Why is this? Hills grassy, trees and shrubs scattered, fire-scourged. Glacier features. Mountains blue in the distance. Had good fortune as usual in finding two pleasant traveling companions, one a Swiss, who kindly shared his fine luncheon with me, as there is no dining car on the train. At night he gave me one of his rugs as there was no bedding on the train. This friend is a professional hunter with headquarters at Nairobi. The other is Arch-Deacon Binns.[1] Two others joined us in our compartment in the middle of the night. Scotch. One who had often been in Dunbar and knew my friends there. Heard him pronounce "John" and knew him for a Scotchman in the dark, though I was half asleep.

Feb. 8

Country more and more distinctly glacial. See hundreds or thousands of hartbeests and other antelopes, some within stone's throw of the track. Large number of wild ostriches. Grassy plains. No trees or shrubs for miles and miles. Great hills and mountains in the distance. Lovely country. Glacial drift common. Arrived Nairobi at 11:15 a.m. Went to Norfolk Hotel.

Feb. 9

At Hotel. Fine scenery. Heavy rain. Great need of increased hotel accommodations. In rare weather conditions Kaillimanjara visible one hundred and fifty miles distant from here. Rained for three days on most of way from Mombasa. Rainy season usually begins in March in this part of British East Africa.

Feb. 10

Left Nairobi for Port Florence at noon. Rainy until after dark. Never saw rain so early in the season in the last fourteen years, though only about a month earlier than usual. Railroad runs through beautiful mountain scenery, patches of forest with open grassy prairies, filled-up lake basins. Views of large main valley, very broad, fine in its main lines. Tawny in

---

[1] Possibly the Unitarian minister Reverend Ottwell Binns (b. 1872), who, under his own name and under the pseudonym Ben Bolt, published more than fifty novels of mystery and adventure including *The Man from Malaba* (1917), *Trail of Adventure* (1923), *Forest Exile* (1933), and *By Papuan Waters* (1938).

color from dry grass. Juniper common. Used for lumber, but splits too freely for some purposes, and as usual all the older trees are eaten with dry rot in the center. This is true of all the many species of juniper. Grand views of the great valley. Was kindly given a blanket and pillow by Mr. Rees, the night being very cold, although almost directly on the equator. The elevation at the highest point the railroad passed over during the night was about 8,000 feet above sea level.

Feb. 11

Arrived at Port Florence about 7:00 a.m. Went aboard the good little steamer *Clement Hill* and started for Antebbe at 10:00 a.m. Wonderful

Sketch made from Lake Victoria, looking back at the hills behind Port Florence, British East Africa (now Kenya)

picturesque scenery. Low, green, half-forested hills with mountains in the distance. Not very high. Some perhaps about 6,000 feet above the sea. The Victoria Nyanza one of the largest in the world. Second in size only to Lake Superior. Hippopotamus common around the muddy and reedy shores. The lake is comparatively shallow, only about 240 feet at the deepest part. Anchored at dark.

Feb. 12

Started at daybreak. Arrived at Antebbe about 11:00 a.m. at head of a beautiful bay. Measured one tree about six feet in diameter a little way back from the shore. Many are three or four feet, with fine, wide-spreading head. One tree, of moderate size, had noble digitate leaves, fourteen or more, eighteen inches wide. Petioles two feet long. Mr. Rees took me to the Uganda Protectorate.[2]

Spathodia nilotica, has very large flowers.
Canarium schweinfurthii, very large tree.
Thevetia nerriforia, red.
Bauhinia triandra, double leaf.
Randia dummetorium.
Solianum macaranthum.
Maesopsis berchemoides.
Pipledenia africana.
Monodora myristica.

Mr. Rees took me to the Botanical Gardens. Saw the Manager, who kindly ordered his head gardener[3] to show me over the garden and give me specimens of all I wished. A bright, scholarly fellow, Singalese, from

---

[2] Established in 1894, the Uganda Protectorate was an immense central African British protectorate that encompassed the former African kingdom of Buganda.
[3] Notes in one of JM's informal address lists in the TMS suggest that the gardener was F. G. Pulle, Head Gardener at the Botanic Gardens in Entebbe. The botanical list preceding this comment was presumably made by JM during his visit to the Entebbe Gardens.

Ceylon. There is a species of mourning dove hereabouts which says "Too hot for anything." A lovely creeper going up straight on smooth-barked tree in regular zigzags.

Feb. 13

Started for Kompali at daylight. Arrived about 9:00 a.m. Ride in jinrikisha from port to village, a distance of about seven miles, through beautiful landscape. Extensive and thrifty banana orchards. The fruit red instead of yellow. Interesting swamps full of the famous papyrus growing here naturally. Charming red, blue and white water lilies in the harbor in glorious abundance. Arrived at Kompali in an hour and a half. Returned in one hour. My jinrikisha was hauled and pushed by three lusty Negroes, two pushing and the other in the shafts. Chanted all the way while trotting, the leader rapidly improvising a line, and the chorus sounded like "Harry *Trunk!* Harry *Trunk!*" The leader would say: "The white man is going to see our pretty town." "Harry Trunk. Harry Trunk." "He sees the black man's fine banana field." "Harry Trunk. Harry Trunk." "He is looking at the birds in the trees." "Harry Trunk. Harry Trunk." "The white man's far from his cold, cold home." "Harry Trunk. Harry Trunk." Etc.

Feb. 14

Started for Jinja at 5:00 a.m. Arrived at 11:30 a.m. From the village I went to see the Ripon Falls at the outlet of the great lake, the main head fountain of the Nile, the distance from the port being only a little over a mile. The fall is only about fifteen or twenty feet over a bar of resisting rock. The Fall is divided into three parts and makes a magnificent show of foam. Large numbers of alligators were sunning themselves[4] on the farther bank at the head of the falls, while fishes in large numbers are constantly springing in wide curves in their attempts to ascend the cascade to

---

[4] Here, at the outlet of Lake Victoria, JM is not seeing alligators but crocodiles—in this case the African, or Nile, crocodile *(Crocodylus niloticus)*, which can attain a length of twenty feet.

enter the lake. The broad stream setting out in rapids on its 3,330 mile course is very impressive.

"In 1852 Sir Roderick Murchison[5] advanced the hypothesis that Africa south of the Sahara Desert was a continent of great antiquity, and simplicity, which had maintained the form of a great basin ever since the age of the new red sandstone. He based his theory on the work of Bain, the pioneer of South African geology, summarized in a paper entitled 'On the Antiquity of the Physical Geography of Inner Africa' by R. Murchison, in which he claims that the country is of interest because it was geologically unique in the long conservation of ancient terrestrial conditions."

The famous Ngrurunga (water holes) from J. W. Gregory's book entitled *The Great Rift Valley.*[6]

Feb. 15

Start for Port Florence at 4:00 a.m. Arrived at 5:00 p.m.

---

[5] The source for JM's interpolated quotation in this paragraph is John Walter Gregory's *The Great Rift Valley, being the Narrative of a Journey to Mount Kenya and Lake Baringo: with Some Account of the Geology, Natural History, Anthropology and Future Prospects of British East Africa* (London: J. Murray, 1896), from which JM has quoted and paraphrased parts of the first and second paragraphs of chapter 12 (pg. 213). In TMS, JM spells the quoted name "Murchoson" in the first sentence of the paragraph and "Murchison" in the second sentence. I have changed the former spelling to the latter, since the person referred to is prominent geographer and geologist Sir Roderick Impey Murchison (1792–1871). The Murchison paper here mentioned is his 1864 presidential address to the Royal Geographical Society of London, published in the *Journal of the Royal Geographic Society* (vol. 34, pgs. 201–205).

[6] The book to which JM refers, which does indeed contain a description of the ngrurunga, is *The Great Rift Valley, being the Narrative of a Journey to Mount Kenya and Lake Baringo: with Some Account of the Geology, Natural History, Anthropology and Future Prospects of British East Africa,* by John Walter Gregory (London: J. Murray, 1896). Chapter 5 of Gregory's book, "On the Uganda Road," describes an experience of Ugandan travel very like JM's own. The region described in Gregory's book—and in other African materials Muir was then reading—would later become crucial to our understanding of human origins and evolution. Olduvai Gorge, one of the most important sites in the history of anthropological archeology, is located near Muir's route, at the eastern edge of the Great Rift Valley in what is now Northern Tanzania, halfway between Mt. Kilimanjaro and Lake Victoria. Here Dr. Louis Leakey (1903–1972) and his wife, Mary Leakey (1913–1996), among others, discovered stone tool and fossil evidence indicating that human evolution centered in Africa (rather than Asia), and thus suggesting older origins for human evolution than had previously been believed.

Feb. 16

Got aboard the train on the return journey to Mombasa at 7:30 a.m. From the Port a long level valley six to eight miles wide looks like a filled-in part of the Port Florence arm of the lake, extending twenty or thirty miles to the southward, bounded on the west by a range of bold bluffs, separated by wide cirques here and there; and on the east by smooth terraces, extending lakeward parallel to the bluffs. Native villages and fields along the valley. Water lilies at Port Florence, and papyrus. *Kigelia* trees in fruit here and magnificent figs. One near Port Florence, green with dark green foliage, had fruit a half inch in diameter. The trunk about eight feet in diameter, with a dense dome-shaped broad head something like the great banyan of India. Wild mountains after leaving the lake plains, through which the railroad has been built at great cost. Twenty or thirty steel trestles over gorgeous and fluting ravines in close succession. Some of the passengers saw a lion by the roadside.

Feb. 17

Very cold night. Slept cold, with heavy underclothing, coat and vest, overcoat, and a thick blanket. Elevation of the region about 6,000 to 8,000 feet above the sea. Colder than the Tuolumne Meadows in the spring, though 3,000 feet higher than here. Passed through dense forests about noon, but the greater part of the way is through grassy hills with only detached patches of brush and trees. Extensive wheat fields here and there. Yesterday afternoon and this forenoon near Nivahsa Station and Lake. This remarkable lake is surrounded by a picturesque mountain and hills. Water said to be fresh, though without any visible outlet. Between Nivasha and Nairoba saw Mt. Kilimanjara and Kenia,[7] and many antelopes and zebra, all within short distances of the railroad, and remarkably tame. The latter most at ease as the train rolled past. This afternoon soon after leaving Nairoba saw hundreds or thousands of antelopes, two droves

[7] Mount Kilimanjaro, the highest point on the continent of Africa (5,895 meters), and Mount Kenya (5,199 meters), to the north.

of zebras, and a few ostriches. Some of the antelopes were lying down within a stone's throw of the track, a few of which lay still. Others rose and gazed at the train, and a few ran off to a distance of a quarter of a mile or so. These fine beasts were on a beautiful treeless shrubless plain or prairie. After coming to a plain dotted with small trees and bushes none of the animals were seen. Some parts of the prairie were roughened with moraine boulders, and some places weathered from the bedrock, which occurs here and there in large patches without any kind of soil, something like glacier pavements, with potholes here and there, weathered out by the rain and wind. Some beds of quartz pebbles with large boulders here and there. The stream channels very shallow. All signs point to glaciation no great geological time ago. Most of the animals seen today were on the Athi plain, and have learned that the nearer the railroad the safer they are from the attack of either men or lions. A strip along the track a mile in width had been reserved as a game refuge, which the animals have been quick to

Baobab trees along the railroad tracks

discover and flock into it, from all the adjacent region. Saw Kilimanjara again this afternoon. Only its broad base was visible. The head and main body cloud-mantled. Saw also many baobabs two hundred and fifty miles or more from Mombasa. One stood near the Makinda Station within six feet or so from the railroad track.

Met Leslie Simson, Rand Club, Johannesburg,[8] a Californian, and college classmate of John Hays.[9]

Feb. 18

Arrived Mombasa at 8:00 a.m. Fine fields and gardens and palm and mango groves. The mango is a particularly fine tree, with a very large, dark green dome. The whole tree forming in some cases an almost perfect sphere, densely leafy and brilliant. The very type of tropical luxuriance and health. Not a single imperfect leaf visible. The largest that I saw were near Klinendina. Here, too, there are several rubber plantations.

Feb. 19

Very hot and breezeless until about 9:00 a.m. Then came the moderating sea breeze. Went to the office of the East African Dutch Line and from the Agent got the number of my cabin on the *General,* which is expected to arrive within a few days. Sauntered about in the Town Gardens, which are near the Hotel. Had Mr. Alsop to dinner.

Feb. 20

Calm and oppressively hot as usual in the morning. Sketched so-called almond trees. Leaves brilliantly red and at a little distance look like flow-

---

[8] Leslie Simson, a hunter, guide, and—somewhat later—conservationist, was a Californian and philanthropist whose gifts to the California Academy of Sciences in San Francisco allowed the Academy to open its African Hall in 1934. Simson was a member of the Rand Club, founded in 1887, an exclusive gathering place for the South African social and economic elites. The Club, located in downtown Johannesburg, South Africa, barred women from membership until 1994, and has admitted black members only since 1997.

[9] Perhaps John Coffee ("Jack") Hays (1817–1883), a soldier and surveyor who came to California in 1849; Hays served as sheriff of San Francisco County during the early 1850s, and later went on to own large real estate and banking interests in Oakland.

ers. These leaves are thick, large, and shiny, like those of the magnolia. Out on coral plateau with Mr. Alsop photographing baobabs.[10] Suffered with the almost intolerable heat.

Feb. 21

Hot as usual. Out again with Mr. Alsop photographing baobabs. The young baobabs are straight and orderly in their general form like conifers, with their branches at regular intervals in whorls around the axis, though they become so wildly grotesque in age. Fine gray bark with minute furrows an eighth of an inch or so apart and less in depth. Branches whorled about as regularly as those of the silver firs.

Feb. 22

Getting ready to sail on the *General* for home.

Feb. 23

Got aboard the fine steamer at noon. Sailed this evening at 6:00.

Feb. 24

Cloudy and warm. Cooler toward noon. Head wind. Heavy swell. Good many passengers seasick. No land in sight.

Feb. 25

Wind abating slightly. Few whitecaps but the swell quite heavy. The sky dingy around the horizon. Nearly clear overhead. No wing, fin, or flipper visible. Expect to reach Wubuschi this afternoon, in British East Africa Protectorate. Arrived about 2:00 p.m. Town of considerable size, situated on the sandy windswept shore of a wide open bay. Stopped at anchor about two hours. Heavy sea. A half dozen large boats manned by eight to twelve rowers, oars long elastic shafts with small blades attached.

---

[10] In this entry and the entry for the following day, February 21, JM indicates that he is photographing—as well as measuring, describing, and sketching—baobabs. Unfortunately, JM's photographs of the trees appear not to have survived.

The black boatmen with long regular strokes displayed fine play of muscles as they pulled alongside against the wind and high over-curling waves. That the boats were not wrecked seemed marvelous. Two or three passengers managed to get aboard with difficulty. Live cattle and sheep were hoisted aboard for ship provisions. So also the mail, etc. The coast to the southward for fifty miles or so, along which we sailed at a distance of three or four miles, is well timbered beyond reach of immense yellow sand dunes. The waves along the shore on the rocky headlands made a grand show of up-dashing spray. A good many of our passengers seasick.

Feb. 26

Fine, clear, calm morning. Swell gone down. Multitudes of small glittering wavelets. Temperature delightful. No wing or fin in sight all day. Clear sunset, the first in many a day.

Feb. 27

Fine, calm, half cloudy morning. Tranquil sea. No life visible outside the ship, though we are not far from the coast. Almost cloudless at evening.

Feb. 28

Off Cape Guardifui. Bold striking mass of mountains. Bluffs wave-beaten. Lofty brush-covered mountains and tableland in the distance. This is the northernmost part of Somaliland.

Feb. 29

Arrived at Aden, at 10:30 a.m. Wonderfully sculptured sharp-pointed crenelated peaks. Barren. Low ground in the distance ahead, with palm groves on Arabian Coast. Fine sunset.

Mar. 1

In the Red Sea. Left Aden about 3:00 p.m. Passed Babelmandeb Straits in the night. Fine bright morning. No land visible. About noon passed a

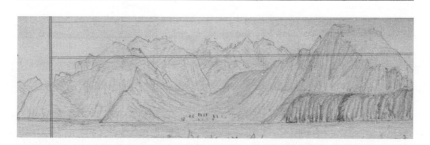

Glacially carved valley in the mountains near 'Adan, at the mouth of the Red Sea

dozen islands, called the Twelve Apostles; some mere rocks; all of them in line, trending with the long narrow sea. They are plain and bold in sculpture, contrasting the sharp-pointed crumbling down-draggled mountains about Aden. Parts of a ridge, perhaps degraded by glacial action.

Mar. 2

Cloudy. Clear towards noon, with brisk east wind, causing fall of temperature so great as to call for heavy clothing. A flock of seventy-five swans or herons followed the ship for a mile or more close alongside. Then turned off to the southward. Talking excitedly. Rising high in beautiful order. Sea dark blue; almost black. Yesterday passed through belt of reddish-yellow alga a mile or so long and cloud-shaped masses which glowed in the sun in changing tones. Very striking. Fine hair-like tresses of delicate filament, turned up from considerable depth.

Mar. 3

Head wind. Steady and cold, coming from Europe. Heavy swelling waves. Ship pitching. Sea dark in color. The top of a rock visible. First land seen since passing the Twelve Apostles. Not a cloud in the sky. Fine bracing weather. First for many a day. At 10:00 a.m. sky half cloudy. Passed three lighthouses about 8:00 p.m.

Mar. 4

Wind abating slightly, but the temperature is still lower. Overcoats now being worn. Fine bracing sunny morning. Lofty hills and mountains on either hand. Some of them apparently metamorphic slate infinitely sculptured, in zigzag forms, others bedded in regular strata. *Trichodesmium erythryaeum* not seen since the N.E. wind began to blow. This is the species of *Confervae* which gives name to the Red Sea.[11] We arrive at Suez about 5:00 p.m. Enter the canal about 7:00 p.m.[12] N.E. wind scarce perceptible, but the temperature still lower. Fifteen passengers left us here at Suez to go to Cairo by a night train to visit the pyramids, expecting to join the ship again at Port Said. In this they were successful, having the romantic pleasure of passing the night in the sand at the foot of the pyramids.

Mar. 5

Fine, cool, calm morning. No clouds, but hazy. The canal is being widened. Many dredges are at work. The banks, too, are being lined with cemented rock and brick work, to protect them from washing, caused by waves from the passing steamers. Arrived at Port Said about 8:00 a.m., a busy place. Thirty or more steamships here. Many of them coal carriers. Departed for Naples about 2:00 p.m.

Mar. 6

Cloudy morning. N.E. wind. Cool overcoat weather. Bracing. Exhilarating. Clearing toward noon. Water dark blue. No land in sight all day. High wind.

---

[11] The Red Sea is normally blue-green in color but occasionally turns a reddish brown after the die-off of extensive blooms of the filamentous alga *Trichodesmium erythraeum*.
[12] The 100-mile Suez Canal, which connects the Mediterranean and Red Seas, was built by the French-owned Suez Canal Company and was completed in 1869 after eleven years' construction.

Mar. 7

Beautiful day. Sea calm. Sky clear. Temperature still low, but the long-continued N.E. wind has at last died away. Crete, where Paul was ship-wrecked,[13] was in plain sight this morning at 7:00.

Mar. 8

High wind. Slight rolling of ship. About 1:30 p.m. Italy in sight. Mountainous. Shows glacial feature on approach to Straits of Messina, whose ruined cities were lately so perfectly desolate, and where over 100,000 people lost their lives.[14] The scenery of the Straits very picturesque.

Mar. 9

Arrived at Naples. Go to Museum, full of the statuary from Pompeii.

Mar. 10

Go to the old Roman town of Pozzuli with Mr. Toplas.

Mar. 11

Make the trip to Pompeii.

Mar. 12

To Vesuvius.

[13] The New Testament book of Acts relates the story of the apostle Paul, who, after being arrested by the Romans and subsequently appealing to Caesar, was sent by King Agrippa as a prisoner to Rome in order to appear before Caesar himself. Paul's journey took him 2,000 miles, from Caesarea, to Myra, to Cnidus, and then to Crete, where his ship landed safely at the port of Fair Havens. The shipwreck JM mentioned occurred not at Crete, but on the way from Crete to Phoenix, when the ship carrying the apostle was blown off course and was wrecked at Malta, an island then inhabited by a people of Phoenician ancestry. Acts 27 and 28 tell the story of the great storm, of the Angel of God who foretells the wreck, and of Paul's subsequent stay on Malta before eventually making it safely to Rome, where he remained to preach the Christian faith to the Gentiles.

[14] On December 28, 1908, one of the most destructive earthquakes in recorded history (magnitude 7.5) struck Messina, Italy. The death toll from the quake and the tsunami it caused is estimated at between 70,000 and 100,000.

Mar. 13

To Capri, whose blue grotto is one of the most wonderful I ever saw.

Mar. 14

At hotel packing. Letter writing, etc. Fine day. The beautiful blue bay sparkling in the sunbeams.

Mar. 15

Go aboard the *Kaiserin Augusta Victoria* at 2:00 p.m. Conducted most kindly by Mr. Toplas, who also planned all my excursions about Naples.

Mar. 16

Cloudy, breezy, cold. Sailed past the north end of Sardinia. Mountains glaciated.

Mar. 17

Cold, clear, sailing close along the mountainous coast of Spain, which shows glaciated features very clearly.

Mar. 18

Arrived at Gibraltar at 6:00 a.m. Sailed at 1:00 p.m. Beautiful Algeria Bay.

Mar. 19

Moderate head wind. Cool, clear or half-cloudy.

Mar. 20

Cloudy. Stiff east wind. Cold. Temperature 50 and 55 deg. Long heavy waves. Our big ship pitching.

Mar. 21

High east wind. Sea rough. Foamy. Sunbeams streaming through chinks in the clouds, and falling with glorious effect on the reflecting side of the large waves.

Mar. 22

Very high head wind. Ship pitching and staggering. Cold gloomy day. Wild sea; foamy; tossing spray.

Mar. 23

Dark and rainy. High head wind.

Mar. 24

Storm wilder than ever. Weltering interfering waves; up-leaping snowy pillars of foam, with streamers like silver hair. All the sea streaked with ribbons of spent wave-foam. The Captain says that this is the stormiest of all the forty voyages that he has made in this ship.

Mar. 25

Wind changed to north. Difficult deck walking.

Mar. 26

Storm over. Lovely clear calm weather.

Mar. 27

Arrive at New York, after my very long voyage, one hundred and nine days sailing, having crossed the equator six times.

Correspondence

Naples, Italy
March 13, 1912
Osborn family

Dear Osborns,

I'm now headed straight homewards. Expect to arrive New York March 26th on the *Kaiserin Augusta Victoria* and fondly hope to find you all well.

Faithfully,

John Muir

Naples, Italy
March 15, 1912
Hooker family

Dear Friends Hookers,

I start today for New York on the *Kaiserin Augusta Victoria,* all my big trip done except the delightful homegoing—fondly hoping to find all well. I may have to linger in N.Y. a few weeks proofreading, etc. Write as soon as you receive this c/o R. U. Johnson, The Century Magazine, Union Square, New York, telling all good Hooker tidings.

Ever Your affectionate friend,

John Muir

P.S. Guess how often I thought of you while here![15]

---

[15] The implication is that JM thought often about the Hookers because they had traveled in Italy a great deal, and because Katharine Hooker had already written her first book of Italian travels, *Wayfarers in Italy* (San Francisco: D. P. Elder and Morgan Shepard, 1902).

Naples, Italy
March 15, 1912
Helen Muir Funk

Hello Darling Helen,

You now seem precious near, for all my wanderings over South America and Africa are done and I start today for New York on the *Kaiserin Augusta Victoria* of the Hamburg American line. So now there is nothing left of the big hard trip but homegoing with fond hopes of finding you all well. I'm quite well myself and have had wonderful luck in my studies, health, and every thing. I suppose the incomparable boy is now quite manly. I'll be in New York by the 26th of March, but may have to read book proof for a week or two. Write to me telling me all about Wanda and her wondrous offspring. C/o R. U. Johnson, The Century Magazine, Union Square, New York.

Ever your devoted father,

John Muir

P.S. Send word to Mrs. Sellers, Mrs. Thompson, and Mrs. Jones.

———

CHAPTER 7

Home to America, California, and Writing: The Fate of John Muir and His South America and Africa Journals

28 March 1912–29 December 1912

I F JOHN MUIR's South America and Africa journey had given him the "most fruitful year" of his life, it would also prove the last great journey of his life. Indeed, Muir's death less than three years after his return gives the 1911–12 adventures special poignancy and importance. In order to fully understand Muir's feelings about the trip—and his literary intentions for the travel journals in which he recorded his impressions of it—it is helpful to examine his correspondence through the end of 1912, the year in which he returned from the southern continents to America and to his home in Martinez, California. These 1912 letters remind us that

Muir's last years included accomplishments and struggles other than the much discussed battle to preserve Hetch Hetchy. Among other things, this correspondence teaches us a great deal about Muir as an international traveler, a family man, and a disciplined writer whose keen awareness of his own mortality both inspired and circumscribed his vast literary ambitions.

When, on March 27, 1911, Muir arrived safely in New York despite the many concerns of his loved ones, he was understandably anxious to return to family and friends in California. Nevertheless, he had important business to attend to in the East, and so would remain for several weeks before heading west in mid-April. Relatively little is certain about Muir's movements and activities during these few weeks between his return to New York and his departure for the West, but we do know that Muir spent a good bit of this time actually in New York, reading the final text of *The Yosemite*, scheduled to be issued the following month by the Century Company. Contrary to Muir's instructions, Century had set type and begun production in his absence, so rather than seeing proof sheets, as he had expected, he returned to a finished book that—despite its handsome appearance—contained scores of errors. In a letter to his friends the Marshalls Muir complained that the first edition of *The Yosemite* "was put up and stereotyped before I saw a single proof. I discovered 51 errors in it which will have to [be] chiseled out of the plates." While in New York Muir also went out to Clara Barrus's chalet in Pelham on April 3 to join the celebration of his friend John Burroughs's seventy-fifth birthday.

Muir also spent time in Boston, where on April 12 he discussed the ongoing Hetch Hetchy controversy with several prominent Bostonians, and where he presumably met with Houghton Mifflin, the publishers of his forthcoming autobiography. It is probable that Muir proofed the autobiography while in Boston, and it is certain that he successfully negotiated its periodical pre-publication: an abridgment of *The Story of My Boyhood and Youth* appeared in four parts in the November and December 1912 and January and February 1913 issues of the *Atlantic Monthly* before being released as a book in March 1913.

In mid-April Muir started West by train, and was scheduled to arrive in Los Angeles on the afternoon of his seventy-fourth birthday, April 21, 1912. He stayed for several days there with his daughter Helen and her family, including his young grandson, Muir Funk. Muir then returned home at last to Martinez, where his daughter Wanda's family had grown to include a third son, Richard.

Although his homecoming at the Martinez ranch must have been gratifying to him after so long an absence, by the end of April Muir had already settled into a domestic routine that he clearly found quite lonely. Muir's correspondence from this period poignantly relates his sense of isolation, uncertainty, and, sometimes, sadness. Part of Muir's loneliness certainly came from living by himself in the big house, so empty of domestic warmth and so full of memories of happier times when his wife, Louie, was alive. The feeling of loss that he now associated with the house must have been exacerbated by the surprising fact that his two daughters, to whom Louie had left the big house in her will, wanted "to sell the blessed old place to an Oakland somebody or nobody stranger"—a plan Muir prevented by buying the house himself, "for the sake of the memories about it," he wrote, "though the poor wanderer may never be able to make it his home."

Though he had saved the Martinez ranch house, Muir was still rattling around in it by himself. "I'm in my old library den," he wrote to Anna Dickey on the first of May, "the house desolate, nobody living in it save a hungry mouse or two." Nearly every letter Muir sent during this period remarks on the beauty and luxuriance of the flowers, bushes, and trees that he had, over the years, collected from his many travels and planted around the Martinez ranch—plants through which he felt a powerful emotional link between his home place and his journeys abroad. Nevertheless, Muir remained uncertain as to whether he could make a real home of the old house, and his troubling doubts only thinly masked a deeper sadness: "there's no good bread hereabouts and no housekeeper," he wrote, "so I may never be able to make it a home, fated, perhaps, to wander until sundown." Muir's feeling of emotional homelessness was linked to a fear that, having toured the hot continents, his best years were now behind him. "Anyhow I've had a glorious life," he wrote with a tone of uncharacteristic resignation, "and I'll never have the heart to complain."

Muir's new life in the old house began with the monumental chore of sorting through eight months' worth of letters that had accumulated in his absence. Having been busy with politics and publishing back East and then absorbed by natural history study during his long trip, Muir now felt a strong need to renew old friendships; he wrote many letters tenderly affirming his affections and loyalties, and expressing his appreciation for friends both here and gone, even as he also intimated the sadness of his own contemplations on old age and mortality. "[F]riends become more and more precious in the serene light of life's evening," he wrote to Annie Bidwell at the end of April. And to his close friend Katharine Hooker he complained of the "eternal unfitness of mundane things" that prevented him from visiting her. "We must look, it seems, somewhere in the sky for a permanent meeting place," he wrote. "Heavens! What long unblazed trails through starry space friends have to trace to get together." "Anyhow," concluded Muir somewhat despondently, "let's be hopeful and grateful for the good ante-death days we have enjoyed."

Muir's letters from the spring of 1912 are particularly interesting as reflections—or, more accurately, *projections*—of his own preoccupations and ambitions. His personal concerns about aging and about the importance of establishing his environmental ideas and values through writing are suggested by a May 10 letter to his Alaska companion William Trelease, in which he wrote, "May you live to be a hundred years young. Anyhow you will live forever in your works." And Muir might have been addressing himself as well as William Trout when he wrote to his old Canada companion that "[f]riends get closer and dearer the farther they travel on life's journey. It's fine to see how youthful your heart remains, and how wide and far reaching your sympathy with everybody and everything. Such people never grow old." In a comment that reflects Muir's own concern about having his desire to study nature eclipsed by mercantile activity, Muir further admonishes Trout that "I only regret your being held so long in mechanical bread winning harness instead of making enough by middle age and spending the better half of life in studying God's works."

Although lonely in his old house, Muir was soon at work organizing his manuscripts and notes in preparation for a number of book projects he was then planning. Indeed, he was soon so engaged by book preparations that he found it difficult to pull himself away even when, on July 17, Helen gave birth to his fifth grandson, Stanley. Muir's letters to family and friends repeatedly lament that he could not free himself from work in order to visit them. At seventy-four, alone in the Martinez "scribble den," and surrounded by what he once described as "moraines" of largely disorganized manuscripts and journals, Muir's mortal contemplations had now begun to fuel his literary ambitions. At mid-summer he wrote to Katharine Hooker that "[j]ust now from every direction grim work is staring me hard in the face crying ''twill soon be dark,' and urging concentration and haste. And alas, the advice seems reasonable." Muir also expressed this sense of urgency in a letter to his sister Mary. "Have notes enough for more than a hundred volumes," he wrote, "but of course I won't live long enough to write that many."

Muir's intentions for his South America and Africa journals are best understood in light of this tension between his considerable literary ambitions and his urgent sense that the time available to complete these many book projects was running out. Only by piecing together scores of unpublished holograph letters that he sent and received during the summer and autumn of 1912—and by tracing in those letters a number of allusions to other Muir letters that have not survived—can we begin to tell the story of the fate of John Muir's 1911–12 travel journals.

It is important, first, to recognize that there were literary expectations of these journals even before they were written. In casual correspondence with friends and in professional correspondence with editors—particularly Robert Underwood Johnson of *Century Magazine*—Muir was often asked about his intentions for the literary presentation of the journey, and urged to share his impressions with others. When Muir returned home from his voyage, holograph notebooks in hand, he was already under pressure—albeit friendly pressure—to turn his journey into words. Although many of his friends and admirers asked when his impressions of the journey would be available, Muir remained hesitant to make specific promises. Typical of these enthusiastic inquiries is the following, written in a fan letter Muir received in June: "When I read that John Muir had returned to America after a tour through Africa and also South America, my heart leapt at the thought of reading your travels. I want to see the great Victoria falls through your wonderful eyes and I hope you won't wait too long before you give us another grand book." Through such letters, which he received before, during, and after the voyage, Muir was often reminded of his readers' expectations of him: that he would not only make the trip, enjoy it, and record its details for his own botanical studies, but also that he would work his travel journals into articles and books through which his audience could vicariously enjoy the exotic places to which he had traveled.

Even more revealing is the frequent and often tense correspondence between Muir and Johnson regarding the possible South America and Africa articles for *Century Magazine*. Having actively solicited such articles even before Muir left on his voyage, Johnson apparently wasted no time in requesting Muir's travel essays once the explorer returned to America, and it is almost certain that the two men discussed the matter when Muir was in New York in late March and early April. At that time Muir's immediate concerns were with the two books he then had in press, and with returning to California, though he expressed hope that he would be able to honor Johnson's request.

Whatever transpired between Johnson and Muir, by the end of April Muir was home again at the Martinez ranch, sequestered in his "scribble den" and trying to clear away accumulated correspondence in order "to get at something worth while." Several of his letters during these weeks discuss the voyage with genuine enthusiasm, thus suggesting momentum toward writing publishable accounts of the journey. In a May 10 letter responding to inquiries about Brazilian trees from his friend Harvard botanist Charles S. Sargent, Muir explains that he had made many sketches, but that—despite the promises of his Brazilian acquaintances—he had not yet obtained decent photographs. He also mentions that he brought home specimen flowers and cones, and that he would gladly divide with Sargent any additional specimens he could obtain from his contacts in South America. As for his literary intentions for the material, Muir concludes the letter with a telling comment: "I had a glorious trip both in S. America and Africa, notes of which I hope to write soon and will send copy."

As of mid-May, then, Muir had not yet begun the work he intended on his travel journals, and several of his missives make clear that it was taking him longer than expected to clear away the deep drifts of accumulated correspondence. Despite the loneliness of these weeks in the old house, the tremendous volume of paperwork that burdened him, and various new Sierra Club concerns, including the purchase of Soda Springs in Yosemite, Muir had—by late May or early June—decided to go to Los Angeles to work on his travel notes in his daughter Helen's bungalow on Formosa Avenue in Hollywood. As of June 10 Muir's letters bear the Hollywood return address, and in a letter written on that day Muir informs Johnson that "I am working on my Amazon notes and will soon be able to tell you if I can get something out of it to make the articles you wish."

Two days later Muir was writing to a California friend, the former Iowa newspaperman J. E. Calkins, of the difficulty of working on the literary record of his "grand saunter over two continents": "I am now writing up some of my notes, but it is a long job to get them in anything like shape, and a harder job than traveling," he added, "even in those hot countries like Brazil and Rhodesia, and the equatorial regions at the head of the Nile." To Mr. Aimers, the fellow Scot whom he had met aboard the *Dennis* in Brazil, Muir wrote on June 20 that "I am now writing up some notes, but when they will be ready for publication I do not know." "I will be glad to send you a copy but it will be a long time before anything is arranged in book form."

Still in Hollywood the following month, Muir wrote to Katharine Hooker a letter on July 2 that contains his most direct statements regard-

the sky was overcast

yesterday.   Last evening heavy, leaden, gloomy clouds *with* / *lead colored*

wonderfully enlivened with wondrous full of lightning sweeping along the eastern horizon.

Very little thunder heard 16th. *heaving in long* Sea foam, purple or violet.

beautifully sculptured into Low swells intermingled with hollows of innumerable wavelets *each* *one of which had its own little hollow + ridge some* *then breaking in* Wonderful cloud mass. *overhead the sky* Jet black, light blue, white and yellow

smoothly brushed, or mackerel clouds back of it. A strange sky. *rippled with*

Most day muddy dingy clouds, cumuli, like those of tropics.

August 17, 1911.   Almost same next morning, 17th, and evening. Glorious tree-like clouds *along the horizon*

August 18, 1911.   Nearly same *this* morning, only white and whitish *more* and luminous. Rows of pillared masses and dense black cloud. *and* White cumulus above *them*.

August 19, 1911.   Almost cloudless.   Sea without a single speck of foam. Wonderful circle of H₂O, dark blue. *water* Sky

Typescript journal page with Muir's editorial notes

ing his preparatory work on the South America and Africa travel journals: the timing of his provisional editing of them, the circumstances under which the typescript version of them was produced, and his intentions for the articles he hoped might be derived from them. "I've been at work here on my African and S. American notes, and Mrs. Thompson has made duplicate typewritten copies of them all," he explained, thus confirming that by early July 1912 Henrietta S. Thompson—who had served as Muir's secretary during his previous literary residencies at the Hooker home in Los Angeles—had completed the preparation of Muir's travel journal and notes in the form of the 160-page typescript on which *John Muir's Last Journey* is primarily based. In an undated letter that must certainly have been written in the late summer or early autumn of 1912 (though the Muir Papers include it with the undated correspondence for 1913) Muir later confirms that "I got my S. American and African notes copied and locked up for safe keeping before I left Los Angeles."

Having completed the considerable task of converting his fragmented, elliptical, and sketch-laden field journals into a form that could be worked with more easily, however, Muir remained uncertain as to the literary fate of what he had produced. "The *Century* editor wants three or four articles out of them [the travel notes]," he explained to Katharine Hooker, "but I don't see much readily available magazine stuff in them, excepting perhaps the Amazon, the Araucaria forests of Chile and Brazil, the Mombasa and Zambesi Baobabs, and the Victoria Nyanza." Although Muir disparages the literary potential of the notes, the parts he identifies as worthy of presentation as articles amount, interestingly, to nearly the entire journal, exclusive of sea voyages and the trip home from coastal Africa through the Mediterranean and North Atlantic. Indeed, the Amazon, the *Araucaria braziliensis* forests of Brazil, the *Araucaria imbricata* forests of Chile, the baobabs of Africa, and the excursion to Lake Victoria comprise the five central chapters into which *John Muir's Last Journey* has been organized.

That Muir had worked so hard on the notes and had identified four or five major sections of the journal that he felt could be turned into publishable essays is somewhat at odds with the mildly disparaging tone of his comments about the South America and Africa materials. By the time he finished the typescript version of his travel journals, Muir was fatigued with "word work," and even seems to have contemplated yet another trip to Alaska in order to escape the burdens of writing. In the meantime, Robert Underwood Johnson continued to apply pressure, asking Muir on July 6, "Can't you let me know definitely about the two articles on the Amazon and the Victoria Falls[?] I'm trying here to get some Amazon pictures. Have you any fine ones [of] Victoria Falls? Or can you tell me where I can get some?"

In mid-July Muir returned to Martinez by automobile, via Santa Barbara, Paso Robles, Sequoia National Park, and Yosemite, arriving at the ranch on the evening of July 22. But he had little rest from the persistent Johnson, who wrote again on July 23 and on July 26 asking Muir to assure him that the articles would be written. By late July Muir was clearly feeling the pressure Johnson was placing on him. Muir's anxiety about the *Century* articles had begun to suggest itself even in letters on other subjects; on July 30, for example, he wrote to Katharine Hooker that "[y]our interesting excursion to the edge of Mexico is so full of good things it might easily be enlarged to a magazine article that would be more readable than anything I could write on Africa or South America."

At last, on August 2, Muir wrote to Johnson to break the bad news: "I had duplicate typewritten copies of my S. American and African notes made before leaving Los Angeles and I find that without a lot of good photographs suitable magazine articles cannot be got out of them, at least in a reasonable time," wrote Muir. "Therefore I'm sorry to say don't count on me." Detailing the few poor photos he did have, Muir further explained that "I have written to friends in Para and Manaos to try to obtain river and forest views for me at any cost. Also to Buenos Aires and Victoria for Argentina and Chile views. Am promised a lot, but when I'll get them or what like they will be none can know." In closing the letter Muir seemed to encourage Johnson not to insist further upon the articles; "Don't worry about those hot continents," he wrote, emphatically.

Muir's claim that he had actively tried to obtain photographs adequate to the production standards of the *Century* is confirmed by a number of letters to Muir from friends and acquaintances in various parts of South America and Africa. Only one of Muir's own letters requesting photos has apparently survived, a June 20 missive in which he reminds Douglas Aimers that "[o]f course you know I shall be glad to get any photographs of Brazilian trees you might chance to get." However, it is clear that many such letters were written, sent, and received: there are no fewer than fourteen extant letters, dated between June 3 and December 13, written to Muir from northern and southern Brazil, Uruguay, Chile, South Africa,

Rhodesia, Kenya, and Uganda, approximately half of which refer or allude to Muir's requests for photographs, and several of which indicate that the correspondent has included photographs with the letter.

Unfortunately for Muir, all too many of his South America and Africa acquaintances reported that they had not been able to obtain photographs, and although many promised to try, none seemed likely to provide the kinds of photographs Muir needed—particularly not in time to meet Johnson's urgent publication deadlines. Of those who did include photos, most apologized for their poor quality: on July 25 Herbert H. Allsop, whom Muir had met in Uganda, sent four prints that were "not as good as they might have been"; on July 29 John Harper, whom Muir had met in Paraná, Brazil, sent "a few photographs from this vicinity" with the apology that "[s]ome of them are very poor" and a repeated apology that he had been "unable to get some which I thought would interest" Muir; on August 24 Juan Hunter, whom Muir had met in Chile, sent ten prints with the explanation that "I have overexposed the plates; that is the cause of the fog."

The evidence of these letters is extremely valuable to our understanding of Muir's literary ambitions for the South America and Africa journals because it confirms that Muir made substantial efforts to obtain publication-quality illustrations for the would-be *Century* articles, that his inability to do so was attributable to circumstances beyond his control, and that his decision not to produce these articles hinged on a lack of requisite illustrations rather than a lack of interest in the project. Muir's own skepticism about the power of photography—especially mediocre photography—to convey natural beauty may also have contributed to his decision. In a later letter in which he notes how many nature photos are "impressively bad," Muir writes, "Strange is it not how photographers with their crystal lenses can make God's holy light tell lies."

Despite Muir's clear statements that the requested articles could not be properly prepared on short notice, Johnson responded with another, more insistent request on August 10. He took a new tack this time, though. Narrowly interpreting Muir's refusal, Johnson asks, "Am I right in thinking that we are to have an article or two on the Amazon but none on Victoria Falls?" And then, in a rhetorical turn that seems intended in jest but which thinly masks exasperation, closes with the assurance that he himself is feeling quite well, "[only] disturbed by such anxieties about my next year's programme as whether we shall have any articles by John Muir—a former friend of mine!"

Having concluded by early August that the *Century* articles could not be produced any time soon, Muir turned his attention to sculpting his voluminous Alaska notebooks and journals into book form. Muir's first mention of the Alaska plan appears in an August 24 letter to Johnson. "As to the Amazon-African articles, I thought I had explained that I would not be able to write them at the time you wanted them and that I was not to be depended on," Muir wrote, adding that "I'm trying to obtain more photographs. It may be more than a year before any of the above stuff is ready for you. In the meantime I'm working on Alaska." Muir's disappointment that he had not yet written essays about the voyage—and his continued hopes that he might eventually do so—also appear in his September 11 letter to Katharine Graydon: "I'm in my old library den all alone, looking over a hundred or more old notebooks and manuscript scraps, planning new books. I've not written a word on my foreign travels as yet. May in a year or two. Am now at work on Alaska." As 1912 began to wane, Muir continued to be at work on Alaska—as he would for the remaining two years of his life.

Muir's final letters of 1912, the year in which he returned from his last journey, are characterized by a generosity and tenderness that are often quite moving. His holiday missives are usually accompanied by thoughtful gifts for children, gestures of deep appreciation for long friendships, and fond wishes for the coming new year. Warm as they are, though, these letters also contain suggestions of Muir's loneliness, and intimations of meditation on mortality. In December 1912, for example, Muir writes to his old Yosemite friend Harry Randall in appreciation for "your kind New

Year greetings showing that you have not forgotten me." "You should visit Yosemite after all these years," importunes Muir. "None you know are left—Galen Clark, Hutchings, Leidig, George Kenney all dead, but," he adds in consolation, "the Valley itself is little changed." And, in what was probably the final letter Muir wrote during 1912, a poignant response to Charles Dwight Willard's remarkable, inspiring letter of Christmas Day— in which Willard, though wracked by fatal tuberculosis, bravely describes having discovered a new appreciation for the gift of life—Muir seems to confront his own mortality and to aspire to meet it with the sort of courage he sees in Willard. "I have been one of your many admirers from the first day we met," Muir writes, "and admiration has been growing ever greater as I saw how bravely you held on your way against deadly odds, digging hard and deep for bedrock foundations, making ladders out of disease and pain, climbing higher into the calm heights of life, like God's strong soaring pine trees, going straight to the heavens, nourished by their own decaying branches and leaves. The lesson of your life all should read, for in it there are some of the finest and divinest things humanity has to show. . . . For, as Thoreau well says, there are infinite degrees of life from that which is next to sleep and death to that which is ever awake and immortal."

The remaining two years of Muir's life, 1913 and 1914, were devoted by turns to family, writing, and preservationist battles. Muir still felt rather unsettled in the old Martinez home, and he continued to mourn the passing of his dearest friends. In lamenting the death of Francis Fisher Browne, for example, Muir noted in May 1913 that many "friends of the dear old leal sort have vanished never to be seen again in this world of light. And now beloved Browne has gone," adds Muir, "and all California seems lonelier than ever." As was characteristic of Muir, such troubles made him want to once again take up wandering, and in a letter written to Katharine Hooker just a week prior to his seventy-fifth birthday, he notes that if he could only see "a few of the Greenland and Antarctic ice-floods, then I'd willingly let my legs rest."

Muir's competing literary ambitions and activist work prevented any more great journeys, however. Indeed, there was no let up in Muir's feeling that he was racing the clock of mortality to complete book projects while he was still able, and his correspondence from 1913 is replete with comments such as this, from a June 4 letter to J. E. Calkins: "All my notes— a huge pile are here—the gatherings of a lifetime, & it's hard to move. Only six volumes published as yet out of material for more than a hundred." Writing to Mrs. Osborn a month later he remarks, "I see no way of escape from the work piled on me here—the gatherings of half a century of wilderness wanderings to be sorted & sifted into something like clear useful form."

Muir's literary plans were unusually focused during 1913. His letters consistently confirm the intention he described in a May letter to Mina Merrill, whose family had nursed Muir as he lay in blindness in Indianapolis in 1867: "I'm now at work on an Alaska book, and as soon as it is off my hands I mean to continue the Autobiography from leaving the university to botanical excursions in the northern woods, around Indianapolis, and thence to Florida, Cuba and California. This will be volume Number 2." Muir even wrote to Houghton Mifflin, the publishers of the first volume of his autobiography, to let them know that he thought he would be "ready to take up the next book in the 'Autobiography' series sometime in 1914."

Unfortunately for Muir's literary ambitions and legacy, work on the Alaska book—and work toward any future books—ground to a halt during 1913. As of October 1912, when he attended a national parks convention in Yosemite, Muir had once again become deeply involved in fighting the Hetch Hetchy battle—a seemingly eternal battle that had intensified, consuming most of his time and energy during 1913. Muir's correspondence from 1913 is not only full of Hetch Hetchy business, but is also regularly punctuated by references to the Hetch Hetchy battle as a trial that is "sadly interrupting my own natural work." Muir's fatigue with fighting for Hetch Hetchy and his frustration with interruption of his writing projects intensified along with his determination to save the Valley. But Muir remained willing, as he had been for nearly a half century, to make the personal sacrifice necessary to try to protect Yosemite. By mid-November he wrote to Helen that "I still think we will win. Anyhow I'll be relieved when it's settled for it's killing me. No matter I've had a grand life in these divine mountains & I may well do something for those coming after me."

Unfortunately for Muir and his preservationist allies, on December 6 the US Senate passed the Raker Bill—which removed Hetch Hetchy from Yosemite National Park and gave it to the city of San Francisco for damming as a water reservoir—and on December 19 President Wilson's signature sealed the Valley's fate. Just after Christmas 1913, Muir wrote to his friends the Kelloggs that "[a]s to the loss of the Sierra Park Valley it's hard to bear. The destruction of the charming groves & gardens the finest in all California goes to my heart. But in spite of Satan & Co.," Muir affirmed, "some sort of compensation must surely come out of even this dark damn-dam-damnation."

Not only had the Hetch Hetchy loss gone to his heart, but 1914, Muir's final year, began poorly. He became quite ill during the first months of the year and was unhappily confined to the cold, empty Martinez ranch house. Despite his troubles, Muir demonstrated a remarkable emotional resiliency, and it was most often Muir who wrote the consoling letters assuring friends that the Hetch Hetchy struggle, though lost, had not been in vain. By early spring he was feeling somewhat better, and was hard at work again on the Alaska book. According to Marion Randall Parsons, who served Muir as secretary during much of 1914, he often worked from seven o'clock in the morning until ten at night, taking breaks only to play with his grandchildren, who lived with their parents in the adobe house on the ranch property. Parsons later commented on "the freshness and vigor of his whole outlook on life." Muir's intellectual and literary abilities remained unimpaired, and "[n]o trace of pessimism or despondency, even in the defeat of his most deeply cherished hopes, ever darkened his beautiful philosophy," she recalled.

Typical of Muir's resilience was his surprising decision, in the fall of 1914, to fix up the old house, which had received almost no attention since his wife's death nine years earlier. He cleaned up the home's sixteen rooms and even had electricity installed. Next, he went to San Francisco and, with the help of his friend Charlotte Kellogg, purchased materials sufficient to completely refurbish the house. After sprucing up the home, Muir got back to work on Alaska, and he worked on the project until mid-December, when he decided to go South to Daggett to visit Helen's family, which now included Helen's third son, John, who had been born in late June.

It was well past midnight when Muir's train arrived at Daggett, where cold winds were blowing hard off the Mojave Desert. Muir developed a cold, which may have exacerbated the lung damage caused by his severe bout with "the grippe" that January, but feeling a bit better the next day, he went back to work on the typescript of the Alaska book. He soon felt worse, however, and the doctors whom Helen called in diagnosed double pneumonia and instructed that Muir be moved by train to the California Hospital in Los Angeles, where he was admitted just before midnight on December 23. After a brief rally the following morning, during which he joked with doctors and asked for his Alaska typescript in case he should feel well enough to work on it, he took a final turn for the worse. John Muir died peacefully, with his unfinished manuscripts within reach, on Christmas Eve, 1914.

Correspondence

New York City
April 12, 1912
Merrill Moores

Dear Merrill, Charles, and all your great family,[1]

You know how I sympathize with you in your bereavement. The sad news came this morning and stirred a thousand blessed dearly cherished memories—your mother's great kindness when I was in darkness, and her sisters and all you children when you were young—reading for me, bringing flowers and love into my dark room. Never in all my wanderings in all these years has anything in the least dimmed the love light of that blessed Indiana Moores-Merrill-Graydon lang syne.

    God bless and comfort you,

        John Muir

---

[1] Merrill Moores (1856–1929), a successful attorney and for a decade a Congressman from Indiana, was ten years old when JM, then a young sawyer, met him in Indianapolis in the spring of 1866. Moores was a nephew of Catharine Merrill, to whom JM was introduced by a letter from Professor James Davie Butler of the University of Wisconsin. Young Merrill Moores also traveled with JM when JM returned home to Wisconsin in 1867, before leaving on his thousand-mile walk. Charles is Merrill's brother, Charles Washington Moores, Jr. (1862–1923). JM considered the family "great" for a number of reasons, not the least of which was the comfort they had given him while he was convalescing from the March 1867 industrial accident that left him temporarily blind. In addition to the Moores and Merrill families, the Graydon family also lived nearby and were great friends to JM; thus, the "Moores-Merrill-Graydon lang syne" refers to JM's fond memories of the kindness of these families during his trials in Indianapolis. The letter itself is written to console Merrill Moores for the recent death of his mother, Julia Dumont Merrill Moores (1829–1912), who had shown JM particular kindness in his hour of need.

New York
April 15, 1912
Helen Muir Funk

Darling Helen,

I expect to reach Los Angeles by the Santa Fe Limited next Sunday afternoon at 2:30.[2]

The Yosemite book is out and looks fine. The Autobiography story[3] will be out soon after parts of it are printed in the *Atlantic* or other magazine. I had lots of proofreading, etc. to do on these two books, and am glad they are at last off my hands. I'm looking forward joyfully to seeing you and your wondrous family and Wanda's. Be sure to let Wanda and Mrs. Thompson know I'm coming. I got your letter with Charlotte's. Also had a telegram from Mrs. Sellers. She is at "The Green Hotel," Pasadena, after passing 4 or 5 months in Chicago.

I was so relieved when I got your telegrams.

Good night, darling.

With love to the child and father,

John Muir

———

Martinez, California
April 30, 1912
Dr. Charles E. Rice[4]

Dr. Charles E. Rice,

Going to God's Mountains is going home.

John Muir

———

[2] Muir's train was scheduled to arrive on April 21, 1912, his seventy-fourth birthday.

[3] The Century Company brought out *The Yosemite* in April 1912; the "autobiography story," published as *The Story of My Boyhood and Youth,* would be brought out by Houghton Mifflin in March 1913.

[4] Although JM had a Wisconsin college friend named Rice, the Rice here addressed is almost certainly Dr. Rice the teacher, whom JM met in Santiago, Chile, in November 1911 and whose scholars he addressed on the evening of November 24. Enclosed with this letter is a photograph of JM and President Theodore Roosevelt in Yosemite, inscribed "To Dr. Charles E. Rice with sincere regards."

Martinez, California
May 1, 1912
Mrs. Anna R. Dickey[5]

Dear cheery, exhilarating Mrs. Dickey,

Your fine lost letter has reached me at last. I found it in the big talus heap awaiting me here.

The bright, shining, faithful, hopeful way you bear your crushing burdens is purely divine, out of darkness cheering everybody else with noble God-like sympathy. I'm so glad you have a home with the birds in the evergreen oaks—the feathered folks singing for you and every leaf shining reflecting God's love. Donald, too, is so brave and happy.[6] With youth on his side and joyful work he is sure to grow stronger and under every disadvantage do more as a naturalist than thousands of others with every resource of health and wealth and special training.

I'm in my old library den, the house desolate, nobody living in it save a hungry mouse or two. The girls, to whom it was left by my wife, were trying to sell it to a stranger, so I bought it myself for the sake of the dearly cherished memories about it and the fine garden grounds full of trees and bushes and flowers that my wife and father-in-law and I planted—fine things from every land.

But there's no good bread hereabouts and no housekeeper, so I may never be able to make it a home, fated, perhaps, to wander until sundown. Anyhow I've had a glorious life, and I'll never have the heart to complain. The roses now are overrunning all bounds in glory of full bloom, and the Lebanon and Himalaya cedars, and the palms and Australian trees and shrubs, and the oaks on the valley hills seem happier and more exuberant than ever.

[5] Anna Ryder Dickey was a nature enthusiast and amateur botanist with whom JM had corresponded since 1902. JM had spent some time in the field with Mrs. Dickey, probably on a Sierra Club trip of July and August of that year.

[6] The son of Anna Dickey, Donald Ryder Dickey (1887–1932), studied at Yale and went on to be a distinguished zoologist who gathered over 50,000 specimens of birds and mammals—a collection that for many years was the largest private collection in the United States.

The Chelan trip[7] would be according to my own heart, but whether or no I can go I dinna ken.[8] Only lots of hard pen work seems certain. Anywhere, anyhow, with love to Donald, I am,

Ever faithfully, affectionately yours,

John Muir

———

Martinez, California
May 6, 1912
Katharine Hooker

Dear Mrs. Hooker,

You will find the missing trees in the new edition of *The Mountains of California*,[9] a copy of which goes to you today by mail.

The news that Fred is going East is good, telling returning health. But that you and Marian, celestial twins, are going north about the time I'll be going south is according to the eternal unfitness of mundane things. We must look, it seems, somewhere in the sky for a permanent meeting place. Heavens! What long unblazed trails through starry space friends have to trace to get together. Anyhow let's be hopeful and grateful for the good ante-death days we have enjoyed.

I took a dusty sore throat cold in my den about a week ago, and until today haven't been able to speak above a choking whisper. Am now getting better.

Ever affectionately,

John Muir

———

[7] In an undated May 1912 letter (I/A/20/11688), Mrs. Dickey wrote to JM, "If you go a-traveling to Chelan or any point of less altitude, do let us know so we may tag, and wherever you are in these parts when Mrs. Hooker is absent, we should love to have you pitch your tent 'at-the-end-of-the-trail' where the Dickey-birds live."

[8] This Scots expression, which means "do not know," was one JM often used.

[9] In an undated May 1912 letter (I/A/20/11692), Katharine Hooker had expressed disappointment that several pictures of trees that she had provided JM did not appear in JM's book *The Yosemite*. "As for me," wrote Hooker, "I almost wept when I discovered those two tree pictures were not in the Yosemite book!" As JM's response makes clear, Hooker's pictures were published not in *The Yosemite*, but rather in the 1912 edition of *The Mountains of California* (first published in 1894).

Martinez, California
May 10, 1912
Charles S. Sargent[10]

Dear Sargent,

I'm very glad you are so hopefully recovering from your dangerous crushing accident.

I made a lot of pencil sketches of *Araucaria brasiliensis,* but got no good photographs. I hope to get some, however, for several of the mill workmen in the Parana forests promised to send me as many as I liked as soon as they obtain a supply of films.

I brought home flowers and young cones, but none mature, as it was in Mid-October when I was in the woods. Perhaps I can get some of the workmen to carefully wire and pack a boxful. If successful I'll divide with you.

I had a glorious trip both in S. America and Africa, notes of which I hope to write soon and will send copy.[11]

With kindest regards to all the family I am,

Ever faithfully yours,

John Muir

———

[10] Charles S. Sargent (1841–1927) was a horticulturist, botanical collector, and writer of considerable talent and renown. He served as the first director of the Arnold Arboretum in Boston, and he introduced a number of Asian plants to American horticulture. Like JM, he was a devoted student of trees, and he accompanied JM on part of JM's 1903–04 world tour.
[11] Within two months of writing this letter JM had indeed written up his notes of the South America and Africa trip, and he had had Henrietta Thompson prepare the typescript of the notes in duplicate. However, it appears unlikely that JM actually sent the duplicate copy to Sargent. Sargent's papers, which are housed at the Arnold Arboretum Libraries and the University Archives at Harvard University, do not include the TMS of JM's notes, nor do they contain any subsequent letter from JM to Sargent.

Martinez, California
May 10, 1912
William Trelease[12]

My dear Trelease,

I'm glad to learn you are now free to go your own flowery way while yet young and able. Happy man! Burdened only with blessed good luck. May you live to be a hundred years young. Anyhow you will live forever in your works. I often think of our Alaska days. Nothing found in them has given greater pleasure than yourself.

I've just returned from a grand trip in South America and Africa. Found lots of good botany and geology. Hoping to see you ere long, I am with good wishes,

Ever faithfully your friend,
John Muir

———

Martinez, California
May 10, 1912
William Trout[13]

Dear William Trout,

In trying to clear away the huge talus of letters a year high accumulated while I was in South America and Africa I find your long interesting letter of March 15th full of good news. I'm always glad to hear from you. Friends get closer and dearer the farther they travel on life's journey. It's fine to see how youthful your heart remains, and how wide and far reaching your sympathy with everybody and everything. Such people never grow old. I only regret your being held so long in mechanical bread win-

---

[12] Dr. William Trelease, Director of the Missouri Botanical Garden in St. Louis, was one of the scientists who traveled with JM on the 1899 Harriman expedition to Alaska.

[13] JM's old friend William Trout was the operator of the sawmill and rake and broom factory near Meaford, Canada, where JM worked between 1864 and 1866; JM had lived with the Trout family while he was a factory employee, until the factory burned down in March 1866.

Muir with fellow naturalist John Burroughs, on April 3, 1912, Burroughs's seventy-fifth birthday; Muir would turn seventy-four a few weeks later, on April 21

ning harness instead of making enough by middle age and spending the better half of life in studying God's works as I wanted you to do long ago. The marvel is that in the din and rattle of mills you have done so wondrous well. By all means keep on your travels since you know so well how to reap their benefits. I shall hope to see you when next you come West. And don't wait until the Canal Years.[14] Delays are more and more dangerous as sundown draws nigh.

I've just returned from a long fruitful trip. First up the Amazon a thou-

[14] JM's reference is to the Panama Canal, which was nearing completion by 1912. JM's comment that his friend should not wait until the canal years to visit because "delays are more and more dangerous as sundown draws nigh" proved prophetic: Trout did not visit JM, and the Panama Canal was completed on August 15, 1914, just a few months before JM's death.

sand miles and return to Para. Thence to Rio de Janeiro, thence to Santos and inland four or five hundred miles in the state of Parana. Thence back to the coast at Paranagua, thence to Buenos Aires stopping at many interesting ports by the way. Thence across the Andes to Santiago, thence south 500 miles and up through grand forests to the snow where I found *Araucaria imbricata*, a wonderful tree forming the strangest woods imaginable. Thence back across the Andes and Argentina to Montevideo. Thence to Teneriffe, thence to Cape Town, Africa. Thence 1,300 miles Northward to Victoria Falls, where I found *Adansonia digitata*, another wonderful tree. Thence to the East Coast at Beira, thence to Mozambique, Zanzibar, etc., to Mombasa. Thence to Victoria Nyanza, Entebbe, Jinji, to the head of the Nile, thence back to Mombasa, around the N. end of the continent[15] to Aden and home by the Red Sea and Naples and New York, thus crossing the equator six times on a journey about 40,000 miles long. Hope to tell you about it some day. In the meantime I am,

   Ever faithfully your friend,
      John Muir

———

Hollywood, California
June 10, 1912
Robert Underwood Johnson

My dear Johnson,
   Never mind the $100 Soda Springs money.[16] We have already raised enough so that Mr. Colby, Mr. Parsons and myself can easily complete the sum required.

---

[15] It is actually the eastern tip of the African continent—at Ras Asir—around which JM sails to 'Adan. Ras Asir is, however, the northernmost point in present-day Somalia.

[16] In early May, JM, along with Parsons, Colby, and Le Conte, had written to Sierra Club members asking for $100 from each, that they might raise the $5,000 necessary to purchase 160 acres around Soda Springs as a buffer to help protect Yosemite National Park (see, for example, I/A/20/11643).

I very much enjoyed your editorial from the June number.[17] I am working on my Amazon notes and will soon be able to tell you if I can get something out of it to make the articles you wish.

Ever faithfully yours,

John Muir

————

Hollywood, California
June 10, 1912
Charles Lummis[18]

Dear Lummis,

I first heard the sad news of your blindness from our blessed old friend, Francis Browne, and as I was at one time threatened with blindness, and was blind for several weeks, I know what that darkness is and am able to sympathize with you.[19]

After my return from a long trip in South America and Africa I have yet found no permanent home or abiding place as yet. But no matter, I shall pay you a visit as soon as I can find my way to you.

I am very glad that you can write, as you say, better than ever. You have seen a great part of the world so well that you can recall it almost as if you were again enjoying God's sunshine.

With all good wishes I am,

Ever faithfully,

John Muir

————

[17] JM here refers to Johnson's editorial from the June 1912 issue of *Century Magazine* (vol. 84, no. 2), "The People's National Parks" (pgs. 313–14), which argued eloquently for the protection of Yosemite's Hetch Hetchy Valley.

[18] JM had met the southwestern author, editor, preservationist, and Native American rights activist Charles Fletcher Lummis (1859–1928) at the studio of his artist friend William Keith.

[19] This sympathetic letter alludes of course to JM's temporary blindness in the wake of the industrial accident that befell him in Indianapolis in March 1867.

Hollywood, California
June 12, 1912
J. E. Calkins [20]

Dear Mr. Calkins,

I have often thought of you since I returned and I assure you that you are far from any danger of being forgotten.

As you say, I have had a grand saunter over two continents, and have had wonderful success not only in finding what I was looking for in particular, but a great deal that I was not looking for and did not expect to see. I am now writing up some of my notes, but it is a long job to get them in anything like shape, and a harder job than traveling, even in those hot countries like Brazil and Rhodesia, and the equatorial regions at the head of the Nile.

I am going to try and get to see you some time when I need a rest, but cannot get away so easily as I used to, since my good old friends, Mr. Hooker and Colonel Sellers, have passed away. [21]

In the meantime, hoping that you all enjoy your California home among the oranges, I am, with thanks for your kind letter and invitation,

Cordially yours,

John Muir

———

[20] J. E. Calkins was an Iowa newspaperman whom JM had met around 1906, when Calkins and his wife, who were considering moving to California, visited JM in Martinez. JM, whose wife, Louie, had died in 1905 and who was then living alone in the big house with Helen, invited Calkins and his wife to share the home, but Helen's poor health prevented the plan from going into effect. The Calkins family later moved to a small home in the country town of San Dimas, east of Los Angeles—the "home among the oranges" where JM occasionally visited them.

[21] Because Hooker and Sellers often hosted and helped JM when he was in southern California—and because Calkins himself is in San Dimas, east of Los Angeles—JM's point is that the death of these men has made his own travels to southern California less frequent and more difficult.

Hollywood, California
June 20, 1912
Mr. Aimers

My dear Aimers,

I arrived home in blessed California in a little over a year after leaving it, after a grand time in your South America and in Africa. Here is an outline sketch of the whole trip, some of the brightest spots of which I owe to your kindness.

After a few extremely interesting days in and about Rio de Janeiro I went to Santos. Thence into the interior of the State of Parana, where I found extensive forests of the magnificent *Araucaria braziliensis,* a species that I have long wished to see growing in its native primeval woods. Thence I returned by way of Curetiba to the Port of Paranagua and sailed thence to Montevideo and Buenos Aires, touching at a great many interesting ports by the way. The mountains remarkably bold, and show glacial features on a grand scale all the way to Santa Catarina and some distance beyond. From Buenos Aires I crossed the Andes to Santiago, Chile, looking for another tree that I had had on my mind for a long time. After a long search I at last discovered it, the *Araucaria imbricata,* five hundred miles south of Santiago near the snowline, where it forms most striking woods. Thence returning to Buenos Aires I crossed over to Montevideo and saw something of the country to the northward for a few days.

At Montevideo I wanted to go to Cape Town. Had to go to Teneriffe to catch a steamer from England. This made a very long roundabout voyage of thirty-two days.[22] From Cape Town I went to the Victoria Falls on the Zambesi, a distance of about thirteen hundred miles. When a short distance from the famous falls I found another great tree that I had long desired to see, the baobab, a wonderful fellow. Found it also at Zanzibar, at Des er Salaam, and at Mombasa. From Victoria Falls I went down to Southern Rhodesia to Beira on the East coast. Thence to Mombasa.

[22] Actually, JM's South America to Africa voyage lasted thirty-five days; or, if his night in Tenerife on December 26, 1911, is excepted, thirty-four.

Thence by rail up through the game region where Roosevelt hunted. Saw thousands of antelopes and zebras on the Athi plains, etc., etc. Thence to Port Florence on the Victoria Nyanza, a region I had long wished to see. Thence to the lower end of the Great Lake to Entebbe, Kampali, and Jinji, and in a short walk from Jinji I saw the remarkable Ripon Falls, the outlet of the lake and main head fountain of the famous Nile. Saw the river starting on its long journey of between three and four thousand miles. Thence returned to Mombasa where I got another steamer and sailed for Naples around by the Red Sea. From Naples, after visiting the famous Vesuvius, Pompeii, and sailing from point to point on the beautiful bay, I sailed to New York, and thence had only the continent to cross to get home.

I am now writing up some notes, but when they will be ready for publication I do not know. I will be glad to send you a copy but it will be a long time before anything is arranged in book form.

I hope you are well, and when you get tired of your wonderful river[23] and its rubber I shall hope to see you in California. In the meantime write me a long letter and give me all the news you can gather about the good people I met. Of course you know that I shall be glad to get any photographs of Brazilian trees you may chance to get.[24] After hearing from you I shall take pleasure in sending you my Yosemite book which has just been published.

With kindest remembrances to all the good people who were so kind to me in Para, and with all good wishes, dear Aimers, I am,

Ever faithfully yours,

John Muir

––––––––––

[23] The Amazon, where JM had met Aimers in Pará in mid-September, 1911.
[24] In an effort to gather illustrations for several articles he intended to write for *Century Magazine,* JM requested photographs from many of his South American and African contacts; ultimately his inability to gather sufficient publishable illustrations was a factor in dissuading him from writing the articles.

Hollywood, California
July 2, 1912
Katharine Hooker

Dear friend,

I was hoping to get another glimpse of you on your return from San Diego until Mrs. Dickey sent word that you had hurried back north. What a load of good work and good pleasure you must be carrying these eventful days. All this southland seems lonely since you left it. From Hollywood the big Eddy science dome[25] is sometimes dimly visible through sea fog and dust, and it marks for me the location of the West Adams home where so many memorable days and weeks and months were spent.

I've been at work here on my African and S. American notes, and Mrs. Thompson has made duplicate typewritten copies of them all. The *Century* editor wants three or four articles out of them, but I don't see much readily available magazine stuff in them, excepting perhaps the Amazon, the *Araucaria* forests of Chile and Brazil, the Mombasa and Zambesi Baobabs, and the Victoria Nyanza. Besides, I'm unsettled as yet. Helen's bungalow is too small for word work, and I'm half or more inclined to seek a short rest and try to get rid of mind rust and dust cough in icy Alaska or the ever-blessed Sierra.

My love to you, dear friend, and to all who love you,

John Muir

Martinez, California
July 30, 1912
Katharine Hooker

Dear Katharine Hooker,

I don't believe you half know how glad good tidings from you make me. Your interesting excursion to the edge of Mexico[26] is so full of good things

[25] The dome of the Second Church of Christ Scientist, which is still in use today, on the corner of Hoover and Adams streets in Los Angeles. "Eddy" is Mary Baker Eddy (1821–1910), who founded the Christian Science movement in 1866.

[26] On July 10, Hooker had written to JM describing her adventures during a recent automobile trip in southern California (I/A/20/11727).

it might easily be enlarged to a magazine article that would be more read-able than anything I could write on Africa or South America. Motoring over oak-dotted valleys and little mountains with a crowd of admiring friends and a shovel and coffee pot, drowning the engine in a small San Diego Amazon, scrambling down precipices, etc., must have been pictur-esque and exciting and not altogether dangerless. But it's well known nothing can stop you in love-work for friends.

I too have been on a crooked high and low gasoline trip from Los Angeles to San Francisco, by way of Santa Barbara, Paso Robles, the giant forest of the Kaweah, and Yosemite, a long journey which accounts for delay in reply to your letter.

A trip to Alaska or anywhere with Ellie and Maude[27] would be accord-ing to my own heart. Fate however seldom allows hearts to have their own way. Just now from every direction grim work is staring me hard in the face crying "'twill soon be dark,"[28] and urging concentration and haste. And alas the advice seems reasonable.

I'm in my little library den looking over notes, plotting and planning and trying to get the lonely old house into something like order, though how long I'll stay in it I dinna ken, or where I'll settle and cease from wan-dering.

God be with you all.

Love to your blessed clan,

John Muir

---

[27] Ellie Mosgrove was a close friend of the Hooker family, whom she often visited and with whom she traveled; Mosgrove first met JM on a Sierra Club outing in the summer of 1902, and she continued to write to him from that fall until his death in 1914. "Maude" may be Maude Thomas, who is mentioned in a letter Mosgrove wrote to JM on October 9, 1914 (I/A/22/12958).

[28] A line from Ralph Waldo Emerson's poem "To J. W.," which JM admired and which he often quoted to friends. JM transcribed the verse of the poem containing this line in a December 1913 letter to Loulu Perry Osborn (I/A/21/12552).

Martinez, California
August 2, 1912
Robert Underwood Johnson

Dear Mr. Johnson,

Your letters of July 6th and 23d and 26th reached me only a day or two ago because I was away on a trip to the Giant forest of the Kaweah and Yosemite. I'm glad you are going to cool Canada after Owen's long dangerous illness.[29]

I had duplicate typewritten copies of my S. American and African notes made before leaving Los Angeles and I find that without a lot of good photographs suitable magazine articles cannot be got out of them, at least in a reasonable time. Therefore I'm sorry to say don't count on me. I have three good photos of the Victoria Falls and a few rather poor ones of the Baobab. Of the Amazon I have none worth anything as illustrations. I have written to friends in Para and Manaos to try to obtain river and forest views for me at any cost. Also to Buenos Aires and Victoria for Argentina and Chile views. Am promised a lot, but when I'll get them or what like they will be none can know. Possibly views of Rio may be obtained in New York.

As to the Freeman report[30] here is all I have as yet seen of it.

Your reply to the *Call* is capital.[31]

---

[29] Robert Underwood and Katherine McMahon Johnson's son Owen McMahon Johnson (1878–1952) went on to become a prolific novelist, journalist, playwright, and politician. At the time of JM's letter Owen would have been thirty-four years old and already the author of nine books; he would publish fourteen more books before his death in 1952. Though Owen was educated at Yale and raised among the social elite, many of his most accomplished novels are explicitly critical of the "snob rule" that he saw operating in American high society.

[30] The "Freeman report" was the work of John R. Freeman, an engineer from Rhode Island, who had been called in by the City of San Francisco to evaluate their plan to acquire Hetch Hetchy Valley as a water source for the city. Freeman's report, which JM had not yet seen, was a 401-page document (entitled *The Hetch Hetchy Water Supply for San Francisco*) which, perhaps not surprisingly, supported the city's argument that Hetch Hetchy should be converted to use as a water reservoir. For further discussion of the Freeman report and the Sierra Club's response to it, see Jones (chapters 4–6).

[31] JM is congratulating Johnson on his recently published editorial in the *Call*—an editorial arguing for the protection of Yosemite National Park. Johnson enclosed a copy of the two-page editorial with his July 6, 1912, letter to JM (I/A/20/11722). An influential editor, effective advocate for national parks, and staunch defender of Yosemite, Johnson often wrote such editorials.

Good luck to you on your Canada rest trip. Don't worry about those hot continents.[32]

Ever Faithfully Yours,
    John Muir

———

Martinez, California
August 14, 1912
Enos Mills [33]

My dear Mr. Mills,

I am glad to hear of your continued good health and good work in the cause of saving samples of God's best mountain handiwork for the benefit of humanity and all our fellow mortals vertical or horizontal.[34] Strange that the Government is so slow to learn the value of parks.

I'm quite well and had a good time abroad, though hard.

It was on what is now called "the Brady Glacier" that Stickeen was so terribly tried.[35]

With all good wishes I am,
Faithfully Yours,
    John Muir

———

[32] This is JM's way of telling Johnson not to be too anxious about receiving South America and Africa articles from him.

[33] In many ways, Coloradan, author, climber, and wilderness advocate Enos Abijah Mills (1870–1922) was JM's successor as the leader of the American preservation movement, and in JM's late letters one can sense the torch passing from JM to the next generation of environmental activists. Mills was inspired to his work by JM's books and public service, and he considered JM his personal hero; indeed, Mills's life and career rather self-consciously followed JM's path, and it has been accurately observed that Mills "wanted to become the John Muir of the Rockies" (Wild 73). Ever since meeting Mills in 1889, JM had encouraged the young man, thirty years his junior, toward preservationist work. Mills succeeded admirably, and, in addition to publishing a number of respectable books, could also take considerable credit for the establishment of Glacier National Park in 1910 and Rocky Mountain National Park in 1915.

[34] That is, both human and nonhuman animals.

[35] The story of the famous dog Stickeen, and his adventures with JM on Alaska's Brady Glacier, is told in JM's book *Stickeen,* published by Houghton Mifflin in March 1909.

Martinez, California
August 24, 1912
Robert Underwood Johnson

Dear Johnson,

I've written to Colby asking him to send you all the clippings on Hetch Hetchy affairs likely to be useful to you in writing your *Century* editorial.

As to the Amazon-African articles, I thought I had explained that I would not be able to write them at the time you wanted them and that I was not to be depended on, though you should know how glad I'd be to serve you. I'm trying to obtain more photographs. It may be more than a year before any of the above stuff is ready for you. In the meantime I'm working on Alaska.

With best wishes,
Faithfully Yours,
John Muir

———

Martinez, California
August [26], 1912
Helen Muir Funk

Darling Helen,

You know how the terrible trials you have been called on to endure distress me, and how great was the relief when assured at the close of your letter that the worst was over and you were on the way to hopeful health again. Spare no expense for help in the house and feel assured I'll stand by you to any extent. And if my presence is wanted telegraph a word and I'll leave everything and take the first train to you.

When I left you I expected to be with you again within a few weeks. But when I got among my notebooks and manuscripts and began planning new volumes for the press the work seemed endless, while moving everything south seems an almost insurmountable difficulty. Nevertheless Darling all this is nothing weighed against your welfare. Send a word and I'll be with you.

In any case ask Buel to send a line of a dozen words or so every day, that I may be able to know how you are as if I were with you.

God bless you darling.

So prays your loving father,

John Muir

———

Martinez, California
September 11, 1912
Katharine M. Graydon[36]

Dear Miss Graydon,

I greatly enjoyed your good letter so full of dear lang syne times. I should have enjoyed more than I can tell a week or two with you all. But after wandering over two continents a thousand voices were calling me home. How delightful your college work must be, right at home in your own town—reveling in literature like a bee in honey bloom.

No great changes are visible in our little valley—only a new house here and there and weeds in the vineyard that I used to cultivate. The Reids, the Colemans, and Swetts are well.[37] So are Wanda and Helen with their five boys. Helen with her two lives in Los Angeles. Brother David in Pacific Grove.

---

[36] Katharine Merrill Graydon, to whom JM later referred as "my dear, frail, wee, bashful lassie and dear madam" (Badè, *Life* 250), was one of the children who read to JM and brought him flowers during his convalescence in blindness in Indianapolis during 1867. "Katie" Graydon went on to become a professor of Greek and English literature, hence JM's reference to "your college work," and it was Graydon who later introduced JM to naturalist David Starr Jordan. In this letter JM is responding to Graydon's letter of August 29, 1912 (I/A/20/11800).

[37] The Reids, Colemans, and Swetts were JM's Martinez neighbors. May Reid Coleman was JM's niece and was married to Arthur Coleman, JM's business manager at the Martinez ranch. JM's brother David Gilrye Muir (1840–1916) had moved West in 1892, after the bankruptcy of his general merchandise firm, Parry & Muir, in Portage, Wisconsin. David first came to the Alhambra Valley and helped work the Martinez ranch, and later settled in Pacific Grove, California, on Monterey Bay.

I'm in my old library den all alone, looking over a hundred or more old notebooks and manuscript scraps, planning new books. I've not written a word on my foreign travels as yet. May in a year or two. Am now at work on Alaska. A first volume of my Autobiography will be published soon—next winter or spring.

Give my love to Mina and your mother, brother and sisters, Charley and Merrill Moores and Hendricks.

Your affectionate friend,

John Muir

Muir, playing with his grandchildren

[Martinez, California]
October [16], 1912
Telegram sent to Theodore Roosevelt in Mercy Hospital, Chicago

Col. Theodore Roosevelt,

I congratulate you and the nation on your providential escape,[38] and with profound sympathy pray for your quick recovery.

John Muir

———

San Francisco, California
October 25, 1912
Mrs. [Mary Muir] Willis Hand [39]

Dear Mary,

I would like to visit you all but it is impossible for me to do so, I am so overloaded with work. If my visits are few and far between, so also are yours, in fact none of the scattered family ever come to visit me. I suppose for the same reason that you are not able to do so. You have no idea what a lot of work I have on hand. The book you referred to, *Yosemite*, is easily obtainable from any of the booksellers. Another book, the first volume of

[38] Theodore Roosevelt, whom JM considered a friend, was shot during an assassination attempt on October 14, 1912, while campaigning as a third-party candidate for a third term as president. While leaving his hotel and entering a waiting car, Roosevelt was shot by John F. Schrank, a mentally unstable anti-third-term extremist, from less than thirty feet away. The bullet penetrated Roosevelt's overcoat, glasses case, and the manuscript of his speech before lodging in his ribs. Roosevelt tried to cough blood and, when he could not, assumed he would survive the shot. He ordered the gathering crowd not to harm the assailant, but instead to bring him forward. Roosevelt stared the man down, eye to eye, before proceeding to his previously scheduled speaking engagement at a political rally. At the rally Roosevelt pulled the manuscript out of his bloodied coat, showed the bullet hole to the crowd, and spoke for an hour and a half before seeking medical attention. After an X-ray exam he was moved to Chicago's Mercy Hospital, where he remained for six days. JM's telegram is undated; the conjectural date of October 16 is likely to be correct within a few days, given the timing of the event, the speed with which such news was then disseminated, and the urgency of JM's message.

[39] JM's younger sister Mary (1846–1928), the sixth of the eight Muir children and the twin of Annie Muir (1846–1903), married Willis Hand in 1878. In this letter JM, who at the time felt lonely as he struggled with his projects while living along in the big house, responds with mild frustration to his sister's complaint that he has not visited recently.

a sort of autobiography, will be out in the spring. Am now at work on an Alaska book and others. Have notes enough for more than a hundred volumes, but of course I won't live long enough to write that many.

Am always glad to hear from you and to get news of all the family.

Ever your devoted brother,

John Muir

Martinez, California
December 28, 1912
Katharine and Marian Hooker

Dear Twins,

Your gifts—involucre, corolla, and book—arrived in fine order, and they are making my den shine and my head blossom like your Los Angeles garden, hopefully foreshadowing a happy new year for,

Your friend,

John Muir

Martinez, California
December 29, 1912
Charles Dwight Willard [40]

Dear Mr. Willard,

I treasure your noble letter as the best of my New Year blessings. I have been one of your many admirers from the first day we met, and admiration has been growing ever greater as I saw how bravely you held on your way against deadly odds, digging hard and deep for bedrock foundations, mak-

---

[40] Charles Dwight Willard (1860–1914) was a journalist, historian, booster, and political reformer in Los Angeles. Nicknamed "Citizen Fixit" by fellow Angelinos, Willard was at the vanguard of many of the most important of the city's progressive reform efforts during the late nineteenth and early twentieth centuries. So active was he in L.A. politics that members of the city council often referred to him as the "Member from the Tenth Ward" during a time when there were but nine wards in the city. Willard became very ill with tuberculosis in 1912 and died on his fifty-fourth birthday, January 22, 1914.

ing ladders out of disease and pain, climbing higher into the calm heights of life, like God's strong soaring pine trees, going straight to the heavens, nourished by their own decaying branches and leaves. The lesson of your life all should read, for in it there are some of the finest and divinest things humanity has to show. Made into a book it could not fail to awaken and encourage many poor drowsy, forespent wanderers on Life's hard roads. For, as Thoreau well says, there are infinite degrees of life from that which is next to sleep and death to that which is ever awake and immortal.[41]

To all who know you, Mr. Willard, you are a hero. I admire and love you, and with warmest enthusiasm congratulate you on the victories you have won in these hard fought battles. May dear God guide and cheer and comfort you all the rest of your way home to the world of Light, so devoutly prays,

Your friend,

John Muir

---

[41] JM's allusion is to a line in Thoreau's journal, January 13, 1857: "There are infinite degrees of life, from that which is next to sleep and death, to that which is forever awake and immortal." JM, a great admirer of Thoreau, read and annotated the entire twenty-volume, 1906 edition of *The Writings of Henry David Thoreau* (Boston: Houghton Mifflin).

APPENDICES

Timeline / Locator

The Timeline/Locator is designed to enable readers to follow the progress of Muir's journey and to identify important activities of each day of the voyage. Rather than simply redacting the information available in the TMS ("typed manuscript") journal, which is sometimes skeletal or elliptical with respect to Muir's activities or the places he visits, the Timeline/Locator combines information from various sources—the TMS journal, the AMS ("autograph manuscript") journal, over 100 letters to and from Muir, and other relevant biographical materials, scraps, memorabilia, sundries, and maps. The aim is to provide the most complete picture possible of Muir's movements and activities during the journey.

Many of the South American and most of the African place names Muir employed have since changed. To allow readers to connect old and new place names throughout the Timeline/Locator the current place name is used, but upon first use it is followed by the place name Muir uses, which appears in quotation marks within parentheses. For further discussion of the details of tracing Muir's movements and the construction of this apparatus, please refer to Appendix B, Editorial Methods.

1911

12 Aug.	Leaves Brooklyn, New York, at 11:00 a.m. on the Booth Line steamship *Dennis,* which stops for several hours at the Statue of Liberty before proceeding south along the Atlantic coast.
13 Aug.	Enters Chesapeake Bay and arrives at 4:00 p.m. in Norfolk, Virginia, where the ship takes on a load of coal.
14 Aug.	In port at Norfolk, the *Dennis* coaling up and trimming.
15 Aug.	Leaves Norfolk at 11:00 p.m., southbound for Barbados ("Barbadoes").
16–20 Aug.	Southbound through the tropical Atlantic, into the Caribbean, and along the Lesser Antilles.
21 Aug.	Passes to the west of St. Kitts ("Christopher Island") during the day, and sails past Martinique at about midnight.
22 Aug.	Crosses through the Lesser Antilles from the Caribbean back into

the Atlantic, arriving at Barbados at 3:30 p.m., with time to record some impressions of the agriculture, geographical features, and trees of the region before departing the island three hours later, southbound for the Amazon.

23–27 Aug. At sea, southbound for the Amazon delta. JM crosses the equator for the first time on his journey at about 6:00 p.m. on the 27th.

28 Aug. Arrives Belém ("Para"), Brazil, at 4:00 p.m. and spends the night aboard ship.

29 Aug. Calls on American Consul in Belém and writes letters in preparation to begin journey up Amazon.

30 Aug. In the morning delivers letters to Consul, changes money, and studies ferns, palms, and the *Victoria regia* in the Botanical Gardens. In the afternoon visits with Mr. F. H. Sanford, Mr. Ross, and others, and visits the city's park. Dines with Mr. Ross and Mr. Southgate and returns to the *Dennis* around 9:00 p.m.

31 Aug. In the morning returns to the Botanical Gardens, where he studies flowering trees, and also visits the Zoological Gardens, where he observes the behavior of monkeys. Returns to the *Dennis* and in the afternoon begins the journey to the Amazon.

1 Sept. Rises at 4:00 a.m. to observe the scenery along the banks. The *Dennis* proceeds up the Pará River, anchoring at 7:00 a.m. in "the Narrows" separating the Pará River from the Amazon proper before proceeding up the latter.

2 Sept. Travels up the Amazon toward Manaus ("Manoas"), noting what he sees along the way. Passes old Portuguese village of Santarém ("Santarem") about 10:00 p.m.

3 Sept. Passes old Portuguese village of Obidos in the morning, and continues up the Amazon.

4 Sept. Arrives Itacoatiara ("Itisoatiara"), near the mouth of the Madeira River, about 10:00 a.m. Bids farewell to many of his fellow passengers, who are going up the Madeira, to its navigable terminus at Porto Velho, to work on the Madeira River Railroad.

5 Sept. Arrives Manaus ("Manoas"), near the mouth of the Rio Negro, about 9:00 a.m.

6 Sept. Remains aboard the *Dennis* in port.

7 Sept. In morning goes ashore with Mr. Sanford, rides trolley to the Flores district, and walks in the forest. Has brunch at the home of Col. May (one of the builders of the Madeira River Railroad), who takes him for an automobile ride around town in the afternoon. Meets Mr. Suabi, who offers to take JM on a Sunday adventure upriver to see the *Victoria regia*. JM's note leaves some doubt as to whether he had

dinner with Col. May or at the home of Mr. Robardia (agent for the Booth Steamship company). Spends the night at Mr. Sanford's home.

8 Sept.   Remains in Manaus. Breakfast at Mr. Sanford's, and both lunch and dinner at Mr. Robardia's.

9 Sept.   Goes with Mr. Sanford and Mr. Robardia to see the town sawmill, electrical machinery, and foundry. In the afternoon is driven around town by Mr. May, with whom he dines and spends the night.

10 Sept.   Goes with Mr. Sanford, Col. May, May's engineer, and the two Suabi brothers on the Suabi's steam tug across the Rio Negro to the head of a reedy bay. The men board skiffs and make their way up an igarepa in an unsuccessful attempt to reach a remote lagoon in order to see *Victoria regia*. Spends the night at Mr. Sanford's.

11 Sept.   Back in Manaus all day. Spends the morning at Mr. Sanford's, reading, and discovers Katharine Hooker's 1902 book, *Wayfarers in Italy*, in Sanford's library. In the afternoon travels by trolley to the home of Mr. Gordon (the head of a rubber company), where he dines. Spends the night at Mr. Sanford's.

12 Sept.   In the morning boards the *Dennis* in preparation for return downriver to Belém.

13 Sept.   Continues downriver, passing Obidos at 11:00 a.m.

14 Sept.   The *Dennis* enters "the Narrows" about 8:00 a.m.

15 Sept.   Arrives Belém about 6:00 a.m. and goes ashore with Mr. Aimers, a fellow Scot whom he met aboard the *Dennis*. Draws thirty pounds sterling and, apparently, accepts the invitation of a Mr. Duff to stay at his home.

16 Sept.   In the morning takes tea and then returns to Botanical Gardens, where he resumes study of the trees and plants of the region. Also revisits the *Victoria regia* and notes changes in its growth since he first observed it there on 30 August.

17 Sept.   Spends the day "in the quietest way, reading, etc." Receives letters and telegrams forwarded to Belém by the Osborns.

18 Sept.   Spends most of the day at the Duff home answering letters.

19 Sept.   Writing letters and reviewing Amazon journal notes.

20 Sept.   Reading and planning the logistics of his journey.

21 Sept.   Spends the day studying world geography.

22 Sept.   Takes solitary walk in the city and loses his way for a time. Has otherwise a pleasant day studying trees.

23 Sept.   Spends the day reading South American history and making lists of books he intends to mail back, in thanks, to people who have shown him hospitality during his Brazilian journeys.

24 Sept.   Automobile ride with Mr. Aimers followed by walks in the Park and in the Botanical Gardens.

25 Sept.   Buys steamer ticket, has lunch at the Duff home, packs, and says goodbye to Mr. Duff, Mr. Cole, and others. Boards the *Sao Paulo* around 5:30 p.m.

26 Sept.   The *Sao Paulo* leaves Belém at 8:30 a.m.

27 Sept.   At sea, southbound off the east coast of South America.

28 Sept.   *Sao Paulo* arrives at the port of Fortaleza ("Ceara") and anchors about 11:00 p.m.

29 Sept.   The *Sao Paulo*'s cargo is unloaded and the ship leaves port at 2:30 p.m., but not before JM has had a chance to describe the town.

30 Sept.   At sea, southbound off the eastern tip of South America, with land in sight all day.

1 Oct.   Arrives Recife ("Pernambuco") before daylight, and enters harbor about 6:00 a.m. *Sao Paulo* discharges cargo of flour and petroleum all day.

2 Oct.   *Sao Paulo* takes on cargo of sugar and cotton and departs at about 10:00 p.m.

3 Oct.   At sea, southbound for Salvador ("Bahia Todos Santos").

4 Oct.   Arrives Salvador at 6:00 a.m.

5–6 Oct.   At sea, southbound for Rio de Janeiro ("Rio").

7 Oct.   Arrives Rio de Janeiro at about 7:30 a.m. Goes to Hotel Avanido with Mr. Mendel, takes long walks around the city, and calls upon the American Consul, Mr. Lay.

8 Oct.   In the morning, walks in the rain to the landing to check on Mr. Harell (whom he met on the ship from Belém). After the weather clears, about 1:30 p.m., he travels up Corcovado Mountain by cog railroad.

9 Oct.   Accompanies Mr. Harell and others to the Rio de Janeiro Botanical Gardens. Buys a ticket aboard the steamer *Voltaire* for Santos.

10 Oct.   Boards the *Voltaire* at 8:30 a.m. with Mr. Mendes. Mr. Harell introduces him to Mr. Bouchet, Superintendent of the Paraná Lumber Company, who invites JM to accompany him to a lumber camp in a deep forest of *Araucaria braziliensis* the company owns in the Brazilian state of Paraná, thus saving JM a longer trip up the Uruguay River in search of the tree. Sails for Santos at 5:00 p.m.

11 Oct.   Notes glacial scenery all along coast between Rio and Santos, and admires the view of foam-encircled islands. At 4:00 p.m. arrives in the lovely port of Santos, goes to town with the sawmill party, and lodges in a modest hotel.

12 Oct.	Leaves Santos at 10:15 a.m. by rail, bound northwest for São Paulo. JM finds specimens of *Araucaria braziliensis* growing on the plateau outside São Paulo. He reaches the city at 12:50 p.m. and stays the night in a hotel near the train station.
13 Oct.	Spends day walking around São Paulo in the rain. Leaves town at 4:20 p.m. by rail, southbound for Porto Amazonas ("Port Amazons") on the Iguacu ("Iguassu") River.
14 Oct.	From the train JM views *Araucaria braziliensis* by the thousands, and begins to note specific features of the *Araucaria braziliensis* forests. In the afternoon the landscape begins to open out to wide prairie dotted with discrete groves of *Araucaria braziliensis*. Arrives Porto Amazonas on the Iguacu River, where he spends the night at the home of a Portuguese farmer.
15 Oct.	Leaves Porto Amazonas at 2:30 p.m., traveling down the Iguacu River on the small river steamer *Iguassu*.
16 Oct.	At 8:00 a.m. the *Iguassu* turns up a tributary and travels less than an hour to the lumber mill.
17–23 Oct.	JM spends most of each day in the forest of *Araucaria braziliensis*, making precise observations of the tree's characteristics.
24 Oct.	Leaves the lumber camp about 6:00 p.m., and begins sailing up the lovely Rio Negro (not the Rio Negro that is a main tributary of the Amazon but the very small Rio Negro that is a branch of the Iguacu River, just east of present-day União da Vitória), bound for the village of the same name.
25 Oct.	Arrives in the village of Rio Negro about 6:30 a.m. When train engine breaks down, delaying his scheduled 1:20 p.m. departure for Curitiba ("Curytiba"), JM spends the day further studying the nearby forests of *Araucaria braziliensis*. Train finally leaves Rio Negro at 7:30 p.m.
26 Oct.	After an uncomfortable night, JM arrives in Curitiba at about 2:30 a.m., and observes *Araucaria braziliensis* by starlight as he walks to his hotel. In the morning he walks around town viewing gardens and trees, but feels lonely after bidding farewell to the men he had met during this part of his journey.
27 Oct.	Departs Curitiba at 6:30 a.m., bound by rail for Paranaguá ("Paranaguay"). Continues to study *Araucaria braziliensis* from the train, and praises the glacial scenery along the way. Arrives Paranaguá 10:30 a.m. and goes to Johnsker Hotel, to which he was directed by a German he met in Curitiba. A young English-speaking German in Paranaguá takes JM to a western movie.
28 Oct.	Purchases a ticket to Montevideo aboard the *Sirio*, which is sched-

uled to depart at 3:00 p.m. JM waits in the dark at the wharf and in the bay on a tender during delays, and is not permitted to go aboard until after 9:00 p.m.

29 Oct.   In the very early morning the *Sirio* sails south for Montevideo. The ship arrives about 11:00 a.m. at the village of São Francisco do Sul ("San Francisco") and departs several hours later, arriving at Itajaí ("Ityhaya") about 5:00 p.m., where the *Sirio* lays in port for the night.

30 Oct.   Departs at 4:00 a.m., sailing the strait between the mainland and Santa Catarina Island and arriving at Florianópolis ("Florionopolis") at 11:00 a.m. Departs Florianópolis six hours later.

1 Nov.   The *Sirio* creeps through thick fog into the mouth of the lagoon at Rio Grande ("Rio Grande del Sul"), arriving at the town at about 1:00 p.m. JM remains aboard ship, describing the geological formation of Lagoa dos Patos ("Patos lagoon").

2 Nov.   The *Sirio* remains in port at Rio Grande all day, discharging and taking on cargo and passengers.

3 Nov.   The *Sirio* leaves Rio Grande at about 6:00 a.m., and JM spends the day developing a detailed summary of Brazil's geology, geography, and hydrography.

4 Nov.   Arrives Montevideo, Uruguay, at about noon, and makes his way through customs and to the Grand Hotel Barcelona, where he spends the night.

5 Nov.   Calls upon the American Consul, Mr. Goding, whom JM joins for lunch, a walk in the Montevideo Botanical Gardens, and dinner, before returning to the hotel about 11:00 p.m.

6 Nov.   Spends the day with Mr. Goding, buys a ticket to Buenos Aires, Argentina, and departs aboard a southbound steamer at 10:00 p.m.

7 Nov.   Arrives Buenos Aires at 7:00 a.m., where he passes through customs and goes to the Royal Hotel. Calls upon the American Consul, Mr. Bartleman, who gives him several letters forwarded from Belém. The American Vice-Consul General, Mr. Hazeltine, takes JM to the Buenos Aires Zoological Gardens in the afternoon. JM is also interviewed by Mr. Huxton for the *Buenos Aires Herald.* In the evening he has a long talk with the mountaineer Annie Peck.

8 Nov.   JM draws forty pounds sterling at the bank, after which Mr. Hazeltine takes him to the Consulate, the Legation, and the Agricultural Department. Mr. Huxton calls at JM's hotel to get a photograph to accompany the interview of the previous day.

9 Nov.   Departs Buenos Aires westbound by rail for Santiago, Chile ("Chili"), at 8:20 a.m. Reaches Rufino at 4:30 p.m.

10 Nov.   Continuing west by rail. The foothills of the Andes come into view

at 6:00 a.m. Changes train cars in Mendoza, where he uses a two-hour delay to observe the geology and plants in the area. Departs Mendoza at 9:00 a.m. JM describes the mountain geology he sees as the train climbs the treeless heights of the Andes. Spends the night in Los Andes, at the western foot of the range.

11 Nov.   Departs Los Andes about 6:00 a.m. and arrives Santiago at 10:30 a.m. Takes a cab to the Hotel Oddo, and then visits the American legation. JM lodges with Minister Plenipotentiary Mr. Fletcher, and Fletcher's personal driver takes JM to the Santiago Botanical Gardens, where JM searches without much success for information about where *Araucaria imbricata* might be found growing in the wild.

12 Nov.   JM enjoys the hospitality and books in Mr. Fletcher's home, and he identifies the principal peaks of the Andes from the balcony of his bedroom window.

13 Nov.   JM returns to the Santiago Botanical Gardens in search of further information regarding *Araucaria imbricata* and later meets an educator, Dr. Rice, who suggests that his friend, Mr. Smith, a lumberman and sawmill owner living in Victoria, Chile, might be able to help JM locate *Araucaria imbricata*. Rice makes arrangements for JM to visit Smith.

14 Nov.   JM departs Santiago at 5:40 p.m. by rail for Victoria, 500 miles to the south.

15 Nov.   Arrives Victoria at 9:00 a.m. and is welcomed by the Smiths.

16–17 Nov. At the Smiths' home and waiting for backcountry roads to dry enough to be passable, thus enabling access to the upper-elevation Andean forests.

18 Nov.   With backcountry roads still bad, but sufficiently dry to travel, JM and party depart by horse and buggy for the forests of the Andes, arriving at the Smith ranch house at 6:30 p.m.

19 Nov.   JM wanders the fields, sketching volcanic cones and studying trees and shrubs. In the evening he rides to the home of John Hunter, a sawmill operator, who offers to join the party as guide.

20 Nov.   JM prepares for the final push into the higher-elevation forests. Accompanied by Mr. Smith, Mr. Williams, Mr. Hunter, and two Chilean packers, JM crosses ridges, streams, and meadows on his ascent. At last is excited to find the long-sought forests of *Araucaria imbricata*. JM spends the night sleeping out on the ground.

21 Nov.   JM traces the south ridge above the camp, studying the ancient forest of *Araucaria imbricata*, before journeying back to the Smith ranch.

22 Nov.   Returns to Victoria by horse and buggy and stays the night in the Smith house.

23 Nov.	Departs Victoria at 7:20 a.m., northbound by rail for Santiago. Arrives Santiago 10:20 p.m., to find Mr. Fletcher's car waiting for him. Spends the night at Fletcher's house.
24 Nov.	Returns to the Santiago Botanical Gardens during the day; in the evening gives a talk to the students at Dr. Rice's school.
25 Nov.	Departs Santiago in afternoon, northbound by rail for Los Andes, where he arrives at 10:30 p.m.; spends the night in a hotel.
26 Nov.	Departs Los Andes at 6:20 a.m. for return rail trip east across the Andes. Arrives Mendoza, at the eastern foot of the Andes, at about 10:30 p.m., changes cars, and continues journey to Buenos Aires.
27 Nov.	Arrives Buenos Aires at 7:20 p.m. and goes to Royal Hotel.
28 Nov.	At the American Consulate receives letters forwarded from Belém, then goes to the Legation, where he talks with Mr. Bliss, the American Minister. Becomes lost on his way back to the hotel, and must walk 3–5 miles in finding his way back.
29 Nov.	JM declines a number of lunch and dinner invitations, deciding instead to sail to Montevideo in an attempt to find a steamer to Cape Town before the South African vegetation withers for the season.
30 Nov.	Packs up, bids farewell to friends in Buenos Aires, and sails for Montevideo at 10:00 p.m.
1 Dec.	Arrives Montevideo at 7:00 a.m., and goes first to the American Consulate, then to the Hotel Pyramedes.
2–5 Dec.	Still seeking a ship to Cape Town. On 5 December JM finally purchases a ticket to Tenerife ("Teneriffe") in the Canary Islands aboard the *Kurakina,* scheduled to sail on 8 December. On the evening of 5 December JM is the guest of honor at a dinner served at the home of the American Minister, Mr. Nicolay Grevstad.
6–8 Dec.	Waiting for the *Kurakina.* On the evening of the 7th JM addresses the Montevideo YMCA in a "short talk" that lasts at least two hours.
9 Dec.	The *Kurakina* finally arrives, and JM is taken by carriage to the pier by Mr. Goding (the American Consul) and Mr. Bright, and goes aboard at 5:00 p.m. The ship loads coal until 11:00 p.m., and sails sometime during the night.
10 Dec.	JM awakens at 5:00 a.m. and is surprised to find the ship already out of sight of Montevideo, bound for the Canary Islands.
11–25 Dec.	At sea, bound northeast through the equatorial Atlantic.
26 Dec.	After more than a fortnight at sea, the nearly 13,000-foot Pico de Teidè ("Peak of Teneriffe") on Tenerife in the Canary Islands comes into sight. Arriving at the island at 4:00 p.m., JM is happy to go ashore and to the Camachos Hotel.
27 Dec.	JM books passage to Cape Town, South Africa, on the 5,000-ton

Dutch East Africa steamship *Windhuk.* The ship arrives in the evening and JM goes aboard at about 7:45 p.m. Presumably the *Windhuk* sails sometime at night.

28–29 Dec. Back at sea, southbound along the west coast of north Africa.

30 Dec. At sea, JM notes passing a number of large steamers and gains a fine view of the shores of the Cape Verde Islands. Ship is opposite the mouth of the Senegal ("Senagel") River, on the present-day border of Senegal and Mauritania.

31 Dec. At sea, JM notes gulls, dolphins ("porpoises"), and the "Grand New Year Dance" that continues until the early hours of New Year's Day, 1912.

1912

1–9 Jan. Far out at sea, southbound for Cape Town, South Africa, through the South Atlantic. Crosses the equator for the third time on his journey on January 3. On the evening of January 9 a farewell dinner is given for the many passengers who will depart the following day at the German coastal settlement of "Squakum" (probably Swakopmund, Namibia), from which they will make their way about 300 miles inland to the diamond and gold mines at Windhoek ("Windhuk").

10 Jan. Sails down the Skeleton Coast, arrives "Squakum" at 4:30 a.m. Departs about noon, after taking on more than 100 new passengers bound for Cape Town.

11 Jan. Arrives in the picturesque "Rudiret Bay" (probably Lüderitz, Namibia) about 8:00 a.m. The *Windhuk* takes on yet more passengers and departs for Cape Town about noon. JM sees the ship upon which Roosevelt sailed to Mombasa from Naples, and notices a group of seals at play near the mouth of the bay.

12 Jan. At sea, southbound for Cape Town, JM enjoys the wildness of a stormy day on the ocean.

13 Jan. Arrives Cape Town about noon, goes ashore about 2:00 p.m., and drives to the Mt. Nelson Hotel. After lunch JM walks to the Cape Town Botanical Garden.

14 Jan. Spends the day writing letters, enjoying the blooming plants in the gardens at the Mt. Nelson Hotel, and observing trees along the streets.

15 Jan. JM completes many of the travel logistics of his remaining journey when he purchases a ticket that will eventually take him all the way to Naples, Italy.

16 Jan.	Leaves Cape Town by rail for Victoria Falls about 12:30 p.m., stops briefly at 5:15 p.m. at Worcester ("Worsuster"), and then the train climbs steep grades to a vast plateau surrounded by peaks and buttes.
17 Jan.	Traveling by rail all day across the plateau. Crosses a fork of the Orange River and arrives at the diamond mining town of Kimberley ("Kimberly") about 7:20 p.m., departing again at 8:30 p.m.
18 Jan.	Still bound by rail through South Africa's interior.
19 Jan.	Having now traveled through present-day South Africa and Botswana, arrives Bulawayo, in present-day southwestern Zimbabwe, at 7:00 a.m. Has breakfast and walks around the town, admiring the increasing diversity of the forest.
20 Jan.	Arrives at Victoria Falls station, on the Zambezi ("Zambesi") River, near the border of present-day Zimbabwe and Zambia, at 7:00 a.m. and inquires into the proximity of baobab trees, the main object of his journey to this part of Africa. A young boy guides him to baobabs growing within a few miles of the station. After a wonderful morning, departs Victoria Falls by rail at 12:20 p.m. for the return trip to Bulawayo, enjoying the scenery he had passed through at night on the way to Victoria Falls.
21 Jan.	Arrives Bulawayo at 7:00 a.m. Spends the day at the Grand Hotel, resting and writing extensively in his journal about the beauty of Victoria Falls and the baobab forests.
22 Jan.	Draws twenty pounds sterling and departs Bulawayo at 2:00 p.m. by rail for Beira.
23 Jan.	Still eastbound by rail for Beira.
24–25 Jan.	Arrives at Beira, Mozambique, on the Indian Ocean, at 9:40 a.m. Meets the postmaster, Mr. Ayere, and Mr. Stokes, who was a friend of the great botanist Sir Joseph Hooker. Goes to the Savoy Hotel, where he spends the night and much of the 25th awaiting the *Windhuk*, which arrives in port in the evening.
26–27 Jan.	JM goes aboard the *Windhuk*, the same ship on which he had sailed to Cape Town, in the afternoon. He remains aboard as the *Windhuk* discharges and takes on cargo on the 27th.
28 Jan.	The *Windhuk* departs Beira harbor at 10:00 p.m., amid a lightning storm, northbound along the east coast of southern Africa, bound for the Port of Chinde, at the mouth of the Zambezi River.
29 Jan.	Arrives off the Port of Chinde about 10:00 a.m.
30 Jan.	At sea, northbound, arrives Mozambique at 6:30 p.m.
31 Jan–1 Feb.	Departs Mozambique about 1:30 a.m. Sails north, bound for Zanzibar, Tanzania.
2 Feb.	Arrives at the former slave-trading center of Zanzibar at 6:00 a.m.

The *Windhuk* takes on cargo all day and then sails for Dar es Salaam ("dar es Salaan").

3 Feb. Arrives Dar es Salaam in the early morning. Goes ashore, takes a walk, and discovers baobabs within a few miles of town.

4 Feb. Back aboard ship, returning to Zanzibar to pick up mail before sailing north for Pangani ("Panga"), at the mouth of the Pangani River. Arrives Pangani in the afternoon and loads cargo all night.

5 Feb. Departs Pangani at 8:00 a.m., sailing north. Arrives Mombasa, in present-day Kenya, about 2:00 p.m. and goes to the Grand Hotel.

6 Feb. Spends the day in Mombasa, walking in the hot sun and measuring baobabs.

7 Feb. Departs Mombasa at noon, bound inland by rail for Entebbe ("Antebbe"), in present-day Uganda. Notes baobabs, grassy hills, blue mountains, glacial features, and several pleasant traveling companions.

8 Feb. Sees thousands of hartbeests, antelopes, and ostriches before arriving in Nairobi, in present-day Kenya, at 11:15 a.m. and going to the Norfolk Hotel.

9 Feb. Spends the day at the hotel in Nairobi.

10 Feb. Departs Nairobi at noon, bound by rail for Port Florence, south of Kisumu on the shores of the eastern arm of Lake Victoria ("Victoria Nyanza").

11 Feb. Arrives Port Florence at 7:00 a.m., boards the steamer *Clement Hill,* and sails at 10:00 a.m. on Lake Victoria for Entebbe.

12 Feb. Arrives Entebbe at 11:00 a.m. Sometime during the morning JM crosses the equator for the fourth time during his journey. Studies trees near port, and is then taken by Mr. Rees to visit the Uganda Protectorate and the Botanical Gardens.

13 Feb. Departs for Kampala ("Kompali"), in present-day Uganda, at daylight, arriving at about 9:00 a.m. in port and riding the seven miles into town in a jinrikisha. Passes through banana orchards and papyrus swamps, arriving in the city in an hour and a half.

14 Feb. Departs at 5:00 a.m. for Jinja ("Jinji"), at the outlet of Lake Victoria, where he arrives at 11:30 a.m. From the village of Jinja JM travels to Ripon Falls, at the headwaters of the Nile River.

15 Feb. Sails for Port Florence at 4:00 a.m., arriving at 5:00 p.m. JM crosses the equator for the fifth time on his journey.

16 Feb. Departs by rail for Mombasa at 7:30 a.m.

17 Feb. In the morning near Naivasha ("Nivahsa") Lake. In the afternoon sees antelopes, zebras, and ostriches on the Athi plain, and appreciates views of Mount Kilimanjaro ("Kilimanjara") to the south and

Mount Kenya ("Kenia") to the north. Notes many baobabs growing adjacent to the railroad tracks, near Makindu ("Makinda Station").

18 Feb.   Arrives Mombasa 8:00 a.m.

19 Feb.   In Mombasa. Notes heat, saunters in the Town Gardens, and obtains number for his cabin on the East African Dutch steamer the *General.*

20–22 Feb.   In Mombasa, sketching and studying baobabs in the intense heat.

23 Feb.   Boards the *General,* which sails at 6:00 p.m.

24 Feb.   At sea, northbound off the east coast of present-day Kenya and Somalia ("Somaliland"). Sometime this day, JM crosses the equator for the sixth time on his journey.

25 Feb.   Arrives "Wubuschi" (probably Muqdisho, Somalia) about 2:00 p.m. Sails again at about 4:00 p.m.

26–27 Feb.   At sea, northbound off the east coast of Somalia.

28 Feb.   Admires the wave-beaten bluffs off Ras Asir ("Cape Guardifui") as the *General* enters the Gulf of Aden.

29 Feb.   Arrives 'Adan ("Aden"), in present-day Democratic Yemen ("Arabian Coast"), at 10:30 a.m. Departs 'Adan about 3:00 p.m., passing through the Bab al Mandab straits ("Babelmandeb Straits") and into the Red Sea during the night.

1–2 Mar.   In the Red Sea. Passes a line of islands he calls "the Twelve Apostles" (perhaps Jazâ'ir az Z'ubayr) about noon. Ship passes through a mile-long bed of reddish-yellow alga.

3 Mar.   Probably nearing the tip of the Sinai Peninsula, Râs Muhammad, by around 8:00 p.m. Later that night the *General* passes through the Strait of Gûbâl into the Gulf of Suez.

4 Mar.   Arrives El Suweis ("Suez"), Egypt, about 5:00 p.m., where fifteen fellow passengers disembark to take a night train to Cairo in order to see the pyramids before rejoining the *General* at Bur Sa'id ("Port Said"), Egypt, the following day. The ship enters the Suez Canal about 7:00 p.m.

5 Mar.   In the Suez Canal. Arrives Bur Sa'id about 8:00 a.m., departing by 2:00 p.m. for Naples, Italy.

6–8 Mar.   At sea in the Mediterranean Sea, bound for Naples via the Stretto di Messina ("Straits of Messina") separating Sicily from the Italian mainland.

9–13 Mar.   In Naples, visiting local attractions including the museum, the old Roman town of Pozzuoli ("Pozzuli"), Pompeii, Mount Vesuvio ("Vesuvius"), and Capri.

14 Mar.   Spends day at his Naples hotel, writing letters and packing for his journey home.

15 Mar.	Boards the Hamburg-American line steamship *Kaiserin Augusta Victoria* at 2:00 p.m., and sails sometime that day.
16 Mar.	Sails through the Strait of Bonifacio between Sardinia and Corsica.
17 Mar.	In the Balearic Sea, sailing along the glacially sculpted mountainous coast of Spain.
18 Mar.	Arrives Gibraltar ("Gibralta") at 6:00 a.m., departing again at 1:00 p.m. and sailing across Algeria Bay and through the Straits of Gibraltar into the Atlantic Ocean.
19–26 Mar.	At sea in the North Atlantic, westbound for New York.
27 Mar.	Arrives in New York after his thirty-week, 40,000-mile-long voyage.

Editorial Methods

Textual editing might be described as the painstaking, challenging process by which an author's literary remains are sorted through and reconstituted into texts that, if properly executed, are both accurate and alive. Because the work of the textual editor involves so many difficult problems and choices, it is important to make clear what sorts of archival materials were used, how the condition of those materials influenced the rendering of the final text, and what editorial policies and procedures were adopted in order to assemble, shape, correct, and present the archival materials in book form. This appendix thus describes the history, physical characteristics, and condition of the archival materials used in preparation of *John Muir's Last Journey*, and explains the methods and principles of documentary editing that I have employed in rendering these materials in book form.

History and Condition of the Journal Manuscripts and Correspondence

While on his South America and Africa journey—which lasted from August 12, 1911, until March 27, 1912—JM kept daily notes of his observations, studies, and adventures. There are three separate journal books from this voyage; all three were carried in the field, all were written in soft lead pencil, and all contain many sketches and drawings as well as text. The first of these journals, containing entries for August 12 through October 23, 1911, is of red leather, and is only 13 × 8 centimeters in size; it bears an octagonal tag which reads "55a" (presumably the cataloguing number assigned it by William F. Badè, Muir's literary executor), and it contains 123 pages on 62 lines per page. The second journal, containing entries for October 24 through November 13, 1911, is of scuffed brown leather, and is somewhat larger than the first, at 17 × 10.5 centimeters; it bears an octagonal tag with the catalog number 55, and it contains 43 pages on 23 lines per page. The third journal, containing entries for November 14, 1911, through March 27, 1912, is of scuffed tan leather, and is slightly larger than the first and smaller than the second, at 15.5 × 10 centimeters; it contains 124 pages on 63 lines per page and its catalog number is 55b. All three journals are included in the microform edition of the John Muir Papers, reel 30. There is also a fourth journal book associated with Muir's last journey, to be found in reel 33. It contains Muir's reading and commonplace notes rather than diary entries or field notes. This fourth notebook, which is con-

tained in a small, promotional calendar notebook distributed in 1911 by the Union
Well Supply Company of Los Angeles, California, is 14 × 7 centimeters; its catalog number is 60, and it contains 30 pages on 17 lines per page, with three of those
pages not in Muir's hand. Although some smudging and migration of text and
sketches has occurred, all of these notebooks have received little use; they have
been well cared for, and they are in excellent condition, especially when one considers that they traveled halfway around the world, that they were used in the field
in all weathers, and that their contents were written and drawn in soft lead pencil.

Soon after returning to California in late April 1912, Muir began making plans
for revision and development of the South America and Africa journals (for more
on this, see the introduction to chapter 7). By late May or—more likely—early
June, Muir had traveled to his daughter Helen's modest home in Hollywood, California, and soon began working on the travel notebooks in earnest. He wrestled
with how best to organize the materials, and sometime in late June Muir engaged
Henrietta Thompson, who had done typing for him on several previous occasions, to prepare the revised travel notes and journals in a typescript form that
could be more easily worked with. By early July Thompson had completed, in
duplicate, a 160-page, triple-spaced typescript of the journals and corollary reading notes. This typescript is on bond typepaper, 33 × 20.5 centimeters, and has, like
the holograph journals, been well preserved. Although the duplicate copy has
apparently been lost, Muir's working copy of the typescript has been preserved
intact, and is now housed in the John Muir Papers at the University of the Pacific.
It is also included in the microform edition of the John Muir Papers, reel 30. In
addition to being the product of Muir's own revision of his holograph field journals, this typescript also contains many holograph annotations, insertions, cancellations, transpositions, and revisions in Muir's hand.

After John Muir's death in 1914 his papers remained scattered; many materials
were in the Muir family home in Martinez, while others remained with friends or
family, and yet others were at Yosemite National Park, with the Sierra Club in San
Francisco, and elsewhere. Many of the most important Muir manuscripts were
entrusted to Muir's friend, Sierra Club comrade, and literary executor, William F.
Badè (1871–1936). Badè, who was Professor of Old Testament Literature and
Semitic Languages at Pacific School of Religion (then Pacific Theological Semi-
nary) in Berkeley, California, deposited Muir's papers at PSR while working on
his early books on Muir. In 1937, the year following Badè's death, most of the Muir
papers were turned over to Linnie Marsh Wolfe (1881–1945), the successor chosen
by the Muir family to continue biographical and textual work with Muir's manuscripts (*Son* viii). Apparently Wolfe temporarily stored various materials at the
Alameda County Free Library, though presumably PSR remained the main permanent depository.

For more than a decade after Wolfe's own death, the bulk of Muir's papers remained at PSR. In 1956 the Muir family directed that they be moved from PSR to the Bancroft Library of the University of California, where they remained on deposit, mostly uncataloged and relatively unused for another fifteen years. In 1970 the Papers were moved again, from the Bancroft to the Holt-Atherton Library of the University of the Pacific in Stockton, California. At UOP the papers were cataalogued and made more practically accessible, and in subsequent years the Muir Papers there served as the core of the impressive collection of publicly and privately owned Muir materials contained in Ronald H. Limbaugh's and Kirsten E. Lewis's monumental microform edition of the John Muir Papers, completed in 1986.

The Muir letters included in *John Muir's Last Journey* are held in various public and private archives, but most are housed with the Muir Papers at UOP, and all letters here published or quoted are contained in the microform edition of the John Muir Papers. Because the microform edition of the Papers is not widely available, however, I have documented quotations from letters which have been previously excerpted or published by citing their secondary sources. When quoting from previously unpublished letters other than those included in this book, I have cited the letters by the series, reel, and frame numbers corresponding with the cataloging of the letter in the microform edition of the Muir Papers (e.g., I/A/20/11720). The letters published in this book are not documented individually, but may all be found arranged chronologically in the microform edition of the Muir Papers, series IA, reel 20.

Documentary-Editing Philosophy and Methodology

Because this edition of Muir's journals and correspondence is intended for a general as well as a scholarly audience, I have opted for a clear-text edition rather than a less readable genetic text transcription; thus, I have employed silent rather than overt techniques of emendation, and I have presented an expanded transcription rather than a facsimile transcription (a reproduced image of the page) or diplomatic transcription (a modern-type transcription augmented by symbols indicating insertions, cancellations, etc.). My philosophical approach to the textual editing of these materials adheres to R. B. McKerrow's maxim, paraphrased by Joel Myerson, that "whichever form of the text seems to embody the author's last intentions should be *chosen as a whole* as the base or copy-text" (Myerson 344). Thus, I have accepted the typescript, rather than the handwritten, or holograph manuscript of Muir's journals as the copy-text for *John Muir's Last Journey,* and have used it to set text and to select among both substantive and accidental textual variants. Furthermore, I have taken as final copy-text the *edited* typescript of the journals—that is, the typescript as it would appear if all of Muir's holograph editing adjustments to it had been included in a revision of the typescript text. I have, however, willingly consulted the holograph manuscript for clarification in instances in which the typescript—or the holograph annotations to it—appeared ambiguous, incomplete, or incorrect.

Some textual editors, such as Hershel Parker, Donald Pizer, and Jerome McGann, believe that authorial intent is too abstract a concept to serve as a practical guide for documentary literary editors (Myerson 358–59). On the contrary, I strongly agree with Thomas Tanselle's assertion that "as long as our concern is with authors and their intentions, we cannot reject revisions made by authors simply because we consider them misguided, for we are then placing ourselves, not the authors, at the center of attention" (83). Thus, I have labored to present Muir's words precisely as he wrote them—that is, precisely as they would have appeared had his holograph editorial annotations to the text been incorporated into a subsequent revision. Because both the holograph and typescript manuscripts are extant and in good condition, and because Muir's writing and editing of these materials was not collaborative—thereby allowing us to remove external editors and printers from editorial consideration—the goal of presenting Muir's words exactly as he wrote them was made easier than it might otherwise have been.

Described in the most general terms, the stages of my editorial method were as follows: make photocopies of holograph and typescript materials from microfilm of archival materials; enlarge photocopies and reassemble into oversize folios; working from folios and using magnifying glasses as necessary, transcribe typescript precisely, without correction or adjustment to Muir's text; correct transcription through parallel reading against the typescript; verify corrected transcription through a two-reader recitation of the full text, including all details of spelling and punctuation; using verified, corrected transcription, include all holograph insertions, cancellations, transpositions, and revisions made to the typescript in Muir's hand; correct and then verify correction by the means described above; make silent textual corrections in keeping with the specific editorial principles and policies described below; make silent textual emendations and document them in a Table of Emendations (Appendix F); make silent textual corrections and document them in the Textual Notes; consult the holograph manuscript in cases in which authorial intention remains ambiguous, and document adjustments in the Textual Notes; solve final textual problems and ambiguities by referring to the original holograph and typescript materials archived with the John Muir Papers; and, proofread, checking any problem spots against the copy-text of the original, annotated typescript. A parallel editorial method was used in the textual editing and presentation of holograph and typescript letters from Muir's voluminous correspondence.

Challenges in the Editing of the Text

Perhaps the most predictable challenge was transcription of Muir's holograph letters and his holograph insertions, cancellations, transpositions, and revisions to the typescript. Though Muir wrote a reasonably steady hand, even into his seventies, his late letters are often hurried and/or cramped, and those written during the voyage were often scribbled from bobbing steamer decks or rattling train cars, or in the heavy weather of subequatorial rainforests. Because Muir invariably wrote in soft lead pencil, smudging, migration, and fading have often combined with the adverse circumstances of composition to make these letters difficult to transcribe—even after magnification and recourse to original manuscripts. Some of the same difficulties attend the task of deciphering Muir's annotations to the typescript; in addition to being cramped and faint, many of these notes involve elaborate and multiple cancellations, insertions, and transpositions that are often indicated with various interlocking lines and arrows which leave sentences looking much like birds' nests. In most cases, however, patient work—combined with familiarity with Muir's hand, the circumstances of his life, and his literary style and diction—and recourse to archival materials has made it possible to render accurate transcriptions; where uncertainties exist, explanatory textual notes have been added.

A related challenge has attended the selection and publication of sketches and drawings from Muir's journals. Although Muir's three travel notebooks include a total of more than 160 sketches, many are not practically reproducible. Most of these sketches are fairly small, and some are remarkably tiny. Those sketched on lined paper and those Muir has crosshatched or shaded do not resolve well. Much worse, smudging, fading, and migration have rendered scores of these wonderful images unpublishable. Fortunately, modern techniques of manuscript photography and photographic enhancement enable quality reproduction of many of Muir's field sketches.

In editing and structuring the book, it has also been a considerable challenge simply to *find* Muir—that is, to trace his precise geographical locations during the nearly eight months of his voyage. All too often Muir's journal remains elliptical: the entries are often relatively terse or fairly general, and even when quite specific, often omit and sometimes mistake local place names. For example, Muir might remark on the geologic or climatic features of a place but neglect to include the specific place name by which his location might be verified. Worse yet for the scholar who would trace Muir's precise movements on what is often such slight evidence, many of the place names in South America and perhaps *most* of the place names in Africa have been changed since Muir made his journey. Recall that Muir's voyage took place just a few years before World War I, a contest that resulted in a significant restructuring (and consequent renaming) of the global political landscape—particularly in Africa, where Franco-British forces dislodged the Germans from nearly all of what had previously been a 1-million-square-mile colonial empire in Togoland, Cameroons, German Southwest Africa, and German East Africa. Subsequent political struggles have resulted in many additional changes that have further complicated efforts to locate Muir's exact route. Certain places Muir visited have been renamed several times over since 1912, while others simply disappeared when local colonial efforts failed, or when the introduction of a new railroad or steamship route substantially altered migration or settlement patterns.

In order to trace Muir's route as precisely as possible, I have used several forms of textual, historical, cartographic, and circumstantial evidence. First, I have consulted geographical atlases published in the first and second decade of the twentieth century, military maps drawn during the First World War, and books of travel and natural history published in the years immediately preceding Muir's trip.

Second, I have studied various travel-related items in the uncataloged memorabilia contained in the Muir collection at the University of the Pacific. Perhaps the most helpful of these items has been the List of Correspondents for Letters of Credit that accompanied the Letter of Indication issued to Muir on April 20, 1911, by Knauth, Nachod & Kühne of New York. Listing every location in the world where Muir might draw credit on his Letter of Indication, this list often allows confirmation of place names and spellings. The list has been particularly helpful in identifying locations in Africa, where the extensive network of colonial protectorates that dominated the political landscape of Muir's day has given way to a range of renamed, independent African republics.

Third, I have scrutinized the details of Muir's textual descriptions of place, and have often been able to verify his location by combining the clues provided by various descriptive details: when a headland comes into view, and whether off the port or starboard bows, for example, or the shape of a nearby cape or a distant tableland.

Fourth, I have often combined the details of Muir's physical descriptions of landscape with relevant historical facts—such as the size of towns, the route of railroads, or the speed of ships—in order to identify or estimate his location on any given day.

Fifth, I have also consulted three of Muir's own extant maps that are potentially relevant to the South America and Africa journey; these maps are held with the Muir Papers but remain uncataloged and, to my knowledge, are here described for the first time (for more on this, see Appendix E, Annotated List of Selected Archival Materials). The first is a small, undated map of the Atlantic Ocean (and its American, European, and African coasts), printed in German, while the second is a surviving fragment, printed in French and also undated, which contains the northern half of South America, from around Pôrto Alegre, Brazil, north-ward. The third is a large, 1909 map of South America that has received heavy use and only survives as a number of fragments. However, by literally piecing the map back together I have fortunately been able to recover most of it, and I have dis-covered that Muir's holograph travel journal contains facts and passages clearly derived from the text on the back of the map—thus proving certainly that this is the map Muir carried with him during his travels in South America. In addition to providing an often-definitive means by which to cross-check place names, the map is in some places lightly annotated with circles indicating the places Muir visited, thus offering yet more assistance in locating Muir's movements during the first half of his journey.

Through a combined use of the techniques and materials described above, I have been able (with only a few exceptions) to identify Muir's location on each day of the journey. Appendix A, Timeline / Locator, consists of a fairly detailed time-line that accounts for his daily activities and location. This appendix is also designed to work as a locator and an apparatus by which place names may be ver-ified and / or compared to those currently in use.

Finally, the greatest challenge in editing these manuscripts has been determin-ing how best to present the materials in book form. On the one hand, I remain committed to the fidelity of the text, and so I was resolved to present, to the best of my ability as a textual editor, an accurate text of the journal as Muir himself wrote (and edited) it. On the other hand, I was working with an elliptical journal manuscript which, though fairly finished as a journal, had never been finally pre-pared by its author for publication as a book. If we are to judge from the tech-niques Muir used in preparing other of his journals for book publication, it is probable that the 1911–12 journal would have been heavily revised and substan-tially expanded had Muir lived long enough, as he had hoped he would, to prepare his notes in book form. As a result of the elliptical nature of the journal, a great deal of the personal, emotional, and literary significance of Muir's journey remained, as it were, between the lines. After careful consideration of various structures, I concluded that the full, human story of Muir's last journey could best be told by braiding the narrative of the journey with corollary accounts of the trip presented in Muir's correspondence from this period. Thus, letters were selected so as to avoid unnecessary repetition, strengthen the narrative of the journey, and add information important to understanding Muir's life and work at the time.

The chapters into which *John Muir's Last Journey* is divided are my own, and a word about the logic of these chapter divisions is also in order. The first and sev-enth chapters of the book consist entirely of letters from Muir, and are designed to help set the journey in the context of the events of Muir's life that preceded and followed it. The five central chapters are structured as they are for two important reasons. First, Muir's journey organically organizes itself into a series of five significant quests to see and study specific landscapes or tree species: the Amazon, *Araucaria braziliensis, Araucaria imbricata* (the monkey puzzle tree), *Adansonia digitata* (the African baobab tree), and Lake Victoria (and the headwaters of the Nile). Indeed, Muir's own approach to the stages of the journey as he experienced them expresses a notably deliberate sense that he is moving from one of these quests to the next. Second, Muir's writing about the journey after the fact often groups its major phases according to these five experiences, as in a July 1912 letter in which he notes that the trip material most suitable for presentation as magazine articles would be "the Amazon, the *Araucaria* forests of Chile and Brazil, the Mombasa and Zambesi Baobabs, and the Victoria Nyanza." Thus I've tried to structure this book so as to honor the text, the story behind the text, and the man behind the story. In the end, of course, textual editing remains an act not only of patience and love but of faith, for we can never know precisely how Muir would have organized these materials had he lived long enough to present them in book form.

Transcription Policies and Editorial Principles

The journal copy-text adopted is the typescript version, inclusive of all holograph editing of it and notes to it made in Muir's hand. Annotations not in Muir's hand are described in the Textual Notes. When textual incongruities (such as singular/plural, or capitalization/lowercase) have been created by Muir's holograph editing of the typescript, they have been silently corrected to bring the text into conformity with what appears to be the intended spirit of the edited version. Many lines of text in the typescript are underlined in holograph marking; the underlining may or may not be in Muir's hand, and its existence has not been specifically described in the Textual Notes except in cases where its potential relevance to Muir's intentions was discernible. At a number of places in the typescript, Muir noted the addresses of people he met during his travels; because these addresses were intended only as information for further correspondence, they have been omitted from the text of the journal but are included in the Textual Notes. Muir has chosen not to include in the typescript some comparable inscriptions and notes in the flyleaves of his holograph journal notebooks, and so those notes have not been included here (in many cases these notes are also too confused to be clearly transcribed); readers interested in these notes, which consist largely of addresses and jottings regarding travel logistics, are referred to the holograph journals themselves in the microform edition of the John Muir Papers, reel 30.

No attempt has been made to adjust or correct stylistic idiosyncrasies and infelicities. I have followed the rule of *verbatim et literatum*, except in the case of slips of the pen, which have been silently corrected and subsequently noted in Appendix F, Table of Emendations. In particular, all neologistic "Muirisms" (e.g., "branchlets") have been retained; the "correction" of JM's idiosyncratic diction would, in the case of these manuscripts, be unacceptably invasive.

Standard paragraph indentation has been adopted, though Muir, like many nineteenth-century authors, typically ended paragraphs in midline and then began the subsequent paragraph at the left margin (in the case of the correspondence, he would sometimes finish and begin "paragraphs" on the same line, but would use an exaggerated space to denote the break); however, to the degree they are discernible, Muir's own paragraph breaks have been preserved, both in the journals and in the correspondence.

Some adjustment in formats has been adopted and requires explanation. The presentation of the letters has been regularized, thus: place of composition, date of composition, addressee, greeting, body, close greeting, and signature. Muir's greetings and signatures appear precisely as worded in the correspondence; however, I have standardized greetings so that each is followed by a comma, whereas JM irregularly used commas, dashes, colons, or no punctuation at all. I have also silently added "P.S." to denote postscripts that followed the signature but were not so noted. In the infrequent case in which a letter's envelope is extant, I have not included transcription of the short notes Muir occasionally jotted on the outside of envelopes; readers wishing to further pursue such details are referred to the appropriate correspondence reel in the microform edition. In presenting the journal, I have also standardized the dateline (Muir included the year with each daily entry; I have used the year as a heading, with only the month and day listed). In cases in which Muir's letters were written on letterhead, the content of the letterhead has not been transcribed as part of the text of the letter.

Letters are presented chronologically. I have silently supplied part or all of the date of some letters that Muir failed to date (in particular, he often chose not to write the year on his letters), noting only those cases in which a reasonable doubt about the date of composition remains. Likewise, the names of addressees and places of composition, where unsupplied, have been silently added in those cases where discernible, and noted only in cases where a reasonable doubt remains. When two letters were written on the same day, they are presented in the order they appear in the microform edition of the John Muir Papers unless, as occurred in a number of instances, internal or external evidence led me to discern a probable alternative order of composition, in which case I have placed them in what I believe to be chronological order and have included an explanatory note. For many undated or misdated letters I have been able to supply a probable composition date, and have likewise placed the letter where I believe it belongs, with an explanation given in the Textual Notes.

Throughout the footnotes and appendices, I use several convenient abbreviations. In conformity with the system employed in *The Guide and Index to the Microform Edition of the John Muir Papers,* I refer to the holograph version of the journal as "AMS" ("autograph manuscript") and the typescript version of the journal as "TMS" (typed manuscript). In addition, I abbreviate John Muir "JM," the University of the Pacific "UOP," and the John Muir Papers "MP."

Muir's own abbreviations have generally been allowed to stand if their meaning will be immediately clear to a general reader, though ambiguous abbreviations have been silently expanded and noted in the Table of Emendations. There are several exceptions and additions to this policy, however. Ampersands have been expanded to the word "and" except in the case of proper names (e.g., "Boone & Crockett Club"). The abbreviation "deg." (for "degrees") has been allowed to stand, but has been standardized to lowercase. JM would often abbreviate a person's first or last name by using the name's first letter (e.g., "Mr. S." rather than "Mr. Sanford"); in cases in which the referent of the abbreviation is not in doubt, I have silently replaced the abbreviation with the proper name. "US" has been supplied in place of all other abbreviated forms of "United States" (e.g., U.S., U. S.). Directional abbreviations such as N., S., SE, have been allowed to stand, and directional words such as "northeast" have remained unregularized when JM chose, instead, to spell them out.

Commas have been added to numbers (e.g., 1000 becomes 1,000) to conform with modern usage. I have also regularized "A.M." and "P.M." to "a.m." and "p.m." throughout, and I have added those designations where time of day is mentioned, in cases where forenoon or afternoon is not otherwise obvious. Since JM usually uses numbers (e.g., "10:00") rather than words (e.g., "ten o'clock") in reference to times of day, I have standardized temporal notations by changing his occasional use of words to numbers, except in the case of narrative locutions such as "half past ten."

With respect to spelling, slips of the pen have been silently corrected and noted in the Table of Emendations, while irregular variant spellings (for example, of place names or plant names) have been allowed to stand. Capitalization is presented as found in the copy-text but is standardized to uppercase in the first word of a sentence, and in geographical names, personal names, and the first word of Latinate binomials. Contractions have been retained, but apostrophes have been silently added where necessary (e.g., "it's"). Nonstandard hyphenation of compound words has been allowed to stand (e.g., "wave-tops," "foam-masses," "sun-glow," etc.) except where noted otherwise in the Table of Emendations, but hyphenation has not been supplied in cases in which JM chose to omit it from such compound words (again, a few exceptions are noted in the Table of Emendations). Dashes have been regularized to modern usage, but JM's end-line hyphenations have been universally omitted. Commas have been added only where clarity requires it, and endline punctuation has been silently supplied where missing. Scientific names have been rendered according to modern practice, but taxonomic nomenclature has been neither standardized nor modernized. The titles of books and names of ships and boats JM mentions have been uniformly capitalized and italicized.

John Muir's Reading and Botanical Notes

In preparation for, and even during, his last voyage, JM read widely in texts that might provide insight into the cultures and, especially, the botany, geology, and natural history of the regions to which he intended to travel. As he often did for other projects, JM kept separate reading notebooks in which he recorded facts and ideas of three kinds: natural history information; thoughts jotted in response to the authors' insights; and, most often, quotations from the books (sometimes called "commonplace notes"). JM's 1911–12 reading notebook, described in Appendix B, Editorial Methods, has fortunately survived in good condition and is included in the microform edition of MP under the title "Amazon Notes, etc." (III/A/33/01887). Although it has not been possible to date the notebook's specific entries, it is certain that all were made between January 1911 and June 1912, with the bulk of them made either during the journey or in the months immediately preceding it.

Although JM never lived to prepare these materials for publication, he considered these reading notes, however casual and fragmentary, as part of his working manuscript for a would-be book or articles on the South America and Africa journey. In June 1912 he engaged Henrietta Thompson to prepare a clean, typed manuscript of his South America and Africa travel journals; interestingly, he also instructed her to type up these reading notes, which now comprise pages 148–160 of the 160-page TMS. In many cases these notes, even the simple commonplace notes in which JM has roughly quoted an item of interest from the text he was reading, show us not only *what* JM was reading, but *how* he was reading—that is, what he was noticing, and what the pattern of his notes suggests about his concerns, interests, and ambitions at this stage of his life. For example, we recognize JM's sensibility in his detailed botanical notes, and in his concerned observations regarding human pride and the environmental destruction it often precipitates. In addition, JM seems particularly moved by passages that refer to the benefits of international travel, or that meditate upon solitude, old age, or mortality.

In JM's own notebook—and even in the TMS that is based upon it—the titles of the thirteen texts included here are usually incomplete and fragmentary, and occasionally abbreviated or even partially incorrect. I have made every effort not only to determine complete and accurate titles and publication information for these texts (silently included in the heading of each entry), but also to obtain them in the editions JM is likely to have read, in order to examine the pattern of JM's notes and to understand what information and attitudes may have conditioned his approach to the landscapes he visited. Although I have expanded and corrected the headings, the entries themselves are rendered as they appear in the TMS. Brief commentary on each of these texts and their authors will be found in the italicized headnotes.

Following JM's reading notes from the 1911–12 journey, in Appendix D, I have also included a selected list of South America and Africa books owned by JM. These books, though not specifically mentioned in the context of the 1911–12 journey, are very likely to have stimulated JM's desire to visit and study the "two hot continents."

Agricultural and Pastoral Prospects of South Africa, by Owen Thomas
(London: Archibald Constable, 1904)

TMS lists this volume as "The Flora of South Africa, by Call Owen Thomas," though JM probably intended a reference to Owen Thomas's 1904 book Agricultural and Pastoral Prospects of South Africa *(perhaps intending the chapter on "Vegetation"), listed here. It is not known whether JM actually saw this book, or if he simply noted it as a reference. Although JM's note "Khaya tree, very large" might suggest that he had begun to read the book, the repetition of that note under the following reference leaves the matter in doubt.*

Khaya tree, very large.

The Uganda Protectorate, an Attempt to Give Some Description of the Physical Geography, Botany, Zoology, Anthropology, Languages and History of the Territories Under British Protection in East Central Africa, between the Congo Free State and the Rift Valley and between the First Degree of South Latitude and the Fifth Degree of North Latitude, by Sir Harry Hamilton Johnston
(London: Hutchinson, 1902)

In TMS, JM has noted "vol. II" after the title of Johnston's book. However, volume two consists primarily of anthropological observations, while the notes JM has made here seem to derive from the first volume. The fact that JM had long known of Johnston's important work—which included the discovery of a number of new African species—is confirmed by a clipping JM kept (now in the "Scraps" files with the MP at UOP) of a January 26, 1902, San Francisco Examiner article ("A Whole Menagerie of Strangely Colored Animals Is Discovered in Africa") describing Johnston's expeditions and discoveries.

Khaya tree, very large.

The *Borassus* Palm and gardenia, very fragrant trees.

Musa sapiantum (plantain, native of equatorial Africa).

Hartabeest antelopee caama, common throughout the greater part of the continent.

Anthocleista. (Loganaceae, with crown of very large leaves on branchless stem.) Like samples of the unexplored splendors of the primeval forest of Brazil. Most of these gigantic trees belong to the class of sterculiae or the boswelliae or caesalpiniae. The rubiaceae are smaller.

Kniphofia. (Red hot pokers).

Acanthus arboreas.

Podocarpus folcatus.

Kigelia, fruit like sausages, two feet in length, two or three inches in diameter; trunk with rough bark like that of black oak. Common in Equatorial Africa. Has a purple tulip-like blossom.

Bambusa abbysinica, the common bamboo of the Upper Nile, about thirty feet high, one to two inches in diameter.

Notes on the Botany of Uruguay, by David B. Christison
(Edinburgh: Neill and Co., 1878) No. 8 in a volume with binder's title:
*Pamphlets. "From the Transactions of the Botanical Society of Edinburgh,
vol. XIII, Session 1877–78"*

JM's use of this very specific and very rare botanical publication suggests his devotion to learning as much as possible about the plants he encountered in his travels. This item may have been given or recommended to him by F. G. Pulle, Head Gardener at the Botanic Gardens in Entebbe, which JM visited on February 12, 1912.

Very few daisies or goldenrods.

39 Species of *Baccharis* and 22 species of *Senecio.*

34 species of *Paspalum,* 39 species of *Panacum,* 6 of *Melica.*

Pterocoulon, also common in the *Araucaria* forests of Brazil.

Escalonia montevidensis (saxafrage).

Also *Sellowyiana* (saxafrage) common also to Brazil. Bushes are small trees; along streams and around meadows.

Combreta terminala, Australian tree, 20 or 30 ft. high.

Combretum leprosum, 7 to 10 ft. high.

*Araucaria*s of Vulk Tolhuaca.

Species of Order *Myrtacea,* like Eucalyptus, perhaps *Myrtus.* Large tree, small leaves.

Pernettia—heathwort, red berries.

Cytharoxylon, spiny shrub at ranch—Homaliaee.

Homalium, nat. order sansydacae and type of the tribe. Large tree with compound leaves.

Embothrium coccinum—red-flowered shrub.

Laureliana aromatica, large tree.

Azarole, cretegus-like—*Bixaceai*—shrub.

Fagus obliqua, large tree.

Drimys winteri—Magnoliaceae—1 Sp. in So. America, 2 in Australia, 1 in New Zealand and 1 in Borneo—5 in all. *(Podocarpus)*

Fagus procira, 6 sp. in Chile, 5 called Roble—large.

Fagus dombeyi.

Fagus obliqua.

Persea lingue, large tree. Order Laurinae (Lauraceae) about 100 species widely distributed, Asia, etc; and from Virginia to Chile.

Drimys, Greek, meaning sharp, acid, pungent, referring to the taste of the bark. It is distributed along the Western coast of South America from Mexico to Cape Horn. It is much used both by the Indians and whites as a medicine. This tree belongs to the Magnoliaceae.

The cone of the Oolitic *Araucaria* is hardly distinguishable from that of existing species. Ferns, club mosses, and coniferie, some of which are generically identical with those now living, are met with as far back as the carboniferous epoch.

Travels in West Africa, Congo Français, Corisco and Cameroons,
by Mary Henrietta Kingsley
(New York: Macmillan, 1897)

Traveling alone and without a knowledge of African languages, Mary Kingsley explored the villages and wildernesses of West Africa for two years between 1893 and 1895. Her Travels in West Africa *is among the best-written and best-known works of women's travel writing from the late nineteenth century, and it is still of considerable scholarly interest today. Although modern abridgments of the book tend to excise the substantial scientific observations included in the first edition (1897), JM would of course have deeply valued such observations. JM's commonplace notes here also suggest that, like many readers, he appreciated Kingsley's adventurous spirit and her keen aesthetic appreciation for the inspiring majesty of the West African landscape. The subsection of JM's notes labeled "Mts." is derived from chapters 12 and 13 of Kingsley's book, which describe the great mountain peaks of West Africa.*

Rubber vine of W. Africa, *Landolphia florida (Ovariensis).*

Pandanus candelabrum, making dense thickets, with prickly stems, leaves and thick aerial roots.

"Armchair explorers."

"Lamb-like calfheadedness."

"Suburban agnostics."

On all sides rises the colossal liane-hung forest mirrored with the sky in the rivers. Natives live and die in the universe of forest, river and sky. In the tornado season lightning comes down into forests in great forked plashes, and howling winds rush through it, claiming as many victims among its giants as the lightning does.

The heavy, brooding, suffocating heat and evident apprehension of all living things when the storm bursts and roar of rain—

Behind it lie many of its noblest trees with all their bravery of foliage and vines, etc.

Pistia stratiotes, makes floating islands, some slowly swirling round and round in eddies.

The great rollers of the Atlantic meeting here their first check since they left Cape Horn.

Natives say if you fire the grass too soon or when there is no wind, you kill it outright. But if you wait until it is very dry and the fire is fanned by the wind, it sweeps rapidly over it without heating the roots, instead of smoldering long enough to kill them.

The happy cocksureness of stay-at-home suburban agnostics regarding God and the universe.

Mts. "The magnificent Mungo Mah Lobeh—The Throne of Thunder." The great peak of Cameroon, 13,760 feet high, rising suddenly right up out of the sea while close at hand to westward towers the lovely island mass of Fernando Po to 10,190 feet. Every time you pass it by, its beauty grows on you with greater and greater force, though it is never twice the same. Sometimes wreathed with indigo-black clouds, sometimes softly gorgeous with gold, green, and rose-colored vapors tinted by the setting sun. Sometimes smothered in dense clouds so that you can't see it at all, but when you once know it is there, it is all the same and you bow down and worship. Sometimes crested with snow.

There are only two distinct peaks. The Big and Little Camaroon Mountains. Most striking when you first see it after coasting for weeks along the low shores and mangrove fringed rivers of the Niger Delta.

"My business never takes me up mountains."

"Colossal sweeps of color."

When I reached the S.W. end I saw the South Atlantic down below like a plain of frosted silver. Out of it barely twenty miles away rose Fernando Po with that majestic grace peculiar to volcanic mountains. Soon the white mists rose from the mangrove swamps and grew rose color in the light of the setting sun as they swept up above over the now purple foothills, and this mist sea rose toward me, changing to lavender color, and was soon at my feet, blotting out the under world, leaving only the two summits, Cameroon and Fernando Po, then down came the rain.

Slippery *Amomum* stems.

To me it seems unthinkable that there can be anything more perfect in loveliness, majesty, color and charm (than this Cameroon region).

Travel and Adventure in South-East Africa, Being the Narrative of the Last Eleven Years Spent by the Author on the Zambesi and its Tributaries; With an Account of the Colonisation of Mashunaland and the Progress of the Gold Industry in that Country, by Frederick Courteney Selous
(London: Rowland Ward, 1893)

The first of JM's reading notes from Frederick Selous's 1893 work is taken from a passage near the end of the book and suggests that JM may have intentionally searched the text looking for indications of where he might find the long-sought baobab tree. Selous's account of seeing baobabs near Victoria Falls on the Zambezi River may have influenced JM's decision to travel to that area in search of the tree.

Camped beneath an immense baobab tree close to Wankie's Town on the Zambesi 150 miles below Victoria Falls.

The country we passed through was far from monotonous and uninteresting. Scattered here and there over the alluvial plain were patches of sandy soil covered with bush and tall forest trees, amongst which the dark leaved evergreens, which grow so thickly on the brink of Victoria Falls, were conspicuous. Here and there, too, a fantastic baobab, with its huge gouty-looking stem and long, leafless limbs, met the eye. (July)

Rain season November to April.

The high plateau of Mashunaland, remarkable for its many huge naked masses of granite rising abruptly from grassy downs, some 600 or 700 feet high. The plateau itself 6,000 ft. high, perhaps the highest part of East Africa.

These domes now being guttered by heavy rain.

Lightning.

Suddenly I saw splinters fly from a tree near me whilst all the cattle standing beneath it fell to the ground. On going up to see what had happened I found thirteen fine oxen lying dead.

Some years ago I lost one of my best friends by lightning.

African elephants $10\frac{1}{4}$ and $10\frac{1}{3}$ feet high at shoulders. Ears $5\frac{1}{2}$ ft. long, $3\frac{1}{4}$ wide.

Lion weighing over 400 lbs.

The Story of an African Farm, by Olive Schreiner
(London: Chapman and Hall, 1883)

Olive Emilie Albertina Schreiner (1855–1920), the daughter of a German peasant serving as a Protestant missionary in Africa, was born in Wittebergen, South Africa (then Cape Colony), on the edge of the Great Karoo desert of the central South African tableland. Schreiner wrote the autobiographical novel The Story of an African Farm, *published in 1883 under the pseudonym Ralph Iron, in the late 1870s, while in her early twenties. Later accepted into political and artistic circles in England, Schreiner became a leading literary proponent of women's rights, writing several novels with strong feminist themes, including* Women and Labour *(1911). Schreiner was also an energetic political activist who worked on behalf of the Afrikaners—and therefore against the British and the leading proponent of British colonial efforts in Africa, Cecil Rhodes— during the Boer War (1899–1902).*

"Dear old man, to such as you time brings no age. You die with the purity and
    innocence of childhood."
"Never a great man who had not a great mother."
As intellect grows love strikes deeper.
Stars looking down in glory.
"Oh, little hand! Oh, little voice! Oh, little form!"
"Around God's throne there may be choirs and companies of Angels, Cherubim
    and Seraphim, rising tier above tier, but for one of them all does the soul cry
    aloud; only perhaps for a little human woman full of sin that it once loved."

African Game Trails: An Account of the African Wanderings
of an American Hunter-Naturalist, by Theodore Roosevelt
(New York: Charles Scribner's Sons, 1909)

Although his seemingly insatiable appetite for killing wild game earned him the contempt of some, Theodore Roosevelt's famous 1909 African safari made his African Game Trails, *which documents the killing of more than 500 animals, a celebrated book. Although JM recognized the limits of many of Roosevelt's conservation views, he liked him anyway, and he owned and carefully read most of Roosevelt's books. JM had camped with Roosevelt in Yosemite in 1903, and he had attended Roosevelt's Pasadena lecture (and a dinner party afterward) on "A Zoological Trip Through Africa" on March 21, 1911, shortly before JM came to the East Coast to prepare for his own journey to the southern continents. JM's journals and correspondence suggest that as he traveled through that part of British East Africa that is now Kenya, he was quite conscious of following Roosevelt's trail—though he preferred observation to hunting of the remarkable animals he saw on the east African plains. JM probably knew* African Game Trails *well, for Roosevelt had inscribed a gift copy of the book (still housed with the MP) "To*

John Muir with the Best Wishes of Theodore Roosevelt" on April 21, 1911, JM's seventy-third birthday. Like the book itself, JM's notes suggest an uneasy combination of lyrical celebration of nature and triumphant pride in the hunter's conquest of wild animals.

The climate is delightful and healthy. A white man's country. (British East Africa.) No danger to health greater than going to the Riviera.

The best timber is got from the tall Mahogo tree—a kind of sandal wood. Often killed by the wild fig which begins as a parasitic vine and ends as one of the largest, most stately and shady.

Death by violence, cold, starvation—are the normal endings of the stately and beautiful creatures of the wilderness. Life is hard and cruel for all the lower creatures and for man also in what sentimentalists call a state of Nature.

The sentimentalists who prattle about the peaceful life of nature do not realize its utter mercilessness.

The curious "lily trotters," or jacanas running across the lily pads.

If they (hippos) are found in a pool with little cover, and if the shots be taken close by from firm ground, there is no *sport* whatever in killing them.

The bulbuls sang well.

Three men who had been mauled by lions informed me that the actual biting caused them at the moment no pain whatever.

In this part of Africa where flowers bloom and birds sing all the year round, there is no such burst of bloom and song as in the northern spring and early summer.

Saw the heavens redden and the sun flame over the rim of the world.

Ostrich (male) weighed 263 lbs. Hen 240 lbs.

Koodoo, handsomest and stateliest of all the antelopes.

We several times followed honey birds which in each case led us to bee trees!

A sight to gladden any hunter's heart as he lay, (an elephant) a giant in death.

Frogs with queer voices.

A Prince of Europe (Helianthus),
by Ouida (pseudonym of Louise de la Ramée)
(New York: Macmillan, 1908)

A Prince of Europe *was the posthumously published last novel of prolific and popular female novelist Louise de la Ramée (1839–1908), whose celebrated nom de plume was, simply, "Ouida." The book was published by Grosset & Dunlap as a Macmillan's Standard Library edition in 1908 under the title* A Prince of Europe *(with the parenthetical subtitle* Helianthus*); the 1909 Tauchnitz edition was published under the title* Helianthus. *Although the novel is too maudlin to have much appeal for twenty-first-century readers, JM's reading notes from the book, when compared to the text, are quite*

interesting. For example, his notes regarding the "deviltry of man" thwarting the "kind-
ness of nature," the hunter enjoying "the sheer pleasure of seeing the agony of their game,"
the "insane impulse of the sportsman to kill everything," and the idea that "the exercise
of mercy is the most divine attribute of human nature" are all sharp commentaries on the
ethical consequences of certain kinds of "sport." The fact that JM's notes focus so insis-
tently on the novel's fairly minor critique of hunting is especially interesting, given that
in both the AMS and TMS sources these notes immediately follow JM's notes on
Theodore Roosevelt's African Game Trails.

The kindness of Nature is generally thwarted by the ingenuity and deviltry of
    man.
Hunters who are hungry and who have children at home are excused, but not
    those who hunt for the sheer pleasure of seeing the agony of their game.
He is conscientious. All disagreeable people are.
Guardian angel in uniform ever watching over him.
The armed shape that his heavenly father's protection assumed.
He believed in himself first, and then in the Deity, as the creator and defender of
    himself.
The insane impulse of the sportsman to kill everything. Would eat any amount
    of dirt in the service of anybody provided that the dirt was the washings of a
    gold pan.
Has he not enjoyed life and have not all the good physicians been busy all the
    world over brewing serum to put sap into his worn-out _____.
His throne was planted on a solid bed of gun metal set around with half a mil-
    lion bayonets.
They have qualities in common.
The exercise of mercy is the most divine attribute of human nature.
The glories of sunrise seemed with every daybreak to be the new birth of the
    world. The solitude, the silence, the sanctity, the majesty of these everlasting
    hills, were dear to him.
The calmness, stillness, the deep shadows, the clear lights, the sunsets beyond
    the distant sea, the sense of nearness to a great past.
Indecision is an intellectual defect. It accompanies acute perfection. Belongs to
    philosophic doubt. But it paralyzes action.

The Daughter of an Empress, by Louise Mühlbach
(New York: Collier, 1893)

Although the TMS lists the author of this work as popular novelist Ouida (see note
above), Louise de la Ramée apparently never published a book by this title. JM may
have confused Ouida with her contemporary Louise Mühlbach (1814–1873), who did

publish a novel called The Daughter of an Empress *in 1893 (New York: Collier). I have therefore listed Mühlbach, as she is the more likely author of the book. JM's reading notes from this work suggest his Thoreauvian contemplations of the challenges and rewards of solitude. JM was invigorated by his solitary travels while also sometimes admitting, as Thoreau so rarely did, that he felt lonely.*

One must be very happy or unhappy to love solitude.

To seek in it what is so seldom found among men, repose for happiness or consolation for sorrow.

For the happy solitude provides the most delightful festival, but it also provides a festival for the unhappy memory of past joys, etc. For the children of the world, for the striving, for the seeker of inordinate enjoyment, for the ambitious, for the sensuous, solitude is but ill adapted.

Love that ennobles the heart and strengthens it for holy resolutions.

Rupert of Hentzau: From the Memories of Fritz von Tarlenheim,
by Anthony Hope
(New York: Henry Holt, 1898)

Along with its companion novel, The Prisoner of Zenda *(published four years earlier, in 1894) this lesser-known sequel novel,* Rupert of Hentzau *(1898), tells the story of the fictional kingdom of Ruritania. JM's sole commonplace note from Hope's novel suggests that JM, now in his seventies, was attempting to make peace with the transience and ephemerality of his own life.*

Times change for all of us. The roaring flood of youth goes by, and the stream of life takes to a quiet flow. In the aged and ailing the love of peace breeds hope of it.

Fighting the Slave Hunters in Central Africa: A Record of Twenty-six
Years of Travel & Adventure Round the Great Lakes and of the
Overthrow of Tip-pu-tib, Rumaliza and Other Great Slave-Traders,
by Alfred J. Swann, with an Introduction by H. H. Johnston
(Philadelphia: Lippincott, 1910)

Alfred J. Swann's book is a personal narrative of twenty-six years spent in central and east Africa between 1882 and 1909. Although the book contains natural historical and cultural observations, its primary concern is the Arab-run African slave trade that flourished in these regions of Africa until the late nineteenth century. Swann was one of several devoted international abolitionists whose efforts may be credited with breaking the slave system as it was then operated, in the Congo and around the shores of the great lakes, by powerful Arab traders including Tippu Tip and Rumaliza. Perhaps JM had the concerns of this book in mind when, in his journal entry for February 2, 1912, he laments the "woeful, slave-ful history" of Zanzibar. (In the entry below, the misspelling of Livingstone is JM's own.)

My youthful enthusiasm was fired by Livingston's stories of slavery in that vast
   wilderness.

"So long" is a sailor's phrase for "until we meet again."

The rains were now over (June or July) but as yet the grass about six feet high
   was not burned up by those devastating fires which annually sweep over
   nearly all tropical Africa, destroying or stunting most of the young trees. It is
   this repeated scorching which partly accounts for the wretched specimens of
   trees growing in most districts of East Africa, making charcoal deserts.

Blantyre on the Shire tributary of the Zambesi, named after the birthplace of
   Livingston. At Shupanga under a gigantic baobab tree a pure white cross
   marks Mary Moffatt's grave (Mrs. Livingston.)

Diseased persons who were left outside the village walls once taunted a roaring
   lion, disdaining any attempt at defense. They challenged the brute to do its
   worst. "Come this way. Don't go creeping around those poles. You know you
   can't jump over. Your voice is like thunder, but it's the lightning that kills. You
   are not the lightning. Go and hide your clumsy head in a hole of the forest
   pig and take care the rabbit does not bite your nose." Strange as it appears, I
   never heard of lions attacking any of those isolated wretches.

Boys teasing the last boat crew in a race on Lake Tanganyika: "You fellows know
   more about pushing porridge down your throats than pushing a canoe." "Get
   out and carry the boat, it will go quicker."

Cecil Rhodes thought in continents.

Some Negroes at a mission inquired of the minister: "Why do you keep on praying to your God? Is he always watching for an opportunity to injure you?
   Does he get tired of preventing bad spirits putting medicine into your porridge? Our spirits never sleep, and we let them alone as much as possible."

My Story, by Sir Hall Caine
(London: W. Heinemann for Collier & Co., 1908)

The critic, novelist, and dramatist Hall Caine hailed from the Isle of Man, in the Irish Sea off the southern coast of Scotland. JM may have been interested in My Story *because it is a literary autobiography of the sort he seems to have been contemplating for one or more of the intended subsequent volumes of his own autobiography,* The Story of My Boyhood and Youth. *JM's commonplace notes from Caine's book emphasize the link*

between sensory experience and memories of place, assert the ennobling value of poverty,
and suggest the wisdom of the British Romantic poets. JM's revealing note that "[c]at-
like devotion to home, believing one's own country the best, is an amiable fallacy" might
be read as a comment on his own globetrotting, and as an indirect assertion of his own
devotion to global botany, natural history, and environmental conservation.

A thrilling sense of the vastness of the world and the mighty things of Nature.

What I felt fifty years ago about the Isle of Man, that it was the whole world in
   little, that all the interest, all the passion, and almost all the experiences of
   mankind, lay there on that rock in the Irish Sea, has been the motive inspiring my book, for if I have learned anything by five and twenty years of almost
   continuous travel, it is that humanity is one and the same everywhere, and
   that nothing I had known of the tiny Man race was out of harmony with
   what I saw in races great and small at the farthest corner of the earth.

She could see a good heart through a clear countenance as she saw stones at the
   bottom of a well.

Poverty, so sweet, so clean, so free from want, more human and beautiful than
   wealth, I have even seen.

When I now smell a turf fire I am fifty years younger in a minute.

Poverty, if it is sweet and not bitter, is in my view a condition far more blessed of
   God than wealth, bringing hearts closer together in mutual dependence and
   brotherhood.

Cat-like devotion to home, believing one's own country the best, is an amiable
   fallacy.

As to Shelley, it is really a mercy that he has not been hatching yearly Universes
   till now.

Rosetti was born in London, in 1828.

Work your metal as much as you like, but first take care it is gold and worth
   working. Rosetti.

Sloth jaundiced all, and from my graspless hand dropped friendship's precious
   pearls like hourglass sand. I weep yet stoop not, the faint anguish flows, a
   dreamy pang in mourning's feverish doze. Coleridge.

"I assure you," said Rosetti, "that Chatterton was as great as any English poet
   whatever, and might absolutely had he lived have proved the only man in
   England's theater of imagination who could have bandied part with Shake-
   speare."

The Naturalist on the River Amazons: A Record of Adventures,
Habits of Animals, Sketches of Brazilian and Indian Life, and Aspects
of Nature Under the Equator, During Eleven Years of Travel,
by Henry Walter Bates, F.R.S.
(London: John Murray, 1910)

Henry Walter Bates's influential book of Amazonian travel and natural history was first published in 1863, but it was the 1910 Popular Edition that JM owned and read. His copy, still held with the MP, is heavily annotated, with more than 100 individual notes (indexed by page number) jotted in the flyleaves. Several of JM's notes are dated to mid-January 1912, suggesting that he carried Bates's volume with him on his South America and Africa voyage.

JM thought highly of Bates, whose work in Amazonia was an important contribution to the development of mid-nineteenth-century evolutionary theory as it is more commonly associated with Charles Darwin and Alfred Russell Wallace. Indeed, Bates's 1848 expedition to the Amazon was a joint venture with Wallace, and after Wallace returned to England in 1852, Bates remained in the region for seven years more, not returning to England until 1859. Bates's findings in the Amazon—a "Garden of Eden" that became to him what the Galapagos were to Darwin—convinced him of the accuracy of the Darwinian theory of natural selection. Darwin himself wrote "An Appreciation" of Bates that was published in Natural History Review *(vol. 3) in 1868 and reprinted as the foreword to the Everyman's Library edition of* The Naturalist on the River Amazons *(London: Dutton, 1910). Darwin credits Bates with an astounding Amazonian specimen collection of nearly 15,000 species, "of which about 8000 were previously unknown to science" (Everyman's Library ed., vii).*

JM's respect for Bates—and for the evolutionist work of Darwin, Wallace, and others—is clearly suggested by an appreciative comment he made to the New York Times *shortly after returning from his last journey: "Sixty years ago Alfred Russell Wallace and Henry W. Bates traveled all over this region; Wallace was there four years, Bates eleven," remembered JM, accurately. "Afterwards I met Wallace, and have enjoyed his friendship ever since. I have frequently heard him speak of his travels on the Amazon, and that, with Bates's masterly book, 'The Naturalist on the River Amazons,' gave me a taste for exploring it myself" (NYT, April 21, 1912, pg. 12). It is not surprising that at one time JM's personal library included at least a half dozen works by Darwin and Wallace.*

JM's reading notes from The Naturalist on the River Amazons *are not included, as are all previous reading notes, in the AMS notebook (MP III/A/33), but were apparently added to the TMS when JM was editing his travel notebooks in June or early July 1912. JM's long note on the sand wasps* (Bembex ciliata) *is a commonplace note derived verbatim from Bates's chapter VIII ("Santarem"), but the long, parenthetical paragraph beginning "(The above agrees . . .)," which comments on the keen navigational abilities of honeybees, is probably JM's own observation.*

Instinct

Whilst resting in the shade during the great heat of the early hours of afternoon, I used to find amusement in watching the proceedings of the sand wasps. A small pale green species *(Bembex ciliata)* was plentiful near the bay of Mapiri. When they are at work, a number of little jets of sand are seen shooting over the surface of the sloping bank. The little miners excavate with their fore feet, which are strongly built and furnished with a fringe of stiff bristles; they work with wonderful rapidity, and the sand thrown out beneath their bodies issues in continuous streams. They are solitary wasps, each female working on her own account. After making a gallery two or three inches in length, in a slanting direction from the surface, the owner backs out and takes a few turns around the orifice, apparently to see whether it is well made, but in reality, I believe, to take note of the locality, that she may find it again. This done, the busy workwoman flies away, but returns, after an absence varying in different cases from a few minutes to an hour or more, with a fly in her grasp, with which she reenters her mine. On again emerging, the entrance is carefully closed with sand. During this interval she has laid an egg on the body of the fly, which she had previously benumbed with her sting, and which is to serve as food for the soft footless grub soon to be hatched from the egg. From what I could make out, the *Bembex* makes a fresh excavation for every egg to be deposited; at least, in two or three of the galleries which I opened there was only one fly enclosed.

I have said that the *Bembex* on leaving her mine took note of the locality; this seemed to be the explanation of the short delay previous to her taking flight; on rising in the air, also, the insects generally flew round over the place before making straight off. Another nearly allied but much larger species, the *Monedula signata,* whose habits I observed on the banks of the Upper Amazons, sometimes excavates its mine solitarily on sand-banks recently laid bare in the middle of the river, and closes the orifice before going in search of prey. In these cases the insect has to make a journey of at least half a mile to procure the kind of fly, the *Hadrus lepidotus,* with which it provisions its cell. I often noticed it to take a few turns in the air round the place before starting; on its return it made without hesitation straight for the closed mouth of the mine. I was convinced that the insects noted the bearing of their nests, and the direction they took in flying from them. The proceeding in this and similar cases (I have read of something analogous having been noticed in hive bees) seems to be a mental act of the same nature as that which takes place in ourselves when recognizing a locality. The senses, however, must be immeasurably more keen, and the mental operation much more certain, in them than they are in man; for to my eye there was absolutely no landmark on the even surface of sand which could serve as guide, and the borders of the forest were not nearer than half a mile. The action of the wasp would be said to be instinctive; but it seems plain that the instinct is no mysterious and unintelligible agent, but a mental process in each individual, differing from the same in man only by its unerring certainty. The mind of the insect appears to be so constituted that the impression of external objects, or the want felt, causes it to act with a precision which seems to us like that of a machine constructed to move in a certain given way. I have noticed in Indian boys a sense of locality almost as keen as that possessed by the sand-wasp. An old Portuguese and myself, accompanied by a young lad of about ten years, were once lost in the forest in a most solitary place on the banks of the main river. Our case seemed hopeless, and it did not for some time occur to us to consult our little companion, who had been playing with his bow and arrow all the way whilst we were hunting, apparently taking no note of the route. When asked, however, he pointed out, in a moment, the right direction of our canoe. He could not explain how he knew; I believe he had noted the course we had taken almost unconsciously. The sense of locality in his case seemed instinctive.

(The above agrees in every particular with what I have observed in the actions of honey bees in the woods. When I had imprisoned a bee in a box containing honey, after it had eaten its fill, and I removed the lid of the box, instead of flying away directly homeward, it flew several times around the box, examining it narrowly as if fixing its appearance in its mind. It then flew around my head and looked me in the face as if making sure that it would know my face when he saw me again . . . as a mark leading to the box. It then flew to the top of the nearest oak tree and cleaned its legs of the honey it was smeared with. Then it examined the branch hung out nearest to the box, then rose above the treetops and made several circles in the air, then made a bee line for its hive, which I afterwards found was in a hollow log in a fence, about half a mile distant. After it had gone home and deposited its honey it came back for more. I saw it return to the outleaning branch of the oak above mentioned, thence it came direct to my head, buzzed a moment in my face, lighted on the edge of the box and entered. After it had started the second time to its hive, in order to satisfy myself that it had the position of the honey box in its mind, I removed with the honey box to one side only a distance of two or three rods, and stood with the honey box in front of me set on the top of a stake as before. When the bee returned the second time I saw it visit the overhanging branch of the oak, then it descended in a straight line to where the box had stood, and finding nothing, it buzzed around in the air in the spot where I stood with the box the first time, and although I was only a short distance away, it failed to find me.)

In proportion as a country is wild, the so-called instinct of domestic animals improves in address and sagacity. When the mules on the dangerous trails on the Andes feel themselves in danger they stop, turning their heads to the right and to the left, and the motion of their ears seems to indicate that they reflect on the

decision they ought to take. Their resolution is slow but always just, if it be spontaneous; that is to say, if it be not thwarted or hastened by the imprudence of the
rider. On the frightful roads of the Andes during journeys of six or seven months,
across mountains furrowed by torrents, the intelligence of horses and beasts of
burden is manifested in an astonishing manner. Thus the mountaineers are heard
to say: "I will not give you the mule whose step is the easiest, but the one which is
most intelligent, the most rational." This popular expression, dictated by long
experience, bears stronger evidence against the theory of animated machines than
all the arguments of speculative philosophy.

South America and Africa Books Owned by Muir

Although JM's personal library has not survived intact, approximately 600 of the books he owned are with the MP at UOP, while more than 100 others are at the Huntington Library in Los Angeles. Of those books, the following are relevant to JM's interest in South America and Africa, and may have influenced his decision to study the landscape and natural history of those continents. All volumes are with the MP at UOP unless otherwise noted; volumes containing JM's annotations are noted "Ann."

Agassiz, Louis, and Mrs. Louis. *A Journey in Brazil.* Boston: Ticknor and Fields, 1896. Ann.

Agassiz, Louis. *A Journey in Brazil.* Boston: Houghton Mifflin, 1909. Ann.

Baker, Sir S. W. *Exploration of the Nile Tributaries of Abyssinia.* Hartford: O. D. Case, 1871.

Bates, Henry Walter. *The Naturalist on the River Amazons.* London: John Murray, 1910. Ann.

Bingham, Hiram. *Across South America: An Account of a Journey from Buenos Aires to Lima by Way of Potosí, with Notes on Brazil, Argentina, Bolivia, Chile, and Peru.* Boston: Houghton Mifflin, 1911. Ann.

Bryce, James. *South America Observations and Impressions.* New York: Macmillan, 1912. Ann.

Budge, Sir Ernest Alfred. *The Nile: Notes for Travellers in Egypt.* London: Thomas Cook, 1902. Ann.

Buell, J. W. *Heroes of the Dark Continent and How Stanley Found Emin Pasha.* San Francisco: Pacific, 1890.

Clark, Francis E. *The Continent of Opportunity.* New York: Fleming Revell, 1907.

Conway, Sir William Martin. *The Bolivian Andes; A Record of Climbing & Exploration in Cordillera Real in the Years 1898 and 1900.* New York: Harper & Bros., 1901. Ann.

Curtis, William Eleroy. *Between the Andes and the Ocean.* New York: Duffield, 1907.

Cutler, Harry Gardner. *Panorama of Nations; Or, Journeys Among the Families of*

Men: A Description of their Homes, Customs, Habits, Employments and Beliefs; Their Cities, Temples, Monuments, Literature and Fine Arts. Chicago: Western Publishing House, 1889.

Goldsmith, Rev. J. *Geographical View of the World, Embracing the Manners, Customs and Pursuits of Every Nation.* Hartford: D. F. Robinson, 1831.

Hartwig, Dr. G. *The Polar and Tropical Worlds.* Springfield: C. A. Nichols, 1878.

Hooker, Joseph Dalton, and John Ball. *Journal of a Tour in Marocco and the Great Atlas.* London: MacMillan, 1878.

Humboldt, Alexander, and Aime Bonpland. *Personal Narrative of Travels to the Equinoctial Regions of America During the Years 1799–1804.* London: George Bell, 1907. Ann.

Le Vaillant, Francois. *Voyage de M. Vaillant Dans L'interieur de L'Afrique par Le Cap de Bonne-Esperance, Dans les Annes 1780, 1781, 1783, 1784, 1785.* Paris: Chez Leroy, 1790.

Peck, Annie S. *A Search for the Apex of America.* New York: Dodd, Mead, 1911.

Prescott, William H. *History of the Conquest of Peru.* Philadelphia: David McKay, 1847.

Roosevelt, Theodore. *African Game Trails: An Account of the African Wanderings of an American Hunter-Naturalist.* New York: Charles Scribner's Sons, 1909.

Whymper, Edward. *Travels Amongst the Great Andes of the Equator.* New York: Charles Scribner's Sons, 1892. Ann.

Annotated List of Selected Archival Materials

The following annotated list includes all known archival materials related to JM's South America and Africa journey of 1911–12, including manuscript fragments, newspaper articles, scraps, memorabilia, sundries, botanical specimens, and maps. The range of these materials—and their sheer number—indicates that JM's interest in the southern continents was intense and abiding; that so many of these materials have not previously been described also suggests that scholars of Muir's life and work have remained largely unaware of their existence. Taken together, these various archival materials help to describe the pattern of JM's interest in particular aspects of the physical geography and natural history of South America and Africa.

A few of these materials are in the microform edition of the MP; many more are manually catalogued in the archives at UOP; some are in the UOP archives but remain unidentified and uncataloged; a few have been discovered elsewhere.

Manuscript Fragments

I have found only three holograph manuscript fragments possibly related to JM's South America and Africa journey. These are listed and transcribed below.

FRAGMENT #1

Listed as "South American Note Fragment" in the MP (III/47/12877), this extremely small fragment was found tipped into the AMS of JM's South American Journal; it appears to contain botanical observations from the Amazon.

Ata- White flrs 4 to 6in
orii (broad + gourd-like
fruit about a foot long
agascariensis
   Red flrd

FRAGMENT #2

Listed as "South American Notes" in the Muir Papers (III/34/02138), this note may be related to JM's search for *Araucaria imbricata,* since it mentions South America, the pine genus, and the Andes.

S. Am. has Oaks but not a single pine
    Humboldt
True vegetation ceases on the Alps at 6000
On the Andes at 12000—tree line
Reaching farther N in the interior of N Am
[Main] along the coasts—69°

FRAGMENT #3

Not included with the Muir papers, this fragment of holograph manuscript was tipped into a first-edition copy of Linnie Marsh Wolfe's 1938 book *John of the Mountains: The Unpublished Journals of John Muir* (Boston: Riverside / Houghton Mifflin). During the late 1990s the book, with manuscript leaf included, was sold as lot number 8777 by Buddenbrooks Fine Rare Books, Manuscripts, and Prints, of Boston, Massachusetts. Written on a torn piece of paper—apparently torn before it was inscribed—this fragment could be a commonplace note from JM's reading or an original note or letter fragment suggesting his Humboldtian ambitions in South America.

> Of the Amazon & Orinoco with their "boundless conti[guity] of shade" through which the explorer may toil for months in constant gloom creeping through dank vine-tangles & under = = brush like ants in grass Almost every tree holds its arms wide open to the sun & [torn]

Newspaper Articles

The fifteen newspaper articles I have located from 1911 and 1912 that are of immediate relevance to JM's South America and Africa journey are listed below. These articles are useful in several ways: they provide a view of how the popular media and its readers understood JM as a celebrated public figure; they suggest that JM's travels were of genuine interest not only to Americans, but also to readers in the countries through which he passed; and, they offer some wonderful moments in which JM comments on the value of his international journeys and on his own sense of himself as a traveler.

Because only a few of these have been previously noticed by scholars, I include all available citation information as well as a brief description of each article. There are no bylines for the articles unless otherwise noted. None of these articles are included in the microform edition of the MP, though many exist as clippings in various locations within the archived MP at UOP (in which case a parenthetical citation has been added to identify the location of the item in the MP).

"Goes to Chili [sic] to See Tree: Naturalist Tells Alpine Club How Much Trip Means." June 18, 1911. Source unknown. (MP: Scraps/John Muir/Travels—South America)

Although listed as "date unknown," the date of this article must be June 18, 1911, for it mentions the Alpine Club dinner given "last night" in Muir's honor at the Hotel Manhattan. The talk Muir gave at the June 17 event was later published in the *Sierra Club Bulletin* (12 [January 1924]: 43–46). The brief article on the event, probably from one of the New York dailies, explains that "Mr. Muir is about to start for Southern Chili [sic] to see one tree," referring undoubtedly to *Araucaria imbricata,* and notes that "[t]he naturalist has been worried for a long time over the fact that he has not seen this particular tree." According to the article, Muir was "most enthusiastic last night because at last it appeared as though he would be permitted to enjoy what he termed a 'great treat'."

"John Muir, at 73, to Trace Amazon." June 25, 1911. *New York American.* (MP: Scraps/John Muir/Travels—South America)

Although its date is listed without month or day, and with the year as "191[0]," the date of this article must be June 25, 1911, for its clipping service header clearly notes the month and day, while the year, although illegible in the source, can only be 1911, since the article describes JM's immediate preparations for the voyage. According to the article, Muir was "at last to fulfill the ambition of forty years" by "going to explore the Amazon"—an area that "has long held a curious interest for Muir." "He set out for it forty years ago," the article explains, "but caught the fever in Cuba and had to return," which is how he came to settle in California. Since reaching California in the 1860s, JM has been "planning to resume his trip to the Amazon, but, in his own words, he hasn't had time." The article concludes by noting JM's continued vigor and health: "He is seventy-three years old, but he can take a mountain with the same vim that a small boy vaults a baseball fence."

"A Naturalist of International Renown: An Interview with Prof. John Muir." November 15, 1911. *Buenos Aires Herald.* By Mr. Huxton (though no byline). (MP: Kimes materials; also listed in Kimes bibliography, item A26)

This two-column article, published in English, was based on an interview Muir gave on November 7 with a Mr. Huxton, who also called on him the following day to obtain the photograph that would accompany the article. In mentioning the interview in his journal, JM notes his surprise that "my fame has traveled thus far, though I am not acquainted with a single person in the whole of this great city."

Huxton's article offers a biographical sketch of the naturalist, with an emphasis upon JM's contributions to American conservation and his discovery of Alaskan glaciers. When asked about his literary ambitions, Muir apparently declared, "'I am not going to write books to any extent until I give up my present occupation'." "And what may that be?" Huxton asked. "'Tramp,' came the answer with grim Scotch gravity. 'I am seventy-four and am still good at it'." (Muir, who was actually seventy-three at the time, sometimes misstated his age, and often seems to have done so for effect). When asked if he had a "particular object" in coming to Brazil, Argentina, and Chile, JM replied unhesitatingly that "I am studying the trees of South America," and went on to describe *Araucaria imbricata* and his upcoming journey to Chile in search of it. JM next responds to a question about Buenos Aires by noting its Zoological Gardens, trees, and fertile soil. Huxton concludes by commenting appreciatively that JM's conversation demonstrated "a simplicity and a lack of egotism which was delightfully refreshing to a newspaper correspondent whose daily routine brings him into contact with many personalities but with few who, with so much right, have so little inclination to claim attention."

"Y.M.C.A." (apparent fragment of illegible title). December 7, 1911. *Montevideo Times.* (MP: Scraps/John Muir/Travels—South America)

This one-column article, printed in English, announces the talk that JM would give that evening at the Montevideo YMCA. The piece gives some biographical information, including a list of JM's travels and some note of his conservation work, literary productions, and honorary degrees. The article also mentions that JM's visit to Uruguay was anticipated by a letter of introduction from US President Taft himself, and concludes by predicting that JM's adventures and his skills as a storyteller will combine to make the event unique and memorable.

"El Dr. John Muir en Montevideo." December 7, 1911. *El Tiempo* (Montevideo). In Spanish. (MP: Scraps/John Muir/Travels—South America)

This piece manages to cover, albeit briefly, JM's background in science, study at the University of Wisconsin, association with Emerson (and Emerson's oft-quoted proclamation that JM is "more wonderful than Thoreau"), his 1903–04 world tour, tree studies in South America, honorary degrees, conservation work, President Taft's letter of introduction, and his impending departure for South Africa.

"Hombres de Ciencia: El Doctor John Muir, Su Permanencia en Montevieo [sic]." December 7, 1911. *La Tribuna Popular* (Montevideo). In Spanish. (MP: Scraps/John Muir/Travels—South America)

Although formatted differently, the text of this article is identical to that of "El Dr. John Muir en Montevideo," described above.

"An Evening with John Muir." December 7, 1911. Source unknown. (MP: Scraps/John Muir/Travels—South America)

This one-page announcement of JM's December 7 talk at the Montevideo YMCA consists of three sections: (1) the title and date, along with a photograph of JM and John Burroughs in Yosemite, over a caption reading "Neither man nor the scenery ever had better companionship"; (2) the title "One of North America's Greatest Scientists Visits Montevideo," and a short sketch of JM's life and accomplishments; and (3) the particulars of the event, and mention that JM's talk will be in English.

"El Doctor John Mouir [sic]: Su Conferencia en las Asociacion de J. C." December 9, 1911. *El Dia* (Montevideo). In Spanish. (MP: Scraps/John Muir/Travels—South America)

This brief article notes JM's December 7 talk at the Montevideo YMCA, mentions Muir's previous work and travels, and comments that the talk was engaging, instructive, and well-received.

"John Muir Returns: Botanist Hunted the 'Monkey Puzzle' Tree in Brazil." March 27, 1912. *The Morning Sun* (New York). (MP: Kimes materials; also listed in the Kimes bibliography, item A27)

Although listed as "date unknown," this article must have been published on March 27, 1912, for it mentions that Muir "returned to-day by the Hamburg-American liner *Kaiserin Auguste* [sic] *Victoria.*" The article announces JM's return to America and focuses on his tree studies abroad. Although the piece contains several factual errors (that JM is seventy-four rather than seventy-three; that his 1911 departure from New York was on April 20 rather than August 12; that the monkey puzzle tree is found in Brazil rather than Chile), it does give a clear sense of JM's voyage as a pilgrimage to study the *Araucaria* and *Adansonia* trees. The article concludes with this note: "A coincidence of Mr. Muir's trip home in the *Kaiserin Auguste* [sic] *Victoria* was that he met Mrs. Charles T. Boal of Chicago on board. In 1871 Mrs. Boal was the only woman member of a party that he guided through the Yosemite."

"John Muir Returns Hearty: Naturalist Back from Year's Trip in Remote Forests at 74." March 28, 1912. *New York Tribune.* (MP: Scraps/John Muir/Travels—Miscellaneous)

Although listed as "ca. 1912," this article must have been published on March 27, 1912, for it mentions that Muir "arrived here yesterday" from his trip abroad. The article announces JM's return, and, although it erroneously claims that JM found *Araucaria* forests along the Amazon, it accurately represents the voyage in terms of the tree quests that inspired it.

"John Muir at 74 Back From Quest for Queer Trees: Veteran California Naturalist Climbed Mountains of South America and Africa." March 31, 1912. *New York World.* Pg. 6N. (MP: Scraps/John Muir/Travels—Miscellaneous; also with MP: "Scraps/John Muir/Interviews and Reports)

The source and date of this article are noted along the article's margin, though in a hand other than JM's. Here the unnamed reporter asks JM about his journey. "You wish me to tell all about my trip? But I can not tell you all. There are so many things and it would take me one year to go through my notebooks," said Muir. "But you can tell me something particularly interesting and wonderful?" counters the reporter. "Well, everything was interesting and wonderful," replies JM, characteristically. The bulk of the article is then given to JM's own description of his journey, with special emphasis given to the Amazon, *Araucaria,* and *Adansonia.* "I have material to write almost a hundred books," JM notes, "but I feel I am wasting my time when I write books. If I keep on writing books I will have no time to climb mountains."

"John Muir's Tree Pilgrimage." April 13, 1912. *Boston Transcript.* By Allen Chamberlain. (MP: Scraps/John Muir/Travels—Miscellaneous)

Chamberlain begins by noting that JM is once again visiting Boston (a fact of which scholars have apparently remained unaware), and its author takes pleasure in comparing JM's challenging and austere wilderness journeys with the more common, touristic approach most travelers take. Chamberlain takes an engaging, narrative approach to JM's travels, thereby offering readers an unusual opportunity to understand the drama, as well as simply the facts, of JM's last journey. Organized, like the journey itself, around a series of tree quests, the article does a particularly good job of helping readers to appreciate how JM's talents as a naturalist led him to rare botanical quarry where other travelers had failed. The article also demonstrates a rare awareness of the endangerment of the landscapes through which JM traveled. In emphasizing the rarity of the *Araucaria braziliensis,* for example, Chamberlain quotes JM and then offers a prescient observation of his own: "'And they told me in the States that this tree was very likely extinct,' exclaimed Mr. Muir. But while far from extinct today, that fate may not be far hence, for the lumbermen are at them with sinister intent, and armed with all the modern appliances for complete destruction."

This article may also be unique in including JM's own dramatization of his first sighting of the baobab tree to which he was led by a young African boy whom he met near Victoria Falls. "'Well, sir,' said Mr. Muir in telling of the hunt, 'when I saw that tree I burst out laughing, and you should have seen that little "muggins" of a boy look at me. He probably thought me crazy. The tree was perhaps thirty feet through at the base, but short in the head, and with the smoothest and most human-like skin that you can possibly imagine, and all wrinkly at the elbows. It was fantastic'." And, although it only indirectly addresses the issue of the journey as the completion of a lifelong dream, the article does mention JM's temporary blindness in 1867 in the context of his subsequent wilderness journeys.

"A Future Paradise for Mankind in South America: John Muir, Famous Naturalist of the Sierras, Home from a Year's Trip Abroad, Describes the Vast Possibilities of the Amazon Valley and Tells of the Dangers That Threaten Yosemite National Park." *The New York Times.* April 21, 1912. Pg. 12.

This lavishly illustrated, seven-column article in the Sunday *New York Times* ran on Muir's seventy-fourth birthday (though the article does not note this fact), and is probably the most extensive coverage his South America and Africa journey ever received. As the title of the article suggests, the reporter has chosen to emphasize the economic potential and instrumental value of Amazonia over the scientific, aesthetic, and spiritual values that actually motivated JM's journey. Although JM often noted the impressive fecundity and immensity of the Amazon basin, he did not—as the article unfortunately suggests—appreciate the region primarily for its "vast possibilities for the human race." While JM was most interested in talking about trees and his pilgrimages to see and study them, the rhythm of the interview suggests the journalist was more interested in JM's views of lumber, rubber, agriculture, and the possibilities for development of the region. And while JM predicted that shortages of food might compel future generations to settle the region more actively, he casually noted that such future development might happen "in two or three centuries, perhaps." One further senses that words are being put in JM's mouth when, for example, JM is reported to have described the scenery of the Amazon as "somewhat monotonous," "lacking in diversity," and, by implication, in need of "the vigor and the enterprise that accomplishes great things"— characterizations inconsistent with JM's observations in many other interviews, journals, and letters.

Despite the instrumentalist rhetoric of this article, its sheer length allows some of JM's travel story to emerge, and some discussion of JM's curiosity about rare trees, the expansiveness of the Amazon river system, and the influence of the writings of Alfred Russell Wallace and Henry W. Bates on JM's desire to travel to South America. "It seemed strange," the reporter observes, "to hear John Muir, who is so closely identified with the scenic glories of the Pacific Coast, talking of a trip in lands so foreign as South America and Africa." Also valuable is a shift in the article, from the journey to the "scenic glories of the Pacific Coast," which allows JM to discuss the Hetch Hetchy controversy and the urgent need to protect the endangered landscapes of Yosemite National Park. This final section ends with the concluding words of JM's *The Yosemite,* just published by the Century Company: "Dam Hetch Hetchy! As well dam for water-tanks the people's cathedrals and churches, for no holier temple has ever been consecrated by the heart of man." The article reprints three illustrations: a photograph of "John Muir and His Friend John Burroughs," almost certainly taken at Burroughs's seventy-fifth birthday party on April 3; a lovely, left-profile sketch of JM made from a photograph; and a photograph, with additional penciled art in the foreground, of "John Muir in the Famous Grove of Great Trees, California."

> "Future Paradise for Mankind in South America: John Muir, Famous Naturalist of the Sierras, Home from a Year's Trip Abroad, Describes Vast Possibilities of the Amazon Valley." *The Dallas Morning News.* May 4, 1912. Pg. 12. No byline. (Kimes bibliography, item A28)

Although this article is listed in the Kimes bibliography, the Kimes were apparently unaware that this article is an abbreviated reprint of the April 21, 1912, Sunday *New York Times* article described above.

> "John Muir Comes Here to Take Rest: Famous Naturalist, Now 74 Years Old, Visiting Daughter After Years of Research." [Los Angeles] *Herald.* April 23, 1912. (MP: I/A/20/11636)

Article describing JM's arrival in Los Angeles to visit Helen at his journey's end. JM is reported to have said that "he is now ready to rest and visit with his daughter after undergoing so many dangers and hardships."

Scraps

I have found twenty-two scrap items (other than newspaper articles about JM's journey, described above) that bear on JM's interest in and travels to South America and Africa. These scraps consist primarily of newspaper clippings JM kept, and they often provide insight into his interests, reading, and experiences as they relate to the South America and Africa travels.

These materials are not included in the microform edition of the MP, but exist in folders and boxes in the archived MP at the UOP. Materials referred to as "scraps" are collected in "MS 48, Series VI: Related Articles and Scraps," and the locator terms used here may be cross-referenced to the alphabetical "Inventory of Scraps" in order to ascertain the box and folder location of each item. Because few of these items can be accurately dated, I have organized the scraps described below topically. Within each topical category items appear alphabetically, according to the UOP inventory headings and subheadings. Following the formal heading/subheading I have provided an abbreviated title/description and an annotation of the item. Sources and dates of items should be assumed as unknown unless listed.

SOUTH AMERICA SCRAPS

Books—Miscellaneous. "South American Relations: Two Important Books"

A double book review of *The Monroe Doctrine, an Obsolete Shibboleth*, by Prof. Hiram Bingham (New Haven: Yale Univ. Press, 1913), and *The Two Americas*, by Gen. Rafael Reyes (London: T. Werner Laurie, 1914), former President of Colombia. Discusses South American travel, exploration, and politics, and includes a strong critique of Theodore Roosevelt's actions in Panama.

Books—Miscellaneous. "The Lower Amazon: A Remarkable Record of Exploration in Para." *San Francisco Chronicle.*

Book review of Algot Lange's *In the Amazon Jungle: Adventures in Remote Parts of the Upper Amazon River, Including a Sojourn Among Cannibal Indians* (New York: Putnam's Sons, 1912), focusing on Lange's exploration of the Amazon and his accounts of hardship, wildlife, and Indian artifacts.

Books—Nature. "Camera Shots at Big Game. By Mr. And Mrs. A. G. Wallihan."

Brief advertisement for the Wallihans' book of big game photographs, which JM may have clipped because his friend Theodore Roosevelt wrote the book's introduction.

Drawings—Indians. "Indians Halting Near Mocoa, South America."

Book or magazine plate illustration of indigenous people of what is now western Colombia making camp in the jungle while a white traveler looks on.

Envelopes—South America. Mark Kerr Note.

Empty envelope on which JM has written "*Ex South America.* Mark Kerr." The envelope may once have contained the clipping described below (see South America—Andes Mountains).

Forests—South America. "Forest Resources of South America."

Clipped from a publication with the running head "Conservation," this article fragment describes the character of tropical forests, primarily in the Amazon basin.

Photographs—Trees. "Pawpaw Tree, Brazil."

Book or magazine plate illustration of a well-dressed Brazilian planter posing before a large pawpaw tree.

South America—Andes Mountains. "Far Up in the Andes: The Journey of a Young San Franciscan."

Illustrated article about Mark Kerr's explorations in the Ecuadorian Andes. Kerr, a San Francisco civil engineer who had formerly been with the USGS, read a paper on his explorations at a Sierra Club meeting. The description of Andean natives is somewhat racist in tone, but the article also offers what must have been, to JM, an interesting account of travels at the upper elevations of the western flank of the Andes.

South America—Colombia "Tree Pilgrimage." "The Lhasa of South America." By Arthur Ruhl. *Everybody's Magazine.* 591–604.

Lengthy, undated, heavily illustrated magazine article by Ruhl, author of *The Other Americans: The Cities, the Countries, and Especially the People of South America* (New York: Charles Scribner's Sons, 1910), who had recently returned from the jungles near the Amazon's headwaters. Much of the article, which is rather racist in tone, describes Bogotá and the native lifeways and peoples of Colombia.

South America—Rubber Industry. Rubber Plantations and Prices Fragment.

Brief newspaper fragment listing then current prices for Brazilian rubber, noting that those prices have fallen, and explaining that plantation grown rubber in other parts of the world has begun to compete with the harvest of wild Amazonian rubber. JM may have clipped this in part because the plunge in rubber prices rendered the famous Madeira Railroad, which was in its final stages of construction while JM was in Brazil, economically untenable and therefore virtually useless.

Travel—Miscellaneous. Florence Jackson and Harriet Cory Talks.

Two-part newspaper clipping describing, first, an upcoming lecture by Mrs. Florence Jackson, editor of the *Overland Monthly,* on the subject of "The Eastern Republics of South America"; and, second, the recent return of Californian Harriet Cory from travels in Brazil and Europe.

Africa Scraps

Africa. "A Whole Menagerie of Strangely Colored Animals Is Discovered in Africa." *San Francisco Examiner.* January 26, 1902.

A dramatically illustrated article about the ten species of animals—including the singing ostrich, five-horned giraffe, ant bear, and white-bearded chimpanzee (as well as "a new race of pigmies")—discovered by Sir Harry Johnston in Africa.

Illustrations depict the three-horned *Chamaeloeon johnstoni* and the zebra-like *Okapia johnstoni*. Given the date of the article, which coincides with the 1902 publication of Johnston's two-volume book *The Uganda Protectorate*, this clipping probably relates most directly to JM's 1903–04 world tour. However, JM did read and take notes from *The Uganda Protectorate* in association with his 1911–12 journey.

Africa. "The Niger-Soudan Campaign."

An article describing the progress of an expedition to the source of the Niger River. Describes some of the flora and fauna of the region and offers reports about the supposedly cannibalistic natives among whom "the human foot is a great delicacy."

Africa. "Horseless Age is Promised in Africa: Zebras Are Now Being Domesticated for Use in Black Man's Country."

Short notice of attempts to domesticate the zebra in the East African Protectorate. "The domestication of the zebra," the article begins, "is no longer regarded as hopeless."

Africa. "Heart of Africa."

Article on the remarkable progress of railroad building in the Congo Free State. During his trip to Lake Victoria and the headwaters of the Nile in February 1912, JM traveled by rail to and from Port Florence, south of Kisumu on the shores of the eastern arm of Lake Victoria.

Africa. "The Victoria Falls." *The National Geographic Magazine.*

This clipping from a *National Geographic* article consists of little text but includes five full-page photographs of Victoria Falls and the forest surrounding it. Interestingly, good-quality prints of photographs nearly identical to these (and, in at least one case, absolutely identical) are held with the MP (IV/8/373; IV/9/398-403). The photo credits on the prints in the MP and on the photos published in *National Geographic* both indicate that copyright is held by a photographer named Pedrotti, of Bulawayo. The text of the *National Geographic* article also mentions that the photos there printed were provided by the Royal Geographical Society of London, which had recently published a description of the falls in its own journal. Given the great difficulty JM had in obtaining photographs adequate to illustrate the would-be South America and Africa articles Robert Underwood Johnson wanted him to write for *Century Magazine,* JM may have clipped this piece in order to track down good photos of Victoria Falls through *National Geographic,* the Royal Society, or Pedrotti himself. Indeed, the presence of the Pedrotti prints in the MP would suggest that JM was successful in this effort, though the *Century*

Magazine articles were never written. These are probably the photos to which JM refers in his August 2, 1912, letter to Johnson, when he comments that "I have three good photos of the Victoria Falls. . . . "

Animals—Miscellaneous. "How Dr. Egan Ministered to Duke, the Young Lion." *San Francisco Examiner.* August 1, 1897.

Illustrated article describing how a San Francisco doctor, W. F. Egan, treated the illness of a lion cub named Duke. The early publication date of this clipping may suggest that JM had African fauna in mind long before his international journeys began.

Books—Africa (also filed under Roosevelt, Theodore—Hunting). "In Darkest Africa, and Other Lands." By H. E. Cobblentz. *The Dial.* June 1, 1909. 364–367.

An omnibus book review of seven recent books on foreign travel, four of which concern Africa: Winston Spencer Churchill's *My African Journey* (Toronto: William Briggs, 1909); A. F. R. Wollaston's *From Ruwenzori to the Congo: A Naturalist's Journey Across Africa* (London: John Murray, 1908); John M. Springer's *The Heart of Central Africa: Mineral Wealth and Missionary Opportunity* (Cincinnati: Jennings & Graham, 1909); Decima Moore's and Major F. G. Guggisberg's *We Two in West Africa* (London: William Heinemann, 1909). The review essay includes a lengthy critique of Theodore Roosevelt's famous 1909 African hunting expedition, on which Roosevelt, his son Kermit, and their party killed more than 500 animals. JM may have clipped this because of the connection to his friend Roosevelt or because of his ethical concerns about the treatment of animals, but he would also have been interested in books on the natural history of Africa, particularly in the years just before his own voyage there.

Drawings—Plants. "Liberian Coffee Plant."

Book or magazine illustration of a single, young plant, above the caption "Liberian Coffee Plant."

Envelopes—Trees. "Baobab."

Empty envelope on which JM has written "*Trees* / Baobab— / Spruce far North / The biggest. Hugh Miller." This may simply be a note about large trees, or a list of the envelope's contents, which may once have included items related to the large tree species mentioned. Muir studied the baobab, *Adansonia digitata,* in central and east Africa during January and February 1912.

Roosevelt, Theodore—Miscellaneous. "Mr. Roosevelt's Jungle Book." *The Dial.* Sept. 16, 1912.

Fragment of a lengthy review of Roosevelt's *African Game Trails: An Account of the African Wanderings of an American Hunter-Naturalist* (New York: Charles Scribner's Sons, 1910). The anonymous reviewer, while careful to be respectful of Roosevelt, suggests that the 510 animals Roosevelt's party killed far exceeded the imperatives of specimen gathering, and thus implies there was more barbarism than science in Roosevelt's celebrated African safari. As a friend of Roosevelt's, and as someone who had traveled on the game-rich east African plains, JM would have been doubly interested in this review. Indeed, Roosevelt had inscribed a gift copy of *African Game Trails* to JM on April 21, 1911, JM's seventy-third birthday, and just four months before JM's own journey. That volume, which is still housed with the MP, is inscribed "To John Muir with the Best Wishes of Theodore Roosevelt, April 21, 1911."

Trees—Miscellaneous. "Very Aged Trees."

Brief clipping about the prodigious size of the baobab tree. Humboldt is quoted as having declared baobabs the "oldest living organic monument on our planet," and it is noted that "a room large enough to furnish comfortable quarters for thirty men has been cut out of the trunk of a baobab, which continued to grow and flourish."

Memorabilia

I have found thirteen items of memorabilia that relate to JM's South America and Africa travels. In calling these materials "memorabilia," I am simply adopting the term used to denote several boxes of random, uncataloged materials in the MP collection at UOP, though many of these materials are quite similar to the items formally classified archivally as "scraps," described above.

South America Memorabilia

Letter of Indication

While in New York preparing for his journey abroad, JM purchased a Letter of Indication—roughly equivalent to what we would now call a traveler's check—which allowed him to draw credit at various banks around the world. The letter of indication, signed by JM, is dated April 20, 1911, and was issued by the firm of Knauth, Nachod, and Kühne in the amount of 1,000 pounds. The letter of indication is accompanied by a set of instructions for use and the 1910 List of Correspondents to whom JM could apply, worldwide, to obtain cash.

"Peruvian Rubber and International Politics." *The American Review of Reviews.* Circa 1912. 325–328.

An article describing atrocities inflicted upon indigenous peoples working as rubber harvesters in the Putumayo district of Amazonian Peru. The article states that a recently released report describing these atrocities prompted the Peruvian government to begin reforms that included more strict policing of rubber barons, whose "atrocious crimes against the Indians" included forms of torture "which the spoken word cannot easily describe." The fact that JM saved this article suggests that he was sensitive to the issue of native exploitation in the Amazonian rubber industry.

"An American Adventure in Brazil: A Search for Gold that Led 5,500 Miles, to the Source of the Amazon, up the Riberao Rapids, through the Jungle, across the Pampas, and Down the Paraguay." By Alexander P. Rogers. *The World's Work*. Circa 1912. 625–640.

A lengthy article describing Rogers's journey up the Amazon from delta to headwaters, then south through Brazil and Argentina to Buenos Aires. In addition to offering an account of this epic journey, the article describes the conscription and torture of indigenous peoples by the rubber barons of the Amazon region.

Postcard of Florianópolis, Brazil

Postcard with photograph of the Brazilian seaside village of Florianópolis, through which JM passed on his way south, spending the day of October 30, 1911 there.

Page with Contacts for Acquaintances in Brazil

A typewritten page with names and addresses for five men JM met in Belém and Manaus, Brazil: F. H. Sanford, W. S. Gordon, R. H. May, Douglas Aimers, and A. Duff. JM seems to have used this sheet of addresses to correspond with these men after his return to Martinez.

Postcard of "La Piedra Movediza"

Small postcard with a photograph of a large boulder balanced on a rock face. The card reads "Rep. Argentina—Tandil—La piedra movediza." In barely legible typestrikes, someone has noted on the face of the card that the pictured boulder has since tumbled from the position depicted in the photo.

Annie Peck Andes Photographs

A series of nine postcards with photographs of Andean villages and mountains taken by mountaineer Annie Peck. The views are of the village of Yungay, the Llanganuco Gorge, and Mount Huascaran, and each is credited with a 1908 copyright; most are by Annie S. Peck, with a few credited to Harper & Brothers. It is likely that these postcards were given to Muir by Peck herself, on November 7,

1911, in Buenos Aires, for JM's journal entry for that day reads as follows: "Had long talk with Miss Annie Peck, the mountaineer, who called in the evening and showed many Andean photographs." Interestingly, the advertisement on the back of each card is for Singer sewing machines, thus setting up a strange rhetoric by which a woman mountain climber so intrepid as to have discouraged native Andean porters is, in effect, being sponsored by a primary cultural agent of women's domestic manufactory.

Envelope labeled "14 Photos of Andes."

A reused envelope once forwarded to him in Martinez by the US Delegation offices in Buenos Aires, on which JM has written "14 Photos of Andes /101 Mendoza & Los Andes / Along R.R. Pass." Presumably this envelope stored the series of twenty-seven Edmund Carpenter photos of the Argentinean pampas and eastern Andes that are now contained in the MP (IV/22/1200–1207).

AFRICA MEMORABILIA

Postcard of "Santa Cruz de Teneriffe"

One side of this postcard is a photograph of an airy room, which the caption identifies as a "Patio in Santa Cruz Hotel." The reverse side contains a brief description of the city of Tenerife, explaining, for example, that the city has been the capital of the Canary Islands since 1821, and that it then had a population of approximately 50,000. JM stopped briefly at Tenerife on December 26–27, 1911, on his way from South America to Africa.

Rhodesian Time Table

Called "The Rhodesian 'Where Is It' Time Table and General Information," this January 1912 brochure lists the stations (with height above sea level) on the Beira, Mashonaland, and Rhodesia Railways. JM's markings adjacent to the station names suggest that he used this document while traveling through southeast Africa during the early weeks of 1912.

"Baobab Mombasa" Envelope

Empty envelope on which JM has written "Baobab Mombasa/ & French Congo near / Stanley Pool—." This envelope may perhaps have contained the two rare photographs of baobab trees that exist in the MP (IV/8/369-370)—undoubtedly the same photographs JM was referring to when, on August 2, 1912, he wrote to Robert Underwood Johnson that "I have . . . a few rather poor [photographs] of the Baobab." Though the MP lists the trees in these two photos as "unidentified," they are clearly *Adansonia digitata,* the baobab. The blur in the photos suggests that they were taken from the window of a moving train.

Postcard of "A Fallen Baobab Tree, Mombasa B. E. A."

The photograph on this postcard shows a person standing atop the fallen trunk of an immense baobab. JM studied and sketched baobab trees near Mombasa on February 20–22, 1912.

Steamer *General* Menu

The March 8, 1912, menu from the Dutch East Africa Line steamer ship *General*, on which JM sailed from Africa to Europe during February and March 1912. Below an illustration of the ship, the evening's dinner choices are listed in both German and English.

Sundries

The four items here listed as "sundries" are either glued or tipped into a large, uncataloged scrapbook, formerly a ledger, which is a fairly recent addition to the MP. It is not known when or by whom the scrapbook, which contains primarily materials relating to Alaska, was assembled.

"Mr. Whymper in the Andes."

Article about Edward Whymper, mountaineer and author of *Scrambles Amongst the Alps in the Years 1860–69* (London: J. Murray, 1871) and *Travels Amongst the Great Andes of the Equator* (New York: Charles Scribner's Sons, 1892), both of which JM owned.

"Eighteen Hundred Miles Through Central Africa." By Earnest S. Cox.

Illustrated magazine article describing Cox's journey by foot through central Africa, with emphasis on descriptions of native porters, hunting adventures, and the various difficulties encountered by the traveler.

"Flowers in Liberia."

Various drawings of west African flora.

"The Duke of the Abruzzi, the Conqueror of Ruwenzori, the Hitherto Unscaled African Range."

Article on mountaineers who first ascended several celebrated African peaks.

Botanical Specimens

A substantial part of JM's own herbarium survives in files in the basement of Muir's old home, now the John Muir National Historic Site in Martinez, California. Although not well organized or cataloged, many of the approximately 800 specimens remain in surprisingly good condition. JM gathered these stems, leaves, seeds, flowers, and cones during his botanical studies around the world, and at least eight specimens can be identified with certainty as having come from the 1911 travels in South America (the incomplete cataloging of the herbarium makes it difficult to discern how many other specimens may also have come from South America or Africa). Among these specimens, now contained in the H-4 and H-5 divisions of the herbarium, are ferns from the wilderness of southern Brazil and wisteria from near Buenos Aires.

Maps

A large, uncataloged map file in the MP contains a number of JM's own maps—and fragments of maps—from various periods of his life. Three of these appear relevant to the South America and Africa journey. To my knowledge, none has been previously described.

Small Atlantic Map (including the Atlantic Ocean, South America, the east coast of North America, western Europe, and the west coast of Africa). Printed in German. Undated.

Of unknown provenance and in very good condition, this map may have been used by JM as he was homeward bound from Europe to America on the Hamburg-American line steamer *Kaiserin Augusta Victoria* in March 1912, or it may be an artifact dating to his 1903–04 world tour.

Small South America Map Fragment. Printed in French. Undated.

This map survives as a fragment containing approximately the northern half of the continent, from around Pôrto Alegre, Brazil, northward. The way the map has been torn and folded suggests an interest in the northern half of the continent generally and the Amazon specifically, which leads me to wonder if this might be the map JM mentions studying in Indianapolis in 1867, before he began his thousand-mile walk to the Gulf (*Thousand-Mile*, xvi). That the map is printed in French may indicate that JM acquired it while traveling and working in lower Canada in 1864–66. Unfortunately, neither the content nor the condition of the map allows for a conclusive dating of it.

Large South America Map. Printed in English. 1909.

This very large map has received heavy use and has only survived as a stack of well-worn fragments. Nevertheless, by literally piecing the map back together I have been able to recover most of it. In doing so I have discovered that Muir's holograph travel journal contains facts and passages quite clearly derived from the text on the back of the map—thus proving certainly that this is the map Muir carried with him during his travels in South America. Indeed, much of the holograph journal entry for November 3, 1911—an entry that is itself a conspicuous departure from JM's usual journalistic style—is borrowed rather directly from the "Description physique" section of "Le Brésil," the essay printed on the back of this map. This essay is also annotated with marginal notes in which JM has done the calculations necessary to convert the height of South American peaks, which the map gives in meters, to feet. The face of the map is also lightly annotated with circles indicating some of the places Muir visited, thus making this original map not only a genuine artifact of JM's last journey, but also a valuable research tool.

APPENDIX F

Table of Emendations

This appendix presents simple emendations in tabular form, with the emendation in the left column and the typescript reading in the right. A few emendations have been so numerous as to make it awkward to include them in the table. Throughout the JM texts, the country name "Chili" has been emended to "Chile"; the closing greeting "goodby" has been standardized with no hyphen and no final letter "e"; "H.H.," "H'y," and related abbreviations have been replaced by "Hetch Hetchy"; "Ar.," "Arau.," and related abbreviations have been replaced by *Araucaria*; "Portugese" has been emended to "Portuguese"; and the words "negro" and "negroes" have been capitalized. All other simple emendations are noted in the following table.

EMENDATION		TMS READING
Chapter 1: Correspondence		
Feb. 11	San Francisco	S.F.
Mar. 2	Wisconsin	Wis.
Mar. 2	Wisconsin University	Wisc. Univ.
Mar. 2	book manuscript-like	bookms.-like
Mar. 31	drafts	draughts
Mar. 31	to	yo
May 14	Autobiography	Autobio-
May 24	San Francisco	S.F.
May 24	enclosures	inclosures
May 24	Marian	M.
May 30	Sellers's	Sellers
May 30	Sellers's	Seller's
June 13	San Francisco	S.F.
June 27	Nature-love	Nature love
June 27	uncontrollable	uncontrolable
June 27	conferred	confered
July 14	natural.	natural. ....

Chapter 2: Journal

Aug. 16	mackerel	mackeral
Aug. 20	whitecaps	white caps
Aug. 22	railroad	R.R.
Aug. 25	woolly	wooly
Aug. 26	whitecaps	white caps
Aug. 29	mosquito	mosquitoe
Aug. 30	thunderstorm	thunder storm
Aug. 31	Zoological	Zooological
Aug. 31	Manoas	Manos
Sept. 2	panicles	pannicles
Sept. 2	tablecloth	table-cloth
Sept. 4	goodwill	good-will
Sept. 5	coastlines	coast lines
Sept. 6	midday	mid-day
Sept. 6	has	had ("Sanford, had")
Sept. 6	midday	mid-day
Sept. 6	sometimes	some times
Sept. 10	ropy	ropey
Sept. 12	company	Company
Sept. 14	semicircle	semi-circle
Sept. 16	diameter	dia.
Sept. 16	failed	faded
Sept. 16	Handsome	handsome
Sept. 22	long	l.
Sept. 22	leguminous	leguminus
Sept. 23	*Harnsworth*	Harnsworth
Sept. 25	downtown	down town

Chapter 2: Correspondence

Sept. 18	every way	everyway

Chapter 3: Journal

Sept. 26	cloudy	clouds
Sept. 27	Cadaverous	cadaverous
Sept. 29	coconuts	cocoanuts
Oct. 1	Great Barrier Reef	great barrier reef
Oct. 4	waterfront	water front
Oct. 10	Superintendent	Supt.
Oct. 10	fjord	fiord
Oct. 10	scarcely	scarce

Oct. 11	sawmill	saw-mill
Oct. 12	Sao	Soa
Oct. 12	landslide	land-slide
Oct. 12	Sao	Soa
Oct. 12	hotel	Hotel
Oct. 13	Sao	Soa
Oct. 14	tableland	table-land
Oct. 14	arrowhead	arrow-head
Oct. 14	Some	Same
Oct. 14	Iguassu	lguassu
Oct. 15	grows	grow
Oct. 16	downstream	down stream
Oct. 21	monoecious	monocious
Oct. 23	has	have
Oct. 24	herbaceous	herbacious
Oct. 27	sawmill	saw-mill
Oct. 28	waterfront	water front
Nov. 1	thunderstorm	thunder-storm
Nov. 3	in	In ("In the Sierra de . . . ")
Nov. 3	de	De ("In the Sierra de . . . ")
Nov. 3	Sao Paulo	Soa Parlo
Nov. 3	states	States
Nov. 3	affluents	affluence
Nov. 3	Sao Francisco	Soa Francisco
Nov. 3	separates	seperates
Nov. 4	lighthouses	light-houses
Nov. 7	Buenos Aires	Buenoa Aires
Nov. 7	Zoological	Zooological

Chapter 3: Correspondence

Sept. 26	steamer	stmr
Oct. 10	fjord	fiord
Oct. 10	account	acct.
Nov. 8	well-being	wellbeing
Nov. 8	fjords	fiords

Chapter 4: Journal

Nov. 10	firewood	fire wood
Nov. 10	suddenly	suddonly
Nov. 10	papilionaceous	papilonaceus
Nov. 10	there is	thereis

Nov. 13	sawmills	saw-mills
Nov. 14	snow	Snow
Nov. 19	rapidly	rapudly
Nov. 20	sawmill	saw-mill
Nov. 20	rhombs	rombs
Nov. 20	alligator	alligators
Nov. 21	epiphytes	epiphypes
Nov. 21	eight	wight
Nov. 25	10:30	10.30
Nov. 25	overnight	over night
Nov. 26	mountainsides	mountain sides
Nov. 26	10:30	10.30
Dec. 2	*Kurakina*	*Kuritina*
Dec. 9	The	Tho
Dec. 10	journeys	journies

Chapter 4: Correspondence

Nov. 29	4 or 5 hundred	4 or 500
Dec. 6	was	were
Dec. 6	mountains	mtns.
Dec. 6	though	tho
Dec. 6	on my way	on way
Dec. 9	account	acct.

Chapter 5: Journal

Dec. 16	northeast	north-east
Dec. 18	cumuli	cumili
Dec. 18	heartbeats	heart-beats
Dec. 23	pattern	lattern
Dec. 26	zigzag	zig-zag
Dec. 28	5,000-ton	5000 ton
Dec. 30	shore	store
Dec. 30	Lighthouse	Light-house
Jan. 16	boulder-strewn	bowlder-strewn
Jan. 16	S. California	S. Cal
Jan. 18	sandstone	sand-stone
Jan. 19	boundary	bounday
Jan. 21	numbers	number
Jan. 21	leguminous	liguminous
Jan. 22	boulders	bowlders
Jan. 24	mountains	mtns

Jan. 24	railroad	R R
Jan. 28	zigzag	zig-zag
Feb. 5	huge-trunked	huge trunked

Chapter 5: Correspondence
[no entries]

Chapter 6: Journal

Feb. 9	accommodations	accomodations
Feb. 9	British East Africa	B. E. A.
Feb. 11	lake	Lake
Feb. 12	digitate	digited
Feb. 12	Petioles	peteols
Feb. 13	jinrikisha	Jirinkshaa
Feb. 13	distance	disrance
Feb. 13	jinrikisha	jirinksha
Feb. 13	man's	Man's
Feb. 14	falls	Falls
Feb. 14	hypothesis	hypotheosis
Feb. 14	continent	contintent
Feb. 14	*Great*	great
Feb. 17	spring	Spring
Feb. 17	boulders	bowlders
Feb. 17	potholes	pot-holes
Feb. 17	boulders	bowlders
Feb. 18	mango	mangoe
Feb. 25	East Africa	E.A.
Feb. 25	windswept	wind-swept
Feb. 28	tableland	table-land
Feb. 28	northernmost	north-most
Feb. 29	crenelated	crennaleted
Mar. 2	alga	Alga
Mar. 4	Red Sea	red sea
Mar. 4	canal	Canal
Mar. 5	canal	Canal
Mar. 14	hotel	Hotel
Mar. 20	east	East
Mar. 20	waves	wave
Mar. 21	east	East
Mar. 25	north	North

Chapter 6: Correspondence
Mar. 13   Expect   expect

Chapter 7: Correspondence
April 15   Autobiography   Autobio
April 15   proofreading   proof reading
April 15   months   mo's
May 1   Godlike   God-like
May 10   some   som
May 10   workmen   workman
May 10   far reaching   farreaching
May 10   bread-winning   bread winning
June 20   snowline   snow line
Aug. 2   typewritten   type written
Aug. 2   notes   note
Aug. 14   though   tho
Aug. 24   though   tho
Sept. 11   reveling   revelling
[Dec. 29]   bedrock   bed-rock

Muir's Reading and Botanical Notes (referenced by page in TMS)
Pg. 148   vol.   Vol.
Pg. 150   smoldering   smouldering
Pg. 151   Sometimes   sometimes
Pg. 151   baobab   Baobab
Pg. 153   an   An
Pg. 154   conscientious   conscientous
Pg. 155   birthplace   birth-place
Pg. 158   reenters   re-enters
Pg. 159   analogous   analagous
Pg. 159   landmark   land-mark
Pg. 160   treetops   tree-tops

Notes to Editor's Introductions

The following documentary and explanatory notes pertain to the general introduction and chapter introductions in *John Muir's Last Journey*.

Introduction

xxiii   *"to abandon the profession of my choice"*   Turner 122

xxiii   *"of becoming so successful"*   Wolfe, *Son* 100

xxiv   *"My right eye is gone"*   Turner 125

xxiv   *"[t]he sunshine and the winds"*   Wolfe, *Son* 104

xxv   *"gave you the eye within the eye"*   Wolfe, *Son* 104–105

xxv   *"This affliction has driven me"*   Wolfe, *Son* 105

xxv   *"wildest, leafiest, and least trodden way"*   Badè, *Thousand* 1

xxv   *"I bade adieu"*   Badè, *Thousand* xix

xxvi   *"Boys are fond of the books of travelers"*   Muir, *Story* 145

xxvi   *Alexander von Humboldt*   For further discussion of the influence of Humboldt on JM, see Hall and Mark; Holmes.

xxvii   *"For weeks"*   Badè, *Thousand* xvi

xxvii   *"For many a year"*   Badè, *Thousand* xviii

xxvii   *"destination of [Muir's] long-deferred dreams"*   Turner 147

xxviii   *"I had long wished to visit"*   Badè, *Thousand* 96

xxviii   *As he began his long recovery*   Badè, *Thousand* xxi–xxii; Wolfe, *Son* 114; Holmes 189; MP I/A/1/611 and I/A/1/603

xxviii   *When a ship arrived in Cedar Keys*   Badè, *Thousand* 85

xxviii   *"After passing a month"*   Badè, *Thousand* 96

xxviii   *product of reading notes*   Badè, *Thousand* xxii

xxviii   *"[i]t seems strange"*   Badè, *Thousand* 96

xxix   *"I could not find a vessel of any sort"*   Clarke 58

xxix   *"There, I thought, I shall find health"*   Badè, *Thousand* 96

xxx   *wrote to his brother David*   Holmes 199–200

xxx   *"a few months will call upon me"*   Badè, *Life* 110

xxx   *Even when the "attractions of California"*   Wilkins 59

xxx   *In September 1869*   Holmes 208; MP 2:745

xxx   *"The Amazon and Andes"*   Badè, *Life* 123

xxx *Nevertheless, it was difficult* Holmes 218; MP 2:898–900. The primary reason JM's arrival in the Sierra has been viewed as a decisive and immediate discovery of his place in the world is JM's own dramatic account of this arrival in *My First Summer in the Sierra*. However, as Holmes explains, the earliest *surviving* account of JM's mystical entrance into the Sierra comes not from the original notebooks of the late 1860s, which are now lost, but from three notebooks from 1887—notebooks that are clearly heavily revised and cannot be depended upon for a clear view of JM's actual feelings at the time he came to California (200). Thus, I agree with Holmes's claim that JM "did not suddenly *find* a new home in Yosemite, but rather *made* one there over the course of years" (201). Seeing JM's experience of coming to feel at home in California as a gradual one helps us to better understand how urgent his immediate dreams of the Amazon might have seemed, even well into the 1870s.

xxx *Another year in California* Holmes 228n; MP 2:955

xxxi *"continued to write of California"* Homes 190

xxxii *"You do not know how loathe"* I/A/20/11295

xxxii *"I do not quite like the idea of this trip"* I/A/20/11371

xxxiii *"If you do make that southern trip"* I/A/20/11397

xxxiii *"[A]re you melting away"* I/A/20/11439

xxxiii *"John Muir, Esquire"* I/A/20/11422

xxxiii *"It will be a big load off my mind"* I/A/20/11459

xxxiv *"[y]ou probably know best"* I/A/20/11465

xxxix *pocket-sized travel journals* For more information about the provenance, physical characteristics, and condition of these journals, see Appendix B, "Editorial Methods."

xl *sixteen biographical and critical studies* These studies, which are listed in the Bibliography, are those by Badè, Wolfe *(Son)*, Wolfe *(John)*, Winkley, Jones, Smith, Lyon, Stewart, Clarke, Fox, Cohen, Turner, Stanley, Wilkins, Holmes, and Ehrlich.

xl *fewer than a dozen pages* For example, many book-length studies of Muir dispense with this epic journey in a sentence or two, and several—including John Winkley's study of Muir as a naturalist—devote not a single word to Muir's last journey. Herbert Smith's Twayne Series book devotes two sentences to Muir's world travels: the first sentence notes that such travels occurred; the second unaccountably asserts that "[t]hese travels have no place in his writing, however" (122).

xli *discussed inaccurately* Examples of these inaccuracies are disturbingly common. In her edited volume of landscape writing by Muir and his contemporary Mary Austin, for example, Ann Zwinger—herself a gifted naturalist and usually a precise writer—has unfortunately introduced a number of errors in the story of Muir's travels: that Muir's 1867 injury occurred when "a piece of wood flew in his right eye" (it was the tang of a file) (xii); that Muir decided while in Florida to cancel his South America plans (this did not occur until he was in Cuba); that he changed his plans because of poor health and thin pocketbook (he was also unable to find passage south from Havana); that his experience in Cuba "sparked a life-long wanderlust" (he had dreamed of travel long before, as his long walk toward South America shows); that, having given up the Amazon, he arrived in California in April 1868 (it was March) (xiii); and that, "[a]fter six years in Yosemite, Muir left, having lost the battle for Hetch Hetchy" (not actually lost until 1913, thirty-nine years after Muir left Yosemite in 1874) (xxiii).

Zwinger is by no means alone in misrepresentating Muir's travels. Robert Dorman explains that Muir's walk to the Gulf was prompted by an eye injury that occurred in "mid-1866" (it was early March 1867) (105). Edwin Way Teale writes that the 1911 trip allowed Muir to realize his "dream of visiting the araucaria forests of the Amazon" (Muir found *Araucaria braziliensis* in southern Brazil and *Araucaria imbricata* in the Andes, but no *Araucaria* of any kind in the Amazon basin) (231). Laurel Bemis echoes this mistaken claim that Muir went to the Amazon in order to "see araucaria trees in their original habitat," and also incorrectly identifies Muir's departure date from New York as "April 20, 1911" (it was August 12) (1). James Mitchell Clarke reports of Muir that, in order to seek the monkey puzzle tree in Chile, "with two companions he journeyed five hundred miles south" from Santiago to Victoria (Muir traveled alone, and only after arriving in Victoria was joined by others) (314). In her recent book on Muir, Gretel Ehrlich incorrectly claims that Muir went by buggy to the monkey puzzle forests "[f]rom Buenos Aires" (213) (he actually traveled a thousand miles from Buenos Aires across the South American continent to Chile before discovering the monkey puzzle tree growing high in the Andes). Furthermore, Ehrlich's map of Muir's travels from South America to Africa erroneously depicts a straight course from Montevideo to Cape Town (in fact, Muir took a month-long, 10,000-mile voyage north to the Canary Islands before returning south along coastal Africa to Cape Town) (18–19). Even Linnie Marsh Wolfe, who certainly knew better, slips when describing Muir's sixty extant journals as spanning the period "from 1867 to 1911" (at least one of the two final journal notebooks, which includes the end of Muir's last journey, was written in 1912) (*John* ix). Furthermore, it is routine for critics to mistakenly describe

Florida as the goal of Muir's 1867 walk, and accounts of Muir's age when he undertook the 1911–12 trip variously report it as seventy-four, seventy-five, and seventy-six, in addition to the correct figure of seventy-three. It should be added, however, that many of these errors in reporting JM's age are traceable to JM's own misstatements of his age, either from forgetfulness or, equally likely, as a way of exaggerating his strength and accomplishments (when giving inaccurate reports of his age, JM seems always to have represented himself as slightly older than he actually was).

xli   *ignored Muir's international travels*   In the only published piece of Muir scholarship to carefully examine the importance of Muir's international journeys, C. Michael Hall and Stephen Mark correctly assert that the "non-North American travels" are "only given footnote status in accounts of Muir's life" (218).

xli   *"Americo-centric"*   Hall and Mark 218
xli   *"travelled a good deal in Concord"*   Thoreau 2
xliii   *"with muscles firm braced"*   Muir, *Mountains* 252
xlv   *"If the record"*   Badè, *Thousand* xxiv
xlv   *Indeed, readers today*   Teale xv
xlvi   *"[t]he world's big"*   Wolfe, *Son* 331
xlvii   *"We all travel the milky way together"*   Muir, *Mountains* 256

Chapter 1

5   *"Don't forget that we want your impressions"*   I/A/20/11215
6   *"[a]ll continues to go well"*   I/A/20/11224
6   *"the San Francisco thieves and robbers"*   I/A/20/11292.   JM's letter is actually an enclosure in an April 6, 1911, letter from Taft to Secretary of the Interior Walter Fisher and does not, therefore, appear in chronological order in the MP. Taft also wrote to JM on April 6, acknowledging the receipt of the letter and assuring JM that "[n]o action will be taken until the Commission of Army Engineers has sent in its report. You may be sure of that" (I/A/20/11290).
6   *"A Zoological Trip through Africa"*   I/A/20/11225. Roosevelt's lecture was later published in the *Bulletin of the Throop Polytechnic Institute* 20.51 (July 1911): 3–26.
7   *"a very brilliant and in every way Rooseveltian affair"*   I/A/20/11275

Chapter 2
[no entries]

Chapter 3
[no entries]

Chapter 4

106   "*to hear from the heart of so notable a scientist*"   I/A/20/11547

Chapter 5

127   "*had little intention of going to South Africa*"   Gifford 883
133   "'*monstrous' and 'horrible*'"   Wolfe, *Son* 346

Chapter 6

[no entries]

Chapter 7

185   "*was put up and stereotyped*"   I/A/20/11654
186   "*to sell the blessed old place*"   I/A/20/11637
187   *monumental chore of sorting*   I/A/20/11645
187   "*[F]riends become more and more precious*"   I/A/20/11640
189   "*When I read that John Muir had returned to America*"   I/A/20/11712
189   "*to get at something worth while*"   I/A/20/11645
192   "*I got my S. American and African notes copied*"   I/A/21/12554
192   "*[c]an't you let me know definitely*"   I/A/20/11720
194   "*not as good as they might have been*"   I/A/20/11733
194   "*a few photographs from this vicinity*"   I/A/20/11740
194   "*I have overexposed the plates*"   I/A/20/11791
194   "*impressively bad*"   I/A/21/12136
195   "*[only] disturbed by such anxieties*"   I/A/20/11764
195   "*your kind New Year greetings*"   I/A/20/11958
196   "*friends of the dear old leal sort*"   I/A/21/12228
196   "*a few of the Greenland and Antarctic ice-floods*"   I/A/21/12136
197   "*All my notes*"   I/A/21/12240
197   "*I see no way of escape*"   I/A/21/12274
197   "*I'm now at work on an Alaska book*"   I/A/21/12235
197   "*ready to take up the next book*"   I/A/21/12348
197   "*sadly interrupting my own natural work*"   I/A/21/12288
198   "*I still think we will win.*"   I/A/21/12492
198   "*[a]s to the loss of the Sierra Park Valley*"   I/A/21/12542
198   "*the freshness and vigor*"   Parsons 35

Textual Notes

The following textual notes attempt to leave a scholarly trail for those who might wish to follow the edited version of these materials back to their sources. I document here ambiguities, discontinuities, temporal anomalies, editorial conjectures, excisions and insertions, and instances of interesting tensions between the TMS and JM's holograph annotations to it. To enhance clarity throughout these textual notes, JM's words are rendered in italics. For simple emendations, please consult Appendix F, Table of Emendations.

Chapter 1: Correspondence

Feb. 11 / letter to Charlotte Kellogg . . . this side of the great river. : the word *of* has been supplied to clarify JM's meaning.

Mar. 2 / letter to Betty Averell Your letter came perilously . . . : As it appears in the MP, this letter is a rough draft and has perhaps been transcribed, since it appears in TMS form. At several places in the (presumably) transcribed letter an abbreviation has been expanded in brackets (e.g., "Yo[semite]"), or a bracketed word has been added to the text. In each case I have silently included these bracketed expansions and additions.

Mar. 31 / letter to Helen Muir . . . your letters of March 28th . . . : TMS reads only *your letter of March 29th.* JM has made a holograph correction of *letter* to *letters* and has inserted *& 28th* after *29th*. I have simply added the holograph correction and insertion, and restored the chronological order of the references.

June 27 / letter to Charlotte Kellogg . . . those I love most . . . : the word *those* is indiscernible in the AMS letter; it is probably *those,* but might be *these.*

June 27 / letter to Charlotte Kellogg . . . book work here and in Boston, : the comma after *Boston* has been added to clarify JM's meaning.

Aug. 2 / letter to Katharine Hooker : Contextual evidence strongly suggests that this undated letter was written on—or within one day of—August 2, 1911. Thus, I have dated it August 2 and placed it here.

Aug. 10 / letter to Katharine Hooker . . . let him sacrifice his own . . . : The words *him* and *his,* though probably correct, are indecipherable in the AMS.

Chapter 2: Journal

Aug. 12 Left Brooklyn . . . : Before these first words, at the top of the first page of the TMS, JM has written *Full notes from NY to NY 1911 & 1912.*

Aug. 13 . . . over twenty four hours to trim it. : Following this entry there is no journal entry for the next day, in either TMS or AMS. Thus, August 14, 1911, is the only day between August 12, 1911, and March 27, 1912, that does not receive an independent entry in JM's travel journals. However, JM's comment, on August 13, that his ship arrived in Norfolk at 4:00 p.m. and that it required more than twenty-four hours to load and trim confirms that August 14 was spent in port in Norfolk, taking on coal and trimming in preparation to sail.

Aug. 16 The sea is heaving . . . mackerel clouds : JM has edited this material heavily with a number of deletions, insertions, and ambiguous transpositions, thus making placement of some inserted and transposed phrases conjectural. In the final sentence of the entry, *Most of day muddy dingy clouds,* I have supplied *of* to clarify JM's meaning.

Aug. 22 . . . around Madeira Falls did. : TMS reads *around Madeira Falls.* JM's comment about "fifty passengers" does not make sense, given that earlier in the entry he refers to "[a]bout one hundred steerage passengers" who had come aboard. However, AMS includes the word *did* at the end of the sentence, thus making clear that, of the passengers aboard, the fifty who were bound for the railroad at Madeira Falls went ashore despite the inclement weather. Above this final sentence, TMS also includes a holograph annotation reading *Trans back,* which perhaps indicates that JM intended to move this sentence to an earlier position in the manuscript.

Aug. 23 . . . said the waiter at our table. : JM's actual holograph insertions and transpositions at this point in TMS would render the sentence . . . *said the table waiter our our,* an obvious slip of the pen.

Aug. 24 At 4:00 p.m. . . . . : I have replaced TMS *4:00 P.M.* (which JM used as a subheading under the entry for this date) with *At 4:00 p.m.* A comparable adjustment has been made in the entries for August 26 and 28.

Aug. 27 Crossed equator . . . the first time. : In TMS this sentence appears under the entry for August 28, and is phrased *Crossed equator yesterday P.M. a few minutes past six o'clock.* However, above this sentence in TMS is a holograph annotation reading *Trans,* presumably indicating that JM intended to transpose this sentence to the previous day's entry, where it would fit chronologically. Thus, I have moved this sentence to its appropriate chronological position in the entry for August 27.

Aug. 30 . . . Mr. Sanford the banker, Mr. Ross . . . : JM's punctuation may have introduced some confusion here. Since Mr. Sanford is actually a rubber exporter, JM may have meant to place the comma after *Sanford,* instead indicating that Mr. Ross is the banker. Since JM's intention remains unclear, the sentence has been rendered as it appears in TMS.

Aug. 30 Ceiba pentandara . . . : At about this point the word *omit* appears as a holograph note in the left margin of the TMS. A line beginning at *Leaves eight feet long* and running down the left margin through *About sixty fronds* seems to suggest that this material was considered for omission. Because the word *omit* does not appear to be in JM's hand, and because the material in question is not actually canceled, JM's intentions remain unclear, and I have opted to retain this material.

Aug. 31 . . . to start for Manoas . . . : This incorrect variant spelling of Manaus is JM's.

Sept. 3 . . . this morning, old Portuguese . . . : TMS reads . . . *this morning. Both of these are old Portugese* . . . , with the words *Both of these are* canceled by holograph strike-through. The cancellation probably indicates JM's intention to combine these two sentences, thus a comma has been added and the canceled words omitted.

Sept. 4 . . . on to Manoas. . . . Para to Manaos . . . : These incorrect variant spellings of Manaus are JM's.

Sept. 4 And of course all have canoes . . . : TMS reads *All have a few banana trees and palms, and of course all have canoes.* . . . The words *All have* and *and palms* are canceled by holograph strike-through, and the words *All have* appear to be replaced by an inserted ampersand. Evidently JM intended to add *and a few banana trees* to the previous sentence—which appears on a previous TMS page (pg. 23)—not realizing that *a few banana trees* are already mentioned there. Thus, I have deviated from the TMS in omitting the repeated words *a few banana trees.*

Sept. 5 In the rainy season . . . : TMS reads *The water rises in the rainy season about forty feet.* Above *about forty feet* is the holograph note, apparently an insertion, *the rise of the river is.* Thus, it seems JM intended to cancel *The water rises,* include the insertion, and have the sentence read as rendered.

Sept. 5 Strange to say . . . : TMS reads *Strange to say, the Rio Negro in entering the main Amazon, suddenly disappears, flowing underneath the great yellow Amazon flood.* Various holograph insertions, deletions, and lineations appear to alter the sentence as rendered, though JM apparently failed to line out *the main Amazon.*

Sept. 7 After breakfast Col. May . . . . cool airy house . . . : JM's lineation seems to indicate that this material should be inserted after *Madeira River railroad,* as rendered.

Sept. 9 After lunch went . . . : In the TMS the two paragraphs of this entry are in reverse order. I have reordered them to reflect the chronology of the events of JM's day.

Sept. 10 After returning to the tug . . . : JM's editorial changes to this sentence have made it necessary to insert a comma after the words *submerged island* in order to clearly preserve his meaning.

Sept. 10 As an incident of the trip . . . Lives in trees. : JM's cancellations and insertions in this paragraph are clear, but the intended ordering of the sentences is not. My ordering of the first five sentences of the paragraph is conjectural.

Sept. 13 In the afternoon, raggedy cumuli . . . : I have replaced TMS *P.M.* (which JM used as a subheading under the entry for this date) with *In the afternoon.*

Sept. 15 . . . Mr. Aimers, a good Scot from Galashiels.: There is a discrepancy between "Aimer" (the spelling JM used in the TMS) and "Aimers" (the spelling he used on his address list and in his subsequent correspondence with the man). It would seem that JM's formal address list and his later correspondence (which used "Aimers" several times) would be more likely to be correct than his first impressions of the man as recorded in the TMS. Thus, I have changed "Aimer" to "Aimers" throughout.

Sept. 16 The *Victoria* flower failed to bud . . . : TMS reads *flower faded to bud.* However, the context of the sentence and a consultation of AMS suggests that JM intended *failed* rather than *faded.*

Sept. 24 . . . with Mr. Aimers for three hours . . . : *for* has been added to clarify JM's meaning.

Chapter 2: Correspondence

Sept. 19 / letter to Katharine Hooker . . . these long weary years . . . : The word *these* is indiscernible in the AMS letter; it is probably *these* but might be *those.*

Sept. 19 / letter to Katharine Hooker . . . fevers I have had . . . : TMS reads *fevers have had. I* has been added to clarify JM's meaning.

Chapter 3: Journal

Sept. 26 Dull black cloudy evening. : TMS reads *Dull black clouds evening.* However, the context of the sentence and a consultation of AMS suggests that JM intended *cloudy* rather than *clouds.*

Sept. 29 Most of them, however, are low. : TMS ellipses after *low* have been replaced with a period.

Sept. 30 Then fleecy wisps and bundles. : TMS ellipses after *bundles* have been replaced with a period.

Sept. 30 plunged together . . . between them. : In TMS this material is unusual in several respects. First, the material from *plunged together* (which begins TMS pg. 43) to *between them* is marked with a vertical line in the left margin. Second, the material from *plunged together* to *numerous droves* has been underlined by hand. Third, the insertion *on the tops of waves* which follows *now appearing,* appears not to be in JM's hand. The reasons for these idiosyncrasies remain unclear.

Sept. 30 . . . of the horizon, changing as it sank . . . : TMS reads *changing thus as it sank,* with the sentence followed by a very rough pencil sketch of a setting sun. Because the sketch was not practically reproducible as an illustration, *thus* has been omitted in rendering the sentence.

Oct. 5 . . . arching films. : TMS reads *arching films, colored thus—*, with nothing following. AMS reads *arching films, thus—*, with the words followed by a very rough pencil sketch of a sunset. Because the sketch was not practically reproducible as an illustration, JM's phrase has been slightly abbreviated to omit introduction of the sketch.

Oct. 9 . . . with long walks and waits. : On TMS pg. 49, between the entry for October 9, 1911, and that for October 10, 1911, a holograph note reading *From here* appears in the left margin. Although the note does not appear to be in JM's hand, a marginal note reading *To here* in the same hand appears on TMS pg. 65, immediately following the entry for October 26, 1911. The seventeen-day period covered by the entries for October 10 through October 26 does form a logical narrative unit. Beginning as JM sails from Rio de Janeiro to Santos, and concluding when he bids goodbye to his traveling companions and departs Curitiba by rail for Paranaguá, this "chapter" of JM's journey concerns his search for and study of the *Araucaria braziliensis*. The author and the intention of the two marginal notes remain unknown. The notes may pertain to JM's speculation that this span of text might form the basis of an article such as those he was then contemplating for *Century Magazine*.

Oct. 10 . . . so near the Equator; : TMS reads . . . *so near the Equator. To find glacier. . . .* I have replaced the period with a semicolon to clarify JM's intention to offer the second sentence as evidence in support of the observation being made in the first.

Oct. 14 Seems to bear fire . . . : TMS reads *Seems to bear fire better than other trees.* Above the TMS line, JM's holograph insertion reads *yet it has evidently driven to rocky hilltops.* In his insertion, JM seems to have inadvertently omitted the word *been*, which I have supplied to make his meaning clear.

Oct. 14 . . . young trees all aspire. : Both TMS and AMS read *young trees all aspire thus—*, and in AMS these words are followed by a very rough pencil sketch of two small *Araucaria braziliensis* with upturned crown branches. Indeed, this page in AMS contains ten small drawings of *Araucaria braziliensis*, with the visual emphasis upon a comparative study of differences in crown structure. Because the sketch of the two young trees was not practically reproducible as an illustration, JM's phrase has been slightly abbreviated to omit introduction of the sketch.

Oct. 17 . . . one and a half feet . . . : TMS reads *one and half feet.* I have added *a*, which JM inadvertently omitted.

Oct. 23 Of other species of trees . . . : TMS reads *Other species of trees.* I have added *Of* at the beginning of the sentence in order to make JM's meaning more clear.

Oct. 23 . . . an inch wide at base . . . : The word *base*, which is part of a holograph insertion, appears in cramped hand at the far right edge of the TMS page and is therefore nearly illegible; thus, *base* is a likely but uncertain rendering.

Oct. 23 . . . four feet and six inches . . . : TMS reads *four feet high, and six inches high.* I have omitted the repeated word *high* in order to clarify JM's measurement.

Oct. 25 This species is said. . . . A row . . . : In TMS, nearly all the material from *This species* to *A row* (that is, most of the material on TMS pg. 64) is underlined by hand. JM or his typist, Henrietta Thompson, may have wanted to emphasize the need to review this material, which appears to have been at least temporarily lost. Support for this conjecture comes from a holograph note, in JM's hand, at the top of TMS pg. 65, which reads: *Pg 64 Missing.*

Oct. 26 . . . and felt very lonely. : See note under October 9, (". . . with long walks and waits").

Oct. 27 . . . and saw me off. : JM has followed this sentence with a note in the right margin: *(Send (him a (book.* The left parentheses were used to separate the note from the main text of the journal.

Oct. 27 . . . in finding the Johnsker Hotel. . . . has yet arrived here. : Through the length of this passage a vertical line is drawn in the left margin. No indication of the purpose of this line is discernible, though it may be related to the misplaced paragraph described in the note for Oct. 28, below.

Oct. 27 . . . has yet arrived. : TMS reads . . . *has yet arrived here.* The final word of the sentence, which unnecessarily repeats the first word of the sentence, has been omitted.

Oct. 28 Around Paranagua in gardens . . . the latter much taller. : In the TMS this paragraph appears on pg. 69, after the October 29 entry that ends *We lay here all night.* It is set off from the main text of that entry by strong vertical lines, in type, both before and after the paragraph. In the left margin, immediately preceding this set-off paragraph, is a holograph note, in JM's hand, and boldly circled, that reads *Trans back.* Since the October 29 entry describes the voyage to and arrival at San Francisco, it is clear that JM intended to move this paragraph, which describes various species of palms he observed in Paranaguá, back to one of the Paranaguá entries, either October 27 or October 28. The precise placement JM intended for this moved paragraph remains uncertain, however, and AMS shows the paragraph, with related drawings, out of chronological place, just as in the TMS. My placement of the paragraph at the start of the entry for October 28 is thus conjectural.

Oct. 28 Around Paranagua . . . : JM has sometimes rendered the name of the town of *Paranaguá* correctly, as he does here, while at other places in the TMS he has rendered it *Paranaguay.* JM's various renderings of this name have been allowed to stand.

Nov. 1 continuation of the Rio Grande de Sul . . . : TMS reads *continuation of the Rio Negro de Sul.* It is virtually certain that JM intended to identify Rio Grande de Sul here. Since JM had already sailed on two different rivers named Rio Negro during the trip, it's likely that this error was simply a slip of the pen. If JM was consulting maps while writing, it is also possible that he was distracted by yet another Rio Negro—a tributary of the Uruguay River that is south and east of Rio Grande de Sul. JM has also variously rendered the name of Pôrto Alegre as *Alligre, Allagre,* and *Alegre,* all of which have been allowed to stand.

Nov. 2 ... Tilley left the *Sirio* here.: TMS reads *Mr. Hector J. Tilley, whose address is C/o Miss C. R. Johnson, 949 Ogden Ave., Bronx, New York City, left the Sirio here.* Because JM's notes of addresses were intended only as information for further correspondence, they have been omitted from the text of the journal.

Nov. 2 ... come aboard from Rio Grande ... : TMS reads ... *come aboard from Rio Negro.* For a likely explanation for JM's error, see note for Nov. 1, above.

Nov. 3 Left Rio Grande ... : TMS reads *Left Rio Negro.* For a likely explanation for JM's error, see note under Nov. 1, above.

Nov. 3 Brazil is said to form ... : Readers may note the uncharacteristic tone of this day's entry. Most of this material—both the facts and, in some cases, the language—are borrowed from the "Description Physique" section of "Le Brésil," the essay printed on the back of the large South America Map (1909) that JM carried with him while traveling.

Nov. 3 Its culminating points ... Itambe 5,924 feet.: JM has irregularly used both periods and commas in this series of peak names and heights. I have supplied semicolons to make the series more clear and the information more readable.

Nov. 3 ... Serra Canastera, 4,166 feet ... : The comma following *Canastera* has been added.

Nov. 3 ... Montes Pyreneus, 7,774 feet. : The comma following *Pyreneus* has been added.

Nov. 3 ... kilometers and crosses the states of ... : TMS reads ... *kilometers and the state of.* ... Apparently JM inadvertently omitted a word. I have supplied *crosses* and pluralized *state* to clarify the sentence.

Nov. 3 Also the Vassa-Barris ... : TMS reads *The Vassa-Barris.* ... I have supplied *Also* to clarify the sentence.

Chapter 3: Correspondence

Oct. 10 / letter to Helen Muir ... you and family are.: The word *are,* though probably correct, is indecipherable in the AMS.

Oct. 28 / letter to Helen Muir : The MP lists this undated postcard as "Nov.? 1911." However, it is probable that the card was written and mailed on October 28, 1911, since JM boarded the *Sirio,* bound for Montevideo, during late evening of that day. I have thus dated the card October 28 and placed it here.

Nov. 8 / letter to Helen Muir ... this far from home.: Though probably correct, *this* is indecipherable in the AMS and might be *thus.*

Chapter 4: Journal

Nov. 10 9:00 a.m., two hours . . . : The comma after *a.m.* has been supplied.

Nov. 10 . . . lake basin, well watered . . . : The comma after *basin* has been supplied.

Nov. 10 Especially fertile is the one . . . : The TMS reads *Especially the one. . . .* I have supplied *fertile is* to clarify the sentence.

Nov. 13 . . . went to Mr. Rice's school, which . . . : TMS reads *In the afternoon to Mr. Rice's school which. . . .* I have supplied *went,* and the comma following *school,* to clarify the sentence.

Nov. 19 One of the Myrtacaeae . . . : TMS reads *myrtacaea.* I have added the *e* to clarify JM's reference to the Myrtle family.

Nov. 19 *Podocarpus chilense* . . . : The final letter of the word *chilense* is not discernible in JM's holograph correction to the TMS. In any case, there is no podocarp (*Podocarpus* is a large genus of at least ninety-four species of evergreen shrubs and trees) in current taxonomy that resembles *chilense*. JM was likely referring to one of the half-dozen species now organized under the *Podocarpus* section *Capitulatis,* a group native to the Andean highlands of central Chile and southern Brazil.

Nov. 19 Only on a small scale . . . : TMS reads *Only on small scale . . .* I have supplied *a* to clarify the sentence.

Nov. 20 At 6:00 a.m. packing . . . : TMS reads *Six o'clock packing . . . ,* preceded by *At 6:00* canceled by type. In order to clarify the sentence I have restored the cancellation.

Nov. 28 Had many visitors . . . : The material in this paragraph appears in a separate entry in the TMS, but the entry is, like that preceding it, dated *Nov. 28.* The same error occurs in the AMS. Because the two entries for November 28 appear on two different pages in the TMS (TMS pg. 92 and 93), it is likely that JM inadvertently repeated the entry for that date. Here, the two entries have been combined under a single heading.

Nov. 28 . . . to dinner, etc., . . . : The comma after *etc.* has been supplied.

Nov. 29 . . . find steamer to Capetown . . . : JM sometime uses *Capetown* and other times *Cape Town.* These variants of the name have been allowed to stand.

Dec. 7 . . . Minister, in English, . . . : The comma after *English* has been supplied.

Dec. 10 . . . beginning of dinner to tell him . . . : TMS reads *. . . told me at the beginning of dinner, told me to tell him what I wanted. . . .* Obviously JM failed to notice the repeated words *told me,* which I have omitted for the sake of clarity.

Chapter 4: Correspondence

Nov. 29/letter to Henry F. Osborn . . . would that the confounded . . . : I have supplied *would.* There appears to be a word missing here, and in the TMS there is an upward carat with an empty circle above at this spot, apparently suggesting that JM or another reader of the TMS also felt that a word had been left out.

Nov. 30 / letter to Wanda Muir Hanna . . . hope that this has proved true . . . : I have deleted the inadvertently repeated word *has* in *hope that this has proved true.*

Chapter 5: Journal

Dec. 12 Long, narrow-winged birds.: I have omitted the comma that, in TMS, followed *winged.*

Dec. 13 At 8:00 a.m., brightening . . . : TMS reads *8:00 A.M. brightening. . . .* I have added *At* and the comma after *a.m.* to clarify the sentence.

Dec. 13 At noon, growing . . . : TMS reads *Noon: growing. . . .* I have added *At* and the comma after noon, to clarify the sentence.

Dec. 22 At 6:30 a.m., sea . . . : TMS reads *6:30 A.M. Sea. . . .* I have added *At* and the comma after *a.m.,* to clarify the sentence.

Dec. 24 . . . of shuffle-board . . . quoit pitching.: Adjacent to this material in the left margin of TMS is a holograph note, which appears not to be in JM's hand, that reads *Christmas Eve.* Above the words *quoit pitching* is another holograph note, also apparently not in JM's hand, that reads *Piety kept them.* The purpose of this note remains unclear.

Dec. 25 Dawn rosy . . . : Above these words is a holograph note, apparently not in JM's hand, that appears to read *Christmas day next.*

Jan. 9 . . . a village called Windhuk.: In TMS JM has followed the name of the town with a question mark in parentheses, as if to express doubt about his identification of the village. Since JM was, however, correct in referring to *Windhuk* (Windhoek, Namibia), the parenthetical question mark has been omitted.

Jan. 16 . . . grades (7 or 8 %) . . . : I have omitted the type question mark which appears above the parenthetical estimate of the grade.

Jan. 18 . . . wide plain, green . . . : The comma following *plain* has been supplied.

Jan. 18 . . . rounded moutonnée masses . . . : The word *moutonee* appears in TMS as a holograph insertion noted in the right margin. Although the insertion does not appear to be in JM's hand, I have included it on the grounds that this is a word a glaciologist, rather than a typist, would have inserted. The AMS, which includes *moutonee* in its proper place, confirms that JM intended to use the word, and that the holograph insertion was intended to correct the inadvertent omission of the word from TMS.

Jan. 20 Arrive at Victoria . . . : On TMS pg. 116, between the entries for January 19 and 20, 1912, a holograph note *From here,* which is not in JM's hand, appears in the left margin. A marginal note reading *To here* in the same hand appears on TMS pg. 123, following the entry for January 23, 1912. The four-day period thus marked does form a logical narrative unit, that of his search for and study of the "long-dreamed-of" baobab tree, *Adansonia digitata.* The author and intention of the two marginal notes remain unknown, but the notes likely have to do with JM's speculation that this unit of text might form the basis of a single article such as those he was then contemplating writing for *Century Magazine.*

Jan. 20 . . . near Sierra Leone. : Following this sentence in TMS JM has made a holograph note reading *See Humboldt.*

Jan. 23 . . . glacial rocks, noble in size and form. : TMS reads . . . *glacial rocks, of noble forms,* with *forms* canceled and the words *in size & form* noted as a holograph insertion above the cancellation. The phrase as JM edited it would read . . . *glacial rocks, of noble in size & form.* I have thus omitted *of* in rendering the sentence.

Jan. 24 Hot, dim, cloudy . . . the railroad track. : In TMS this material, obviously added once TMS pg. 123 was completed, is typed single-spaced in the right margin of the page. However, there is no question regarding its intended placement.

Jan. 24 That is, the stations . . . : I have omitted the comma after *That* which appears in TMS.

Jan. 28 . . . 10:00 p.m., time of . . . : I have supplied the comma following *p.m.*

Chapter 5: Correspondence

Jan. 31/letter to Helen Muir Funk : Immediately preceding the greeting of this letter, JM has added the following note: *Near Mozembeque and Madagascar where Wanda was supposed to go mountaineering if you'd only ask her.* JM seems to refer to a would-be international mountaineering trip that his daughters never took, but the exact meaning of the reference remains uncertain.

Jan. 31/letter to Helen Muir Funk . . . trip to Lake Victoria . . . : AMS letter reads *Lake Nyanza.* JM has inadvertently mixed *Lake Victoria* and *Lake Nyanza* (*Nyanza* also means "lake"). I have substituted *Victoria* to clarify his meaning, both here and in his letters of Feb. 2 and Feb. 4.

Chapter 6: Journal

Feb. 7 This friend is a professional . . . : In the TMS text, as well as in its right and bottom margins, JM has included a number of names and addresses of traveling companions. They are as follows: *O. M. Rees, P.O. Box 53, Nairobi, B E A; L. Barbizet, Norfolk Hotel, Nairobi; Ven. Arch-Deacon Binns, Mombasa, B. E. A., via Capetown; H. H. Allsop, Mabira Forest, Junja P.O. Uganda.; Captain Cary, East African Police, Mombasa.; G. H. Eyre, Salisbury, Rhodesia.; F. M. Stokes, Box 73, Salisbury, Rhodesia.; Dr. Hunter, 33 Palmerston Place, Edinburgh, Scotland.; James Wiley, Glen Haw, Kloof Road, Capetown, So Africa.* Because JM's notes of addresses were intended only as information for further correspondence, they have been omitted from the text of the journal.

Feb. 7 Heard him pronounce "John" . . . : I have supplied the quotation marks around *John* to clarify that it is the vocalization of this name that allows JM to identify the speaker as a fellow Scotsman.

Feb. 12 . . . the Uganda Protectorate. : Following this sentence in TMS, JM has included a parenthetical note to himself that reads *(See the book entitled Uganda Protectorate, two volumes, by Sir Harry Johnston.)*. The book to which JM refers is Sir Harry Hamilton Johnston's two-volume work *The Uganda Protectorate, an Attempt to Give Some Description of the Physical Geography, Botany, Zoology, Anthropology, Languages and History of the Territories Under British Protection in East Central Africa, between the Congo Free State and the Rift Valley and between the First Degree of South Latitude and the Fifth Degree of North Latitude* (London: Hutchinson, 1902). That JM had long known of Johnston's important work—which included mention of the discovery of a number of new African species—is confirmed by a clipping JM kept (now in the "Scraps" files with the MP at UOP) of a January 26, 1902, *San Francisco Examiner* article ("A Whole Menagerie of Strangely Colored Animals Is Discovered in Africa") describing Johnston's expeditions and discoveries.

Feb. 13 . . . improvising a line, . . . : The comma following *line* has been supplied.

Feb. 13 The leader would say . . . : At the bottom of pg. 132, TMS reads *The leader would say,*. At the top of pg. 133, TMS reads *would say:*. Thus, TMS actually reads *The leader would say, "would say:*. The repetition was obviously a mistake caused by the mid-sentence page break.

Feb. 21 . . . with Mr. Alsop photographing baobabs. : Following Allsop's name (which JM misspells), TMS includes the parenthetical clarification *(H. H. Alsop)*, which I have omitted. Following this sentence, TMS includes the parenthetical sentence *(His address 93 Queen's Road, Liverpool, England, until August, 1912)*. Because JM's notes of addresses were intended only as information for further correspondence, I have omitted the parenthetical sentence.

Feb. 21 . . . as those of the silver firs. : Following this sentence, the TMS contains a final sentence that reads *See illustration made Feb. 21st*. In AMS, the illustration adjacent to the entry for February 21 depicts the symmetrically whorled branches of a young baobab tree.

Mar. 5 . . . from washing, caused . . . : TMS shows a semicolon following the word *washing*. I have changed the semicolon to a comma to clarify the sentence.

Mar. 5 . . . 8:00 a.m., a busy place. : The comma after *8:00 a.m.* has been supplied in order to clarify the sentence.

Mar. 6 High wind. : Following this sentence, TMS reads *Marc*. Since this is at the end of the entry for March 6, *Marc* is obviously a false start for the next entry, March 7, and has been omitted.

Mar. 17 . . . glaciated features very clearly. : To clarify the sentence, I have omitted the comma that in TMS appears following the word *features*.

Chapter 6: Correspondence

Mar. 13/letter to Osborn family : Although the location of composition of this letter is unidentified and is not speculated upon in the MP, the date of the letter suggests that it must certainly have been written from Naples. Thus, I have identified it accordingly.

Chapter 7: Correspondence

May 10/letter to Charles S. Sargent . . . I can get some of the workmen . . . : TMS reads *some of workman.* I have added *the* and emended *workman* to *workmen* to clarify JM's meaning.

May 10/letter to William Trout . . . six times on a journey . . . : The holograph letter reads *times on journey.* I have supplied *a* to clarify JM's meaning.

June 10/letter to Robert Underwood Johnson : Although the location of composition of this letter is clearly identified—both on the TMS and in the MP—as Martinez, California, it was almost certainly written from JM's daughter Helen's bungalow on Formosa Avenue in Hollywood, California. JM wrote at least two other letters on this same day, both of which identify the Hollywood address, and a comparison of the type used in the three letters confirms that this letter to Johnson, though labeled "Martinez," was composed on the same typewriter as all of JM's Hollywood letters. It is not certain why JM used the Martinez return address on this particular letter.

June 20/letter to Douglas Aimers : JM's journal and correspondence refer to this addressee only as "Aimer" or "Mr. Aimer." However, an uncataloged item of memorabilia in the MP identifies "Douglas Aimers," thus, I have silently expanded the addressee's name here. It is uncertain whether this unsigned TMS letter is a draft of a letter or a transcription, thought the latter is more likely. I have added JM's standard signature to the signature line.

Aug. 2/letter to Robert Underwood Johnson . . . don't count on me. : In the holograph letter, JM has inadvertently omitted *me.*

Aug. [26]/letter to Helen Muir Funk You know how the terrible trials . . . : The MP lists this undated letter with the undated correspondence for August 1912. Helen's letter assuring her father of her restored health has apparently not survived, thus making it impossible to date JM's letter precisely. However, it seems fairly certain that this letter was one of several that JM wrote out of concern for his frail daughter, who had given birth to her second child, Stanley, on July 17, 1912. The timing of Stanley's birth and Helen's recovery, combined with evidence from JM's August 23, 1912, letter to Helen—in which he frets that "I'm anxious for a word from you. Have heard nothing for more than a week" (I/A/20/11787)—leads me to believe that this letter must have been written within a few days of August 26. Although this letter also carries no place of composition, JM's other correspondence from late August makes clear that he was in Martinez at the time.

Oct. 16 / telegram to Theodore Roosevelt : Although the MP tentatively lists this telegram as having been sent from Martinez, JM had left Hollywood on October 13 and gone directly to Yosemite, where he attended the National Parks Convention held there. It is more likely that the telegram was sent either from Yosemite or while JM was in transit; he may simply have used his permanent return address of Martinez.

Oct. 25 / letter to Mrs. [Mary Muir] Willis Hand . . . *the first volume of a sort of* . . . : In TMS letter JM has inadvertently omitted *the*, which has been supplied in order to clarify the sentence.

Dec. 29 / letter to Charles Dwight Willard : The MP includes a TMS transcription of this letter from JM to Charles Dwight Willard, which is identified as the "[r]ough draft of letter found in an envelope dated Dec. 29, 1912." However, the transcription also bears a bracketed date of "[Jan., 1913]" (I/A/20/11945). I have adopted the draft date on the envelope, which is presumably the date of initial composition.

Muir's Reading and Botanical Notes (referenced by page in TMS)

Pg. 148 / Muir's Reading and Botanical Notes : I have supplied this title; in TMS the reading notes simply begin on page 148, with no title or header. To the degree necessary for clarity, I have also regularized the format of the notes themselves, and I have omitted the TMS words *Notes from* which preceded most entries.

Pg. 148 The Flora of South Africa . . . : The first half of TMS pg. 148 consists primarily of a list of names and addresses, as follows: *John D. Hunter, Victoria, Chili, So. America; Mr. Fletcher, Legacion Americana, Alameda 1584, Santiago, Chili; D.M. McNaught, 69 Tremont Ave., San Francisco; Wm. Henry Smith; The Ven. Arch-Deacon Binns, Mombasa, B. E. A. via Capetown; G.H. Eyre, Postmaster General, Salisbury, Rhodesia; T. M. Stokes, Box 73, Salisbury, Rhodesia; F.G. Pulle, Head Gardener, Botanic Gardens, Antebbe, Uganda; Captain Carey, East Africa Police, Mombasa, B. E. A.; O.M. Rees, P.O. Box 53, Nairoba, B. E. A.; James · Wyllie, Sr., Glenhaw, Kloof Road, Capetown, S. Af.; H.H. Allsop, Mabira Forest, Jinji P.O., Uganda; [H.H. Allsop,] 93 Queens Road, Liverpool, England; Dr. Hunter, 33 Palmerston Place, Edinburgh, Scotland; L. Barberzet, Norfolk Hotel, Nairoba, B. E. A.; Leslie Simson, Rand Club, Johannesburg, a Californian who studied with John Hays.* Because JM's address notes were intended only as information for further correspondence, they have been omitted from the text of the journal.

Pg. 149 Fagus Obliqua. : JM has used quotation marks to indicate that the word *Fagus* is to be repeated from the previous listing for *Fagus Dombeyi*. I have replaced the quotation marks with the intended word, *Fagus*.

Pg. 154 . . . *to kill everything.* : I have omitted an apparently inadvertent half-dash that follows this sentence in TMS.

Pg. 154 his worn-out _____. : The subscript line following *worn-out* is not an editorial insertion, but appears just so in TMS.

Pg. 156 . . . on Lake Tanganyika: : In TMS, the word *Tanganyika* is followed by a period; I have substituted a colon to make clear that JM intends to introduce the taunt that follows.

Pg. 159 (The above . . . to find me.) : In TMS this material is single-spaced, apparently to indicate that it is a gloss on the primary source, rather than an extract from it. I have added the closing parenthesis, inadvertently omitted in TMS.

Pg. 160 saw me again . . . as a mark . . . : Between *saw me again* and *as a mark* there is a blank line with no typewriter strike marks in the TMS.

Pg. 160 . . . domestic animals improves . . . : I have omitted an extraneous comma that in TMS appears following the word *animals*.

Bibliography

Most, though not all, of the materials included in *John Muir's Last Journey* are held in the John Muir Papers, Holt-Atherton Library, University of the Pacific, Stockton, California. Most of the materials in the Muir Papers at UOP are also included in the microform edition of the John Muir Papers (51 microfilm reels, 53 microfiche cards), edited by Ronald H. Limbaugh and Kirsten E. Lewis, who have cataloged the works in *The Guide and Index to the Microform Edition of the John Muir Papers, 1858–1957* (Alexandria, VA: Chadwyck-Healey, 1986).

Materials that are in the Muir collection at UOP but not included in the microform edition have typically remained uncataloged. These materials, along with some found in other collections, are listed and briefly described in Appendix E, Annotated List of Selected Archival Materials.

Full citations for works mentioned in the chapter footnotes appear with the notes and are not repeated here. Likewise, books and pamphlets mentioned in JM's South America and Africa reading, botanical, and commonplace notes are cited in Appendix C, John Muir's Reading and Botanical Notes, and do not appear here. This bibliography thus contains only those items cited in the book's general and chapter introductions.

Badè, William Frederic. *The Life and Letters of John Muir.* 1924. In *John Muir: His Life and Letters and Other Writings.* Ed. Terry Gifford, 13–380. Seattle: The Mountaineers, 1996.

———, ed. Introduction to *A Thousand-Mile Walk to the Gulf,* by John Muir. 1916. San Francisco: Sierra Club, 1992.

Bemis, Lauren. "John Muir in the Amazon Basin." *The John Muir Newsletter* 3.3 (Summer, 1993): 1+.

Clark, Jean Hanna, and Shirley Sargent. *Dear Papa: Letters Between John Muir and His Daughter Wanda.* Fresno, Calif.: Panorama West, 1985.

Clarke, James Mitchell. *The Life and Adventures of John Muir.* San Francisco: Sierra Club, 1979.

Cohen, Michael P. *The Pathless Way: John Muir and American Wilderness.* Madison: Univ. of Wisconsin Press, 1984.

Dorman, Robert L. *A Word for Nature: Four Pioneering Environmental Advocates, 1845–1913.* Chapel Hill: Univ. of North Carolina Press, 1998.

Earl, John, ed. *John Muir's Longest Walk*. Garden City, N.Y.: Doubleday, 1975.

Ehrlich, Gretel. *John Muir: Nature's Visionary*. Washington, D.C.: National Geographic, 2000.

Fox, Stephen. *The American Conservation Movement: John Muir and His Legacy*. Madison: Univ. of Wisconsin Press, 1981.

Gifford, Terry, ed. *John Muir: His Life and Letters and Other Writings*. Seattle: The Mountaineers, 1996.

Greg, W. W. "The Rationale of Copy-Text." *Studies in Bibliography* 3 (1950–51): 19–36.

Hall, C. Michael. "John Muir's Travels in Australasia, 1903–1904: Their Significance for Conservation and Environmental Thought." Chapter 13 in *John Muir: Life and Work*. Ed. Sally M. Miller. Albuquerque: Univ. of New Mexico Press, 1993.

————, and Stephen R. Mark. "The Botanist's Last Journey: John Muir in South America and Southern Africa, 1911–12." Chapter 11 in *John Muir in Historical Perspective*. Ed. Sally M. Miller. New York: Peter Lang, 1999.

Holmes, Steven J. *The Young John Muir: An Environmental Biography*. Madison: Univ. of Wisconsin Press, 1999.

Jones, Holway R. *John Muir and the Sierra Club: The Battle for Yosemite*. San Francisco: Sierra Club, 1965.

Kimes, William F. and Maymie B. *John Muir: A Reading Bibliography*. Palo Alto, Calif.: William P. Wreden, 1977.

Lyon, Thomas. *John Muir*. Boise: Boise State College, 1972. Western Writers Series, pamphlet no. 3.

Muir, John. *Edward Henry Harriman*. New York: Doubleday, Page, 1911.

————. *John of the Mountains: The Unpublished Journals of John Muir*. Ed. Linnie Marsh Wolfe. 1938. Madison: Univ. of Wisconsin Press, 1979.

———— *John Muir: Nature Writings*. Ed. William Cronon. New York: Library of America, 1997.

————. *Letters to a Friend: Written to Mrs. Ezra S. Carr, 1866–1879*. Dunwoody, Ga.: Norman S. Berg, 1973.

————. *The Mountains of California*. 1894. New York: Dorset, 1988.

————. *My First Summer in the Sierra*. 1911. New York: Penguin, 1997.

————. *The Story of My Boyhood and Youth*. 1913. San Francisco: Sierra Club, 1989.

————. *Travels in Alaska*. Boston: Houghton Mifflin, 1915.

————. *The Yosemite*. 1912. San Francisco: Sierra Club, 1988.

Myerson, Joel. "Colonial and Nineteenth-Century American Literature." In *Scholarly Editing: A Guide to Research*. Ed. D. C. Greetham, 351–364. New York: Modern Language Association, 1995.

Parsons, Marion Randall. "John Muir and the Alaska Book." *Sierra Club Bulletin* 10.1 (January 1916): 33–36.

Smith, Herbert F. *John Muir.* New York: Twayne, 1965.

Stanley, Millie. *The Heart of John Muir's World: Wisconsin, Family and Wilderness Discovery.* Madison, Wis.: Prairie Oak Press, 1995.

Stewart, John. *Winds in the Woods: The Story of John Muir.* Philadelphia: Westminster Press, 1975.

Tanselle, Thomas G. *A Rationale of Textual Criticism.* Philadelphia: Univ. of Pennsylvania Press, 1989.

Teale, Edwin Way, ed. *The Wilderness World of John Muir.* Boston: Houghton Mifflin, 1954.

Thoreau, Henry David. *Walden and Resistance to Civil Government.* 1854. Ed. William Rossi. New York: Norton, 1992.

Turner, Frederick. *Rediscovering America: John Muir in His Time and Ours.* San Francisco: Sierra Club, 1985.

Wild, Peter. *Pioneer Conservationists of Western America.* Missoula, Mont.: Mountain Press, 1979.

Wilkins, Thurman. *John Muir: Apostle of Nature.* Norman: Univ. of Oklahoma Press, 1995.

Winkley, John. *John Muir: Naturalist.* Nashville, Tenn.: Parthenon, 1959.

Wolfe, Linnie Marsh. *Son of the Wilderness: The Life of John Muir.* Madison: Univ. of Wisconsin Press, 1945.

Zwinger, Ann, ed. *Mary Austin and John Muir: Writing the Western Landscape.* Boston: Beacon Press, 1994.

Acknowledgments

All books are, ultimately, collaborative projects, and it is my genuine pleasure to have the opportunity to thank the many people whose assistance made this project possible. All errors of fact and judgment, of course, remain my own.

In the Noble Getchell Library of the University of Nevada, Reno, I wish to thank the reference staff, especially librarians Betty Glass and Richard Grefrath, for assistance with on-line and secondary and tertiary materials; Laura Trounson, for help with microform materials; Bob Blesse and the staff of special collections, for assistance with rare Western Americana; and Carol Keith and Virginia Roecker, who helped to locate the many obscure South American and African materials that I requested through Interlibrary Loan. I would also like to thank UNR Map Librarian Linda Newman, of the Mary B. Ansari Map Library in the De La Mare Library, for helping me access various period maps to verify locations in Muir's travels; and Vicki Davies of the UNR Bookstore, who helped me to get so many in-print titles on such short notice.

For their valuable research assistance I am deeply grateful to two very dedicated graduate student scholars and friends: Dana Zaskoda, whose meticulous transcriptions of microform versions of Muir's holograph and typescript journals and correspondence during 1997–98 allowed me to begin textual editing in earnest; and Madison Furrh, whose inspired, tenacious bibliographical and historical research during 2000 helped me to complete many of the notes that support the text of this book.

At the University of the Pacific, in Stockton, California, repository of the John Muir Papers, I wish to thank the many devoted scholars and archivists who are working to preserve Muir's legacy for future generations: Ron Limbaugh, the dean of Muir scholars, without whose magisterial microform edition of the John Muir Papers much of the Muir scholarship of the past fifteen years would quite simply have been impossible; Sally Miller, Director of the John Muir Center for Regional Studies at UOP and editor of *The John Muir Newsletter;* Daryl Morrison, Director of Special Collections in the Holt-Atherton Library; and Janene Ford, Archivist in the Muir Papers, whose knowledge of the collections and infinite patience were indispensable during my several research trips to UOP. To these people, and others who work with them, all Muir scholars owe a deep debt of gratitude.

At the John Muir National Historic Site, in Martinez, California, I'm indebted to all the staff who work to keep Muir's old home and gardens accessible to visitors and scholars. I'm especially appreciative of David Blackburn, Chief of Interpretation at the JMNHS, whose assistance led me to various Muir materials not elsewhere cataloged and not otherwise available.

I have also received valuable assistance from archivists, curators, and librarians in the reference and special collections departments of the following institutions: the Bancroft Library, University of California, Berkeley; the University of California, Davis Libraries; the California State Library; the San Francisco Public Library; the California Historical Society; the Historical Society of Southern California; the Henry E. Huntington Library, Art Gallery, and Botanical Gardens; the Stanford University Libraries; the Houghton Library, the Gray Herbarium, the Arnold Arboretum Libraries, and the University Archives at Harvard University; the Beinecke Rare Book and Manuscript Library and the Alumni Records and University Archives at Yale University; the Richter Library, University of Miami; the Clifton Waller Barrett Collection, Alderman Library, University of Virginia; the University of Wisconsin Libraries; the American Institute of Arts and Letters; the Division of Rare and Manuscript Collections, Cornell University Library; the New York Public Library; and the Braun Research Library, Southwest Museum. Thanks also to my UNR colleague Eric Rasmussen for bringing to my attention a previously unknown Muir fragment, and to Stephen Pepple and Ann Weinkle of Buddenbrooks Fine & Rare Books, Manuscripts, and Prints, for providing me a facsimile copy of the fragment. I also wish to express appreciation for the valuable assistance with genealogical research that I have received from Stu Branch. And thanks to Deb and Dale Hoagland for giving me a home away from home during research trips to Stockton, Martinez, and Berkeley.

At Island Press I have a number of colleagues whom it is a special pleasure to thank. Foremost is Jonathan Cobb, executive editor of Shearwater Books, whose concern for the quality of this project has been exemplary at every stage of editing and production; if all editors were as devoted and talented as Jonathan, authors and readers alike would have a great deal more to be thankful for. For her early encouragement of the project, I wish to thank Laurie Burnham, former Director of Shearwater Books at Island Press, without whose early vision for the project this book would not have been possible. And thanks to Murdo MacLeod and Kent Redford for bringing these Muir manuscripts to the Press's attention. Cecilia González did fine and fast work to keep this project moving toward publication, and copyeditor Erin Johnson and proofreader Shana Harrington helped ensure the accuracy of the text. Dave Bullen's graceful design made this book a thing lovely to look at as well as to read. And Island's impressive efforts to help this book find its audience may be credited to the good work of Sam Dorrance, Krista Fisher, Lea Kleinschmidt, and Elizabeth Coxe.

It is a delight to be able to express gratitude to my friend Robert Michael Pyle, whose wonderful Foreword graces this volume. Bob is a talented scientist and writer whose work is carrying John Muir's spirit into the twenty-first century. I can offer Bob Pyle no greater compliment than to say that I believe John Muir would have deeply appreciated and enjoyed his sensibility and his impressive gifts as a literary naturalist.

For their careful readings of parts of this book manuscript, I'm grateful to SueEllen Campbell, Madison Furrh, and Leslie Ryan. And for their helpful and generous readings of the entire manuscript, special thanks go to Eryn Branch, Stu Branch, and Michael Cohen.

Over the years I've also enjoyed provocative conversations about Muir—and about environmental writing and philosophy generally—with hundreds of eco-critics, environmental historians, nature writers, archivists, and activists, among whom I'd like especially to mention Ann Ronald and my other colleagues in the Literature and Environment Graduate Program in the English Department at the University of Nevada, Reno. Thanks also to the many students with whom I've been fortunate to work in that program. Special thanks to Scott Slovic, Michael Cohen, and Dan Philippon, whose friendship and scholarship have meant so much to me.

For the opportunity to publish various articles and reviews on John Muir, my thanks to the following editors and the books and journals in which the pieces appeared: Tom Lyon, *Western American Literature;* Sally Miller, *John Muir in Historical Perspective* and *The John Muir Newsletter;* Steven Rosendale, *Representing Place: Essays on Literature, Theory, and the Environment;* Ken Womack, *Interdisciplinary Literary Studies;* Kate Boyes, *Western American Literature;* Scott Slovic, *ISLE: Interdisciplinary Studies in Literature and Environment;* Caroline Ash and Gavin Swanson, *Endeavour: A Quarterly Review of the History and Philosophy of Science;* and Emory Elliott, *The Literary Dictionary.* And for the opportunity to share my ideas on Muir in invited lectures and conference papers, my thanks to the following associations and institutes: American Literature Association, Association for the Study of Literature and Environment, Pacific Ancient and Modern Language Association, Western American Literature Association, California History Institute, and North American Interdisciplinary Conference on Environment and Community; and, at the University of Nevada, Reno, the Elder Hostel Program, Environmental Studies Distance Education Lecture Series, English Department Literature and Environment Colloquium Series, and Nevada Institute.

For their concern and foresight in preserving John Muir's books, manuscripts, maps, and memorabilia, the deep thanks of all Muir scholars goes to the Muir family; and for permission to publish various previously unpublished Muir journals, letters, sketches, and photographs, my personal thanks to the Muir-Hanna Trust, and to the various libraries and museums listed in the credits.

All our thanks go to the countless unsung heroes of the environmental movement who—through activism, philanthropy, parenting, writing, scholarship, or teaching—are working toward the global preservation of the endangered places, flora, and fauna that Muir so loved. A portion of the proceeds from the sale of this volume will be donated to the Sierra Club, the Holt-Atherton Library at the University of the Pacific, and the John Muir National Historic Site in Martinez, to help support their ongoing work in preserving John Muir's legacy for the benefit of future generations.

I offer my continual thanks to my folks, Sharon and Stuart Branch. My deepest and most "unletterable" gratitude goes to my wife and best friend, Eryn.

Credits

The Huntington Library, San Marino, California, for JM letters to: Katharine Hooker, August 2, 1911 (HM31152); Katharine Hooker, September 19, 1911 (HM31154); William Trout, May 10, 1912 (HM31540[4]); Enos Mills, August 14, 1912 (HM31336).

The Houghton Library, Harvard University, Cambridge, Massachusetts, for JM letters to Houghton Mifflin Co., Boston, August 2, 1911 (bMS Am 1925 [1287]). The Gray Herbarium Archives, Harvard University, for JM letter to Charles S. Sargent, May 10, 1912.

The American Academy & Institute of Arts & Letters, New York City, for JM letter to Robert Underwood Johnson, January 26, 1911.

The Clifton Waller Barrett Library, John Muir Collection, University of Virginia, Charlottesville, Virginia, for JM letter to Dr. Charles E. Rice, April 30, 1912.

The Division of Rare Manuscript Collections, Cornell University Library, William Trelease Papers, Cornell University, Ithaca, New York, for JM letter to William Trelease, May 10, 1912.

The Braun Research Library, Charles F. Lummis Papers, Southwest Museum, Los Angeles, California, for JM letter to Charles Lummis, June 10, 1912.

The New York Public Library, The *Century* Collection, New York City, for JM letter to Robert Underwood Johnson, August 24, 1912.

The National Park Service, John Muir National Historic Site, Newman Collection, for JM letter to Mrs. [Mary Muir] Willis Hand, October 25, 1912.

Index

Adanson, Michel, xli, 147
Adansonia digitata:
 bark, 131, 149, 175
 correspondence after the end of the
  journey, 192, 207
 correspondence during South Africa
  trip, 159, 160
 diameter of, 132, 147, 156
 end of a long journey, 166
 first glimpse of, 131, 147
 Mombasa, 155–56
 overview, xli–xlii
 range of, 147–48
 recognized at distance of several
  miles, 149
 sketches and photographs, 148, 156,
  163, 173, 175
 smaller when leaving the coast, 166
 trunk/branches/leaves, 131, 147, 175
Adansonia gregorii, 148
Adansonia madagascariensis, 148
Aden, 164, 176
Africa, East/Lake Victoria and headwaters of the Nile, xlii
 correspondence, 182–83
 end of a long voyage, 165–66
 Gulf of Suez, 164
 Italy, 165
 journals, travel, 166–81
 Kampala, 163
 Mombasa, 163
 Nairobi, trip to, 161–62
 pyramids, 164–65
 Ripon Falls, 163
 route, expected travel, 161

Somalia, 164
Spain, 165
Yemen, 164
Africa, South/Zambezi River and
  Adansonia digitata:
 Adansonia digitata, first glimpse of, 131
 Andes trip, end of, 105–6
 Canary Islands, 127, 129
 Cape Town, arrival in, 130
 colonialism, 132–33
 correspondence, 133–35, 157–60
 journals, travel, 135–56
 landscapes, cultivated/wild, 131
 Mombasa, 132
 overview, xli–xlii
 sea voyage involved, 129–30
 Victoria Falls, 131
*African Game Trails: An Account of the
  African Wanderings of an American
  Hunter-Naturalist* (Roosevelt),
  257–58
*Agricultural and Pastoral Prospects of
  South Africa* (Thomas), 252–53
Aimers, Douglas, 60–62, 74, 98, 190,
  193, 210
Alaska, xv, xxv, xxxv, 70, 72, 195, 197, 198
Albatrosses, 78, 135
Alexander Archipelago, 93
Algae, 177, 178
Algoas, 96
Alligators, 163, 170
Allsop, Herbert, 174, 175, 194
Almond trees, 163, 174–75
Altar Mountain, 111
Amaryllis, 90

Amazon:
  contradictions, Amazonia as a place
    of, 37–38
  correspondence after the end of the
    journey, 206–7
  correspondence during the trip,
    63–68
  Earth's greatest river, 15
  end of a long journey, 166
  first views of the Amazon, 36–37
  Hooker, Katharine, 39–40
  hydrographic system of Brazil, 96
  journals, travel, 40–63
  loneliness, 39
  postponement of first South Ameri-
    can trip, xxxii–xxxiii
  return to coastal Brazil, 39
  start of the trip, 35–36
  traveler than scientist, journals more
    the work of, 37
  valley, xxxii
American Alpine Club, 21
American nature writer, Muir's identification as an, xlv
Andean forests, xlvi
Andes, southern Brazil/Uruguay/
  Argentina/Chile and into *Araucaria
  imbricata* forests of the, xxiii, xxxii
  correspondence, 106–7, 120–26
  deforestation, 104, 105
  glaciers/glacial landscapes, 103,
    108–9
  journals, travel, 107–20
  South Africa, planning to go to,
    105–6
  Victoria, 103–5
  writer, nature, 102–3
Antarctic, 196
Antelope, 172, 173, 211
"Antiquity of the Physical Geography
  of Inner Africa" (Murchison), 171
Ants, black, 88
Apoccinia, 61
Arab influence on east Africa, 132
Araguay River, 96
Ararangua River, 96

*Araucaria angustifolia, see Araucaria
  braziliensis*
*Araucaria araucana, see Araucaria
  imbricata*
Araucaria bidwillii, xxvi
Araucaria braziliensis:
  ants, black, 88
  bark of, 85
  bottom land, growing on rich, 90
  branchlets, 86–87
  Branner, John C., 80
  correspondence after the end of the
    journey, 192, 204, 210
  correspondence during trip through
    forests of the Andes, 107, 125
  correspondence during trip up Brazil
    (coastal) and up Iguacu River,
    99–100
  cross section of tree bole, 89
  diameter of, 84–86, 88
  end of a long journey, 166
  field sketches, xliii
  first glimpse of, 71
  forests of, unbroken, 71, 83, 84–85
  hermaphroditic, 86
  other species of trees scattered
    among, 87–88
  Paraná, 70
  São Paulo, 82
  seedlings and saplings, 84
  Sequoia-like physiognomy, 88
  shade, cast little, 88
  stony hills, 91
Araucaria cunninghamii, xxvi
Araucaria imbricata:
  bark, 115
  beech and laurel groves, lone *Arau-
    caria* growing in, 116
  Botanical Gardens, Santiago, 103,
    110, 111
  correspondence after the end of the
    journey, 192, 207, 210
  correspondence during trip through
    forests of the Andes, 121, 123, 125
  end of a long journey, 166
  first glimpse of, 105, 115

monkey puzzle tree, so called because
    monkeys can't climb it, 103
overview, xl–xli
Archival materials, annotated list of
    selected, 269–86
Argentina, xl, 72–73
    see also Andes, southern
        Brazil/Uruguay/Argentina/Chile
        and into *Araucaria imbricata*
        forests of the
Artemisia, 108
Assu River, 96
Athi plains, xlii, 161, 163, 211
Atlantic Monthly, 185, 201
Atlantic Ocean, North, xxiii, xlii, 161,
    165, 166
Australia, xxvi
Averell, Elizabeth, 13–16
Ayere, Mr., 152
Azarole, 113

Bab el Mandeb Strait, 164
Babelmandeb Straits, 176
Badè, William F., xlix
Bahia, 96
Bahia Todos Santos, 77
Ballinger, Richard, 4
Banana trees, 50, 170
Baobab, African, *see Adansonia digitata*
Barbados, 35, 40, 42
Barrus, Clara, 185
Bartleman, Richard M., 98, 118
Bates, Henry W., 263
Bauhinia triandra, 169
Bedrock, 173
Beginning of the trip, 35–36
Beira, 131, 152–53, 158, 210
Belém, xxxix, xl, 36, 39, 44, 60, 64
Belgian colonialism, 132
Berberis, 113
Berlin Conference of 1884–1885, 132
Bibliography, 313–15
Bidwell, Annie, 187
Binns, Ottwell, 167
Black Sea, xxvi
Blindness, temporary, xxviii–xxix, xxxi

Bliss, Robert W., 117
Blue Mountains, xxvi
Boer War, 133
Bombax, 60
Books owned by Muir, South America
    and Africa, 267–68
Boone & Crockett Club, 19
Boston, xxxvi, 8, 24, 185
Botanical Gardens:
    Belém, 36, 39, 60, 61
    Buenos Aires, 72
    Cape Town, 130, 144
    Montevideo, 72–73, 79
    Rio de Janeiro, 70
    Santiago, 103, 110, 111, 117
    Uganda, 162, 169
    see also Reading and botanical notes,
        John Muir's
Botanical study, Muir's method of, 36
Botswana, 131
Bouchet, Mr., 70, 79, 91
Brady Glacier, 215
Branner, John C., 80
Brazil (coastal) and up the Iguacu
    River:
    Araucaria braziliensis, 71
    Buenos Aires, 72–73
    correspondence, 73, 99–101
    hydrographic system of Brazil, 96
    journals, travel, 74–99
    Paranaguá, 72
    Rio de Janeiro, 70
    São Paulo, 70–71
    start of trip, 69–70
    see also Amazon, southbound and
        up the great; Andes, southern
        Brazil/Uruguay/Argentina/Chile
        and into *Araucaria imbricata*
        forests of the
Bright, Mr., 97, 98, 119
Brooklyn, xxiii, xxxix
Browne, Francis F., 196
Buenos Aires, xxiii, xl, xli, 72–73, 98,
    103, 105–7, 117, 207, 210
Buenos Aires Herald, li, 72
Bulawayo, 131

Burns, Mr., 52

Burroughs, John, xxxix, 4, 6, 8, 26–27, 185, 206

Bur Sa'id, 164

Buzzards, 55

Cactus, 108, 110

Caine, Hall, xlv, 261

Cairo, xxvi, 178

California, arrival in, xxxiii–xxxiv

Calkins, J. E., 190, 197, 209

Calvinism, xxvii

Canada, xxv–xxvii

Canarium schweinfurthii, 169

Canary Islands, xli, 127, 129, 130, 140

Candelabra tree, *see Araucaria brazil-iensis*

Cannon, Joseph, 7

Cape Guardifui, 164, 176

Cape of Good Hope, 129

Cape St. Roque, 95

Cape Town, xli, 130, 144, 158, 210

Capiberive River, 96

Capri, 180

Caraca Mountains, 95

Caribbean Sea, xxxix

Carr, Jeanne, xxix, xxxiv

Cassia, 60

Cassurinas, 153

Castilloa uleia, 60

Castle Rock, 8–9, 26

Cattle, 50, 52, 107, 176

Caucasus Mountains, xxvi

Ceara, 75

Cedar Keys, xxxi–xxxii

Ceiba pentandara, 46, 59, 61

Central Valley, xxxiv

Century Company, xxxvi, 8, 157, 160, 185

Century Magazine, 5, 183, 188–95, 212

Cereus chilensis, 110

Ceylon, xxvi, 79

Chamberlain, Mr., 60

Chameleon, 57

Chile, xl, xlvi, 103

see also Andes, southern Brazil/Uruguay/Argentina/Chile

and into *Araucaria imbricata* forests of the

China, xxvi

Chinde, 154

Christison, David B., 253

Christopher Island, 41

Chrysophillum excelsumrsorva, 60

Chuy River, 96

Civil War, xxvi, xxxi

Clark, Champ, 7

Clark, Galen, 196

Clement Hill (steamer), 162, 168

Clouds, projection of arboreal forms onto, 129–30

Coarym River, 96

Colby, William E., 7, 16–17, 19–20, 66, 160, 207

Coleman, Arthur, 217

Coleman, Mary R., 217

Colombia, xxxii

Colonialism, 38, 48, 132–33

Colorado River, 4

Columbia River, 59

Conard, P. A., 106, 118

Confervae, 178

Contas River, 96

Coral, 76

Corcovado Mountain, 70, 78, 79

Corn fields, 153

Correspondence:

Amazon, southbound and up the great, 63–68

Andes, southern Brazil/Uruguay/Argentina/Chile and into *Araucaria imbricata* forests of the, 106–7, 120–26

before the trip, 10–33

Brazil (coastal) and up the Iguacu River, 98, 99–101

East Africa/Lake Victoria and headwaters of the Nile, 182–83

home to America and writing, 184–85, 187–88, 195–98, 200–221

South Africa/Zambezi River and *Adansonia digitata,* 133–35, 157–60

Corsica, 165

Cotantins River, 96
Cotton, 155
Cream of tartar tree, 148–49
Crete, 179
Crocodiles, 163, 170
Cryptomerias, 90
Cuba, xxxii
Cupressus, 90
Curitiba, 71–72, 80, 90, 91, 210
Currityba, 80, 90, 91
Cycas circinatis, 46–47
Cytharoxylon, 113

Daggett, 4, 199
Danish colonialism, 132
Dar es Salaan, 148, 155, 156, 210
Darwin, Charles, 136
Daughter of an Empress, The
 (Mühlbach), 259–60
Dead rat tree, *see Adansonia digitata*
Deforestation, 104, 105, 114
Dennis (steamer), 35, 39, 55, 58, 190
Deodar trees, xxvi
Dickey, Anna R., 186, 202–3
Doce River, 96
Dolphins, 75–76, 138
Dutch colonialism, 132

Ecuador, xxxiv
Edward Henry Harriman (Muir), 7
Egypt, xxvi, xlii, 164–65, 178
El Gîza, 164
Embothrium, 113
Emendations, table of, 287–92
Emerson, Ralph W., xxv, xxxvi
England, xxvi, 38
English colonialism, 132, 133
English Lake District, xxvi
Entebbe, 162, 166, 169, 211
Equator, 44, 81, 129–30, 166, 181
Erythima tomentosa, 150
Erythrina christagalli, 97
Espidium, 88
Ethiopia, 164
Eucalyptus, 90, 107

Eucalyptus ficifolia, 144
Europe, xxvi, xxxi
 see also individual country
European sycamore, 14

Fairview Dome, 81
Ferns, 88–89
Fighting the Slave Hunters in Central
 Africa: A Record of Twenty-six Years
 of Travel & Adventure Round the
 Great Lakes and of the Overthrow of
 Tip-pu-tib, Rumaliza and Other
 Great Slave-Traders (Swann),
 260–61
Finland, xxvi
Fisher, Walter, 7
Fleming, Arthur, 6
Fletcher, Henry P., 103, 110
Florida, xxix, xxxi
Florionopolis, 93
Formoso River, 96
Fortaleza, 69, 75
Forts, network of jungle, 48
France, xxvi, 38
Freeman, John R., 214
French colonialism, 132
French Guinea, 96
Funk, Buel, xxxvii, 4
Funk, Helen M. (daughter), xxxvii,
 xxxviii, 3–5, 9
 correspondence after the end of the
  journey, 186, 201, 216–17
 correspondence before start of trip,
  17–18, 20, 22–23, 30, 32
 correspondence during Amazon
  River trip, 65
 correspondence during East Africa
  trip, 183
 correspondence during South Africa
  trip, 157–58
 correspondence during travel up
  Brazil (coastal) and up the Iguacu
  River, 73, 98, 99–101
 correspondence during trip through
  forests of the Andes, 121–22, 134
 death of John Muir, 199

Funk, Muir, 5, 186
Funk, Stanley, 187

Garrison on the Hudson, 9
General (steamer), 158, 163–64, 174, 175
German colonialism, 132, 133
Germany, 38
Gibraltar, 165, 180
Gilder, Richard W., 11, 26
Glacier Bay, xxv
Glaciers/glacial landscapes:
  Alaska, 72
  Andes, trip through the forests of the,
    103, 108–9
  Brady Glacier, 215
  Brazil (coastal) and up the Iguacu
    River, 72, 73
  correspondence during South Africa
    trip, 158–60
  East Africa trip, 167, 173, 177
  Mueller Glacier, xxvi
  Muir Glacier, xxv
  Norway, xxvi
  Patagonia, 81
  Rio de Janeiro, 70, 78, 125
  Santos, 82
  Sardinia, 180
  South Africa/Zambezi River and
    Adansonia digitata, 131, 146, 151, 152
  Spain, 165, 180
  Yosemite Valley/National Park, 72
Gleason, Herbert, 6
Goding, Frederic W., 72, 97, 106, 118,
  119
Goodyear, Mr., 91
Gordon, Mr., 57
Goyaz Mountains, 95, 96
Graite, Mr., 97
Grand Canyon, 4
Graydon, Katharine M., 195, 217–18
Great Barrier Reef of Australia, 76
Great La Plata, 135
Great Rift Valley, The (Gregory), 171
Greenland, 196
Gregory, John W., 171

Grevellia, 144
Grewstad, Nicolay, 119
Guadua superba, 46
Guayaquil, xxxiv
Gulf of Aden, 164, 176
Gulf of Mexico, walk to the, xxv–xxxi,
  xliv
Gulf of Suez, 164
Gurupy River, 96

Haeckel, Ernst von, 136
Hall, C. Michael, xlv
Hand, Mary M. (sister), 188, 219
Hanna, John, 5
Hanna, Stentzel, 5
Hanna, Thomas R., 4
Hanna, Wanda M. (daughter), 4, 5, 63,
  106, 120–21, 124, 186
Harell, Mr., 70, 78–80
Harnsworth History of South America, 61
Harper, John, 194
Harriman, Edward H., xxv, 4, 7
Harvard University, 8
Havana, xxxii
Hawaii, xxvi
Hazeltine, Mr., 98
Herero peoples, 133
Herons, 177
Hetch Hetchy Valley, xxiv, xxxvi,
  xxxviii, xlvii, 4–7, 9, 19, 185, 197–98,
  216
Hevea brasiliensis, 46, 59
Himalayas, xxvi
Hingu River, 96
Holmes, Stephen, xxxv
Homatia, 113
Home to America and writing:
  activist work, 196, 197–98
  book projects, 188, 195, 197
  Boston, 185
  correspondence, 184–85, 187–88,
    195–98, 200–221
  death of John Muir, 199
  health, failing, 198
  Hetch Hetchy Valley, 197–98

journals, Muir's intentions for his
  South America/Africa, 188–95
loneliness, 186–87
Los Angeles, 186
Martinez, arrival in, 186
mortality, meditation on, 195–96
New York, staying several weeks in,
  185
photographs, attempts to obtain,
  193–94, 211
ranch home, 186–87, 199
Hooker, John D., xxxviii, xxxix, 4–5, 23
Hooker, Joseph D., 153
Hooker, Katharine, xxxvii, xxxix, 5, 7, 9
  correspondence after the end of the
    journey, 187, 188, 190–91, 193, 196,
    203, 212–13, 220
  correspondence before start of trip,
    21–23, 29, 31
  correspondence during Amazon
    River trip, 39–40, 60, 67–68
  correspondence during East Africa
    trip, 182
  correspondence during South Africa
    trip, 159–60
  correspondence during trip through
    forests of the Andes, 106–7,
    124–26, 134–35
  Wayfarers in Italy, 39, 57, 68
Hooker, Marian, 60
Hope, Anthony, 260
Horses, 107
Houghton Mifflin, xxxvi, 8, 28–29, 98,
  197
Humboldt, Alexander von, xxxii, xxxix
Hunter, John, 114, 194
Hura crepitans, 46
Huxley, Thomas H., 136
Huxton, Mr., 98
Hydrographic system of Brazil, 96

Igarape, 56
Iguacu River, xl, 70, 71, 84, 96, 166
  see also Brazil (coastal) and up the
    Iguacu River

Iguana, 57
Iguapo River, 96
Iguassu (steamer), 71, 84
India, xxvi
Indianapolis, xxvii–xxiv, xxxiii, li
Indian Ocean, xlii, 131, 161, 163
Indigenous cultures, 49, 52–53, 132–33
International travels in Muir's life, vital
  role of, xxv–xxvii, xlv–xlvi, 185
Iowa, xxvii
Ipojuca River, 96
Iquitos, 39, 58
Ireland, xxvi
Isthmus of Panama, xxxiii
Itacoatiara, 37, 50
Itacolomy Mountains, 95
Italian colonialism, 132, 133
Italy, xxvi, xlii, 165, 178–80, 211
Itambe Mountains, 95
Itapicura River, 96
Itatiaya Mountains, 95
Ityhaya, 93

Jaguariba River, 96
Jananda River, 96
Japan, xxvi
Jaquitimhonha River, 96
Jary River, 96
Jeffersonville, xxix
Jinja, 170
Johannesburg, 174
John of the Mountains: The Unpublished
  Journals of John Muir (Wolfe), xlv
Johnson, Robert U., xxv, xxxvi
  correspondence after the end of the
    journey, 207–8, 214–16
  correspondence before the trip, xxxvi,
    10–11
  Hetch Hetchy Valley, 19
  requesting essays from the trip, 5,
    188–95
Johnston, Harry H., 252
Journal manuscripts, history and condi-
  tion of, 239–41
Journals, travel:

Amazon, southbound and up the great, 37, 40–63

Andes, southern Brazil/Uruguay/Argentina/Chile and into *Araucaria imbricata* forests of the, 107–20

Araucaria braziliensis, 71

Brazil (coastal) and up the Iguacu River, 74–99

East Africa/Lake Victoria and headwaters of the Nile, 166–81

Muir's intentions for his South America/Africa, 188–95

overview, xliii–li

South Africa/Zambezi River and *Adansonia digitata*, 135–56

Juniper, 168

Jupura River, 96

Jurua River, 96

Jussieu, xi

Jutahy River, 96

Kaiserin Augusta Victoria (ship), 165, 180, 182, 183

Kampala, 163, 170, 211

Keith, William, xxv, xxxviii, xxxix, 4, 17, 22

Kellogg, Charlotte H., 8, 11–12, 18, 23–25, 60, 199

Kellogg, Charlotte J., 18

Kellogg, Vernon L., 18

Kenney, George, 196

Kent, William, 16

Kentucky, xxxi

Kenya, xlii, 131, 161
  see also Africa, East/Lake Victoria and headwaters of the Nile

Kigelia, 150, 172

Kimberley, 131, 145

Kingsley, Mary H., 254

Kipling, Rudyard, 81

Kisumu, 162

Korea, xxvi

Kurakina (ship), 106, 118

Lake Nyanza, 157, 169, 192, 211

Lakes of Killarney, xxvi

Lake Victoria, xlii, 135, 158, 161, 162, 163, 166, 168, 192

Lamb, Charles, 42

Laurelin, 113

Lay, Julius G., 78

Libya, 133

Lilies, 113, 170, 172

Lindula larch forest, xxvi

Livingstone, David, 132

Logging, xlvii

Lombardy poplars, 108, 112

Loneliness, 39, 186–87, 195–96

Los Andes, 108, 109, 117

Los Angeles, 186, 190, 199

Louisville, xxix

Lummis, Charles, 208

Lunam, Margaret H., 73, 99

Madeira-Mamoré railway, 51–52, 55

Madeira River, 50, 96

Madrona, 113

Maesopsis berchemoides, 169

Makinda Station, 174

Malaria, 52, 54

Malaysia, xxvi, 11

Malisia paraensis, 60

Malvaceae, 148

Manaus, xxxix, 37–39, 53, 55, 58, 67

Manchuria, xxvi

Mandahu River, 96

Mangoes, 155, 163, 174

Mark, Stephen R., xlv

Marshall, Robert B., xxxvii, xxxix, 27–28, 185

Martinez (California), 184, 186, 193

Matobo National Park, 151

Matterhorn, xxvi

Mattogroso, 96

May, Col., 55, 56, 58

McFarland, Mr., 58

Meaford, xxvii

Mearim River, 96

Mediterranean Sea, xxiii, xlii, 161, 164, 165

Mempituba River, 96
Mendel, Mr., 78
Mendes, Mr., 79
Mendoza, 108, 117
Merriam, Clinton, xxxiv
Merrill, Mina, 197
Methodist Episcopal Church, 111
Mills, Enos, 215
Mimosa, 151
Minas Geraes, 95–96
Mojave Desert, 199
Mombasa, 132, 148, 155–56, 158, 161, 163, 172, 174, 210, 211
Monkey bread tree, *see Adansonia digitata*
Monkey puzzle tree, *see Araucaria imbricata*
Monodora myristica, 169
Montagu Pass, 109, 116
Mont Blanc, xxvi
Montenegro (steamer), 50
Montes Pyreneus Mountains, 95
Montevideo, xl, xli, 72, 95, 100, 106, 118, 210
Moores, Merrill, 200
Mopani, 150
Moraine boulders, 173
Mortality, meditation on, 195–96
Mosgrove, Ellie, xxxvi–xxxvii, 213
Mosquitoes, 49, 50
Mossoro River, 96
Mountains of California, The (Muir), 7–8, 203
Mt. Cook, xxvi
Mt. Kenya, 163, 172
Mt. Kilimanjaro, 163, 167, 172, 174
Mt. Ritter, xxv, xlvii
Mt. Shasta, xxv, xlvii
Mt. Vesuvius, xlii, 179, 211
Mozambique, 131, 148, 154
Mucury River, 96
Mueller Glacier, xxvi
Muhlbach, Louise, 259
Muir, David G. (brother), xxxii, xxxiv, 33
Muir, John, death of, li, 199

Muir, Louie, xxxv
Muir Glacier, xxv
Muqdisho, 164
Murchison, Roderick I., 171
Murray, Capt., 149
My First Summer in the Sierra (Muir), 4, 6, 8
My Story (Caine), xlv, 261–62

Nairobi, xiii, 161–62, 167
Naivasha Lake, 163, 172
Nama peoples, 133
Namibia, 130, 131
Naples, xlii, 178, 179
Naturalist on the River Amazons, The: A Record of Adventures, Habits of Animals, Sketches of Brazilian and Indian Life, and Aspects of Nature Under the Equator, During Eleven Years of Travel (Bates), 263–66
New Haven, xxxvi, 8, 24
New Orleans, xxxii
New York, xxxiii, xxxvi, xlii, li, 7, 8, 36, 165–66, 181, 185, 211
New Zealand, xxvi, xlvi, 104, 114
Nile River, xxiii, xxvi, xlii, xliv, 129, 131, 132, 135, 161, 163, 164, 166, 170
Norfolk, 35
North Carolina, xxxi
Norway, xxvi
Notes on the Botany of Uruguay (Christison), 253–54
Nymphia odorata, 108

Obidos, 50
Ochroma lagopus, 46
Ohio River, xxix
Orange River, 145
Orgaos Mountains, 95
Orinoco Basin, xxxii
Osborn, Henry F.:
    Castle Rock, 8–9, 26
    correspondence after the end of the journey, 197
    correspondence before start of the trip, 12–13

correspondence during Amazon
River trip, 60
correspondence during East Africa
trip, 182
correspondence during South Africa
trip, 158–59
correspondence during trip through
forests of the Andes, 106, 123, 134
Hetch Hetchy Valley, 6
invitation to accompany Muir, xxxix
South Africa/Zambezi River and
Adansonia digitata, 127
Osborn, Loulu (Lucretia), 31–32, 39,
64, 197
Osgood, Smith & Co., xxvii–xxiii
Ostriches, 162, 173
Ouida, *see* Ramee, Louise de la
Oypock River, 96

Palm trees, 48, 49, 59, 85, 88–89, 92, 150,
153, 155, 163
Pampas, Argentinean, 103
Panama Canal, 206
Pandanus veichii, 46
Panga, 148, 155
Papyrus, 170, 172
Pará, xxxix, 36, 39, 44, 60, 64, 125, 207
Paraguay River, 95, 96
Parahyba del Norte River, 96
Parahyba do Sul River, 96
Paraná, 70, 80, 95–96, 125, 207
Paranaguá, 72, 91–92, 100, 207
Paranahyba River, 96
Paraná Lumber Company, 70, 79
Parana pine, *see Araucaria braziliensis*
Parana River, 96
Park, Mungo, xxx
Parkia pendula, 46
Parsons, Marion R., 198, 207
Parythain, 96
Paso Robles, 193
Patagonia, 81
Patos lagoon, 94
Paul (apostle), 179
Pearaguassu River, 96

Peck, Annie, 72, 98
Pelham, 185
Pernambuco, 76, 96, 138
Pernettia, 113
Perry, Mr., 91
Persia lingue, 113
Philippines, xxvi
Pico de Teidè, 130
Piedade Mountains, 95
Pindare River, 96
Pinheiro, *see Araucaria braziliensis*
Pipledenia africana, 169
Plants, *see* Trees/plants
Podocarpus chilense, 113
Polomba Mountain, 111
Pompeii, xlii, 179, 211
Poplars, Lombardy, 108, 112
Porpoises, 75–76
Port Allagre, 94–95
Port Amazons, 84
Port Darwin, 76
Port Florence, 162, 163, 168, 171–72
Porto Amazonas, 71
Port of Chinde, 154
Port of Paranagua, 210
Porto Velho, 50
Port Said, 164, 178
Portugal, 38, 48
Postponement of first South American
trip, xxxii–xxxiii
Pozzuli, 179
Praia, 79
Praia Flamingo, 78–79
Preparation for the journey, 3–9
see also before the trip *under* Corre-
spondence
Prince of Europe, A (Helianthus),
258–59
Prussia, 38
Pulle, F. G., 169
Purus River, 96
Puryassu River, 96
Pyramids, xxvi, 164–65

Quartz pebbles, 173
Queensland, xxvi
Quercus pedunculata, 144
quoits, 140

Rainy season, 167
Raker Bill (legislation), 198
Ramee, Louise de la, 258
Randall, Harry, 195–96
Rand Club, 174
Randia dummetorium, 169
Ras Asir, 164
Râs Muhammad, 164
Reading and botanical notes, John
   Muir's:
   *African Game Trails: An Account of the
      African Wanderings of an American
      Hunter-Naturalist* (Roosevelt),
      257–58
   *Agricultural and Pastoral Prospects of
      South Africa* (Thomas), 252–53
   Daughter of an Empress, The
      (Mühlbach), 259–60
   *Fighting the Slave Hunters in Central
      Africa: A Record of Twenty-six Years
      of Travel & Adventure Round the
      Great Lakes and of the Overthrow
      of Tip-pu-tib, Rumaliza and Other
      Great Slave-Traders* (Swann),
      260–61
   My Story (Caine), 261–62
   *Naturalist on the River Amazons, The:
      A Record of Adventures, Habits of
      Animals, Sketches of Brazilian and
      Indian Life, and Aspects of Nature
      Under the Equator, During Eleven
      Years of Travel* (Bates), 263–66
   Notes on the Botany of Uruguay
      (Christison), 253–54
   overview, 251–52
   Prince of Europe, A (Helianthus),
      258–59
   *Rupert of Hentzau: From the Memories
      of Fritz von Tarlenheim* (Hope),
      260

Story of an African Farm, The
   (Schreiner), 257
*Travel and Adventure in South-East
   Africa, Being the Narrative of the
   Last Eleven Years Spent by the
   Author on the Zambesi and its
   Tributaries; With an Account of the
   Colonisation of Mashunaland and
   the Progress of the Gold Industry in
   that Country* (Selous), 256
*Travels in West Africa, Congo Francais,
   Corisco and Cameroons* (Kingsley),
   254–56
Recife, 69
Red Deer River, 123
Red Sea, xxiii, xlii, 176, 178, 211
Rees, Mr., 168
Rhodes-Matopos National Park, 151
Rice, Charles E., 111, 201
Riley, Henry, xxix
Rio de Janeiro, xl, 69, 70, 78, 100, 125
Rio Grande de Sul, 93–96, 100, 125
Rio Grande (town), 94, 95
Rio Negro River (northern Brazil), 37,
   38, 53–56, 58, 67, 166
Rio Negro River (southern Brazil), 71,
   90, 96
Rio Negro (village), 71, 90
Ripon Falls, xlii, 163, 170
River system of Brazil, 96
Robardia, Mr., 56, 58
Roblo, 113
Rochester, 8
Roosevelt, Theodore, xxxvii, l, 3, 6–7,
   219, 257
Royal Ponciana, 153
Rubber, 54
Rudiret Bay, 143–44
Rufino, 107
*Rupert of Hentzau: From the Memories
   of Fritz von Tarlenheim* (Hope), 260
Russia, xxvi, 38

Sahara Desert, 171
Salvador, 69

Sanford, Frederic H., 46, 54–57, 67

San Francisco, xxxiii, 5, 93, 96, 198, 199

Santa Barbara, 193

Santa Catarina Island, 93

Santa Catarina River, 96

Santarem, 50

Santiago, xli, xlii, 103, 105, 107, 109–10, 116–17

Santos, xl, 70, 79, 82, 100, 125

Sao Francisco River, 95, 96

São Paulo, 62, 70–71, 82–83, 96

Sao Paulo (steamer), 69, 99

Sardinia, 165, 180

Sargent, Charles S., xxvi, 189–90, 204

Saudi Arabia, 164

Schreiner, Olive, 257

Scotland, xxvi, xxvii

Scottish Highlands, xxvi

Seamen's Fund, 137

Seascapes rather than landscapes Muir's descriptions of, l

Sellers, A. H., xxxviii, 22, 72

Sellers, Fay, xxxviii, xxxix, 60, 72

Selous, Frederick C., 256

Senegal River, 141, 148

Sequoia National Park, 193

Serra Bertentes Mountains, 95

Serra Canastera Mountains, 95

Serra Central Mountains, 95

Serra do Espiuhaco Mountains, 95

Serra Mattodacorda Mountains, 95

Shangane Hills, 151

Shanghai, xxvi

Sheep, 107, 176

Shubert, Mr., 118

Siberia, xxvi

Sierra Club, xxiv, xxxvi, xlvii, 4, 6, 73, 190

Sierra Club Bulletin, 127

Sierra de Mantiquiara Mountains, 95

Sierra de Mar Mountains, 95

Sierra Leone, 147

Sierra Nevada Mountains, xxiv, xxxiii, 72–73

Simla, xxvi

Simson, Leslie, 174

Sinai Peninsula, 164

Sirio (steamer), 72, 92, 100

Sitka, 79

Smith, Mr., 84, 111, 112, 114

Smith, Mrs., 91

Smiths, 104

Social man, hesitancy in thinking of Muir as a, xlviii–xlix

Soda Springs, 190, 207

Solianum macaranthum, 169

Somalia, 164, 176

Spain, xlii, 165, 180

Spathodia nilotica, 169

Squakum, 130, 143

Stanford University, 4

Stickeen (Muir), 4, 8

Stokes, Mr., 152

Stone, Mr., 52

Story of an African Farm, The (Schreiner), 257

Story of My Boyhood and Youth, The (Muir), 8, 185, 201

Strait of Bonifacio, 165

Straits of Gibraltar, xlii

Straits of Messina, 179

Suabie, Mr., 55–57

Sudan, 164

Suez Canal, xlii, 164, 178

Sugar Loaf Rock, 78

Swakopmund, 130

Swann, Alfred J., 260

Swans, 177

Swedish colonialism, 132

Swiss Alps, 70

Switzerland, xxvi

Sycamore, European, 144

Table Mountain, 130, 144

Taft, William H., xxxvi, xxxvii, 4, 7, 16, 73, 103, 110

"Tam o' Shanter" (Burns), 158–59

Tapajoz River, 96

Teffe River 7, 96

Telegraph cable, 51

Tenerife, 125, 130

Tennessee, xxxi

Textual editing:

  challenges involved, 243–46

  copy-text, 246

  documentary editing (philosophy and
    methodology), 241–42

  history and condition of the journal
    manuscripts and correspondence,
    239–41

  stylistic issues, 247–49

  transcription policies and editorial
    principles, 246–49

*Theobroma,*47, 50, 60

Thevetia nerriforia, 169

Thomas, Maude, 213

Thomas, Owen, 252

Thompson, Henrietta, xxxvi, 191–92

Thoreau, Henry D., xli, xlv, xlvii, 196,
  221

Thousand-Mile Walk to the Gulf, A
  (Muir), xxxi

Thuja, 90

Tiffucas River, 96

Tilley, Hector J., 94

Timeline/Locator, 225–37

"To J. W." (Emerson), xxxvii

Toplas, Mr., 179, 180

Transcription policies and editorial
  principles, 246–49

*Travel and Adventure in South-East
  Africa, Being the Narrative of the
  Last Eleven Years Spent by the Author
  on the Zambesi and its Tributaries;
  With an Account of the Colonisation
  of Mashunaland and the Progress of
  the Gold Industry in that Country*
  (Selous), 256

Travels in the Interior Regions of Africa
  (Park), xxx

*Travels in West Africa, Congo Francais,
  Corisco and Cameroons* (Kingsley),
  254–56

Trees/plants:

  Adansonia gregorii, 148

Adansonia madagascariensis, 148

almond, 163, 174–75

Amaryllis, 90

Apoccinia, 61

Araucaria bidwillii, xxvi

Araucaria cunninghamii, xxvi

Artemisia, 108

Azarole, 113

banana, 50, 170

Bauhinia triandra, 169

Berberis, 113

Bombax, 60

cactus, 108, 110

Canarium schweinfurthii, 169

Cassia, 60

Cassurinas, 153

Castilloa uleia, 60

Ceiba pentandara, 46, 59, 61

Cereus chilensis, 110

Chrysophillum excelsumrsorva, 60

clouds, projection of arboreal forms
  onto, 129–30

cream of tartar tree, 148–49

Cryptomerias, 90

Cupressus, 90

Cycas circinatis, 46–47

Cytharoxylon, 113

deforestation, 104, 105, 114

Douglas Fir, li

Embothrium, 113

*Erythima tomentosa,*150

Erythrina christagalli, 97

Espidium, 88

Eucalyptus, 90, 107

Eucalyptus ficifolia, 144

ferns, 88–89

Grevellia, 144

Guadua superba, 46

Hevea brasiliensis, 46, 59

Homatia, 113

Hura crepitans, 46

international travels in Muir's life,
  vital role of, xxvi

juniper, 168

Kigelia, 150, 172

Laurelin, 113
lilies, 113, 170, 172
Madrona, 113
Maesopsis berchemoides, 169
Malisia paraensis, 60
Malvaceae, 148
mangoes, 155, 163, 174
Mimosa, 151
Monodora myristica, 169
Mopani, 150
Nymphia odorata, 108
Ochroma lagopus, 46
palm, 48, 49, 59, 85, 88–89, 92, 150, 153, 155, 163
Pandanus veichii, 46
papyrus, 170, 172
parasites and epiphytes, 115
Parkia pendula, 46
Pernettia, 113
Persia lingue, 113
Pipledenia africana, 169
Podocarpus chilense, 113
poplars, Lombardy, 108, 112
Quercus pedunculata, 144
Randia dummetorium, 169
Roblo, 113
Royal Ponciana, 153
Sargent, Charles, correspondence with Muir, 189–90
Sequoia, xli
Sierra Nevada Mountains, 72–73
Solianum macaranthum, 169
Spathodia nilotica, 169
sycamore, European, 144
Theobroma, 47, 50, 60
Thevetia nerriforia, 169
Thuja, 90
Victoria, 60
Victoria regia, xxxix, 36, 38, 47, 55, 56
vineyards, 108
Zutahy, 61
see also *Adansonia digitata; Araucaria braziliensis; Araucaria imbricata;* Appendix C. John Muir's Reading and Botanical Notes

Trelease, William, 187, 205
Trichodesmium erythryaeum, 178
Trout, William, 187–88, 205–7
Tubarao River, 96
Tuolumne Meadows, 81, 131, 152, 172
Turner, Frederick, xxxi
Twelve Apostles Islands, 164, 177
Tyndall, John, 136
Tyrrhenian Sea, 165

Uganda Protectorate, 161, 162
see also Africa, East/Lake Victoria and headwaters of the Nile
University of California, Berkeley, 4
University of Wisconsin, xxvii, 8
Upside-down tree, see *Adansonia digitata*
Ural Mountains, xxvi
Uruguay River, 70, 80, 96
see also Andes, southern Brazil/Uruguay/Argentina/Chile and into *Araucaria imbricata* forests of the

Vassa-Barris River, 96
Venezuela, xxxii
Victoria, xli, 103–5, 112, 116, 121
Victoria Falls, 131, 134, 145, 147, 150, 157, 158, 160, 210
Victoria Nyanza, 157, 169, 192, 211
Victoria regia, xxxix, 36, 38, 47, 55, 56, 60
Vineyards, 108
Volcan Copahué, 113
Volcanic cones, 113
Volcan Llaima, 113
Volga Valley, xxvi
Voltaire (steamer), 70, 79
von Trotha, Gen., 133

Walden, xlv
Washington, D.C., xxxvi, 5, 7
Wasps, 50
Water color in Amazonia, 53
Wayfarers in Italy (Hooker), 39, 57, 68
West Indies, xxxi

West Point, 9
Whales, 69–70, 75
Wheat fields, 172
Willard, Charles D., 196, 220–21
Williams, Mr., 114
Wilson, Woodrow, 198
Windhoek, 130, 133
Windhuk (ship), 130, 131, 140, 153, 158
Wireless technology, 51
Wisconsin, xxvii, xxix
Wolfe, Linnie M., xlv
World War I, 133
Writer, nature, xxv, xxxv, xlv, xlix, 7–8,
   102–3, 129–30
   see also Home to America and writ-
   ing; Reading and botanical notes,
   John Muir's
Wubuschi, 164, 175

Yale University, 8, 20, 21, 24
Yatta Plateau, 163
Yellow fever, 54
Yemen, 164
YMCA, 106, 118
Yosemite, The (Muir), 8, 9, 185, 201
Yosemite Valley/National Park, xxiv,
   xxxiii, xxxiv, xlvii, 4, 6, 73, 193, 198
Youthful Muir, our preference for the
   image of a, xlvii

Zambezi River, 131, 154, 157, 158, 160, 210
Zambia, 131
Zanzibar, 134, 154, 155, 166, 210
Zebras, 172, 173, 211
Zimbabwe, 131
"Zoological Trip Through Africa, A"
   (Roosevelt), 7

MICHAEL P. BRANCH is Associate Professor of Literature and Environment at the University of Nevada, Reno. A co-founder and past president of the Association for the Study of Literature and Environment (ASLE) and current book review editor of *ISLE (Interdisciplinary Studies in Literature and Environment)*, he is author of more than eighty articles and reviews and more than one hundred invited lectures on nature writing and environmental literature. He is also a co-editor of several books, including *The Height of Our Mountains: Nature Writing from Virginia's Blue Ridge Mountains and Shenandoah Valley* (1998) and *Reading the Earth: New Directions in the Study of Literature and Environment* (1998). He and his wife, Eryn, live in the desert north of Reno, Nevada, where the western Great Basin and eastern slope of the northern Sierra Nevada meet.

ROBERT MICHAEL PYLE was born and raised in Colorado, schooled on the West and East coasts, held conservation jobs in the Sierra Nevada, Papua New Guinea, England, and Cascadia, and founded the Xerces Society. The author of *Wintergreen, The Thunder Tree, Where Bigfoot Walks, Chasing Monarchs,* and *Walking the High Ridge: Life as Field Trip,* he has also written several butterfly books, including the *Audubon Society Field Guide to North American Butterflies* and, with Brian Boyd, edited *Nabokov's Butterflies.* Pyle's regular column "The Tangled Bank" appears in *Orion Afield,* as well as his essays, poems, and stories, here and there. A Guggenheim Fellow and John Burroughs medalist, Pyle has lived for many years in the Lower Columbia River watershed of Washington State with his wife, Thea Linnaea Pyle, a gardener and botanical artist.